A Joy Forever
Latvian Weaving

TRADITIONAL AND MODIFIED USES

Jane A. Evans

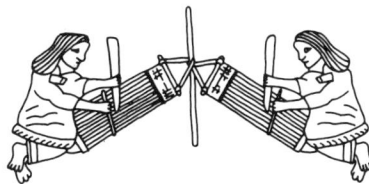

DOS TEJEDORAS FIBER ARTS PUBLICATIONS

SAINT PAUL, MINNESOTA

DEDICATION

To the memory of my mother,
Ruth Everts,
an especially fine person.

Book design by Patrick Redmond
Edited by Karen Searle
Text formatted in QuarkXPress™ with Adobe™ Garamond typefaces
Compugraphic output by Accurate Press, New Brighton, Minnesota
Printed by Kaye's Printing, Fargo, North Dakota
Editorial and production assistance provided by Catherine Fleischman, Susan Larson-Fleming,
Daniel Life and friends, Bill Mertes, Margaret Miller, Mary Skoy

Photo and illustration credits are listed on page *iv*. Photos not credited are by the author.

All drafts were computer-generated by the author using the *Patternland*™ weave program.

Front cover photo: Weft-faced blanket, collection of the Royal Ontario Museum, Toronto, Ontario.
See page 44 for details.

ISBN 0-932394-16-7
Library of Congress Catalog No. 91-075152

Published by

DOS TEJEDORAS FIBER ARTS
P. O. Box 14238
Saint Paul, MN 55114

Contents

Figure Credits

BLACK-AND-WHITE PHOTOS

The author gratefully acknowledges the following sources of black-and-white photographs in this book. Unlisted figures are by the author. AK Photos, Grant Kernan, Saskatoon, Saskatchewan: 4.29; 5.9; 6.15; 6.55; 6.64; 7.8; 8.3; 8.12; 8.24; 9.3; 11.3; 13.3; 14.A; 14.6; 14.10; 14.13; 14.15; 14.18; 14.20; 14.22; 14.24; 14.26; 14.28; 14.32; 14.33; 14.35; 14.37; 14.39; 14.40; 14.46; 14.48; 14.54; 14.55; 15.58a; 14.58b; 14.60. Mr. P. Alexandrovitch, East Orange, New Jersey: 1:10. Mrs. A. Alsupe, Riga, Latvia: 1:9. Available Light Photographics and Design, Gary Robins, Regina, Saskatchewan: 12.B. Erik Dzenis, Thornhill, Ontario: 12.11. Thomas Evans, Grandora, Saskatchewan: 3.3; 4.55; 5.22; 6.29; 12.A; 12.1; 12.3; 12.5a; 12.5b; 13.1; 13.5; 14.11; 14.30; 14.43; 14.45; 14.52; 14.61. Paul von Hahn, Winfield, British Columbia: figs. A, B. Liena Kaugars, Kalamazoo, Michigan: 1.14. Vija Ratz, Saskatoon, Saskatchewan: fig. D. The Royal Ontario Museum, Toronto, Ontario: 3.6; 4.16; 4.21; 4.35; 4.51; 4.53; 4.65; 4.71; 5.24; 5.29; 5.34; 5.40; 5.51; 6.19; 6.51; 6.53; 6.57; 6.62; 7.1; 8.26; 10.10. Irene Ositis-Schmeiser, Saskatoon, Saskatchewan: 1.5; 1.11. State Historical Museum, Riga, Latvia: 2.4 (Plate CVVM74006). Alvis Upitis, Minneapolis, Minnesota: 1.12; 3.A.

COLOR PLATES

Eric Dzenis, Thornhill, Ontario: Plate 32. Thomas Evans, Grandora, Saskatchewan: Plates 6; 11; 15; 23; 26-30; 35-48. George Gerogakakos, Halifax, Nova Scotia: Plate 34. The Royal Ontario Museum, Toronto, Ontario: Front cover, Plates 8 and 16. Alvis Upitis, Minneapolis, Minnesota: Plate 5.

ILLUSTRATIONS

Computer-generated diagrams by: Jane Evans, fig. 1.2; Lydia Kulesov, fig. 1.3; Daniel Life, fig. 5.16; Carol Skallerud, figs. 2.2, 2.6a and b, 2.7, 2.9, 2.10, 2.11, 2.12, 2.13, 3.1, 3.11, 3.23, 6.10, 11.2, 11.6, 11.12, 13.11, 14.1.

Reproduction illustrations: from J. Stausbergs, *Rīgas vēsture,* fig. 1.1; 1.4; 1.15; 1.16; from Veveris & Kuplais, *Latvijas Etnogrāfiskāja brivādabas musejā*; Plate 1; from P. Viļumsons, *Monday Morning,* fig. 5.43; from P. Viļumsons *Thursday Morning,* figs. 1.8, 1.17, 4.79, 5.43; from P. Viļumsons, *Tuesday Morning,* figs. 1.6, 1.7, 4.62; from P. Viļumsons, *Wednesday Morning,* figs. C, 2.5, 4.61, 7.13, 10.13, 13.13.

Line drawings by Patrick Redmond: figs. 1.13, 2.1, 2.3, 11.5, 11.11.

Preface

Many North Americans have only vague ideas about the country called Latvia. I was no exception, until 1977 when I first ran across examples of Latvian weaving at the Royal Ontario Museum (ROM), in Toronto, Ontario, Canada. Since then I have become increasingly involved with the people and the textile arts of Latvia. It has been a rewarding education. Finding few Latvian weavers and fewer books on the subject, almost all of them in Latvian, I have slowly translated and woven my way into a number of fascinating ideas.

I spent much time reading the texts and talking to the weavers, because I wanted to learn both technical details and the perspective on which Latvian weaving is based. As a North American weaver, I have both an advantage and a disadvantage in studying and conveying information on these fabrics. I had no ready knowledge of the textiles' everyday environment, nor of how written instructions would reveal the traditional thoughts toward weaving. I learned to weave from a set of instructions compiled from British, Swedish, Latin American, German, and colonial North American backgrounds, and others, too, no doubt. These influences have contributed to a methodology and vocabulary for naming specific weave types, and to parameters of weave structures and

Mirdza Silkālne-Strauss was a warm and caring teacher who shared her weaving knowledge willingly. She taught me what to look for in good ethnic design, composition and craftsmanship. When I was just beginning to weave the shawls and sashes and complained about my uneven edges, she often told me, "Don't worry, after weaving a few miles, they will be straight and even" – just another way of saying, "practice makes perfect!"

LIENA KAUGARS

methods. The Latvian background also melds some of the information gleaned from those countries, along with other influences, and sometimes in a different way than is known to weavers in North America.

At one point I thought I could cover the most interesting aspects of Latvian weaving as my major paper for the Guild of Canadian Weavers Masterweaver test program. That effort proved only to begin the communication process. The context of the weavings became important, as did the history of both the people and textiles in general. It all grew to a point where it simply needed to be available to inspire and inform other

people – weavers, as well as anyone sensitive to Latvia's textile heritage.

Intrigued by the woven products, I was curious about their backgrounds. Beginning with the ROM collection, I wrote letters to donors, seeking further facts about the pieces. The responses were more than academically thought-provoking. The study turned into one of the extraordinary events in my life. I came to share a sense of history, pride, spirit, love. I was saddened at accounts of mankind's inhumanities, and lifted by its tenacity. I felt a part of an old community of weavers and their values, values that can not be measured in dollar signs. Items were made to last and to be beautiful. I was awed at the level of craftsmanship and care shown by the old weavings of Latvia. To handle the fabrics reinforced their impact, and to learn their history gave each piece a personality. The textiles live on, speaking to their observers and users, but keeping secrets, too. They have become friends to be shared, as best I can convey them. My fond hope is that you, the reader, partake, enjoy, and benefit from them, too.

Jane A. Evans
Grandora, Saskatchewan, 1991

A. (below left) Baroque gateway on the Daugava river, Zemgale province, Latvia.

B. Windmill in Latgale province, ca. 1940.

Acknowledgements

Many present-day Latvians have been extremely generous in helping me learn about the textiles from their homeland. This book would not exist without the translations, fabrics, discussions, books, and friendship these people shared.

Special help and kindness have come from Mrs. Otilia Mezulis, Zinta Enzelins, Sarmite Vilks, Mrs. Nora Priverts (all of Toronto, Ontario); Mrs. Velta Vilsons (Niagara-on-the-Lake, Ontario); Mrs. Anna Smits (Saint. Paul, Minnesota); Alvis and Lizbeth Upitis (Minneapolis, Minnesota); Ilga Jansens (Bothell, Washington); Mrs. Velta Elksnis (Sydney, Australia); Irene Ositis-Schmeizer (Saskatoon, Saskatchewan); Liena Kaugars (Kalamazoo, Michigan); and Paul and Margaret von Hahn (Winfield, British Columbia).

Without Mrs. Dzidra Šēfers (Toronto, Ontario), a fine weaver trained in Riga, the stick weaving mystery might still be unsolved, along with many other questions. Mrs. Vija Ratz (Saskatoon, Saskatchewan) has been pivotal in translating, clarifying information, adding scope, and giving friendly support. Vita Plūme (Halifax, Nova Scotia) has helped me learn about things both Latvian and artistic through the years. Mr. Peter Alexandrovich (East Orange, New Jersey) was an unexpected benefactor with textiles and information, sending many wonderful additions.

M. Kati Meek (Kalamazoo, Michigan), an American weaver interested in Baltic textiles, has shared her studies in critically important capacities.

Seemingly Fated opportunities presented themselves through other non-Latvians, as well. Ravi Nielsen gave support for his *Patternland Weave Simulator* computer program far beyond the call of duty, smoothing seemingly impossible computer and printer mountains with ease and good cheer. The Royal Ontario Museum personnel made research possible, dating from the days of John Vollmer, who started this all by rummaging through what "you might find interesting." The ROM assistance continued aided by Dr. Brigitta Schmedding, Louise Mackie, Dr. Adrienne Hood, Judy Cselenyi, Greta Ferguson, and Anu Liivandi-Palias. Whether in or out of the ROM, for years one of the most inspiring people has been Dorothy Burnham.

Fate also stepped in to bring Deborah Chandler's editing skills to the rough manuscript, where she added her zest and insights. Madelyn van der Hoogt, Vita Plūme and Mary Skoy provided further technical expertise and encouragement. Patrick Redmond contributed his vast expertise in publication design. And, of course, Karen Searle's patient, talented efforts have actually constructed it all into a book.

A truly heartfelt *thank-you*, to every one of these individuals, and to the many other people who have aided in this study. Some of these people I am happy now to know as friends. Much gratitude also goes to my steadfast, old friends for their encouraging words and smiles over the fluctuating years of this project. (And although they can not read, our dogs Seth and Tansy deserve acknowledgement for bringing their unflagging companionship into the years of solitude.)

Aina Alsupe, an ethnographer in Riga, Latvia, has helped and supported in numerous ways, including correspondence, contributions in books, and through her 1982 book *Audēji Vidzemē*, an ethnographic study of Vidzeme's weaving. Much of the general history of textiles derives from her writings.

The Jean A. Chalmers Fund for the Crafts at the Canada Council awarded two grants toward research expenses for this study. Both the financial and moral boost from those awards are appreciated.

A poet at heart, my late mother shared with me her pleasure of words and of an eye for beauty. Her ready smile and strong spirit have never ceased to inspire and encourage me.

The largest thank-you goes to my husband, Tom. From companion to energizer, he has been the crucial ingredient for all my work. He, my mother, and this whole project have exemplified how the joys of life come from the persistence of caring, heartfelt spirits.

In 1905 a poor Estonian servant girl, Juuli, married the son of a Latvian-born woman, Mrs. Anna Pulles Lammertson. Around 1909, Juuli wove the blanket shown in Plate 20, guided by her mother-in-law, and reflecting Latvian tastes in color and design, rather than Juuli's preference for bright colors and stripes. Juuli raised the sheep and produced the wool weft yarns, coloring them with natural and synthetic dyes. She chose cotton yarn for warp, which was readily available in The Baltics by the twentieth century. The blanket served the family intact until 1944. At that time Juuli's son, his wife, and their two small children emigrated to Sweden as war refugees, taking only this blanket and some diapers. An untended hot iron burned a hole in the precious cover, which was salvaged by cutting and piecing. The blanket retained its comfortable, attractive qualities and was eventually brought to Canada for many more years of use by Juuli and her descendants.

MRS. AUGUST LAANSOO

A Joy Forever

A thing of beauty is a joy forever:
Its loveliness increases; it will never
Pass into nothingness.

– John Keats, *Endymion*

The beauty of designs, colors, skilled craftsmanship – these can give joy to weaver and non-weaver alike.

Always fascinated by unusual weave structures, I began researching weft-faced fabrics many years ago. This pursuit brought unforeseen enrichment from a people and their textiles. In 1977 my weaver's curiosity took me to the Royal Ontario Museum in Toronto, Canada. At that time its textile department stored its collection in oak cupboards piled high with brown boxes. These held treasures of cloth from many nations, including blankets from Latvia. Their attractive designs, pleasing touch, and complex interlacements intrigued me. One blanket in particular (shown on the cover), was eye-catching and sensual with its handsome, soft surface of purple and lavender wool. The blanket's history was mostly unknown; its personality safely rested on its merits. After numerous analyses and pictures, it became an old friend to me and led me to study many other "everyday" Latvian fabrics, all of which deserve to be more widely known. This book evolved in order to share these woven textiles produced by skilled Latvian weavers over the past century.

Some good references for weaving Latvian costumes already exist in English, therefore this book deals mostly with household textiles. The information that is included is chosen to help preserve and document a range of valuable heirlooms, give a small insight into textile history, and encourage further excellence in handweaving. In addition to actual examples, there is a background summary of the information used by typical Latvian handweavers up to World War II. For centuries there were several catagories of weavers using widely-differing techniques. The emphasis here is on weaves that are within the scope of handweavers (be they in old Latvia or present North America) who are somewhere along the spectrum between beginners and masters.

Technical information on each weave is provided for weavers who already understand basic drafting and loom setup, and who seek more exciting, sophisticated information. Both four-shaft and multi-shaft

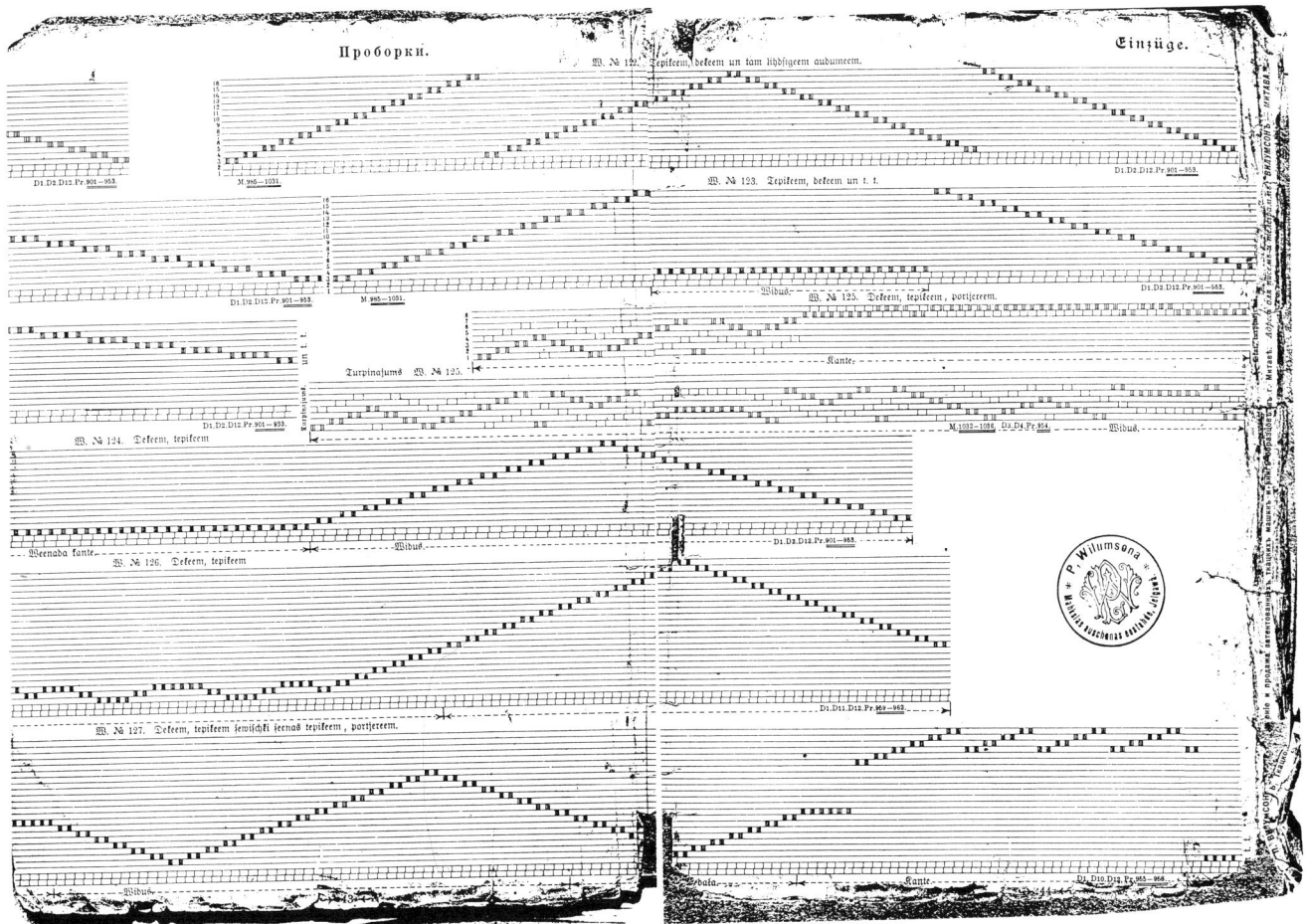

C. *Double page from old Viļumsons book,* Trešdienas rīts *(Wednesday Morning).*

weavers may find challenges in the traditional works and in the modified applications of those works. Latvian texts sometimes used double-harness looms *(see glossary)* with long-eyed heddles *(see glossary)* for complex patterns, and where convenient that drafting is included here. However, most pieces have been analyzed to their most rudimentary drafts for single-harness looms. It is hoped that double-harness loom weavers will re-draft these lengthy drafts to fit their own loom's capabilities.

There are three parts to this book. *Part One* gives background information correlating the textiles to their makers and users, and to significant cultural influences. *Part Two* deals with traditional textiles and contains as much detailed information and history on each piece as possible. It explains the weave structures and theories, emphasizing the perspective of Latvian weavers. *Part Three*, on modified uses of the old weaves, is meant as inspiration for handweavers whose goals may be beyond the original weaves' applications.

Many complex and varied fabrics are possible in handweaving. Endless names are given to distinguish one result from another.

These names are based on everything from structure to site of discovery to whimsy. Rather than get onto semantic carrousels by imposing a rigid classification system, English language nomenclature is from Irene Emery's system in *The Primary Structures of Fabrics* and Dorothy Burnham's book, *Warp and Weft.* A basic glossary of terms is included. A bibliography of both Latvian and English language resources is provided for further information.

There are many technical treats in this book. While journeying through it, the following "landmarks" may reward both average and advanced weavers. Notable features are two sizes of warps alternating in one piece, three concurrent colors of wefts, and turned-lace blocks. Such weaves as weft-faced or warp-faced pattern weaves, derived twills, turned twills, and tied-float units are all worth attention. Above all, the essence of quality, care, and skillful craftsmanship displayed in these textiles will be as great a reward to the spirit as any specific details.

The last great emigrations from Latvia took place during the 1940s. There has been substantial change since then due to politics. Memories of details within technical com-

plexities are hard to recall and even harder to convey in an adopted tongue. The Latvian-language weaving books still extant are scarce. Thus a body of knowledge could fade from the everyday world, and a source of beauty might recede into museum storage. Anyone who appreciates textiles and perhaps wishes to learn from them could miss out on a wonderful resource.

This book is a modest start at displaying this body of textiles for weavers and for anyone who treasures Latvia's legacy. Relevant historical and technical data are included as fully as possible for each piece. Many pieces have been selected because of their special structural qualities, while others use designs or materials for purposes not usual to many handweavers. Some of the items may be of relatively standard constructions but are patterned in attractive, typically Latvian fashion. These textiles are not chosen as laudable but unattainable goals. They are attainable – or at least adaptable – ideas for most moderately adept weavers. The main requirement for these effective, rewarding results is heartfelt control of both one's skills and patience.

D. Rural Latvian scene prior to World War II.

2

PART ONE

The Weaves
CULTURAL BACKGROUND

Along the eastern coast of the Baltic Sea lie beaches once aglow with precious "sunstone" or amber. Beyond the beaches stretch attractive, lowlands holding mixed forests, meadowlands, peat bogs, sandy patches, and marshes. The sea's temperate influence spreads inland, moderating extremes of the damp climate. This site has proven to be one of the crossroads of mankind where Eastern and Western cultures have met over the centuries, often in commercial or political conflicts.

In pre-historic times, Finno-Ugric tribes from the north settled the district called Latvia. Around 2000 B.C. a large group of people, called Balts, moved in along the whole south and southeastern Baltic Sea coast, displacing the previous tribes. From within the many Baltic tribes the Lithuanians and the Letts (or Latvians) established themselves in areas where they remain into the twentieth century as two permanent, identifiable peoples. Lithuanians and Latvians speak the only two surviving Balt languages in the world, ancient branches of the Indo-European linguistic family.

It was almost 1900, and Mrs. Anna Pulles Lammertson was distressed that her future daughter-in-law, Juuli, was a poor serving girl. Farm girls with full hope chests were better marriage prospects. Among the items in her hope chest, a bride customarily brought under-clothes for her husband, but Juuli was too poor to do this. Anna hid her son's existing underclothes, to show her dis-satisfaction at Juuli's poverty. Determined, Juuli enlisted a married sister's help. They bought cotton cloth and made enough underclothes to last into the marriage. By then Juuli's first flax crop would be har-vested, and she would make better-quality thread, fabric, and garments. The marriage took place, and over the years Juuli proved skillful in the many duties of a farmwife, including producing textiles. (See page 115.)

MRS. AUGUST LAANSOO

Thanks to the Baltic Sea and Daugava River, farming and trade have been the basis of life in Latvia for four thousand years. Baltic amber and farm products were traded into the Near East during the Bronze Age (c. 1250 B.C.), and Latvian traders continued to be well received in the Mediterranean Roman Empire until its fall (c. 400 A.D.). Over the Dark Ages (c. 500-1000 A.D.) there were attacks by Scandinavian Vikings, Slavs, Russians, and Danes on various sides of the Latvian districts. Four tribes held kingdoms which today are the Latvian districts of Kurzeme, Zemgale, Latgale, and Vidzeme. See the map in fig. 1.2.

By 1200, German crusaders occupied western Latvia, organizing many small principalities where native Latvians worked under German land-owners. Riga, the capital, was founded in 1201 and developed by Hanseatic merchants into the leading trading center on the eastern Baltic Sea. Serfdom was introduced in 1494. Over the next 500 years, battles and occupations by Russians, Swedes, Danes, and Poles imposed varying forms of government in regions of Latvia. There was restricted freedom and little peace for the farming peasants. In cities, tradesmen and artisans fared slightly better but they, too, lost many legal rights.

Western Latvia remained under German noblemen's rule until the mid-1500s. From their shared German and Swedish influences most of western Latvia and its northern neighbor, Estonia, eventually became similar in culture, history, and Lutheran faith, but not in language.

Years of Polish rule followed in Latvia. This became segmented in the 1600s when Sweden dominated western Vidzeme and Estonia from 1629 to 1710. The Swedes left a somewhat more liberal social heritage in Vidzeme than in the rest of Latvia.

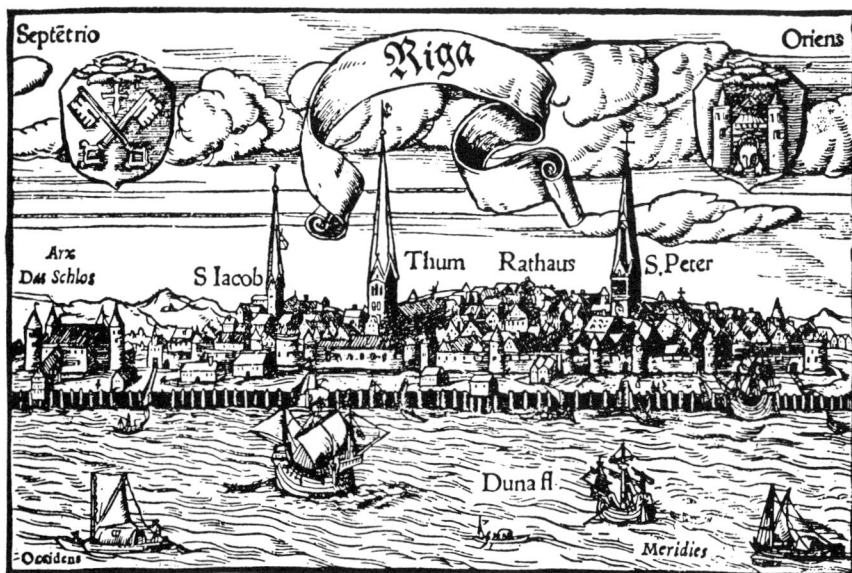

1.1. View of Riga, Latvia, 1559.

Swedish territories fell to the Russian campaign to reach the sea by way of the port of Riga in the early 1700s.

Due to strong dominance by Poland from 1561 to 1772, Latvia's eastern province of Latgale became similar in history, culture, Roman Catholic religion, and language with Lithuania, another Polish possession.

The regions of Kurzeme and Zemgale initially were under German influence. Within Polish rule in the 1600s, a duchy called Courland was formed and covered both regions. Although nominally Polish-Lithuanian, in actuality the area was run by relatively liberal German nobility and remained Protestant. The rulers of Courland emphasized manufacturing activities, colonization in Africa and the Caribbean, and world-wide trade.

Wars continued until Russia obtained the whole Latvian territory by 1795. Although Russia held the district, the old landowning nobility of German origin continued in control of the feudal society. Peasants' personal freedoms were even more rigorously curtailed, within a spectrum of estate owners' policies. Emancipation finally began in the mid-1800s. However, the peasants still could not hold land and were dependent on the German-speaking barons.

In the late 1800s hard-won reforms gradually brought individual freedoms, a cultural renaissance, a new interest in politics, and such educational progress that almost no illiteracy remained in Latvia. An emerging sense of nationalism encouraged pursuit of the Latvian people's folk traditions.

With the collapse of both the German and Russian states during World War I, the severely war-ravaged Latvians declared themselves an autonomous nation in 1918. Inexperienced at independent nationalism, they euphorically sought stability in a volatile era and location. For twenty years Latvians zealously rebuilt their physical and social environment.

In 1940, early in the Second World War, Stalin's Russian troops overwhelmed Latvia, Estonia, and Lithuania, and annexed them as constituents of the U.S.S.R. "The Year of Terror" followed, ended only by German troops who occupied the country until 1944. Thereafter, it became a republic of the Soviet Union, under a program of assimilation in politics and culture.

During Stalin's purges, and especially in 1940 and 1944 when Russia invaded, many Latvians hastily emigrated. These people promoted cultural information in an effort to preserve their heritage in exile. Many books were written in the refugee camps set up in Germany during World War II, while memories were fresh. Many refugees eventually went to North America or Australia.

Within a chaotic history of wars and disasters, the Latvians cherish those years of true independence from 1918 to 1940. A national cultural life proudly blossomed, followed by an ardent, continuous effort to retain it both in and out of present-day Latvia.

This effort triumphed in 1991 when Latvia and its two Baltic neighbors regained their status as fully independent nations.

1.2. Map of Latvia with principlal cities and four districts.

40 Miles

CHAPTER ONE

Latvian Textile Traditions

Centuries of foreign-dominated life in Latvia modified but did not quell its core of individuality as a nation. People had long combined outside influences with old designs and lore, nurturing a sense of their unique history within the incessant occupations. From the mid-1800s and into the 1900s, the nationalism that grew in Latvia fostered a search for cultural identity. This appreciation for tradition created a demand for authentic Latvian music, crafts, folklore, literature, traditions, and costumes.

Crafts that were distinctly Latvian in design flourished. In textiles, for example, a collection of costumes with instructions for making them was produced in 1931. The Latvian Women's National League issued a large book of new and old weaving patterns for clothing and household textiles for home weavers. The State Institute of Crafts was established in Riga, producing many fine craftsmen including weavers. A privately-run school under Mr. Pēters Viļumsons produced master-weavers who wove commercially on their own.

Textile Designs

Geometric motifs have been the only characteristic form in Latvian folk art. As in the arts of many other nations, these geometric forms evolved in prehistoric times from symbols for revered influences in humans' lives: celestial bodies, water, fire, gods and goddesses, trees, etc. An agrarian people, Latvians especially noticed and developed deities from the forces of nature. Figure 1.3 shows some of the primary design motifs. These were widely embellished and adapted to fit the medium, technique, and need of a particular piece. Creativity in blending these recognizable, traditional design elements was valued. Latvian artisans expanded, varied, and re-composed motifs and colors for a rich visual result.

Latvian designs were almost always symmetrical, within each motif and a whole design. Negative space was rarely incorporated into a design. Elements for major focus in a design were put in the center of squares or triangles which served as a frame. If too large, a design often was trimmed at top and bottom equally or cut in half, rather than simplified in ornateness. Borders were commonly placed between a design and the plain background material, avoiding abrupt edges, and often tapering off with complexity into the background. (Dzervitis, 1973.)

LATVIAN DESIGN SYMBOLS

GOD or HEAVEN
This sign combines the solid base line of the earth-mother with the arch of the heavens, topped by the sun's circle. Prior to Christianity, the Balts believed in a god who dwelt near the sun and displayed great power, love, and wisdom. Among the oldest symbols, examples date from Early Iron Age metal jewelry (c. 1000 B.C.).

SUN
Possibly the most predominant of all the Latvian symbols, this is also one of the oldest. Originally a circle, it has evolved so that it usually has eight segments.

CROSS-HATCH STAR
Another simple design unit as old as the God symbol, this star was used to protect its user from evil at night.

MORNING STAR
A complex symbol formed of two interlocked Cross-hatch Stars, the Morning Star is considered very significant and powerful. Called *Auseklis,* it is an extremely popular pattern motif in all Latvian craft media.

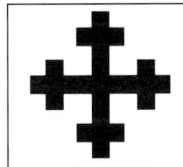

CROSS OF CROSSES
This pre-Christian symbol is a combination of four crosses. Simple crosses and this more complicated sign were used throughout Latvia as decorative elements and to invoke divine favor.

FIRECROSS or THUNDER CROSS
An extremely ancient symbol common to all Indo-European cultures, this is the sign for fire, light, thunder, fortune, health, and prosperity. Its arms may face clockwise or counter-clockwise. It is associated with crops and lightning.

Some motifs based on plant forms filtered into Latvia's designs beginning in the late 1800s. Colorful edge patterns on blankets in the province of Latgale (eastern Latvia) were influenced by Russian designs at that time and changed from rigidly geometric stars to stylized flowers and leaves. Loom-controlled patterns came to range from geometric to extremely descriptive, depending on the capability of the looms on which they were produced. The most representational designs were produced in western Latvia, in particular Kurzeme, where equipment was often complex. (Stepermanis, 1961-1967.)

Outside of these limited floral efforts, most weavers, knitters, and designers for other media used only traditional, geometric motifs for their works.

Woven Textiles

Latvia's textile history displays many competent weavers over the centuries. Card weaving was highly developed for decorative bands by the Iron Age (1000 B.C.-100 A.D.). Artifacts dating back to the second century A.D. include intricately woven horse blankets. Items from gravesites show that clothing became quite ornate between the 600s and 1100s A.D.

Dyed blankets and whole bolts of linen and woolen fabrics have been found in chests from the 1500s. Most fabric probably was made on two-shaft looms, often utilizing laid-in or picked-up patterns.

Fabrics in different areas within the land blended the effects of indigenous and occupying people. This gave distinctive regional types, colors, and means of decorating textiles, as in the following instances.

In the northern Latvian province of Vidzeme and the neighboring country of Estonia, Swedish rule throughout the 1600s encouraged some individual liberty, education, and initiative. One result was the development of proficient master and home weavers, the latter aided by the professionals' examples. By 1685 Vidzeme was exporting block-patterned fabrics, and even the weavers of block patterns, to Sweden. Colors were restrained and woven textures predominated in technically advanced weavings. Farmhome women wove selvage-to-selvage patterns, often in weft-faced plain weave on two shafts, rather than emphasizing inlay or pick-up techniques. Following Russia's take-over of the Vidzeme area in 1721, Germans emigrated to become estate weavers in Vidzeme. Their legacy of block

patterns woven in linen was used by Vidzeme's professional weavers, who substituted familiar twill structures for the satin structures within blocks. By the mid-1800s Vidzeme had developed a large block-woven linen cloth trade, which flourished into the 1900s.

Flemish and German master weavers were directing textile factory production in Kurzeme and Zemgale by the mid-1600s. Local people's skills and taste became more sophisticated from that exposure. In Zemgale, the favorite skirt material became one of brightly colored stripes within which were intricate patterns. These supplementary-weft float patterns, running the width of the cloth, such as the example in fig. 6.3, applied weaving ideas learned in the factories to typically geometric Latvian symbols. By the mid-1800s Kurzeme, like Vidzeme, had its own highly competent center of linen production. Due to more weavers in

1.4. Rural scene from Latvian life in 1701.

1.5. The landmark steeple of St. Peter's Church in Riga. The original wooden church was built around 1200.

Kurzeme being self-employed than in Vidzeme where they worked for large-scale linen merchants, there was more variety of block patterns in Kurzeme than in Vidzeme.

To the east, Latgale's influences were mostly from Russia, Poland, and Lithuania. This is seen in textiles' bright colors (especially red), large patterns, lace trims, and popular structures such as inlays of supplementary wefts, tufts, and lace weaves. These latter techniques, controlled by the weaver rather than the loom, were decorative without the aid of complex machinery. Most of Latgale's handweaving was for use in the farm homes and done by home weavers on simple looms equipped with few shafts.

Pivotal changes in the country's weaving came with each major swing in its political/social/economic history. After the mid-1800s the gradual emancipation of the serfs brought a change to self-directed labour, education, and awareness of cultural traditions. In this atmosphere, all levels of commercial weaving expanded, professional weavers created original designs and products, and home weavers developed in proficiency.

Finnish influences, along with Scandinavian and European ones, were felt by the beginning of the twentieth century. Weaves like *crepe, honeycomb*, certain lace weaves, reinforced weaves, and other structures were not well known until professional weavers began using them at the turn of the century. Home weavers soon learned them. The divergence between Latvia's regions decreased with the spread of similar information, equipment, and skills. For example, during the 1800s the most skillful twill weavers were in Kurzeme and its eastern neighbor, Zemgale. By 1900, with the dissemination of information and more elaborate looms, the weavers in Vidzeme also became adept at the distinctive, complex twill weaves.

Taste within regions still tended to relate to familiar traditions. For instance, lace accents continued to be more common in Catholic areas than elsewhere. The day-blankets of the 1900s, used for decorative covers on beds, were woven of all linen in white and a pale pattern color in Vidzeme, while in other areas they were woven partially of dark wool.

Textile Producers

Undoubtedly home weavers were a mainstay to Latvian textile production across the ages. Professional weavers eventually were part of communities but little information about them is available prior to the 1600s. Within the master/tenant societal structure, weavers fell into five general groups:

Foreign apprentices, journeymen, and masterweavers were at the nucleus of complex weaving until 1800. These were highly-skilled men, often of German background. Most worked on estates in Vidzeme and Kurzeme weaving fashionable fabrics for their employers, and trying to keep up with the latest European trends in both home and garment textiles. Their admired products often set pattern standards that home weavers attempted to copy.

Textile factories of Kurzeme and Zemgale had been directed by foreign (Flemish, Belgian, Swedish, German, and French) masterweavers and staffed by Latvians. These went through a decline in the eighteenth century due to feudalism. They emerged again as significant textile producers in the second half of the nineteenth century, when they spread to Vidzeme.

Cottage-industry producers were virtually unique to Vidzeme until the mid-nineteenth century, where they were a very small percentage of the population. These men and women wove a few products for sale in markets. Weaving time was limited to brief spare time from farming duties.

Tradesmen were quite skilled men and women who did only custom orders. They often were landless persons, working out of a relative's house. The number of tradesmen was very small until the late 1800s because special permission was needed from an estate's owner to pursue other vocations than farming. Nonetheless this group's work was influential as a guide for home weavers.

Home weavers were almost always female family members and servants of the household, who preserved traditional techniques, patterns, and equipment. Farm women were the primary producers of cloth used by country people into the late nineteenth and early twentieth centuries.

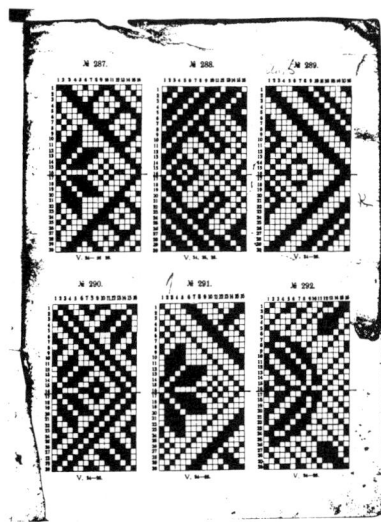

1.6. Page of drafts from Latvian weaving text Tuesday Morning by P. Viļumsons.

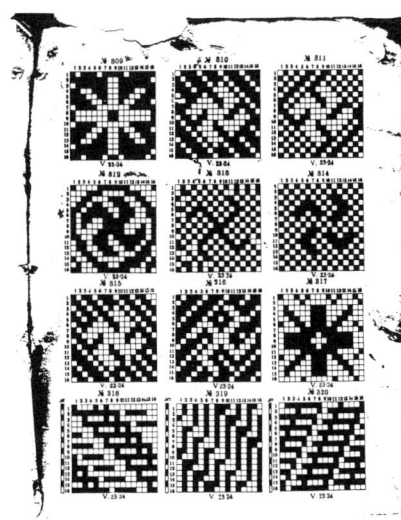

1.7. Page of drafts from Latvian weaving text, Tuesday Morning. by P. Viļumsons.

This was especially the case in Latgale, and slightly less so in Vidzeme. In Kurzeme and Zemgale their work was proportionately less significant because factory-made textiles were somewhat more common there.

Women's role. Up to the twentieth century, primarily women were responsible for all the weaving and spinning, and most of the dyeing and fulling. They were also in charge of all sheep raising and wool processing, and did much of the work of linen processing. Fiber-related jobs were seasonal activities, done when outdoor work was less demanding. Throughout Latvia weaving began sometime after the New Year. In Vidzeme, women spun fiber steadily from November 10 to February 2. Weaving began February 2 and ended April 23, utilizing the lengthening daylight before planting season. Every female in a household helped during the intense activity of cloth production. Young and old members wound bobbins and wove bands. The farmer's wife did the more complicated aspects of warp planning and preparation for everyone. For maximum production, all able women wove in shifts during the daylight, working at one or more looms which were set up in the choice position near the fireplace and windows of the house's main room. Weaving projects were completed in order of the owner's rank, beginning with those of the farm wife and ending with the servant's items. Each year the emphasis shifted to provide one type of needed item, for instance blankets or towels, on a long warp.

Naturally such an annual, intensive effort begot rituals and rules to induce success each year. Projects were best started on odd-number days of the week (Monday, Wednesday, or Friday). If a man entered the room first after a weaving was begun all would go well, but if a woman did threads would snarl. If a young woman did not begin to weave the same day she warped up her loom, she would marry a poor man rather than a rich one. In both Latvia and Estonia it was important to make

1.8. *Cover of P. Viļumsons book,* Wednesday Morning, *or* Trešdienas rīts *in modern Latvian script. This book probably was printed prior to 1918.*

hearty porridge on the day of setting up or finishing a project. This became so entrenched as a tradition that instead of asking if a weaving would be finished a person might ask, "Will you eat porridge today?"

Weaving was greatly respected in the farmhome for its difficulty and importance. With virtually no written books, the home weavers mostly worked from memory, oral exchange of ideas, and items they might encounter. Especially capable home weavers might walk to other farms and help thread complicated weaves. A loom was integral in homes until World War II, although its products might have decreased over the pre-war years. The tradition of mothers teaching their daughters to weave was part of many people's sense

of their cultural heritage. The blanket in fig 8.7 woven by Juuli Lammertson is an example of the legacy of home weaving production.

Commercial Weaving
After serfdom was ended in the mid-1800s farming and the jobs on farms changed. Women found themselves with new tasks which allowed even less time for spinning and weaving. The number of professional weavers gradually increased, and a new category of weaver developed. This was the self-employed producer working out of a small shop, often attached to a mill. For spinning, besides old women who traveled from farm to farm, small shops and commercial home spinners appeared. Home weavers used their precious

1.9. P. Viļumsons sits in the center of one of his 1930s classes of masterweavers. His brother is at the far right. A loom designed by Viļumsons is visible, and many typically Latvian textiles surround everyone.

time to make simple items not practical to buy (everyday clothing, basic bedding, or sacks) or ones that were for special uses. Commercial weavers produced the fancier goods that required complex equipment, time, and expertise.

Weaving Instruction

Pre-1900. For centuries home weavers taught their daughters how to carry on the traditions. Tradesmen or cottage industry weavers learned as best they could, often gleaning ideas from estate and factory weavers. Masterweavers were trained in an apprentice system and seldom were native Latvians until the nineteenth century.

Pattern books were used chiefly by masterweavers. Handwritten books passed among generations of professional weavers, as was common throughout Scandinavia and Europe. The first printed one known in

Vidzeme appeared about 1740 from Saxony in Germany, the European damask weaving center. The book showed block patterns for linens, and all written parts were in German.

In the second half of the nineteenth century textile producers had more books and, eventually, courses than ever before. With education and freedom to move, people were exposed to non-traditional methods and equipment. Finnish and Scandinavian courses were attended by Latvians, who then taught the new ideas and skills back at home. This led to a leveling of differences in methods, patterns, equipment, and taste throughout Latvia. As they took courses from the new teachers, farmhome weavers acquired wider skills and used the information for filling their hope chests and weaving daily necessities. More weavers worked on custom orders out of their rural homes, and

more masterweavers were trained. Popular fashions, personal taste of customers, and ability and taste of the weavers all influenced the trends in patterns, colors, and even uses of textiles. Latvia's textile factories also grew and became more sophisticated to meet the growing market.

Post-1900. In the twentieth century art, craft, and home economics schools were established within Latvia, the most influential of these being in Riga and Jelgava.

In Zemgale, where textile industries were common, Pēters Viļumsons emerged as a figure of consequence in Latvian handweaving. He developed several mechanical looms which made production weaving practical for individual professional weavers. Between 1903 and 1930 he also printed four books called *Monday Morning, Tuesday Morning, Wednesday Morning,* and

Thursday Morning. These contained technical information and many hundreds of patterns. Figs. 1.6 and 1.7 show drafts from two pages of *Tuesday Morning*'s patterns, most using 16 shafts. In his courses, fig. 1.9, he taught the latest Latvian, Russian, and European manufacturing and factory techniques, and incorporated traditional Latvian information. He encouraged his

1.10. Plain weave blouse and skirt for the traditional regional costume of Krustpils in Latgale province. The blouse is of bleached linen, embellished with needlemade laces. Other blouses of the region often had elaborate, four-color embroidery along the collar and lower sleeves. The costume consisted of a blouse, a checkered skirt, a card-woven sash, a beaded headband of red felt, and an embroidered wrap with card-woven trim. The blouse is trimmed with a brooch, made in an old, symbolic geometric design. This "maiden's costume" was made and worn in the early 1930s by Monika Alexandrovitch. A married woman would wear a white cap instead of the felt headpiece. Blouse: early 1930s; Krustpils, Latgale; warp and weft linen, bleached, Z-twist, singles; 19 e/cm (48 epi); 16 p/cm (40.5 ppi); woven by Monika Alexandrovitch. ROM990. 20.14.2. Gift of Mr. Peter Alexandrovitch. See fig. 3.3 and Plate 6 for skirt detail.

students from all parts of Latvia to compile their particular knowledge of patterns and weaves for country-wide dissemination. His influence on weavers' products and methods was prodigious. A blanket in the Royal Ontario Museum collection, fig. 4.63, apparently matches pattern number 603 in *Thursday Morning* and was woven in Zemgale at the time Viļumsons was active. It possibly was a direct result of his teaching.

Two other teachers of note also wrote significant books for weavers. Anna Skuja-Antēne recorded popular nineteenth- and twentieth-century patterns in *Aušans (Weaving)*, 1931, later re-released as *Rokas grāmata audējām (Handbook for Weavers)*, 1949; *Mācies aust (Learn to Weave)*, 1936 and 1939; and *Paraugi audumiem (Samples for Weaving)*, 1940. Recognized as an outstanding teacher, Skuja-Antēne also was an influential author whose books reveal the early twentieth-century emphasis on traditional patterns in modern uses. The books reflect some information related to the Finnish courses which were available at the end of the nineteenth century. Weavers using the books would need skills running from basic to advanced.

Elga Kivicka, a teacher at the national arts trade school, wrote *Aušanas Pašmācība (Teach Yourself*

Weaving) in 1934. This book emphasized post-1890 technical weaving information, such as complex reinforced satins and double weaves rather than the home weavers' popular patterns and methods. Commercial and expert weavers would have found it useful for theoretical bases, and home weavers could also have used it within a more limited extent.

Traditional Textile Uses

With few large cities in Latvia the main users of textiles lived on farms as owners or peasants, the latter being the majority of the population. Commercial, professional, and clerical people formed other strata in society. The class range gave significant diversity in the textile items worn and used. Latvians have long recognized the cultural significance of their textiles, fig. 1.11. The variety of fabrics a person had was determined by wealth, equipment, weavers' skills, materials, taste, and available time.

GARMENTS

Affluent people purchased garments, while poor ones made their own. An average farm person wore simple garments of linen and wool. The main items were long skirts, blouses, shawls, shirts, loose trousers, capes, stockings, mittens, undergarments,

1.11. Located in an old street in Riga, the museum at far right houses functional and "everyday" art objects such as household textiles.

1.12. Costume from Alsunga district, Kurzeme, Latvia. Photographed in Latvia in 1989.

belts, and headpieces. Depending on era and social status, the wealthiest classes wore clothes similar to those of contemporary European fashions.

As in many cultures, Latvians had distinctive special-occasion costumes relating to local regions, as in figs. 1.10, 1.12 and 1.13. The textiles and jewelry displayed separate designs for each region because ancestors, foreign dominance, and trade patterns split exposure within the country. Bronze Age or Iron Age types of metal decorations, card-woven bands, and amber diversely ornamented costumes made centuries later.

HOUSEHOLD TEXTILES

Trained, professional weavers employed on the estates provided household textiles for wealthier families, and some articles were bought from custom weavers or in cities. Fancy weaves such as damask were used on!y in the manorhouses. Weaves requiring over four shafts, and certainly those of more than eight, were seldom woven by home weavers before the end of the nineteenth century. Sheets, pillow covers, towels, blankets, tablecloths, curtains, and rugs were all made of complex

patterns for the gentry class and followed fashion trends. These items were then imitated by home weavers. (Alsupe, 1982.)

For many years a peasant household's textiles were simple versions of basic items: bands, sacks, towels, mattress covers, sheets, pillow covers, blankets, and perhaps a wall or floor mat. It was critical to a girl's marriage prospects to have in her hope chest a substantial part of the clothing and household fabrics her future household would need. Mothers produced much of the fabric, the girl made some, and other relatives might contribute. Even simple sacks were handwoven at home. Cottage industry weavers wove some of the items which were purchased for the dowry, a practice more common after 1860. See Plate 1 and fig. 2.4.

Simple bands were woven on small band-weaving devices for the myriad of domestic uses that small strips can serve, such as lamp wicks, carrying straps, horse reins, or shoe ties.

Towels were woven as one long piece to be cut later as needed. The fabric was rolled up, not folded, and tucked

in the large hope chest. Linen and eventually cotton/linen towels combined bleached, unbleached, and colored threads. There were towels for the face, for sauna, for hands, for dishes, for special occurrences, and for coffins. Sometimes the only difference among these towels was their age, the newest ones being used for better occasions. Showy ones were hung to decorate a room for celebrations or were for guests. A patterned towel was hung near the bed of a woman in labor or near a cradle to bring good luck. In Vidzeme weddings, the bride gave towels to relatives and to the people who carried her hope chest. Coffin towels came into use in the mid-nineteenth century, replacing straps for carrying and lowering a coffin into the grave. A whole set of these narrow towels, ranging from three to six meters long, were part of the household possessions in a well-to-do family. Towels also served on special occasions as cloths for small tables in peasant homes, or covered mirrors or windows during a funeral. By the twentieth century a woman's skill in weaving was on display in the form of a towel prominently hung on a featured hanger.

1.13. Special clothes were stored in wooden chests and boxes in the 1700s and 1800s in Vidzeme.

Tablecloths, although standard accessories in estate homes, were unusual in peasant homes up to the eighteenth century. Thereafter, tablecloths were used by every strata of society, especially on special occasions.

Homemade blankets, simple in pattern and structure, were the main decoration in peasants' single-room houses for centuries. Blankets were still all wool in the 1600s, with linen and cotton warps appearing later. Professionally woven blankets, besides often being fancier in weave structures, frequently were wider and without a seam down the middle.

Wall blankets. These were functional or decorative. Into the nineteenth century the drafty sleeping quarters of poor peasants, such as threshing barns, had insulating wall and window hangings woven of tow linen with various reed wefts. These mats were also thrown on the floor for warmth while dressing. More decorative wall blankets came into use late in the nineteenth century when farm homes began to have plastered walls and were decorated to emulate manor houses. The walls were protected and insulated with blankets. In Latgale and Zemgale bright blankets of sewn-together sashes in traditional patterns were popular for both beds and walls.

Horse and sleigh blankets. Horses were covered in the winter for warmth and in the summer for protection from mosquitoes. Rags or rough linen wefts woven in simple stripes or checks gave two contrasting weights of cloth for the two different uses. Old sleigh blankets in Vidzeme were woven of linen with wool pile tied into the plain weave for warmth. Later sleigh blankets added a leather layer beneath the fabric.

Bed linens were not used on the peasants' plank beds in very old times. Eventually sheets, pillow covers, and mattress covers became more common among all classes of people. In the average peasant farm home, mattresses and pillows were linen bags stuffed with hay or straw. Poultry feathers were used for mattresses by wealthier families in the late 1800s, when cotton yarn became available to weave tighter fabric. Linen sheets began to be used in the 1600s. Interestingly, poor families in parts of Vidzeme slept on top of two short sheets so materials and laundry were conserved; the foot-end sheet could be woven smaller and thinner than the mid-bed sheet. Pillow covers were two layers of linen fabric over feather stuffing. As farm homes became more ornamented in the nineteenth century items such as pillows, sheets, and blankets became showier and

meant for daytime display. Color, pattern, and embellishments like lace were fashionable.

Rugs became desirable in the 1800s when farmhouse floors were wood instead of dirt. The old custom of covering floors with reeds and straw evolved into reed or fir branch mats, then rag or linen rugs. Rugs were usually woven warp-faced as long pieces. In the early twentieth century, several might be placed together to cover an entire floor.

Fancy linens were first used by estate owners, city people, and religious leaders who led the way in patterns and even functions of textiles. Items such as tablecloths or curtains did not appear among the farm people until the trend had been set by the wealthier classes.

Decorative textiles such as cushions, rugs, fancy blankets, and upholstery were prevalent by 1920. Blankets, sheets, or upholstery woven in natural or white linen were considered sophisticated as summer decoration in Vidzeme. They were called *nātns* items, which was the term for natural or bleached linen. In the twentieth century, Latvians' desire for traditional patterns spread to ornate door curtains, wall hangings, and wool table covers - all objects that had not been made previously. The wall blankets and bed blankets of sewn-together sashes flourished at this time, too. Straw-weft mats decorated walls or tables, in contrast to the functional wall and floor covers from poor farms of olden days.

Fibers

Wool and flax, which flourish in the mild climate of the Baltic Sea, have been native to Latvia for centuries.

Wool

All stages of wool production from sheep raising through spinning, fig. 1.14, were done by the farm women. The quality of the wool fibers ranged from very coarse to long and soft. The former was from the average farm

1.14. Mirdza Silkalns-Strauss demonstrates spinning wearing a festive costume. She is surrounded by Latvian craft work. Photographed in 1942 at the Latvian open-air museum, Brīvdabas Musejā.

sheep and the latter came from sheep specially imported by the estate barons. Hand carding of the wool was commonplace late into the nineteenth century. Carding was done in two stages. In the first stage with coarse-toothed cards, one card was attached teeth side up to a bench and the second card was pulled across it. This coarse carding was followed by another on fine-toothed hand cards. Carding mills eventually were favored by people who could afford their services.

Most wool was dyed before carding, to even out the color in the yarn. There were few professional dyers until shortly before 1900 when dyeing shops emerged, often adjacent to carding mills.

Fulling of wool cloth to shrink and soften it was done for centuries at home, mostly by the women. The fabric was soaked in barrels of ash water, washed and agitated until the desired hand was achieved. Called *vadmala*, the fulled cloth also was pressed at home. By 1920 factories existed for these heavy jobs. Figure 1.16 shows a final stage of the work.

Flax

Linen had a pervasive, esteemed position in Latvian life over the ages. Flax was grown and processed on the farms. Men did the heavy labour, fig. 1.15, and women did lighter but more complex aspects of the fiber's growth and preparation. Long fibers made clothing yarn. Short fibers went into sheets, tablecloths, towels, and bedspreads. Bleaching was done by leaving the damp cloth or fiber on the grass in the sun. Occasionally chemicals were boiled with the linen to bleach it. Linseed or rye was boiled for warp sizing. Dyeing of linen was done after spinning.

Used for centuries in ropes and in many household and garment fabrics, linen also became a source of income for farmers. Estate owners and small farmers alike grew flax for marketing, especially in the second half of the nineteenth century. At that time, professionally-woven linen cloth had a wide market so there was a good demand for flax.

Some rituals became attached to the cultivation of this desirable crop. It was considered good luck to sow flax when the juniper tree flowered.

Farmers tried to plant on a day with clouds coming from the west and bearing rain. An old superstition augured that if there had been a death in a house and the body was there, laundry must be rubbed by hand rather than beaten with sticks, otherwise the flax in the fields would turn brown and hard.

OTHER BAST FIBERS
Opposite from linen's rank, *hemp* fibers were occasionally used for making the poorest quality of cloth. Into the nineteenth century some peasants had wall insulators and rugs woven with *rushes* or *fir branches* as wefts. The use of these materials remained popular in Latgale longer than elsewhere.

Cotton

Cotton was imported to a small degree in the eighteenth century. It became readily available in the second half of the nineteenth century. In the twentieth century it was the main warp material. Cotton was used in its natural color or in factory-dyed hues.

Dyes

Textile colors, originally from natural sources, could be delightfully bright and were carefully placed. Due to separate traditions and plants, different regions had diverse colors. For example, in central Vidzeme clothing was somber, while slightly to the south in Krustpils, Latgale, people wore bright colors of red, green, yellow, and blue. For such a small country there was wide variety of taste in colors, traceable to the restricted movement among the peasants.

The main sources for natural dyes were widespread, supplemented by many local additions. Yellow was from marsh marigolds, onion skins, young birch leaves, and crab apple tree leaves and bark. Green, like yellow, was one of the most accessible of natural colors. It came from heather, birch leaves, and moss. Dark green was from soot and urine mixed. Bean flowers gave a lovely blue-green which, unfortunately, was likely to fade. Browns came from pinecones, birch buds, and alder bark and seeds.

1.15. Hackling flax in the 1930s.

Red-brown came from madder (*Glaium boreale*) roots, found locally in clay areas. For centuries madder red was the only red for cloth in Latvia. Beginning in the nineteenth century cochineal (*Cockus cactil*), from dried insects, was imported for a second, scarlet, red. Black came from black alder bark, pitch, or bean leaves and stems. Black generally was held in low regard unless sought as a background for colored designs.

Blue from local woad (*Isatis tinctoria*) and elder (*Sambucus nigra*) berries was acceptable, but the preferred hue was the rich deep blue of indigo (*Indigofera tinctoria*), which required importing the dyestuff. Dyeing with indigo involved a lengthy fermentation with urine in warm conditions. In the 1800s the unpleasant smell of this process was sometimes camouflaged by placing the dye pot in a hole amidst the sheep manure pile, which also provided warmth. To prevent the animals from upsetting the pot or fatally drinking the liquid, an old door or board was placed over the hole. After days of fermenting to form dye, the wool received the liquid in the fermentation vat for several more days. During this time the wool needed to be stirred frequently in the dye bath. By the time the blue wool was rinsed, it had become a valued commodity. Because the fermentation processes for woad and indigo were both time consuming and disagreeable, blue wool was often used sparingly by carding it into grey wool.

Grey yarn could be obtained without dying by carding black and white wool together before spinning.

Synthetic, aniline dyes first appeared in Latvia in the 1860s. Their bright colors and easy application made them popular. Dyeing had not been a separate trade up to this time. Small shops now emerged, attached to carding mills, selling dyes and the dyers' skills. By the early 1900s most yarn used for weaving good fabrics was factory-dyed.

Fabric Care

General laundering was done in a barrel of water. Soap, a precious commodity, was used sparingly for laundry. Ashes were spread on a sack above the water and hot water was strained through them into the barrel. The preferred method was for two young girls to work together, pounding on soaped cloth which was laid over a plank bench. The girls swung their sticks in rhythm, alternating beats on the cloth, singing to the beat. Rinsing was done in a clear stream, then a second washing might be done on items to get them really clean. Finally the laundry was spread to dry on the grass or bushes.

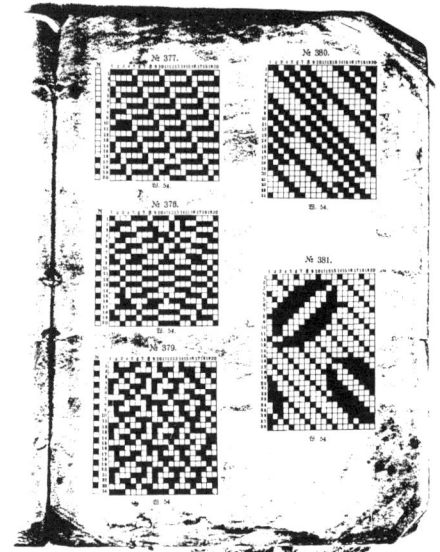

1.17. twill drafts from P. Viļumsons' pattern book, Thursday Morning.

1.16. Rolling the fulled cloth in the 1930s.

14

CHAPTER TWO

Latvian Weaving Equipment

Numerous factors influenced the character of cloth woven in Latvia over the years. Important considerations were materials, societal tastes, outside examples, producers' skills, and available equipment. Looms had a vital effect on the type of textiles produced in Latvia.

Miscellaneous Small Tools

Most Latvian handweaving tools were similar at any given time to those used in many other European and North American cultures. *Raddles, shaft stabilizers,* and flat, wooden *sley hooks* were known as threading aids. *Reeds* were originally handmade of wood, reed, and string and later were factory-made of metal. *Shuttles* took many forms - flat stick shuttles, wooden netting shuttles, boat shuttles, and boat shuttles with rollers on the bottom. Fig. 2.1. *Bobbins* in boat shuttles were made from hollow reeds. *Temples* for maintaining the width of the woven cloth were also used by some weavers.

Over the years various methods of measuring warp threads were devised. In the late 1900s Latvian professional weavers used belt-driven, hand cranked vertical *warping mills*.

Advanced items like *fly shuttles* and *dobby-type mechanisms* were utilized in mills and by some individual weavers in the nineteenth century. Average cottage industry and home weavers in Latvia did not use such aids at that time.

There were regional variations in tool design and their dates of use. Similarly, words associated with weaving were often regionalized. For instance, a system of measuring warps produced a specific terminology in Krustpils, Latgale. An elderly person from a farm in that area recalled how weavers in the 1800s placed a few pegs along the outside wall of the farm house. Warp threads were stretched between the pegs, full length along the wall. The Latvian word for a wall is *siena*, so in that part of the country a warp came to be described in units of length each called a *siena*. Old farmhouses were of similar sizes so a *siena* became a standard length in weaving terms in that district. (Ligers, 1957-1959.)

Heddles

There were several types of heddles in Latvian weaving history. Basic two-shaft or four-shaft looms used simple, continuous heddles up into the 1800s. These were tied or "thrown" by wrapping a continuous cord around an upper stick and then a second, lower, stick. The cord was tied around the lower stick to form the heddles' eyes. The upper stick also was parallelled by another cord for transferring the heddles to the loom. These two sticks were held apart by a board to give a fixed length to all the heddles. The tying process first formed the upper half of the heddles along with an eye 1.5 to 2 cm (1/2 to 4/5 inches) long. Then the lower half of the heddles were tied between the heddles' eyes and a third stick, making the total heddle's height 20-25 cm (8-10 inches). These *thrown heddles,* also called *women's heddles,* were used by home weavers and were made of hemp which was waxed before weaving. (Alsupe, 1982.)

Homemade, continuous string heddles had some disadvantages: they lacked replaceable individual heddles; they were only useful on cloth of up to about one meter's width; and they had a fixed number of heddles per centimetre. Such limitations were generally accommodated by the old farm looms which were about one meter wide and used only two or four shafts. Few home weavers had a wide

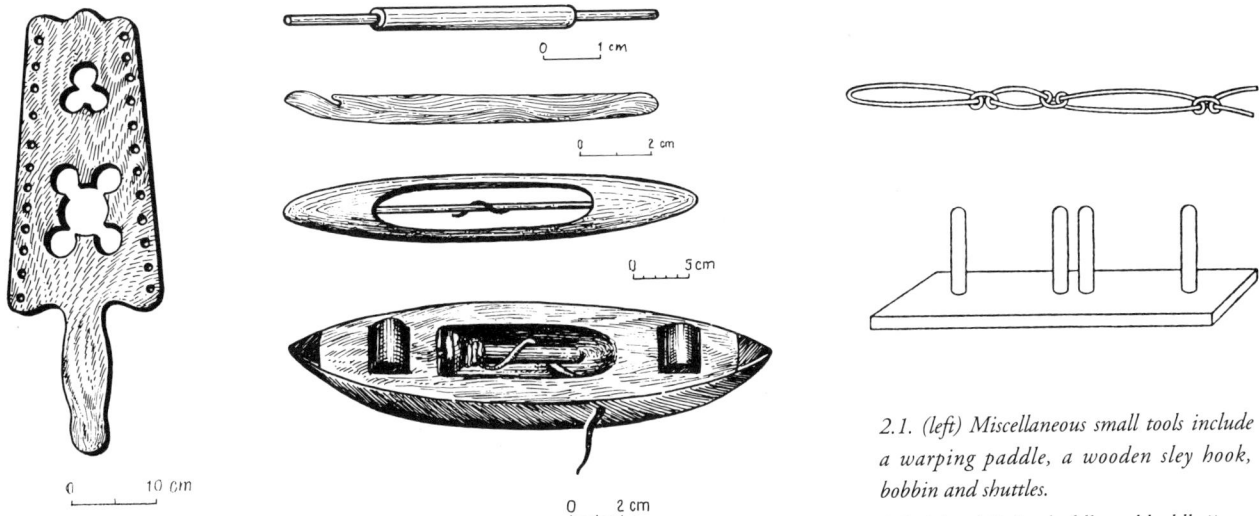

2.1. (left) Miscellaneous small tools include a a warping paddle, a wooden sley hook, a bobbin and shuttles.

2.2. (above) String heddle and heddle jig.

selection of the old, handmade reeds therefore setts for fabrics were determined by the reed and the heddles' density and simply remained limited. Until the second half of the nineteenth century when better equipment was within the realm of farm weavers, the old heddles and looms were acceptably compatible.

It is quite likely that professional weavers in Latvia used long-eyed heddle arrangements in the 1500s. High quality cloth woven in block weaves (*dreļļu audumi*) was produced at that time for home and export markets. Long-eyed heddles were known as *dreļļu nītis* or *block heddles,* associating them with block weaving and dating them from at least the sixteenth century. See pages 69-70.

Professional weavers hand-tied their heddles well into the 1800s, making versatile individual ones on a frame of wood with a removable rod along the center. These heddles still were made in two parts, upper and lower, as were the old, continuous, thrown heddles. Eyes were two to four cm (4/5 to 1 2/3 inches) long.

In the early 1800s new linen, one-part heddles were tied individually, as in fig. 2.2. Jigs were made for tying short-eyed heddles with two to three cm (4/5 to 1 1/5 inches) eyes and for long-eyed heddles with eight to ten centimeters (three to four inch) eyes. As was often the case, the professional weavers introduced these items into general use and by 1900 individual heddles were made for most looms.

In the twentieth century metal eyes could be purchased for heddles, to which linen ties could be added. (Alsupe, 1982.)

Looms

Miscellaneous Small Looms

Narrow bands woven with two sheds are one of Latvia's oldest forms of weaving. These may have been woven with rigid heddles, fig. 2.3, made of slotted boards with holes burned in them. Patterned bands have been made by card weaving in Latgale since at least the eighth century. This technique has evolved into very elaborate work over the ages. Vertical looms were used for wide, simple fabrics throughout middle Europe centuries ago and, although no complete one has been found in Latvia, were apparently also extant there.

Horizontal Looms

Horizontal looms of two, three, and even four shafts probably existed prior to 1200 in Vidzeme. These looms used rollers, rocker-arms (also called *horses* in English), or perhaps even pulleys for *counterbalanced* sheds. Looms counterbalanced with pulleys eventually became the norm throughout Latvia so that in the 1800s one was in virtually every farmhome. Only the peasants' simplest two-shaft looms still used rollers by that time. Rocker-arms were combined with pulleys on some looms for three-or-more shaft weaves.

CONSTRUCTION

For hundreds of years looms were made on peasants' farms and were generally of similar construction principles. See Plate 1. In Kurzeme looms tended to be built heavier and stronger than in other districts. They usually were built with a large, cubic frame of wooden corner pieces that gave much stability to the loom when under warp tension, so very long pieces of cloth wove up evenly. When information began to flow freely through the land in the late nineteenth century, Kurzeme's solid looms' construction was copied elsewhere for basic, home looms.

Pulleys became so intrinsic to all counterbalanced looms that the old name for the pulley was included as part of the loom name: *trīzuļu stāviem* or *pulley loom.* Pulley looms from the 1100s have been found in Latvian archeological digs. They are similar to some looms used on farms in Latgale and Vidzeme in the 1900s. (Alsupe, 1982.) When carpenters standardized parts in the late 1800s, looms and their pulley systems became more uniform. Standardization and better carpentry also made multi-shaft looms more available.

Countermarch looms which used lamms and overhead levers allowed more complex patterning without the limitation of the pulley looms' counterbalanced sheds. Countermarch looms first became known throughout Latvia through the influence of courses in Finland and Scandinavia in the late 1800s.

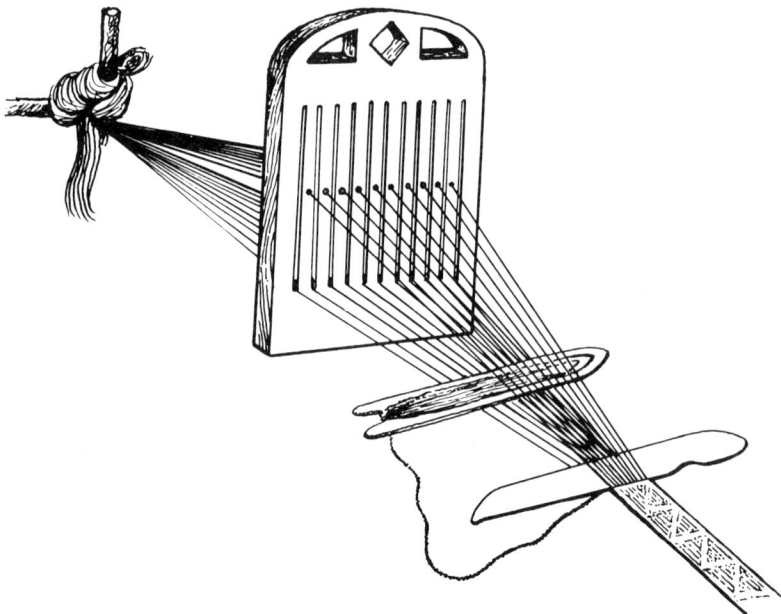

2.3 Rigid heddle loom for weaving narrow bands.

2.4 Latvian home weaver seated at her loom, 1928.

Counterbalanced looms with two, four, or occasionally eight shafts were the average farm looms before 1900. The counterbalance pulley system generally confined weavers to the easiest, most efficient shed formations with even numbers of shafts. The shafts were tied directly to treadles without intervening lamms. Sheds were formed by *double treadling,* or depressing two or more treadles simultaneously. The limited number and action of these shafts meant that for farm weavers the convenient

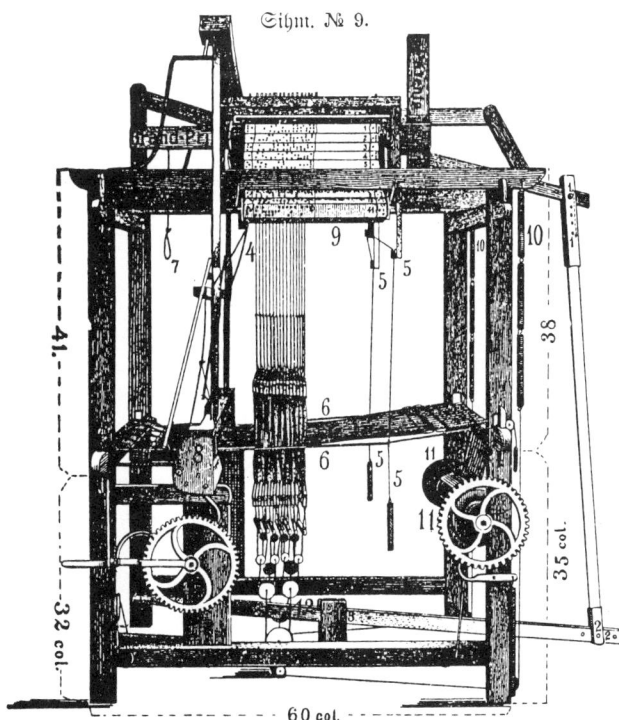

2.5. Loom designed by Peters Viļumsons with a dobby-type head.

textile structures were plain weave and its balanced derivations, 2/2 twills, and four-shaft weaves patterned with supplementary wefts. Most farm looms wove fabric about 70-110 cm (35-44 inches) wide.

Plate 1 shows a typical farm-home loom from the 1800s, using both pulleys and horses for moving the shafts. This facilitates an unbalanced shed for certain weave structures. The loom pictured in fig 2.4 has a particularly large warp beam which apparently was self-tensioned by its own weight.

Professional weavers' looms before the late 1800s usually had 16 or fewer shafts, all operated by a pulley system. Highly trained professional weavers also utilized double-harness looms, which are discussed below. Patterns requiring 32 single shafts were in trade books from the early 1800s, although it is unclear whether 32 separate shafts or a double-harness system was used to weave them. Probably the double-harness setup was employed. Beginning in the second half of the 1800s many professional weavers learned to use double-harness looms.

The professionals' looms were wide so that blankets or tablecloths did not need center seams. Even before the twentieth century, these looms were about 200 cm (78 inches) wide. *Double looms* went up to 270 cm (107 inches) wide so two weavers could catch the shuttle on either side and weave very wide cloth.

Double warp beams were common to the looms of many nineteenth and twentieth century professional weavers. This indicates the weaving of certain complex weave structures which required two warp tensions simultaneously.

PULLEY SYSTEMS

Until late in the 1800s even the looms of professional weavers used pulley arrangements above the shafts and direct tie-ups to treadles, without lamms, below the shafts. Counter-march looms with overhead levers and tie-up lamms were not available in Latvia until the late 1800s. The oldest types of pulleys had one to four grooved wheels and were about 50 cm (20 inches) long. Simple versions of this pulley were still on homemade looms into the 1800s. If this pulley had several grooved wheels it was called a *block pulley (dreļļu trizulis)*. It was for block weaves which needed multiple shafts and was used by professional weavers for many years. In the second half of the 1800s the end of serfdom fostered an increase of tradesmen. Among them were skilled carpenters who began producing smooth-running pulleys of similar sizes. Fig. 2.6A shows one of the well-crafted, sophisticated arrangements allowing 16 shafts to operate from pulleys. This pulley was adopted from the masterweavers' looms by home industry weavers in the late 1800s. By the twentieth century a clever pulley system as in fig. 2.6B was designed for unbalanced sheds, that is, those wherein shafts were moved without evenly counterbalancing each other in numbers. These complicated types of pulley systems probably were of limited occurrence even on professionals' looms because other mechanical actions which were more easily managed became available for complex weaves at the same time.

VIĻUMSONS´ LOOM

About 1900 Pēters Viļumsons built several types of looms for professional weavers. The one of best design was called the *Viļumsons loom,* fig. 2.5. Part of the mechanical head of that loom is seen in the foreground of fig. 1.9. Once the loom was warped and the dobby-like patterning chain established, the weaver only needed to treadle one pedal and operate the fly shuttle. There was an automatic take-up device for the woven cloth, which could be up to two meters wide.

Another loom had double-harness capability (explained below), many pattern shafts, and ease of operation. Viļumsons apparently placed an inverted pulley system for shedding on the front (ground) harness of the loom. The rear (pattern) harness was attached to a mechanical device. The loom cut weaving time of satin-based, block patterned cloth by at least two-thirds.

Due possibly to their cost or to the devastation of World War II, the Viļumsons looms faded from their justified prominence.

TWENTIETH-CENTURY LOOMS

In the twentieth century loom-controlled textile structures became more complex than in previous centuries because looms were built with more versatility in types of actions and in shaft numbers. The twentieth-century professional weaver who was self-employed often had a *half-mechanical* loom with a shedding mechanism akin to a dobby type, often in conjunction with some intricate double-harness arrangement, along with a double back beam, fly shuttle, and automatic take-up.

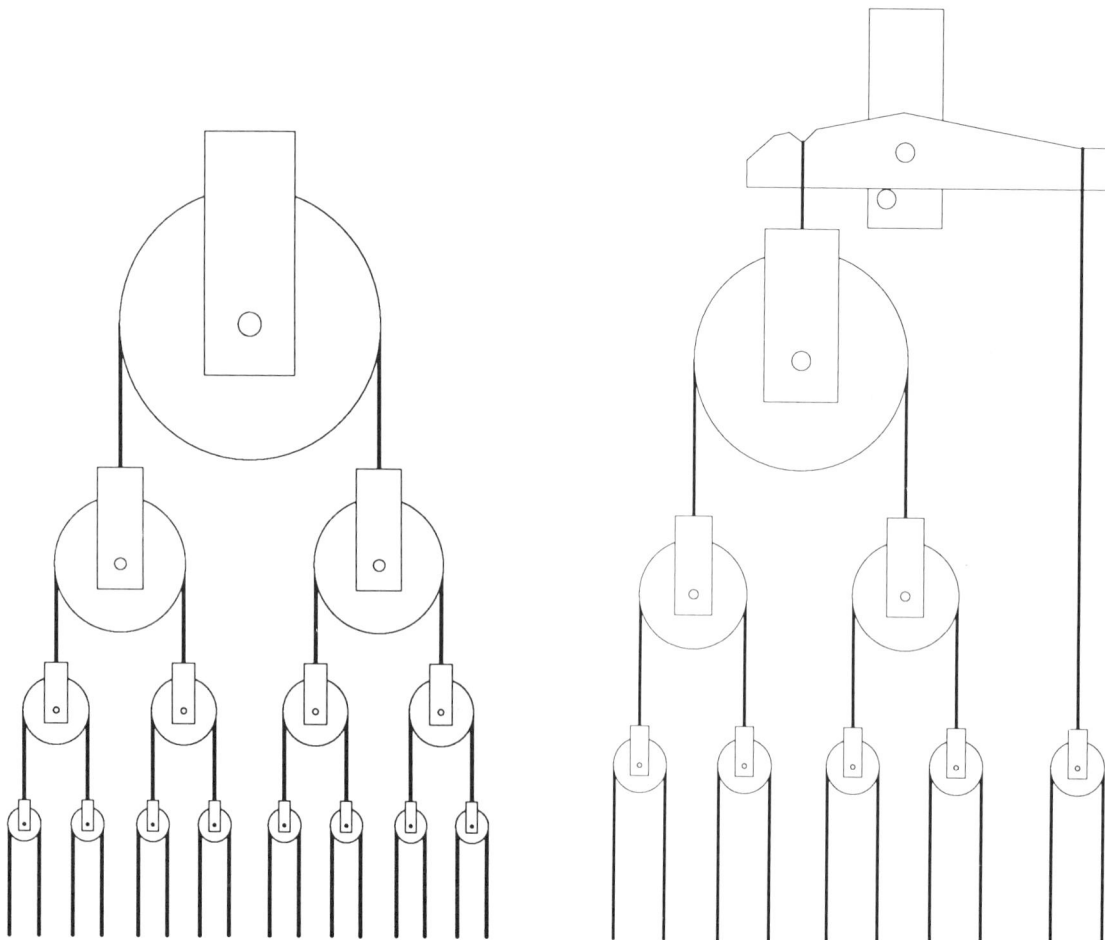

2.6 A & B. A: Pulley arrangement to operate 16 shafts. B. Pulley system for 10 shafts, capable of unbalanced sheds.

Double-harness loom system

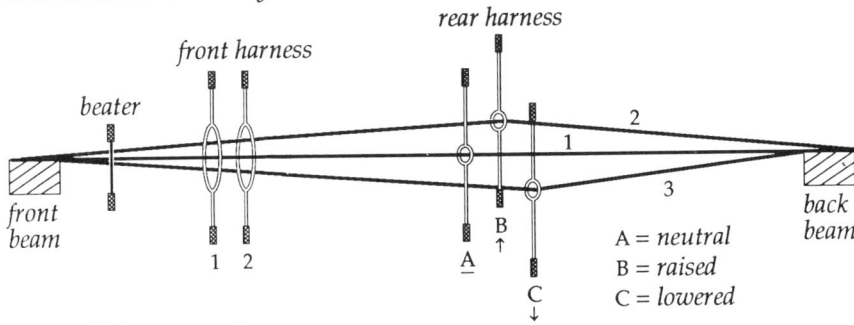

2.7. *Double-harness system's components.*

Double-harness Looms

Several patterned cloth weaves used in Latvia required a great number of shafts and/or treadles to achieve their designs on single-harness looms: supplementary-weft float weaves, unit weaves with tied supplementary-weft floats, turned twill and satin blocks, and patterned double weaves. The preferred way of weaving complex motifs in those cloths was on a double-harness loom.

The double-harness system has been adapted throughout the world. While its general principles are similar everywhere, differing loom constructions have varied its uses. In Latvia, only a very few adept weavers were capable of using double-harness looms through the seventeenth and eighteenth centuries. By the late nineteenth century, the double-harness system was known and used by many skilled weavers there, although it never was a commonplace type of loom. Graduates of craft schools and P. Viļumsons' courses were highly familiar with the advantages of a double-harness loom and quite able to use one.

Fig 2.7 displays the components of a double-harness system. Between the front beam and the back beam are two sets of shafts, each set called a *harness*. As usual, the shafts hold heddles through which the warp threads are threaded.

The harness at the rear of the loom is composed of shafts (collectively called the *rear* or *pattern* harness) which have heddles with regular length eyes. In early twentieth-century Latvia these string heddles were 35-45 cm (14 to 18 inches) long, with an eye of 1-2 cm (3/8 to 3/4 inch) in length.

Shafts on the harness in the front of the loom (collectively called the *front* or *ground* harness) have heddles of a different type, equal in overall length to the rear harness's heddles but with long eyes 8-12 cm (3 to 4.5 inches) long. In contrast to threading a single-harness loom, many or all individual warp threads on a double-harness loom go through two heddles – one on each harness – rather than only one heddle.

For less tension on the warps and better shedding it is best if the rear harness of a double-harness loom is set back from the front harness. The back beam over which the warp passes should be placed farther back from the harnesses than on a usual single-harness loom. Double-harness looms often have an extended back beam to allow for this extra depth.

In a double-harness system, the shafts of the rear harness control groups of adjacent warps that determine the cloth's pattern. Each heddle on these shafts could be threaded with a group of warps if all of those adjoining warps will be

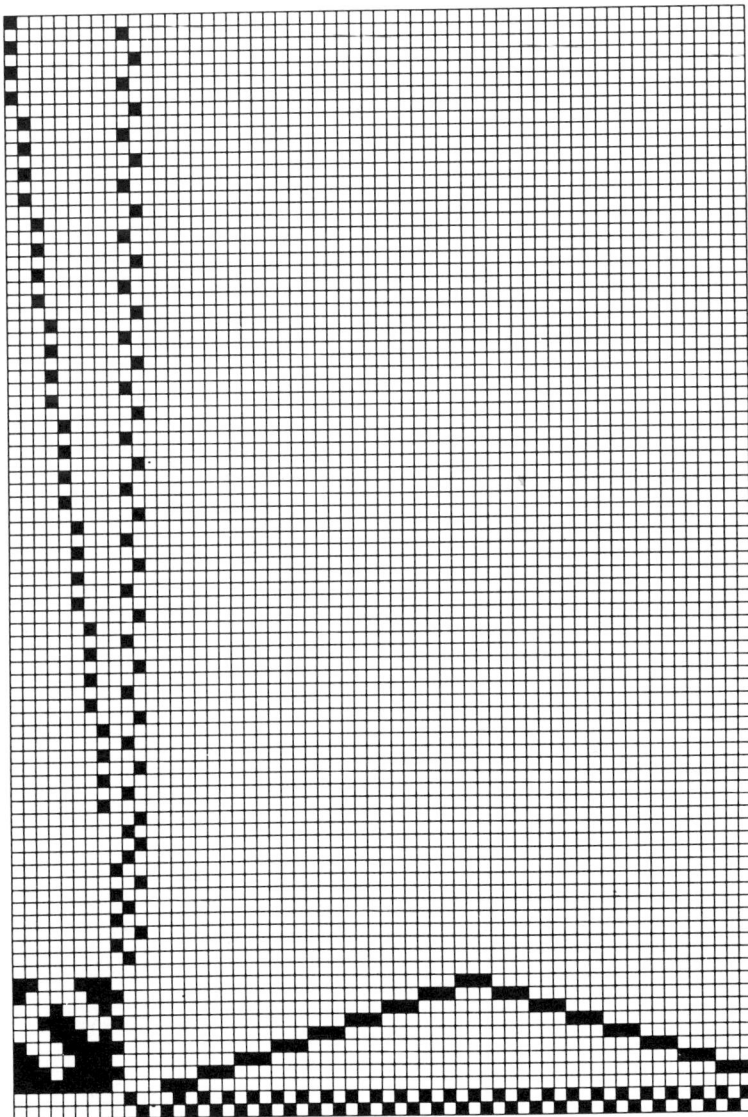

2.8. *Double-harness draft in which each warp goes through two heddles.*

Draw device

draw cords

slots in frame

heddles

small weights

4 shafts

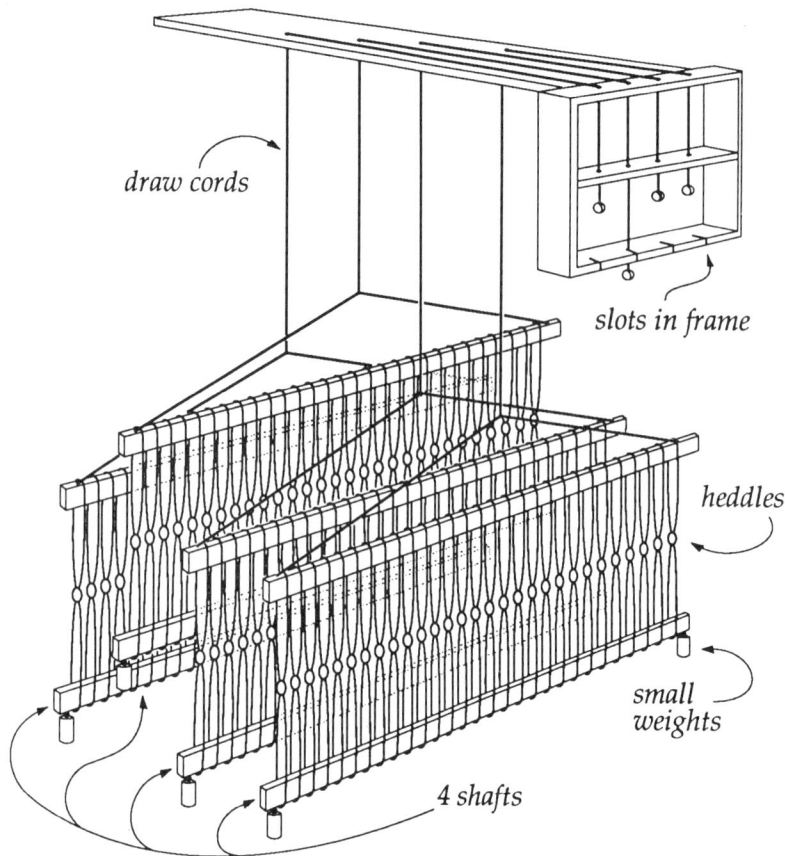

2.9. Draw device for the rear harness on a double-harness loom.

moving similarly within one block in a pattern. The rear harness is also called the *pattern harness.*

After passing through the short-eyed heddles on the rear, pattern harness, the warps pass through the long-eyed heddles on the front harness, also called the *ground harness.* It controls the intrinsic (ground) structure of the cloth, regardless of the design.

Each warp goes through an individual ground shaft heddle in front where it interlaces independently. A double-harness draft, as in fig. 2.8, shows every warp passing through two heddles: a short-eyed pattern shaft heddle in the rear (possibly along with other warps) and a long-eyed ground shaft heddle in front (individually).

Different loom mechanisms might allow for shafts to stay neutral, rise, or sink. The mechanical action of one harness on a Latvian loom could be, and frequently was, different from the action of the other harness.

REAR HARNESS OPERATION
The rear, or pattern shafts operate in one of three ways: with pulleys, countermarch levers, or draw cords.

Pulley mechanisms were common up to the late 1800s. Usually pulleys operated a counterbalanced system, with any raised shaft being countered by a shaft that was lowered. This counterbalancing placed limits on designs by necessitating that equal numbers of shafts be raised and lowered in any given shed. Eventually there were well-built pulley systems capable of making unequally balanced sheds, albeit probably with much careful adjusting that made other mechanisms more attractive. Treadles operated pulley-hung shafts.

Countermarch levers became available for manipulating the rear shafts by the late nineteenth century. This mechanism allowed shafts on the rear harness to move independently, without counterbalancing. A double-harness loom with countermarch rear harness would have been relatively accessible if a weaver already had a single-harness, multi-shaft, countermarch loom and adapted it with a small front harness, as in fig. 2.11. While a loom specifically built for both harnesses would be preferable, a modified loom could serve. Treadles operated shafts on a countermarch system.

Draw cords, part of a draw-shaft device, were also used to operate pattern shafts. The draw device in fig. 2.9 was fitted within or on top of a regular loom frame, behind the front shafts. The resting position of the warp was on the same level as the center of the short eyes of the heddles on the rear shafts, and was near the bottom of the long eyes of the heddles on the front shafts, as shown in fig. 2.10. Shafts on the draw

Draw-loom shed positions due to rear harness

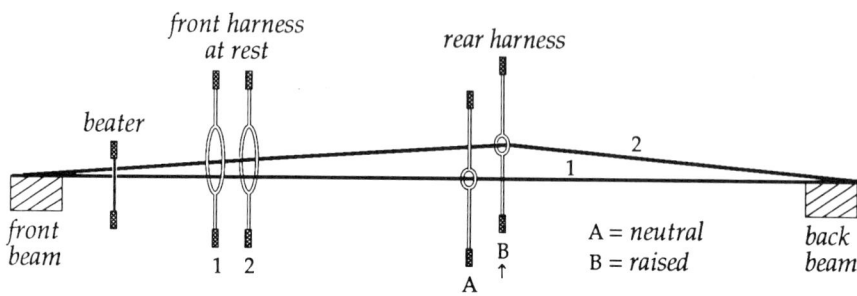

front harness at rest

rear harness

beater

2

1

A = neutral
B = raised

front beam

back beam

1 2

B

A

2.10 Draw-loom shed positions. Front harness at rest, rear harness forming shed.

20

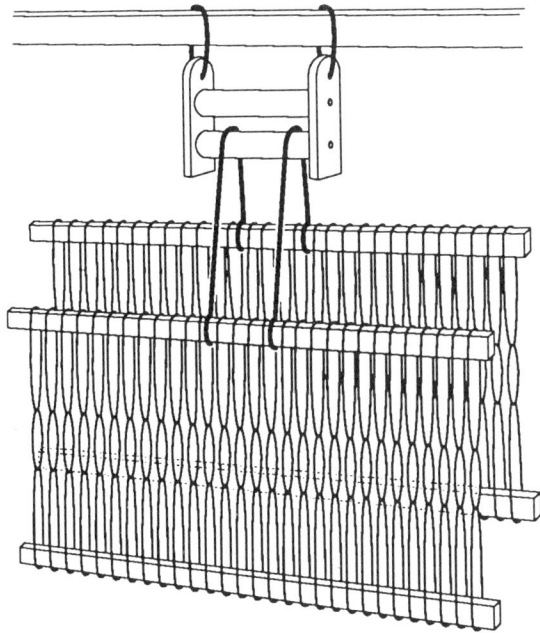

2.11. Roller pulley attachment.

device were lifted individually with a cord that attached in a frame in front of the weaver. Each shaft could be held in the lifted position by securing its cord in a groove of the draw-device's frame. Weights were hung from the shafts to help drawn shafts sink back to resting level. Only a rising shed resulted from drawing a cord to a pattern shaft; no counterbalanced or sinking shed was involved.

Draw devices were especially practical for designs in which pattern shafts remained raised for repeated blocks of pattern, or for complex designs that would require very large numbers of pattern shafts or treadles. Simple draw-shaft devices could be made at home, put on the loom when needed, and removed when not necessary. The whole draw device frame was placed on the loom behind the shafts in the front. Draw devices entered the home weavers' domain around the late nineteenth century. They became more prevalent after World War I when they were added to countermarch looms of the type used in Finland. Plate 5 shows a sophisticated version of a draw loom in use.

FRONT HARNESS OPERATION

In Latvian twentieth-century weaving texts there are references to three means of moving the front harness: levers, pulleys and "roller pulleys."

Levers, mounted on the top of the loom, occasionally were used to move front shafts. This apparently was not a common system on Latvian double-harness looms.

Pulleys were an ancient part of Latvian single-harness looms and a possible, but not preferred means of control for a double-harness loom's front shafts.

Roller pulleys were reputed to give a better shed. There were either one or two rollers, over which cords passed from the frames of the long-eyed heddle shafts. Each roller held two shafts which counterbalanced each other, as in fig. 2.11. If a weave structure had a plain-weave ground, only two front shafts were needed and they both hung from one roller. If the ground weave was in a four-shaft structure, or if turned-twill blocks or double cloth were being woven, four long-eyed heddle shafts were arranged over two rollers.

Treadles were attached to the front shafts for shed selection. It was possible for a front harness to hold two long-eyed heddle shafts along with two short-eyed heddle shafts. This arrangement might have been used in unit weaves with tied weft floats, but there is no clear indication in drafts as to whether this was done.

The counterbalancing of the four front shafts could be arranged differently as required by weave structures. The front harness's cords and rollers are easiest to arrange if shafts 1 and 4 counterbalance and shafts 2 and 3 counterbalance. That was the case in the turned weaves and was the most usual double-harness arrangement on Latvian looms. However, two other combinations on the front harness's shafts are possible:

- shafts 1 and 3 counterbalance and shafts 2 and 4 counterbalance,
- shafts 1 and 2 counterbalance and shafts 3 and 4 counterbalance.

These alternatives were used for patterned double-cloth weaving in Latvia.

SHAFT ARRANGEMENTS

A double-harness system increases the possible number of different sheds on a loom by mixing two shafts' positions for each warp thread. In the rear harness all the heddles have regular, short eyes. These rear shafts may have several positions, depending on the action of their harness. On counterbalanced and countermarch systems a warp might be left in the neutral position (the shed at rest), raised, or lowered by the back harness's shafts, as in fig 2.7. If the rear harness is counterbalanced, any raised shaft must have a countering lowered shaft. On a countermarch mechanism, shafts can be independently in any of the three positions. On a draw device, shafts are either in the neutral (low) or raised position as shown in fig. 2.10.

Front shafts on Latvian double-harness looms had either a counterbalanced or a countermarch action, systems still common in Europe and North America. These arrangements mean that, like the rear shafts, the front shafts can have three positions: raised, lowered, or neutral (the shed at rest). In either case of being raised or lowered the front shafts will over-ride any position warps may have due to the rear shafts. For example, if rear shaft *A* is raised, all the warps within its heddles are raised, as in fig 2.12. The first warp in raised rear shaft *A* can be seen to rise within the long eye of its unmoved front shaft 1. However, if a warp's front shaft is lowered that warp thread ultimately is in a lowered position in the weaving shed even if it is raised by its rear shaft, as shown by the second warp which goes from raised rear shaft *A* through lowered front shaft 2. This double-positioning of one warp thread adds much strain on it, a situation eased by a long distance between the rear harnesses and the back beam.

Similarly the front shaft can over-ride the position of a warp whose rear shaft has been lowered or has remained unmoved. Fig 2.13 shows warp 1 in the lowered shed position from its lowered rear shaft *(A)* and neutral front shaft (#1). Warp 2, from the same lowered rear shaft *(A)*, is raised because its front shaft (#2) is raised. Warp 3, on an unmoved rear shaft *(B)*, is in a raised position in the weaving shed because of its raised front shaft (#3).

If left in the neutral position, a front shaft does not affect the position of a warp passing through it. The front shaft's heddle eyes are long enough to allow a shed formed by the rear shafts to pass through. Double-harness looms are shown in operation in fig. 3A and Plate 5.

In the figures below, *LEH* refers to long-eyed heddles, *SEH* refers to short-eyed heddles.

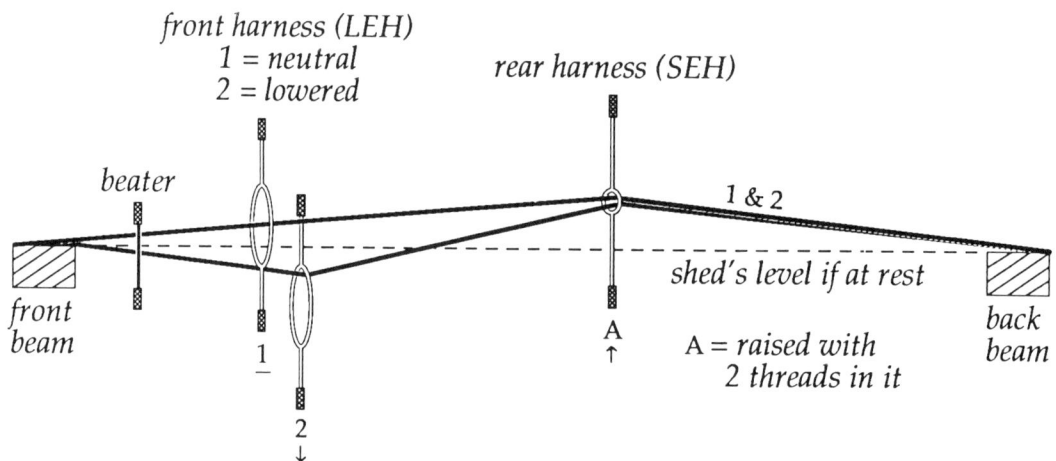

2.12. Double-harness shed with LEH shaft #2 creating the lower level and SEH shaft A causing the upper level.

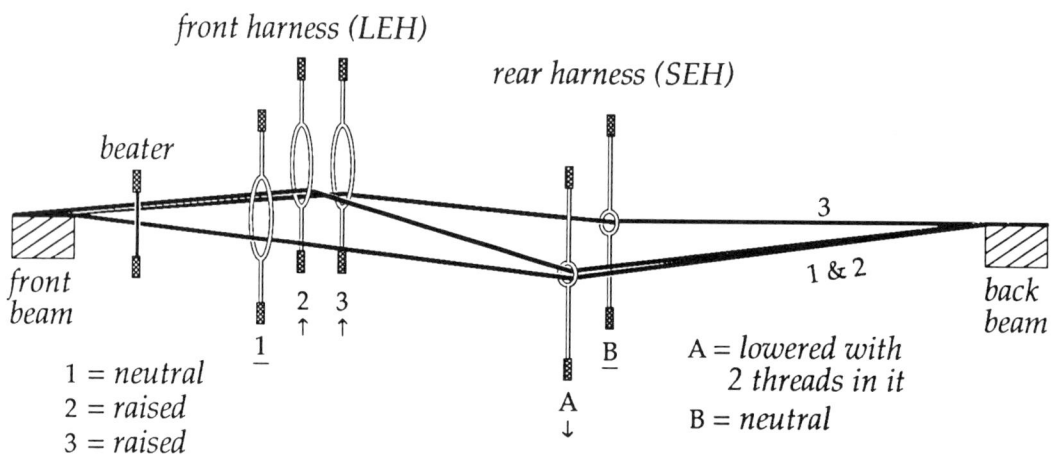

2.13. Double-harness shed with long-eyed heddle shafts #2 and 3 creating the upper level and short-eyed heddle shaft A creating the lower level.

THEORY AND
TRADITIONAL APPLICATIONS

Traditional weaves used in Latvia fall into two basic categories: loom-controlled weaves and hand-manipulated weaves. Loom-controlled fabrics are fairly regular in structure, due to a mechanical repetition of interlacements which are governed by a weaving loom. Looms come in many levels of complexity, starting with those that weave with only two opposite *sheds*. The more complex the loom, the more choices of interlacements the weaver has. These interlacements are varied by controlling the loom's machinations. Once any loom is set up, there are limitations to the structure of the cloth that will come from it as a direct result of the loom's shedding abilities.

Variety can be introduced into the cloth structure by the weaver, either by manipulating threads individually (hand manipulation), or by using the loom to do the intricate manipulations. Most of the traditional textiles presented in this study are *loom-controlled* – the loom was used to manipulate the interlacements in the cloth.

Latvia's loom-controlled fabrics made after the mid-1800s are represented by *everyday garment fabrics* of simple, basic weaves, *ornate costumes* for special occasions, and *household textiles* of weaves that frequently go well beyond simple interlacements. Due to wear and tear, examples of the old, daily garment fabrics are scarce. Fortunately, individual people and museums still have some of the costumes and household textiles from the past century. These fabrics often display careful planning, meticulous workmanship, and deft application of

Mrs. Klavins, a graduate of a home economics institute, worked for the government's agricultural program in Ventspils, Kurzeme, during the late 1930s. She traveled to nearby townships demonstrating, organizing courses, and instructing in home activities such as preserving foods or weaving. Mrs. Klavins offered to weave a blanket as a special thank-you gift to her friend at the district office, Mrs. Laima Kerans. Choosing commercial, locally available yarns of fine, black cotton for the warp and 2-ply wool for the wefts, she set up a wide loom owned by the town's amateur weavers' group. Her skills were on display, so she used a unique weave structure and added special pattern effects. The beautifully woven consequence of such creativity was so cherished by her friend that after sixty years it is still in perfect condition, and is now in the collection of the Royal Ontario Museum. (See fig. 6.19 and Plate 21.)

MRS. LAIMA KERANS

weaving principles. Of course, not every weaver was fully knowledgeable and not every fabric is flawless. Nonetheless, the breadth of the average weaver's abilities appears to have been wide, and there was careful attention to results. This is logical since the products were often to be a part of the maker's life for years.

Theory In Weaving Texts. Prior to the very late nineteenth century there were no weaving texts for the non-professional weaver in Latvia. Books for professionals carried patterns, but little specific technical information, that having been learned in training. By the twentieth century, however, literacy and nationalism prompted an interest in books for home weavers. Textbooks gave instructions on types of weaves and occasional patterns. Pattern books gave designs along with practical details of setting up the loom for the fabric.

There are many similarities between the 1936 major text *Mācies aust* by Anna Skuja-Antēne, and the other textbook of that time, *Aušanas Pašmācība* by Elga Kivicka, first published in 1934. The two books discuss materials, equipment, and loom setup procedures for home weavers. They then explain the loom-controlled weave structures popular with Latvia's numerous cottage industry and home weavers in the late nineteenth and early twentieth century. While there are differing perceptions of the relationships between the more complex weaves, the two writers begin their books with much the same information, presenting the basic weaves (plain weave, twill, satin) in structural terms. The more complex weaves are not discussed on the same analytical basis, however. Instead, many weaves capable of creating *units* of patterns (such as turned twills, supplementary weft weaves, complementary weft weaves, and many others) are grouped with more emphasis on their design functions than on their theoretical concepts. Perhaps this is due to the authors' preoccupation with the practical applications of achieving traditional pattern motifs.

The following chapters contain the Latvian weaving text information organized by the structural relationships between the weaves. While such a format of the chapters reflects later twentieth-century orientation, especially a North American one, the illustrative content of chapters is drawn from pre-World War II Latvian texts, complemented by anecdotes and actual examples from private and museum collections.

The Latvian weaving texts, sources of many of the drafts presented in this book, are referred to by abbreviations in their captions: Ap, *Aušanas Pašmaciba* published in 1934; Ma, *Mācies aust*, published in 1936; Ltm, *Latviešu tautas māksla*, published in 1961; Pa, *Paraugi audumieum*, published in 1940; and Rga, *Rokas grāmata audējām*, originally published in 1931.

Photos from the Royal Ontario Museum's collection list the ROM accession number and donor information in their captions. Yarns, sett, size and other weaving information is also given in the photo captions.

An explanation of the draft formats used in this book appears on page 25.

3.A. Weavers at *Mākslas textilas institutā*, Riga, Latvia, using double-harness looms in the late 1970s.

Drafts included in the following chapters have parts as numbered on the example in fig. 3.B.

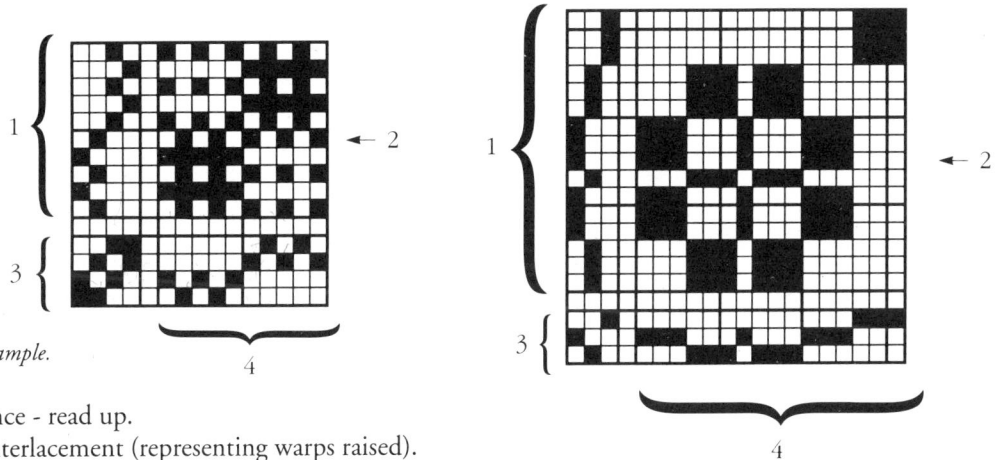

3.B. Threading draft example.

3.C. Profile draft example.

1 = Treadling sequence - read up.
2 = Weave plan of interlacement (representing warps raised).
3 = Tie-up of shafts to treadles (for rising sheds).
4 = Warp threading draft - read from left.

All *treadle tie-ups* (3) are for rising shed looms. Unless noted otherwise, the *weave plan* (2) represents warps raised. *Treadling sequence* (1) reads upward, similar to the woven picks entering the web of cloth being woven.

Warp threading (4) reads left to right. Although drafts in Latvian books read right to left, those drafts are re-written here for the left-to-right orientation if necessary. The shafts here are discussed by number, starting at the lower row of the threading draft, comparable to the front of the loom. In Latvia shaft number 1 is at the top of the draft, comparable to the back of the loom. There has been compensation here if appropriate, so the back/front orientation does not affect the resultant weave structure as presented.

On *double-harness draft*s for looms with long-eyed heddles, the drafts here have long-eyed shafts in the front and short-eyed shafts in the back of the loom and the drafts read from left to right, bottom to top.

TERMS

In this text, *shaft* means one frame with heddles on it; *harness* means a group of two or more shafts. *Tabby* means the two plain-weave sheds. *Use tabby* means alternate the two picks. The drawdown will show this in one of two ways, depending on the clarity and size of the weave plan.
(a) It could include all tabby picks in the drawdown.
(b) It could indicate the two tabby sheds as two weft picks at the edge of the interlacement plan. If only the two picks are shown, the lower tabby would follow the first pattern pick. The upper tabby would follow the second pattern pick. The two tabby picks would then alternate after subsequent pattern weft picks.

A *repeat* is one full threading sequence of a particular pattern or structure. Unless otherwise noted, threading drafts are of one repeat in both threading and treadling directions.

PROFILE DRAFTS

*Profile draft*s are given where it is useful to see an overall design of component squares, called blocks, that form a pattern. In actual threading, individual blocks are assigned a unit of a particular threading, shown in a separate *threading draft*. Profile drafts will be presented as shown in fig. 3.C.

1 = Which blocks combine in a row, comparable to treadling - read up.
2 = Plan of blocks as a design.
3 = Combinations of blocks, comparable to a tie-up.
4 = Sequence of blocks, comparable to a threading – read from left to right.

Unless otherwise noted, profile drafts are of *one full repeat* in both horizontal and vertical directions.

Plate 1. A typical Latvian farm home loom from the 1800s. See also: Plate 5 and fig. 2.4.

Plate 2. Traditional skirt fabric patterned with supplementary weft from Vidzeme province. See fig. 6.3, page 82 for details.

Plate 3. Wool blanket woven by a professional weaver in the 1930s. See figs. 6.5 and 6.6, page 82 for details and draft.

Plate 4. Twill-patterned blanket of homespun wool. See figs. 6.42 and 6.43, page 97 for details and draft.

Plate 5. Weaver at the Mākslas textilas institutu Riga, Latvia, weaving traditional skirt fabric on a double-harness loom.

Plate 6. Detail, skirt fabric worn by Monika Alexandrovitch in fig. 1.10, page 10. See page 35 for details.

Plate 7. Weft-repp blanket woven as a copy of an old blanket in the Latvian Historical Museum in Riga. The wool was raised, processed and dyed at home by the weaver, Miss Berta Mikalis. A few rows of twisted wefts form an arrowhead design. Early 1930s, Vidzeme, County Valka, Township Lugazi; 176 cm (69") L x 146 cm (57.5") W; warp cotton, 2-ply, dark green; weft wool, S-twist, singles, black, white, orange, reds; 4 e/cm (10 epi); 24 p/cm (61 ppi). ROM971.335.1. Gift of Miss Berta Mikalis.

Plate 8. Detail, wool blanket in twill weave. See fig. 4.49, page 53 for details and draft.

Plate 9. Wool blanket woven in a block pattern with side borders and no center seam. 1942; Kurzeme, Ventpils; 176cm (69") L X 136cm (53.5") W; warp, wool, 2-ply, S-ply, grey; weft like warp, brown; 8 e/cm (20 epi); 8p/cm (20 ppi). ROM971.458. Gift of Mrs. Elza Gustavs. See fig. 5.32, page 74 for draft.

Plate 10. Tablecloth in twill derivation woven in 1935. See page 55 for details and draft.

Plate 11. Elaborate twill tablecloth, woven ca. 1940. See page 56 for details and draft.

Plate 12. Blanket in linen and wool, from the 1920s. See figs. 8.5 and 8.6, page 114 , for details and draft.

Plate 13. Blanket woven on opposites in weft-faced repp. See figs. 8.7 and 8.8, page 115, for details and draft.

Plate 14. Blanket in ribbed-block weave, 1892. See figs. 6.45 and 6.46, pages 98 and 99 for details and draft.

Plate 15. Tablecloth in twill blocks, woven as one width on cotton warp with very fine, handspun linen weft. The border design only goes down the sides, indicating a bolt of fabric was cut to the required length. Twentieth century, pre-1945; Latgale; 198 cm (78") L X 140cm (55") W; warp, cotton, 2-ply, S-ply, natural; weft, linen, Z-twist, singles, used double, natural; 18 e/cm (46 epi); 24 (12 working) p/cm (30 working ppi). ROM 990.20.4. Gift of Mr. Peter Aexandrovitch. See pages 72-73 for details and draft.

Plate 16. Wool blanket with supplementary-warp patterning, ca. 1910. See figs. 7.1 and 7.2, pages 107 and 108 for details and draft.

Plate 17. Blanket woven on a 4-shaft loom during the late nineteenth century. See figs. 8.10 and 8.11, page 115 for details and draft.

Plate 18. Blanket in weft-faced tied-unit weave. See figs. 8.21 and 8.22, page 120 for details and draft.

Plate 19. Blanket woven around 1880 in Vidzeme county Riga, twonship Bebri Brenceni; fragment 55 cm (22.5") L X 37 cm (14.5") W; warp wool, Z-twist, 2-ply, S-ply, yellow, grey; weft, wool, Z-twist singles, brown, green, yellow; 11 e/cm (28 epi); 11 p/cm (28ppi). ROM974.165. Gift of Mrs. Irma Loze. See page 53 for details and draft.

Plate 20. Blanket in an elaborate derived twill weave. See figs. 4.51 and 4.52, pages 53-55 for details and draft.

Plate 21. Unusual blanket in 8-block tied-float weave. See figs. 6.19, 6.20 and 6.21, pages 88 and 89 for details and draft.

Plate 22 Cushion patterned with ribbed inlays. See fig. 11.10, page 135 for details.

Plate 23. Close detail of blanket in tied-float weave. See figs. 6.29, 6.30 and 6.31, pages 92 and 93 for details and draft.

Plate 24. Plain-weave blanket with spaced warp. See figs. 3.4 and 3.5, page 35 for details and draft.

Plate 25. Floral coverlet woven in Zemgale about 1900 of extremely soft singles wool in natural white and pale blue. This coverlet has the fine qualities of appearance, drape, and hand that gave damask its high reputation. Zemgale, County Bauska, Township Vecsaule; 188cm (74") L X 143cm (56") W; warp, wool, singles,Z-twist, natural white; weft, wool, singles, Z-twist, used double; 14 e/cm (36epi); 5 p/cm (13 ppi). ROM971.19.1. Gift of Mr. and Mrs. Aleksandris Brivins.

Plates 26 and 27. Reproductions of traditional skirt fabrics. See figs. 12.5 a and b, page 140 for details.

Plate 28. Close detail, tablecloth in combined weaves. See figs. 5.9 and 5.10 , pages 66 and 67 for details and draft.

Plate 29. Detail, table cover in float-block weave. See figs. 12.1 and 12.2, page 139 for details and draft.

Plate 30. Detail, runner in rosepath weave. See figs. 12.3 and 12.4, page 139 for details and draft.

Plate 31. Screen by Velta Vilsons mixes single-layer and double-layer cloth, aceented by sections of tied warp and plexiglass rods. Each panel is 236 cm (93") high by 102cm (40") wide. Wefts of 6-ply linen and plexiglass weave with warps of linen and 6-ply wool. Located at the office of the Metro Chairman, City Hall, Toronto, Ontario. Collection of City of Toronto. See pages 141-142 for details

Plate 32. "Back to the Wall/...kur tauta lai letu?" by Vita Plūme, is composed of tra-ditional supplementary-warp patterned sashes. See fig. 12.11, page 142 for details.

Plate 33. Large woven installation piece by Velta Vilsons. Three panels, each 81cm (32") wide have geometric patterning and bands of color reminiscent of the old, weft-faced plain weave or "repp" blankets in Latvia. Heavy linen warp, sett at 2.5 e/cm (6 epi), is woven with 6-ply wool. Collection of the Latvian Canadian Cultural Centre, Toronto, Ontario. See pages 141-142 for details.

Plate 34. "Latvian Flag II/ Dies, Tava zeme deg," by Vita Plūme features pick-up patterns on a field of ikat-dyed warp. 1983; 229 cm (90") L X 102 cm (40") W; cotton, wool, synthetics. See page 142 for details.

Plate 35. "Maryann's Rug." Weft-faced areas contrast with warp-faced areas. 1983; 114 cm (45") L X 73.5 cm (29") W; tie warp, cotton, 8/4, blue; pattern warp, cotton, 8/8, blue; tabby weft, same as warp; pattern weft, cloth strips, 2.5 cm (1") W, maroon print; 6 e/cm (15 epi); 4.5 p/cm (12 ppi). Designed and woven by Jane Evans. See page 158 for details.

Plate 36. "Ripple II" rug woven on paired-tie draft with warp painting and freeform patterning. See fig. 14.30, page 159 for details.

Plate 37. "Heron II" rug with reversible freeform design. See figs. 14.15 and 14.16, pages 154-155 for details and draft.

Plate 38. "First Hill," weft-faced pictorial weave on paired-tie draft. See figs. 14.33 and 14.34, pages 160-161 for details and draft.

Plate 39. Detail, "Majolica Rug" in tied-Beiderwand weave. See figs. 12.A, page 137; figs. 14.11 and 14.12, page 153 for details.

Plate 40. "Buckle Rug" woven on a twill-tie draft. See figs. 14.48 and 14.49, pages 167 and 168 for details and draft.

Plate 41. Detail, "Blue Shadows Rug" in shadow weave. See fpages 145-147 for details.

Plates 42 and 45. "Weaver's Garden" rug and detail. This rug could be woven loom-controlled on 12 shafts or freeform on 4 shafts, using three large wefts for polychrome patterning. 1990; 114 cm (45") L X 81 cm (32") W; warp and tabby weft, cotton, 12/6, brown; pattern wefts, cotton, flannel, 1.3 cm (.5") strips, various colors; 3 e/cm (8 epi); 4.5 pattern, 1.5 tabby p/cm (12 pattern, 4 tabby ppi). Designed and woven by Jane Evans. See page 168 for details.

Plate 43. Detail, "Victorian House, Eastlake Style" rug in summer/winter weave. See fig. 14.45, pages 164-165 for details.

Plate 44. "Starflowers" rug with freeform patterning. See figs. 14.51 and 14.52, pages 168 an 169 for details and draft.

Plate 46. "Sunset Rug" uses fabric strips for both wefts. 1985; 117 cm (46") L X 68.5 cm (27") W; warp, cotton, 12/6, brown; wefts, cotton, flannel, 2.5 cm (1") W, brown, salmon/mauve ikat; 4 e/cm (10 epi); 3 p/cm (8 ppi). Designed and woven by Jane Evans. See page 158 for details.

Plates 47 and 48. Both sides of "Prairie Sky" rug See fig. 14.43, page 164 for details.

1

2

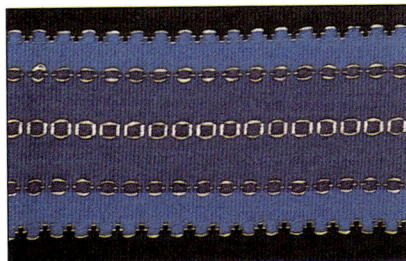

3

4

5

6

7

8

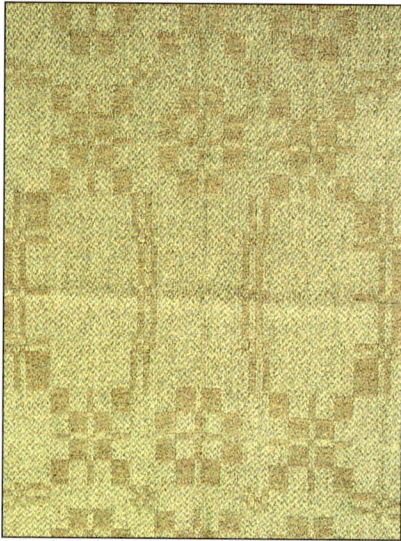

9

10

11

28

12

13

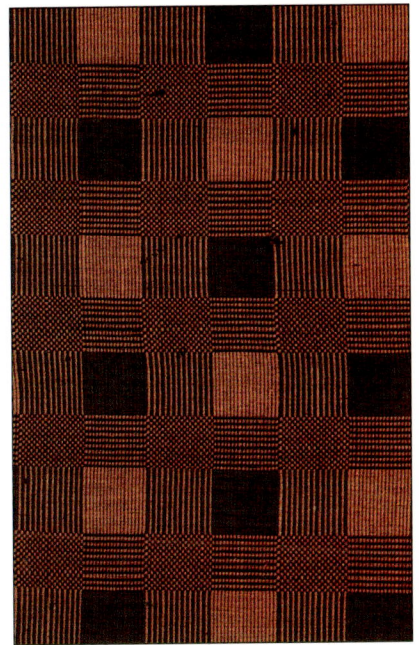

14

15

16

17

29

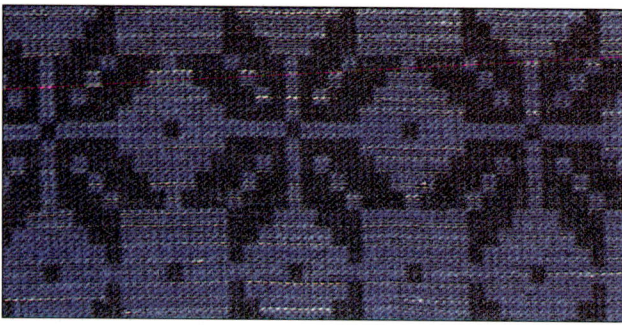

18

19

20

21

22

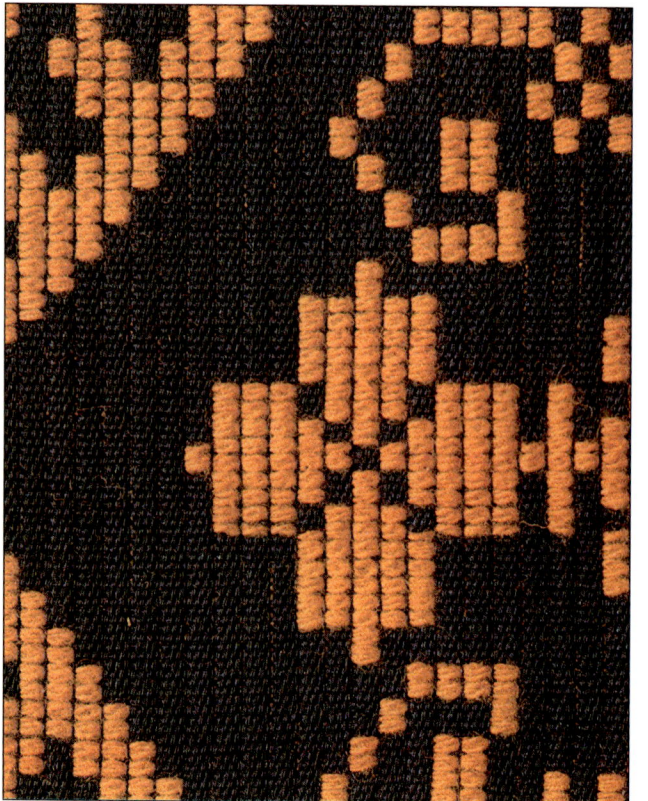

23

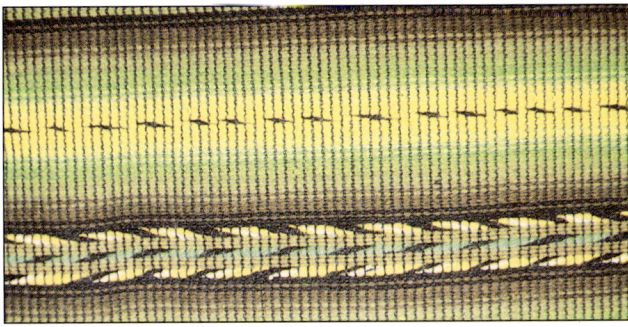

24

25

26

27

28

31

29

30

31

32

33

32

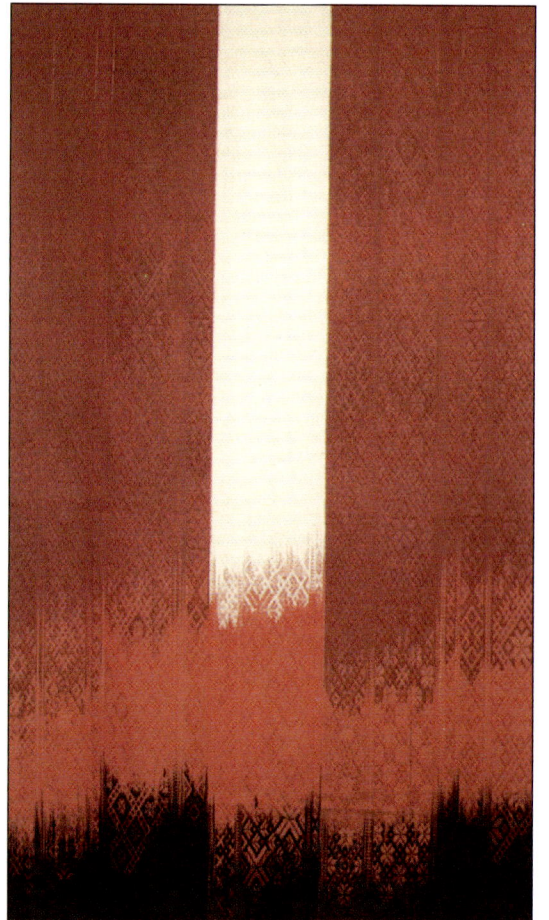

34

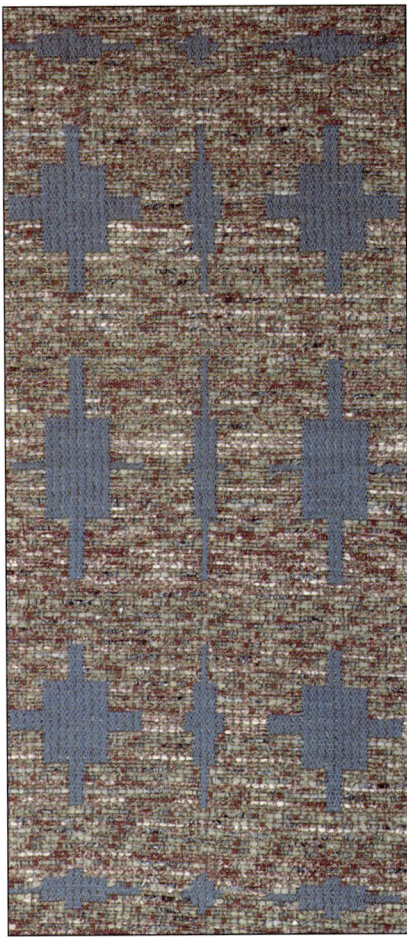

35

38

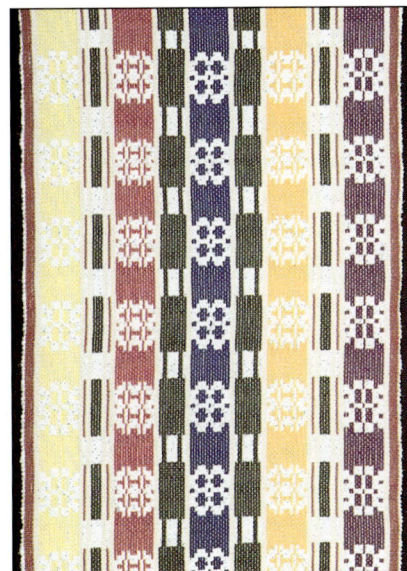

39

36

37

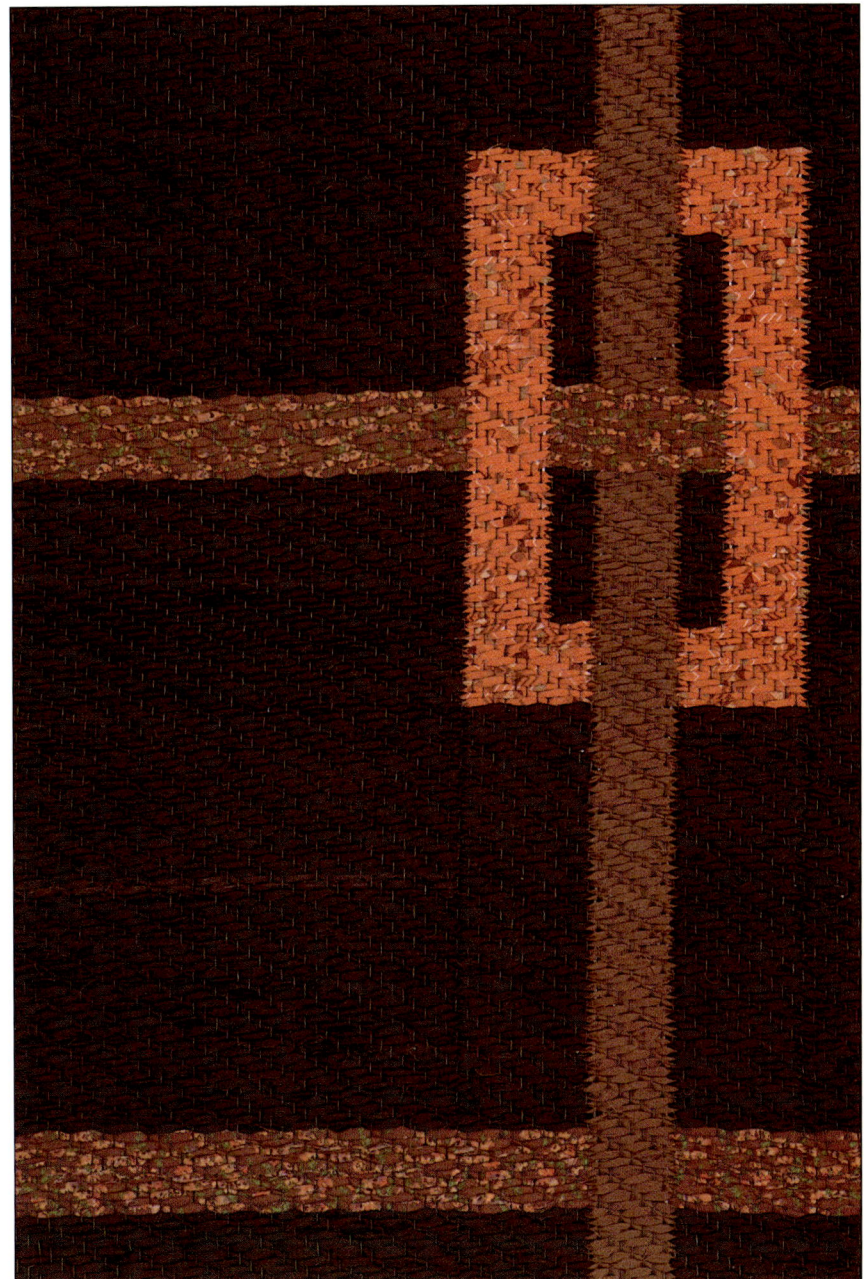

40

33

41

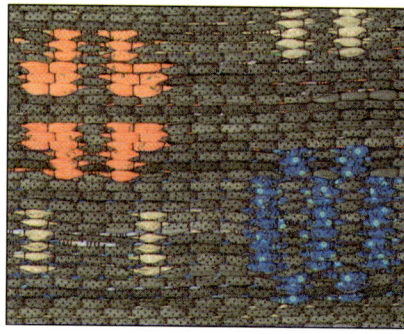

42

43

44

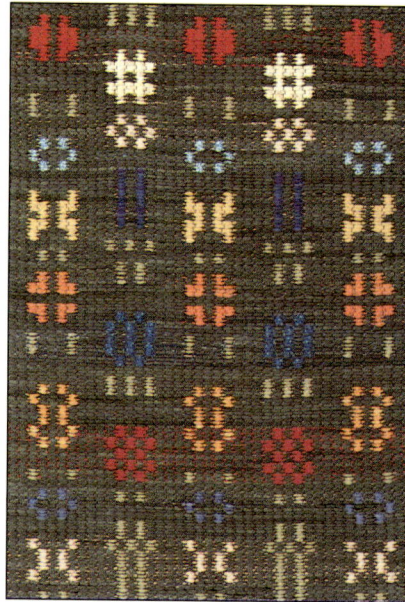

45

46

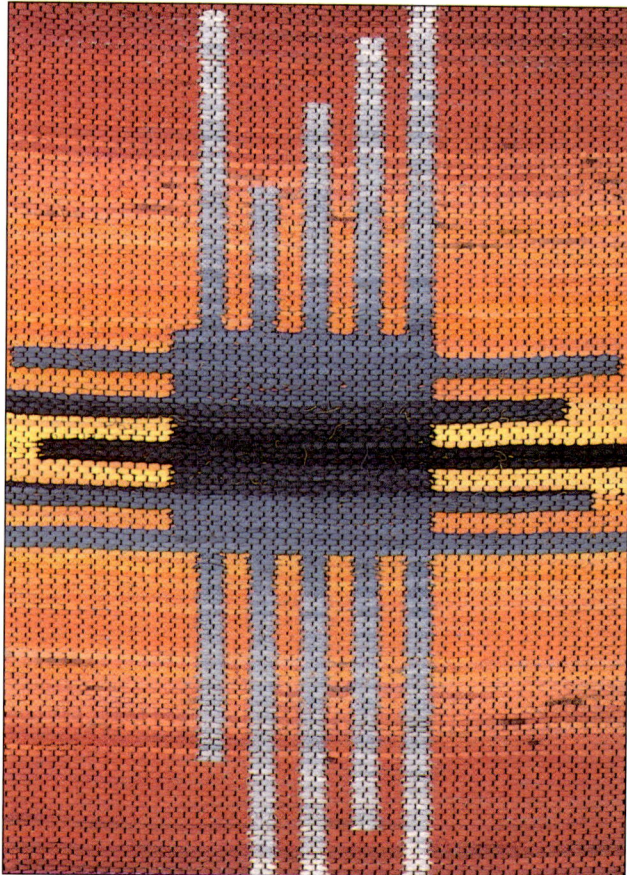

47

48

CHAPTER THREE

Basic Simple Weaves

Simple weaves interlace one set of warp threads and one set of weft threads. Latvian textbooks divided simple weaves into three divisions: *basic weaves, derived weaves,* and *combined weaves.*

Basic Weaves

The most fundamental of woven structures, *basic* weaves, cannot be reduced to any simpler forms of interlacement between one set of warp threads and one set of weft threads. According to many weaving texts, including the Latvian ones, the basic weaves are *plain weave, twill,* and *satin.*

Functional, everyday fabrics in plain weave are not usually saved for collections. The more elaborate,

3.1. (left) Plain weave interlacement. Warps are vertical, wefts horizontal.

3.2. (right) Two repeats of plain-weave draft as in blouse fabric, fig. 1.10.

showy textiles have been carefully preserved as family heirlooms and in museums; however, plain weave and twill textiles were the most common cloths in daily use by Latvian farmers.

Plain Weave

Vienkārtnis

The most basic interlacement formed in weaving is plain weave, which requires only two sheds. In plain weave there are two sets of threads perpendicular to each other. Each thread in a set is called an *element.* Single elements of one set (warp) regularly alternate passing over and under elements of the other set (weft), fig. 3.1. In Latvia this cloth was often referred to as *single cloth,* recognizing its use of one set of elements in each direction. Threads in plain-weave cloth can have different qualities (size, texture, color, twist, sheen) and spacing (sett or beat). The most common variables dealt with color and spacing.

BALANCED PLAIN WEAVE
On the surface of a balanced plain-weave cloth, both the warp and the weft elements are equally visible. The over-under interlacement order of plain weave can be written "1/1." This indicates that the weft goes first under one warp and then over one warp. See fig. 3.1.

Uses. For centuries, uncolored, balanced plain weave was used in Latvia for garments, sacks, and sheets used by peasants which were made in two widths of plain-weave fabric

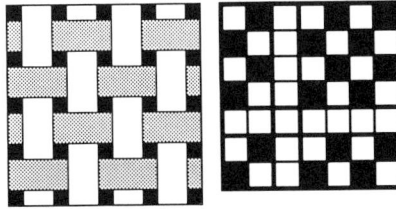

3.3. Detail, plain-weave checkered skirt of fig. 1.10 has seven colors: brick red, white, blue, green, yellow, maroon, and dark blue. Warp color sequence is almost identical to that of the weft. The fabric has been turned 90 degrees so one selvage is in the hem. Seams are machine-stitched and cut edges are hand-overcast. Early 1930s; Krustpils, Latgale; warp and weft wool, Z-twist, singles; 10 e/cm (25.5 epi); 12 p/cm (30.5 ppi); woven by Monika Alexandrovitch. ROM990.20.14.1. Gift of Mr. P. Alexandrovitch. See Plate 6.

sewn together. More decorative plain-weave fabric was woven with differently-colored stripes in warp and/or weft. Striped, checked, and plaid materials were used for clothing, blankets, table linens, curtains, towels – virtually any functional fabrics. It was not unusual to weave a single warp into plain-weave material for garments, a shawl, and two parts of a blanket which were joined into one wide piece. This saved time in loom setup and the products were varied by their colored weft stripes.

The plain-weave fabric draft for the blouse worn in fig. 1.10 is shown in fig. 3.2. Worn along with the costume's blouse was a long, wool checked skirt in plain weave with several accent colors on a warm, brick red base. A detail of the fabric is shown in Plate 6 and fig. 3.3.

In parts of Vidzeme, plain-weave fabric for skirts was decorated by twisting a pair of wefts, one dark and one light, within the same shed. Fig. 12.5a and Plate 26. Narrow bands of colored wefts also accented simple fabrics.

Plain-weave threadings are often made on more than two shafts to avoid crowding and friction among fine warp threads. The pattern book, *Aušanas pašmācība* even recommends using eight or ten shafts if very fine warp yarns are to be threaded. Common Latvian household fabrics like dishtowels might use 16/1 linen at 100 to 120 threads/10 cm (24 to 30/inch). Such fabrics were either of a single color or varied with stripes and plaids.

SPACED PLAIN WEAVE
Unequal spacing of warps adds a decorative element to plain-weave textiles.

Uses. In Zemgale, Kurzeme, and especially Latgale an old, popular, blanket technique depended on spaced warp threads. Warp threads

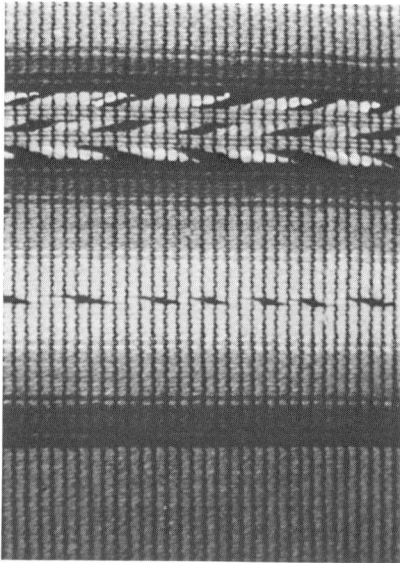

3.4. Warp spacing in blanket with twisted weft accents and center seam. 146cm (57") W; warp, cotton, black; weft, wool, Z-twist, singles used double; 12 warps and 2 spaces/cm (30.5 and 5 epi); 4 p/cm (10 ppi). Collection of Garezera tautas mākslas musejs, Three Rivers, Michigan.

3.5. One repeat of draft for plain weave with spaced warp as in fig. 3.4.

were sleyed in the reed by pairs, leaving wide gaps between each pair of warp ends which were in the same dent. Woven in plain weave, the resulting fabric had a noticeably ribbed appearance. Plate 10 and fig. 3.4 show a blanket in this so-called "tooth" weave. Figure 3.5 gives the draft.

Another example of varying plain weave by spacing of the warp is the nineteenth-century linen towel in fig. 3.6 and fig. 3.7. A stripe results from alternately denting the warp densely (14 ends/cm; 36 epi) and

loosely (10 ends/cm; 25 epi). Each pair of stripes has 12 dense and 8 loose warps. *Leno (see glossary)* twists regularly occur in the widely-dented eight-thread stripes, four twists per stripe. This particular towel also has a decorative band of cut and darned work, plus five bands of drawnwork at each end. Lacework was not common on towels in all regions.

Spacing of warp was also used in sheer fabrics such as curtains. The pattern book *Paraugi audumiem* gives a pattern for plaid, plain-weave curtains. Warp and weft are 24/2 cotton in the color sequence of: 36 red, 12 light blue, 24 and, 12 cornflower blue in a reed of 100 dents/10cm (25 dents/inch). Sleying is: *border* six dents of two threads each; *center section* three threads in a dent, one dent empty, one thread in a dent, one dent empty. Repeat center section as often as necessary; end with another border.

UNBALANCED PLAIN WEAVE OR REPP

Ripss

Unbalanced plain weave has unequal amounts of warp and weft visible. When one set of threads is wholly on the surface, the fabric is called either *warp-faced* or *weft-faced plain weave*. In warp-faced fabric very closely sett warp threads cover the wefts completely. In weft-faced fabric, densely packed weft threads completely cover the widely-spaced warp ends. Long ribs and furrows form in the direction of the hidden threads. The plain-weave interlacement which alternates single warp and single weft threads is maintained in spite of visual predominance by one set of elements.

"Repp," in North American terms, is an inexact term that alludes to any warp-faced and weft-faced textiles with a grooved or ribbed appearance. Likewise, in everyday Latvian weaving terms, apparently a repp fabric had the visual characteristic of a ribbed surface wherein one element wholly covered the other element. The Latvian names might specify *warp repp*, which meant a warp-faced fabric, or *weft repp*, which meant a weft-faced fabric, each with a grooved appearance. Within such a

3.6. This spaced-warp towel with lacework was bought in a market, possibly in Latgale. That was one region that favored lace decorations, but the lace may have been added later. 1800s; Latgale?; 126cm (50") L X 37 cm (14.5") W; warp and weft, linen, Z-twist, singles; bleached. ROM 971.413.4. Gift of Mrs. Aleksandra Dzērvītis.

3.7. Draft for spaced warp in plain weave from towel in fig. 3.6.

3.8. Two repeats of plain-weave draft, called "repp" when woven weft-faced.

simple definition *repps* often meant plain weave woven on two shafts, with a warp/weft balance that resulted in a ribbed surface showing only one of the sets of elements. A draft of a weft repp, or weft-faced plain weave, fig. 3.8, is indistinguishable from a plain-weave draft. In actual weaving, the warp sett was wide enough so that the wefts could slip down and cover the warps. Conversely, warp repp, or warp-faced plain weave, had a very dense warp sett so no weft showed.

Uses. Weft-faced plain-weave blankets, known as *repp blankets*, were favored by generations of weavers, especially in Latgale and Vidzeme.

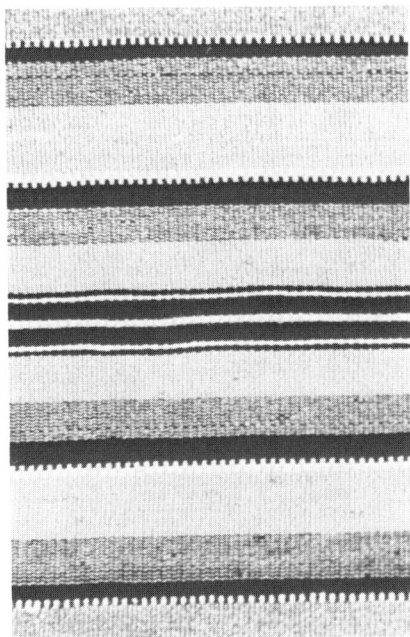

3.9. "Weft-repp" blanket with hand-hemmed ends. 1870s or 1880s; Vidzeme, County Cesuis, Grudzes farm; 215 cm (84.5") L X 148 cm (58") W; warp cotton, 4-ply, dark grey, weft wool, Z-twist, singles, grey, green, black, white; 5 e/cm (12.5 epi); 28 p/cm (23 ppi). ROM 973.37.1.

Prior to the mid-nineteenth century these blankets were woven of all wool, but by the mid- nineteenth century it was more common to use wool over a handspun linen warp. By the twentieth century the warp often was cotton, which had become easily available commercially.

The weft-wise bands decorating these blankets originally were asymmetrical so the blanket's head and foot ends could be distinguished, a consideration when sheets and hygiene were limited by circumstances. Within simple stripe patterns many variations of colors and proportions were developed, especially by tradesmen with skill at designing. There was a huge demand for the weft-faced plain-weave blankets, many of which were made at home in imitation of the tradesmen's designs. Color inspiration originally was from natural surroundings such as sky, landscape, water, and flower hues. "Cornflower," "rose," and "forest edge" became common names for some of the most popular blanket designs. Striped blankets inspired by seasonal colors, rainbows, sunsets, northern lights, or feather were also popular, as in fig. 3.9 or Plate 7.

Dyes for the blankets were initially from natural sources. In the 1860s, there was a shift to using chemical dyes. Blankets with color-shaded striped bands became so popular that the synthetic aniline dyes were sold in multi-hue packages, along with colored ribbon strips to use as guides for dyeing both spun and unspun wool. Another dyeing method involved removing wool skeins from the dye pot at different times, resulting in shades of one color. More dramatic patterns came from tying the skeins before dying so that

parts of the skein resisted the dye's penetration. The resultant variegated yarn could, by skillful placement during weaving, form sinuous patterns of color.

The blankets in Plate 7 and fig. 3.9 share the same structure, drafted in the fig. 3.8: a simple plain-weave interlacement woven weft-faced and known colloquially as *weft repp* or *repp*. Both these blankets were woven double-width *(see below)* on a four-shaft loom, as were many other old ones.

Blanket Styles. There were several style trends in weft-faced plain-weave blanket patterns during the last quarter of the nineteenth century and into the twentieth. These dealt with the width, number, placement, and colors of bands. Eventually a surfeit of bright colors led to more restrained color use, sometimes to the extent of carding in grey wool before spinning and dyeing the yarns. Some blankets even had light and dark threads alternating for grey visual effects. Somber blankets of black accented by white and light grey rows were woven for funerals.

Around 1900, as home and cottage industry weavers became more educated, decorative bands on blankets evolved from simple weft-faced plain weave into ornately-patterned weft-faced weaves interspersed between bands of weft-faced plain weave.

DOUBLE-WIDTH PLAIN WEAVE
Both of the blankets mentioned above were woven double width. Fabric woven in this technique is described as double-woven rather than a "double weave" because two layers of cloth are woven at the same time, one above the other and joined at one side during weaving. (Emery, 1966.) When removed from the loom and

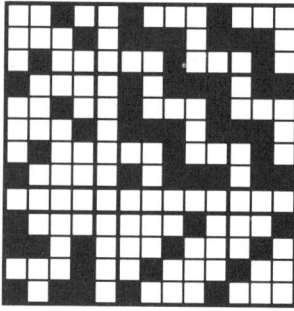

3.10. Draft for weaving double-width cloth in plain weave, two repeats.

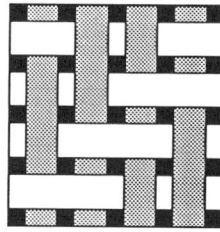

3.11. Straight twill interlacement on four shafts.

3.12. Warp dominant, 2/1 twill, two repeats.

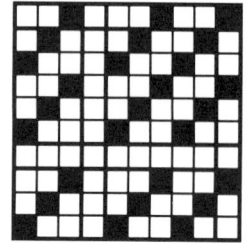

3.13. Weft dominant, 1/2 twill, two repeats.

opened full width, the unfolded cloth – in this case the blanket – becomes a single layer of plain-weave fabric.

Fig. 3.10 is the draft for weaving such a fabric. The number of warp ends is doubled in threading so half of them form each layer of cloth. One shuttle passes through the sheds of both layers so that a fold is created along one side of the cloth. The shuttle must begin on the right-hand side to set up the proper sequence of interlacement between layers. A narrow four-shaft loom is thus able to weave a wider, plain-weave fabric.

Twill Weave

Trinītis

In Latvia, only *straight twill* was considered a basic weave. In twill each weft (warp) thread passes over or under more than one warp (weft) thread during the interlacement sequence before repeating the sequence. Successive wefts picks move over by one warp per pick to form a continuous diagonal line of floats along the surface of the cloth. Figure 3.11 shows the diagonal of one of the most standard twill interlacements, 4-shaft twill. Straight twills form the basis for more complicated twill weaves which the Latvians used extensively in a variety of textiles. Many examples of those twill fabrics are included in *Chapter Four, Derived Weaves*, and *Chapter Five, Combined Weaves*.

Twill floats require a minimum of three warps and three wefts for one repeat of threading and treadling. As seen in its draft form, fig. 3.12, a straight twill has straight progression along threading, tie-up, and treadles.

There are no interruptions to the formation of an unbroken diagonal in the cloth.

Both warps and wefts are visible, although not necessarily equally, on twill cloth's surface. If the warp floats are more dominant due to their length, the cloth is called a *warp twill*, as in fig 3.12. Its reverse side will feature long weft floats and be called a *weft twill*, fig 3.13. A third type of twill, which Latvians called a *mutual twill*, has warp and weft elements passing over the same number of threads that they pass under. Figure 3.11 is this type of twill. It needs a minimum of four shafts as in fig. 3.14. Irene Emery calls this an "even" twill. These designations of warp twill, weft twill, or mutual twill relate to actual counts of threads in float groups, not to whether one set of elements simply appears to be more dense than the other.

As with plain weave, a notation system indicates twill construction, showing the number of warps a weft thread passes under and over in a single sequence before repeating that series in its horizontal journey. A slanted or horizontal line represents the weft thread. Numbers are placed above and below the line to tell how many warp threads go over and under the weft. On a three-shaft straight-twill draft, for example, a weft can go in a 2/1 sequence, fig. 3.12, where it passes under two and then over one warp. Or the weft can go in the opposite sequence, 1/2, shown in fig. 3.13. On four shafts, a straight twill can be drafted in a 2/2 (fig. 3.14), 3/1 (fig. 3.15), or 1/3 (fig. 3.16) sequence. Multi-shaft straight twills rapidly produce even more options.

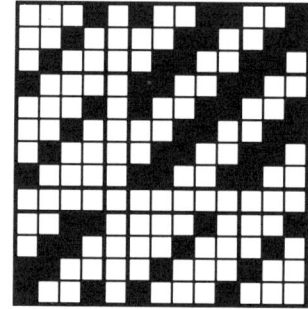

3.14. Mutual twill, 2/2, two repeats, as seen in fig. 3.11.

On six shafts the possible interlacements are 1/5, 2/4, 3/3, 1/1/1/3, 1/2/1/3. In the latter designations the weft passes under and then over warps several times before beginning the series again, as is illustrated by fig. 3.17 of the 1/1/1/3 interlacement.

In the Latvian books, if a twill line slopes to the right its notation has a "+1" added, e.g., fig. 3.14 would be designated 2/2 +1. A left-sloping twill is noted with a "-1," so the twill in fig. 3.18 would be designated as 2/2 -1.

As long as an unbroken, straight twill line is woven, the structure is considered a *basic twill* weave in Latvian texts. Basic straight twills often are made to look complicated by combining several different lengths of floats. These are called *complex twills*, such as the previous six-shaft 1/1/1/3 draft in fig. 3.17, or the 3/3/1/1 twill in fig. 3.19. In the latter each weft can be seen to pass under three warps, over three, under one, over one, and then repeat the series.

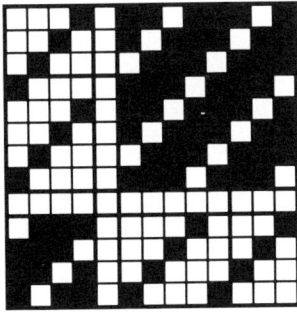

3.15. *3/1 twill, two repeats.*

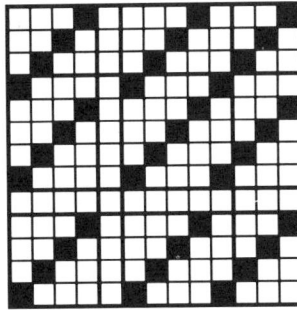

3.16. *1/3 twill, two repeats.*

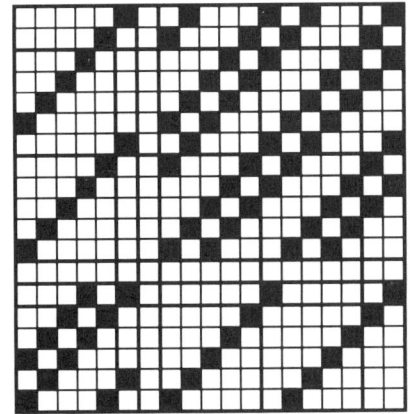

3.17. *1/1/1/3 twill, two repeats.*

3.18. *2/2-1, left-sloping twill, two repeats.*

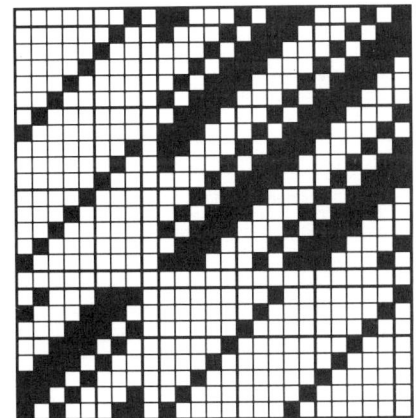

3.19. *Two repeats of complex twill with 3/3/1/1 interlacement, #92 from Rga.*

Uses. In the nineteenth century straight twill was used for linen sheets, mattress covers, and horse blankets. On one long warp of four-shaft weft twill, a weaver might produce several items such as skirt, shawl, and blanket material, simply by varying the colored weft stripes. Recipes for straight twill fabrics in twentieth-century pattern books are given for such items as wash cloths, dress fabric and suiting. Yarns recommended for dish towels and hand towels in three- or four-shaft twill were fine tow linen threads, loosely sleyed to produce an absorbent fabric.

Figure 3.19 is a Latvian draft for a suiting fabric woven of wool warp and weft, probably handspun yarn. It was sett in a 60-70 dents/10 cm reed (15-18 dents/inch), with the warp threads single in heddles and double in dents.

Satin Weave
Atlass

In *The Primary Structure of Fabrics*, Irene Emery analyzes satin weave as springing from twill weave and requiring a rather lengthy, exact definition to become a unique structure. Specifically, satin always forms a structure with: 1) either a warp- or a weft-dominant face, and 2) floats of individual threads positioned such that successive wefts never interlace with successive warps and no warp or weft interlaces at more than one point per threading repeat. See fig. 3.23.

This definition sets up the contrast between the moving, continuous diagonal of straight twills' floats and satin's redistributed, broken advance of the floats' diagonal line. Thus by definition satin weave structure is reliant on, but distinct from, straight twill weave structure.

Satin fabric has, by definition, one warp dominant surface (often referred to as *satin* in English and *warp satin* in Latvian) and its reverse has a weft dominant surface (often called *sateen* in English and *weft satin* in Latvian). Each surface has an unbroken, often shiny visual effect from the dovetailing of floats across its whole face. Satin fabrics are known in handweaving around the world for their desirable luster, created by the floats reflecting light. Plain, single-surface satin does not seem to have been a very common weave in the repertoire of handwoven textiles in Latvia.

Home weaving of satin was limited by a lack of suitable fibers and by the available equipment. A minimum of five shafts was needed, putting even basic satin beyond the range of the average Latvian weavers' four-shaft looms. Satin lends itself to multi-shaft looms, and is the most versatile on complex looms such as double-harness looms. Looms able to produce multi-shaft satin were not available to average weavers until the end of the nineteenth century. Until that time, satin was woven only by highly-skilled professional weavers.

Figs. 3.20 and 3.21 show warp-float faces of definitive five- and eight-shaft true satins. These are two of the satin weaves most commonly used by handweavers. Satin construction can be based on straight twill threadings and treadlings, but the tie-up must be changed to produce satin's interlacing points.

True satin cannot be formed with three, four, or six shafts because the regular skipping of successive interlacing warp threads is not possible.

The four-shaft compromise to satin's smooth surface is a structure called *broken twill*, drafted in fig. 3.22. This is not a true satin because some successive wefts regularly interlace with successive warp ends.

Perhaps because for many years weavers have been ambiguous about satin's relationship with twill, there are often contradictory uses of the word *satin* in weaving sources. This is frequently the case in Latvian books, as well. The book *Mācies aust* notes, "Sometimes four- and six-shaft satin are spoken of, but in truth they belong to derived structures and are broken twill structures..." (Skuja-Antēne, 1936, p. 76.) Nonetheless, all the Latvian texts intermittently refer to four-shaft broken twill as "four-shaft warp satin" or "four-shaft weft satin," depending on the dominant face. However, this "four-shaft satin" name occurs only if the structures are used together in a design of two or more blocks, requiring eight or more shafts. (Examples of these are in *Chapter Five.*) When one block of broken twill is used for an all-over surface of a cloth the structure almost invariably is called "twill."*

The only pattern found in the Latvian books for simple, all-over, five-shaft satin is in the twentieth-century pattern book *Paraugi audumiem.* An upholstery pattern uses 24/2 cotton sett in a 70 dent/10 cm (18 dent/inch) reed, threaded two ends per heddle and two ends per dent. Numerous weft colors of 20/1 linen, wound double on the bobbin, form a weft-faced pattern of horizontal stripes.

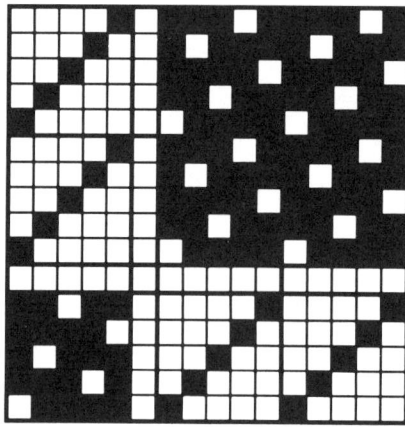

3.20. 5-shaft satin, two repeats.

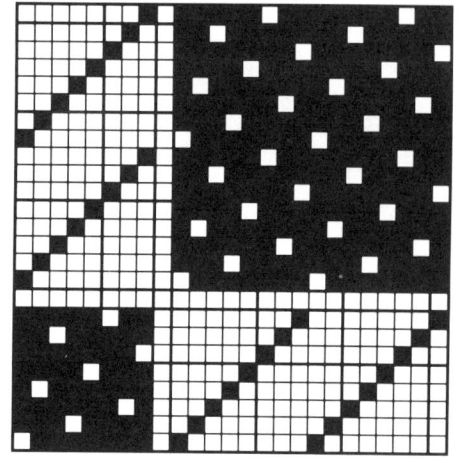

3.21. 8-shaft satin, two repeats.

3.22. 1/3 broken twill, two repeats.

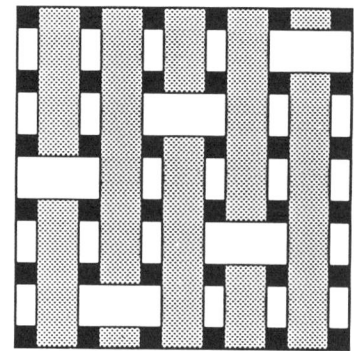

3.23. Satin weave structure.

*The confusing terminology may have roots in the fact the early examples of what came to be called "damask" throughout the world were based on three- and four-shaft weaves. In the 1400s Italian silk weavers established true satin on five shafts as the standard weave in damask. (Becker, 1987.) It is quite possible that the older four-shaft twill had come by association with "damask" to be considered part of the satin family in the general terminology in Europe, from which Latvia's weaving community derived its block weaving information.

CHAPTER FOUR

Derived Simple Weaves

Derived Weaves

Atvasinātie sējumi

These weaves literally derive their structures from the three preceding interlacements - plain weave, twill, and satin. Derived weaves alter the basic weave's structure by changes to weft floats and/or warp floats to create a new, more elaborate fabric surface. This is done by changing the original weave's threading draft, tie-up, and/or treadling order. There is only one set of warp elements and one set of weft elements; both are intrinsic to the fabric structure. If a single warp or weft were removed from this type of cloth the whole structure would be changed.

Handweavers have produced many variations on plain weave, twill and satin, often with only minor differences among some variations. It is not surprising there is little standard nomenclature for all of these weaves. Some names are based on purpose, some on draft, and some on appearance. There is limited unanimity about terminology in Latvian handweaving books, as well. Although the following weaves are titled by the English name that best fits the Latvian concept, it is best not to make assumptions about each draft based on name. The description of each draft and its use is more important than its name.

Derivations Based on Plain Weave

Derived Repps

Ripsa sējumi

In pre-World War II Latvia, just as in present-day North America, there was cloudiness as to exactly what constituted a "repp," so a number of weave structures were included under the term as long as only warps or wefts were visible on a ribbed surface.

The first repp weave, as known in the Latvian vernacular, is discussed on pages 36 and 37 - a warp-faced or weft-faced material in plain weave with ribs along the surface. These colloquial repps have no structural change from basic plain weave, only a change in the appearance of the fabric's surface.

A second type of repp is precisely defined in most Latvian texts as a *derived weave*, identifiable by both its surface ribs and its structural change from plain weave. Its interlacement either changes the plain weave threading by combining warp ends so they act as one thread, or changes the plain weave treadling by combining weft picks so they act as one thread.

Depending on how the threads within the hidden element are combined, derived-weave repps are classified as *regular* or *irregular*.

REGULAR WEFT-FACED REPPS

The covered element is a consistent thickness, resulting in equal-sized vertical ribs on the cloth's surface.

Figure 4.1 shows a *regular* weft-faced repp. Because all of the groups of two warps are equal in size, this is a *regular* weft-faced repp. It also is a *derived weave,* having altered each weft's 1/1 interlacement of plain weave to 2/2 via the threading. The warp still interlaces over and under single wefts.

IRREGULAR WEFT-FACED REPPS

There have unequally-sized groups of warp elements under the visible element. Ribs on the surface are dissimilar in size. Figure 4.2 shows an *irregular* weft-faced repp with groups of one and three (1,3) threads in the warps.

A more irregular weft-faced repp is shown in fig. 4.3. Here the underlying warp groups are ordered 2,3,2,1. While it would not require four shafts for threading, efficiency in weaving and a level warp result from using all four shafts.

REGULAR WARP-FACED REPPS

The covered element is of one consistent thickness, producing equal-sized ribs along the surface. Figure 4.4 shows a warp-faced repp where the wefts under the warps are all tripled.

IRREGULAR WARP-FACED REPPS

There are hidden weft elements of unequal thickness, and the visible ribs vary in size. Figure 4.5 shows a 3,1 weft grouping order.

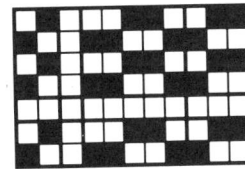

4.1. Two repeats of regular weft-faced repp, #73 from Ap.

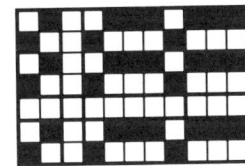

4.2. Two repeats of irregular weft-faced repp.

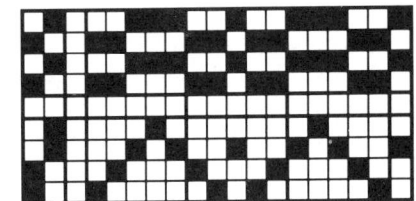

4.3. Two repeats of irregular weft-faced repp.

4.4. Two repeats of regular warp-faced repp.

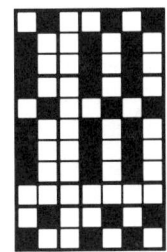

4.5. Two repeats of irregular warp-faced repp.

4.6. Irregular warp-faced repp, two repeats.

A warp-faced repp with several irregular weft elements is shown in fig. 4.6. This is definitely not a common way to weave a warp-faced repp because of the confusion in handling the various weft passes, and the visual distortion of colored patterns. However it is theoretically a viable structure.

PATTERN FROM COLOR

In Latvian repps derived from plain weave, the visible surface element consists of threads of one size. Whether these threads form a colored design is not part of the technical definition of repp. In practice, two or more colors are often alternated to create a visual pattern. Parallel stripes or checks are easy to form, as at the edge of the weft-faced stripes in fig. 3.9. On a warp-faced repp surface, lengthwise (warp-wise) stripes are made by using the same color for several adjacent warps. Cross-wise stripes can also be made by alternating warp-end colors.

GROUPING OF ELEMENTS

Within the Latvian category of repps derived from plain weave (not simply weft-faced or warp-faced plain weave) the hidden element is of a single size of thread grouped so that several threads work together as one. In *warp-faced derived repp*, a shuttle carrying one fine weft yarn is woven several times in a single shed to make the resulting group of wefts lie flat and give vertical growth in the fabric, instead of twisting and forming a thick, round element. See fig. 4.4. At the selvages each weft pick needs to interlace with a warp thread to prevent the weft from raveling on the return pick.

Weft-faced derived repps also have groupings in the hidden element, in this case warp threads. These groupings often are combined so that the warp has two components of different sizes. See fig. 4.2. To

make the warps lie flat within each grouping, the individual warp ends can be threaded in individual heddles so warps do not wrap around their neighbors.

Warp-faced or weft-faced repps may be woven using two or more different sizes of threads for the hidden elements rather than using groupings of the same size threads. If a thicker thread substitutes for a group of several spread-out, thinner ones, the resultant fabric is usually denser and less flexible. This is because a thick thread has more mass in cross-section than a group of thinner ones for a comparable diameter. Latvian weavers have preferred using groups of fine yarns to single, coarse yarns.

Irregular Repps in Unit Drafts

Applying the theories to produce patterns was of the most interest to Latvian handweavers. The old weaving texts present repps from several structural bases including plain weave, as *patterned repps*.

PATTERNED REPPS DERIVED FROM PLAIN WEAVE

These repps are based on *irregular warp-faced repp*, fig. 4.5, or *weft-faced repp*, fig. 4.2. By threading in units of plain weave it becomes possible to design and weave block motifs as either warp-faced or weft-faced ribbed weaves. The fabric has

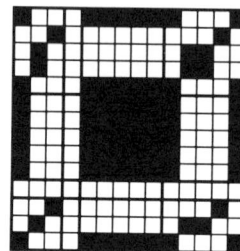

4.7. Profile draft, #189 in Ma.

one set of warp ends and one set of weft threads. The set showing on the surface is of at least two colors. The hidden set is of one thread size and is arranged in two sizes of groupings.

Warp-faced patterned repps derived from plain weave. To arrange to weave a design in a warp-faced repp based on plain weave, first plan its block or profile form, fig. 4.7. Each block in the design requires two shafts, threaded alternately as a pair. The warps always retain the alternating color order of dark/light. The base number of warp pairs to

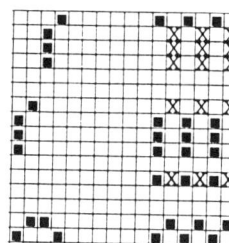

4.8. Three pairs of warps as one block of warp-faced repp Alternating warp colors are indicated above threading.

thread as one unit within a block is then established, e.g., two pairs, three pairs, etc.

The two structures in fig. 4.8 show how one unit of irregular warp-faced repp based in plain weave

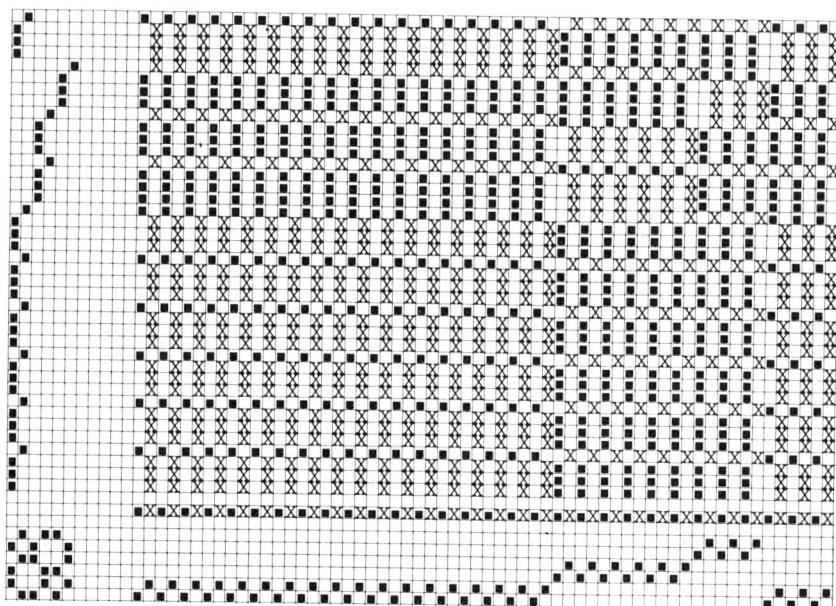

4.9. Warp-faced repp pattern, #190 in Ma. Alternating warp colors are indicated above threading.

4.10. Warp-faced appearance of fig. 4.9.

4.11. Profile draft for warp-faced repp pattern, based on #191 in Ma.

4.12. Four units for warp-faced repp on four shafts. Alternating warp colors are indicated above threading.

interlaces to emphasize either pattern (lower section) or background (upper section). Because the unit is plain weave, these are the only two possible interlacements per block. To achieve one of these two appearances in a block, the enlarged weft must pass under either the *pattern warps* (lower section) or *background warps* (upper section). Compare the tie-ups in fig. 4.8 to see how to control which warp is on the surface:

• for pattern, the pattern warps are tied to treadle 1 and background warps are tied to treadle 2;

• for background, the background warps are tied to treadle 3 and pattern warps are tied to treadle 4.

Each two-shaft unit is tied to all pairs of treadles according to which warps (pattern or background) are to pass over or under the large weft element.

Figure 4.9 shows threading, tie-up, and treadling for a warp-faced pattern of the design in fig. 4.7. Six warps are threaded for each block of the design. The treadling applies the original profile's treadling order for the dominant (pattern) pick. The first treadle opens the shed for the multiple weft threads, so three or more weft picks are put in the same shed (preferably catching selvage threads to avoid unweaving during a return pick). Each enlarged pick is followed by a second single-thread pick for background on the treadle that lifts shafts opposite to the first treadle's shafts. Figure 4.9 shows the resulting patterned repp's structure and fig. 4.10 shows it as warp-faced.

It is possible to weave a four-block design on four shafts, such as the one shown in fig. 4.11. Two pairs of shafts are threaded to the four units

in fig. 4.12. The units are on two opposite pairs of shafts within which two colors alternate in dark/light order. Each unit is four warps wide, and units are repeated as necessary to reach blocks' appropriate widths in a warp-faced sett. When woven with two weft sizes, one color within each unit will become dominant due to having several wefts pass under it. Solid vertical stripes may be threaded

4 12 4 4 4 4 4 4 4 4 4 4 4 4 4 28 8 4

4.13. Partial threading for profile in fig. 4.12. Warp thread colors are indicated above threading.

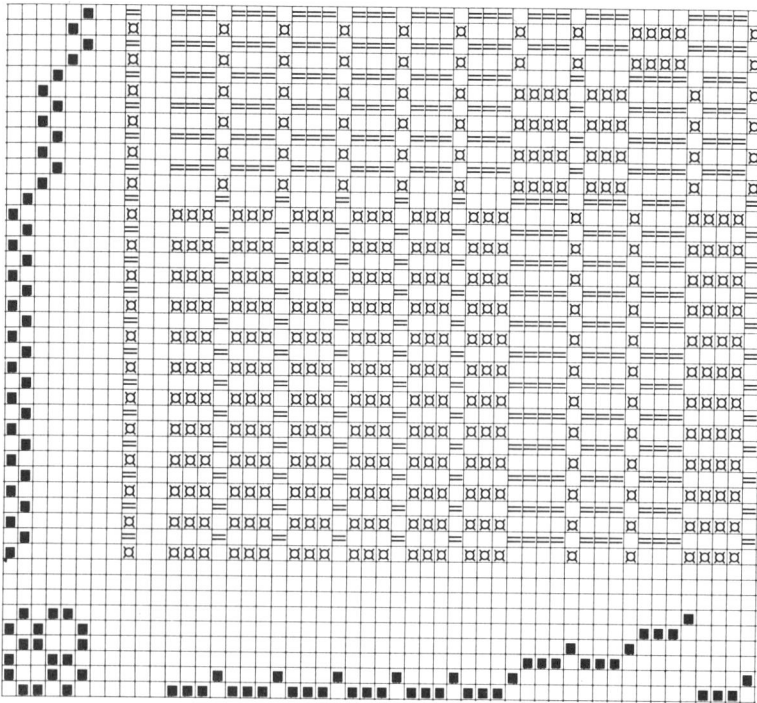

4.14. Weft-faced repp draft for profile in fig. 4.7. Weft color sequence indicated beside treadling order.

4.14 is based on the design in fig. 4.7. The tie-up is made as for the warp-faced repp: two treadles are tied to weave opposite lifts for each pair of shafts. In reverse from sheds in warp-faced repps, the warps in weft-faced repp are lowered rather than raised for the dominant (pattern) weft to show, so the tie-ups for each block are one of the two pairs of treadles shown in fig. 4.15. The treadling follows the original profile draft's treadling order, with the dominant (pattern) pick followed by its opposite (background) pick. This order weaves weft picks *on opposites* and gives areas of unbalanced plain weave. All the colored wefts are the same size.

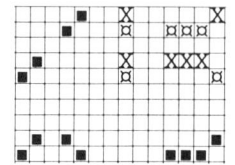

4.15. Weft-faced repp units. Weft color sequence is indicated beside treadling order.

The blanket in fig. 4.16 (also shown on the cover) is a fine example of 16-shaft, weft-faced repp blocks based on plain weave. Its profile draft with two repeats of width is shown in fig. 4.17. A close inspection of the ribbed effect of the blanket reveals that the hidden warps are groups of fine cotton threads. Some groups form a thick band, others form a thin one. The grouping of these hidden warps is as follows: first, eight ends function as one working end, then

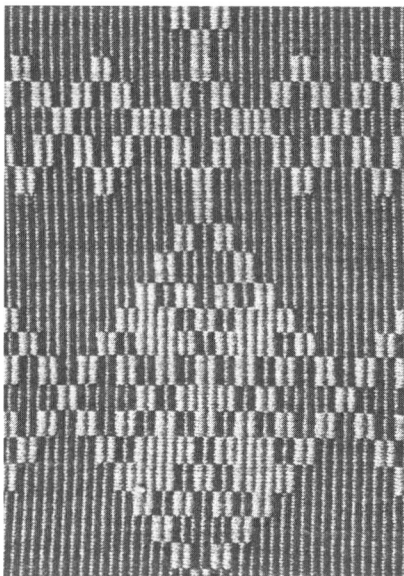

4.16. This blanket, also shown on cover, was made in the 1930s in Vidzeme. It is fascinating in its appearance, structure, and Latvian origin, and initiated the research for this book. The supple, attractive lilac and dark purple handspun wool appeals to both eye and hand. It also is noteworthy to a weaver as a ribbed fabric that is very soft yet functional. Whether this well-crafted, 16-shaft blanket panel was woven by a professional or home weaver is a detail lost over the years. 145.5 cm (57") L X 43cm (17") W; warp, cotton, 2-ply, white, grey, black; weft, wool, S-twist, singles, dark purple and lavender. 3.6 e/cm (9epi); 10 p/cm (25 ppi). ROM971.135.1. Gift of Mrs. Anna Udris.

on any unit, using all light or all dark warp threads. The draft in fig. 4.13 develops this pattern possibility from the left border to the center.

Weft-faced repp patterning derived from plain weave. An adjacent pair of shafts is used for each block of the original design. One size of warp thread is threaded in groups that alternate in wide/narrow order across the whole warp. A two-sized set of warp elements is created, using one size of thread. The warping in fig.

4.17. Profile draft for weft-faced repp blanket in fig. 4.16. One-and-one-half repeats.

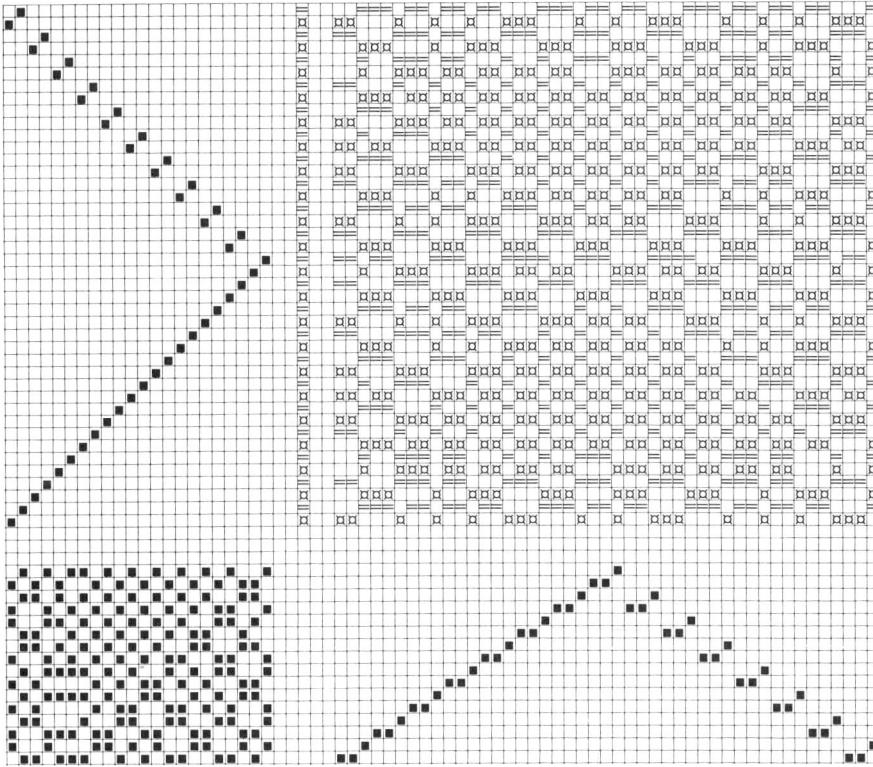

4.18. *Weft-faced repp interlacement for blanket in fig 4.16. Weft color order indicated by symbols beside treadling*

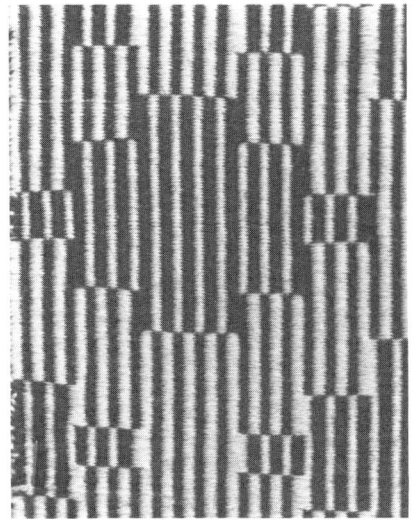

4.19. *Weft-faced repp on two sizes of warp threads, with symmetrical reverses in pattern. Woven by Jane Evans.*

two ends together form a single working warp. This thick/thin alternation is consistent across the warp, with the exception of an added third rib over ten warp ends, as both an eight-end and a two-end group join at the edge of a pattern block. Figure 4.18 illustrates how this combining of warps happens on a partial threading of the blanket's draft.

Two shafts are used per block of pattern. Each shaft is paired with one adjacent shaft. Within a pair, one shaft carries a thick warp group and the other shaft carries a thin warp group. Tie-up and treadling are arranged so that the two shafts of a block are treadled as a pair on opposites.

Moving from one pair of treadles to the next pair means that a thick warp group may be in the same shed as its neighboring block's thin warp group, depending on the blocks' sequence in the design. If these two warp groups are on the same shed they will join into an extra large warp group and give a wider edge to a block, as regularly seen on the blanket.

Because the blocks of threading are always in the order of odd-even (for example, shaft 1, large warp; shaft 2, thin warp) the central point of a motif does not have symmetrically wide edges. To be symmetrical, as in fig. 4.19, the unit's threads would have to be reversed as even-odd (shaft 2, thin warp; shaft 1, large warp) and one warp would need to be added or one warp dropped in the unit forming the reversing point of the pattern. Figure 4.20 is a partial draft for that structure. Whichever way the enlarged edge block is handled, reversed or not, it adds boldness to the pattern areas and also gives a pleasant variety to the proportions of a design. It is unavoidable and will always occur at

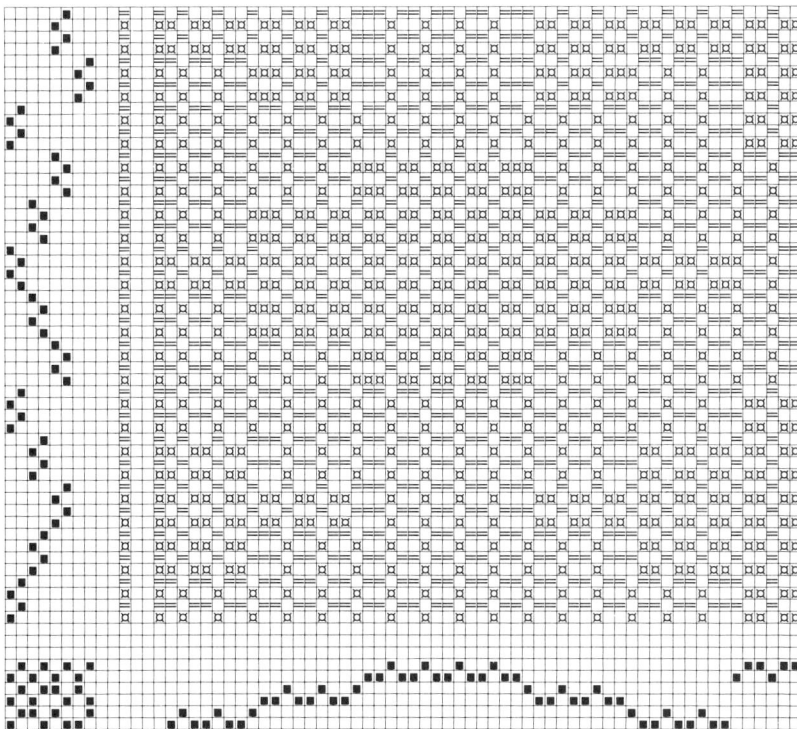

4.20. *Partial draft for fig. 4.19. Weft color order indicated beside treadling order.*

4.21. Fragment of a wall hanging woven about 1940 at the workshop of the Latvian National League of Women in Riga. Like the blanket in fig. 4.16, it is an example of weft-faced patterned repp based on plain weave. The size of the large linen warp threads contrasts to that of the fine cotton warps in the blanket. 22 cm(9") W X 15cm (6") L; warp, linen, 5-ply, natural; weft, wool, 3-ply, blues, pink, yellow,brown, beige; 9 thin and 9 thick e/10cm (23 epi and 23 epi). ROM 972.181.1. Gift of Mrs. Anna Stunda.

the edges of pattern areas threaded as two-shaft blocks and woven *on opposites* to form a diagonal line in a design. This same effect occurs in the 90-degree-turned position on warp-faced patterned repps, such as seen in the earlier fig. 4.9.

Figure 4.21 is a fragment of a wall hanging with large linen warp threads. Its draft is shown in fig. 4.22. Within a unit, one shaft has three consecutive warp threads on it, while its partner shaft has only one warp.

The warps of the blanket in fig. 4.16 were probably threaded as a group of either two or eight threads through a heddle and reed dent, because they appear to twist around

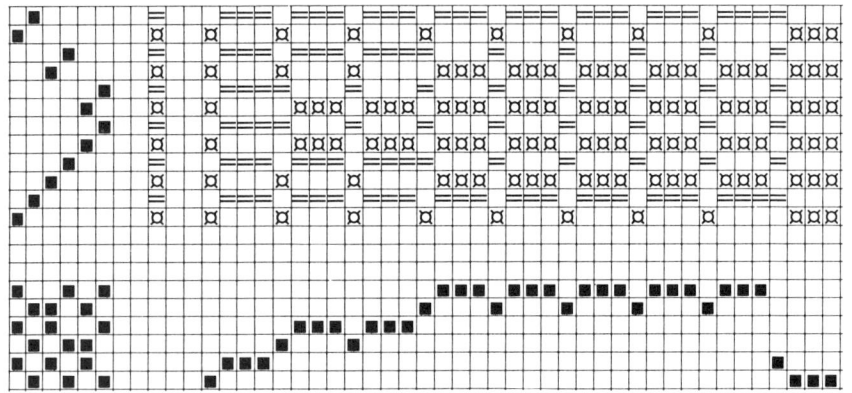

4.22. Draft for fig. 4.21. Weft color sequence indicated beside treadling order.

each other within each group. With large warps, like the warps of the wall hanging in fig. 4.21, it may be preferable to sley them through separate dents in the reed to spread them out flat. If separate dents are used, it is best to also thread the warps through separate heddles or there is a tendency for the threads to twist around each other and resist passing smoothly through the reed during the weaving.

Four-shaft drafts for four-block patterns also can be woven in weft-faced patterned repps. The draft in previous fig. 4.13 simply need be turned 90 degrees. The original warp threading becomes the new, two-colored weft order. The original weft order becomes the new threading for two sizes of warps, which are spread apart. The tie-up is similarly rotated, all leading to fig. 4.23. A weft-faced patterned repp fabric will weave in a block design similar to fig. 4.11.

Uses. Both warp-faced and weft-faced patterned repp cloth were used in pre-World War II Latvia for rugs, uholstery, bed blankets, door curtains, carpets, and other sturdy fabrics.

Basket Weave
Plāces jeb panama sējums
Basket weave is simply an extended version of plain weave's 1/1 inter-lacement. For each single thread within a plain-weave structure, basket weave uses units of two, three, or even four threads in each direction. The unit size chosen for one set of elements is balanced by an equal number in the opposite element. Figure 4.24 shows a

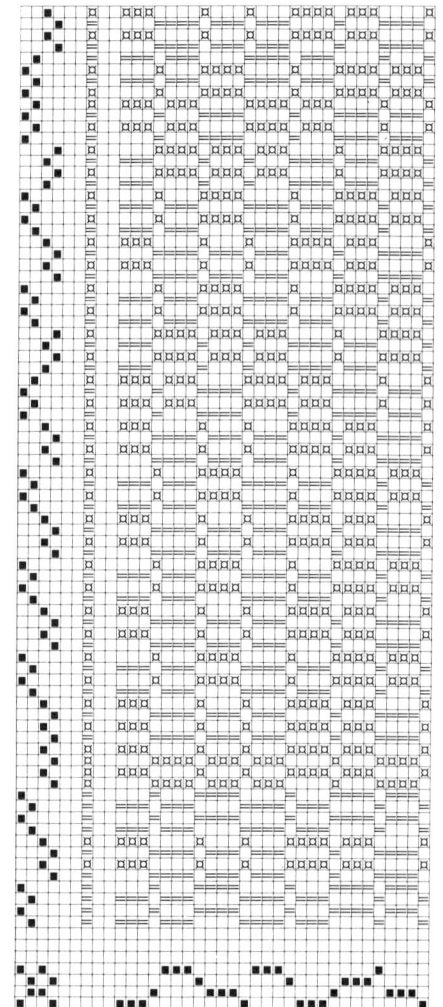

4.23. Four units of weft-faced repp on four shafts.

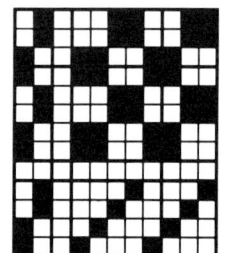

4.24. Two repeats of 2/2 basket weave draft, #66 in Ma.

46

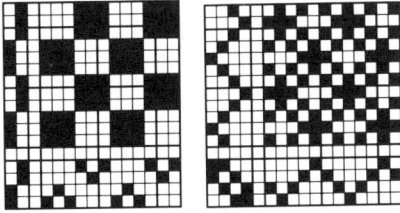

4.25. (left) Two repeats of 3/3 basket weave draft, #67 in Ma.

4.26. (right) Two repeats of canvas weave draft, #135 in Ma.

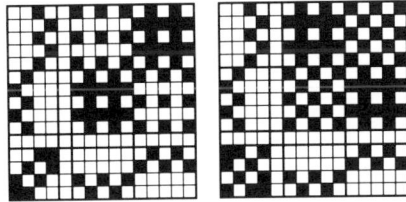

4.27. (left) Draft with canvas interlacement, #137 in Ma.

4.28. (right) Draft with lace interlacement, #139 in Ma.

4.29. Simply changing the tie-up converts the same threading and treadling orders from canvas (upper) to lace (lower) fabric.

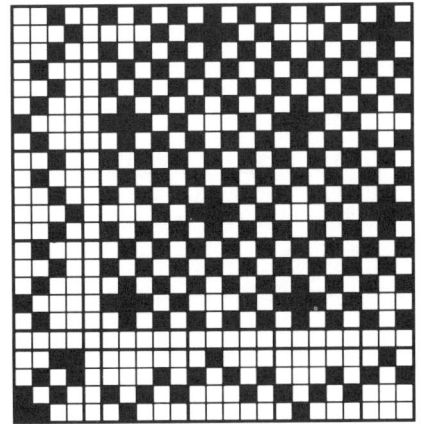

4.30. Two repeats, canvas weave draft suitable for grouped warps and/or two sizes of wefts, #138 in Ma.

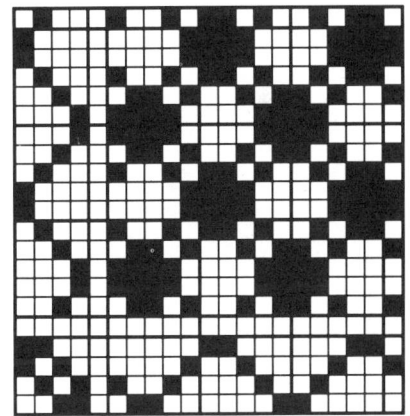

4.31. Two repeats, canvas weave with grouped warps and wefts, #136 in Ma.

2/2 basket weave: two wefts interlace evenly with two warps. Figure 4.25 is a 3/3 basket weave.

Like plain weave, basket weave requires only two sheds. The use of more than two shafts, as in fig. 4.25, allows for threading fewer heddles on each shaft, thus reducing friction between closely sett warp ends.

Basket weave is more effective if the threads within a unit lie flat and give squares of wefts intersecting with equally squared multiple warps. This usually means single weft picks are multiply inserted in the same shed, rather than several weft threads being wound onto one bobbin. In the latter case, the threads wrap around each other as they come off the bobbin and create more depth than if woven individually. Warps are sleyed so they are spread flat by the reed.

Uses. Basket weave is briefly dealt with in twentieth-century Latvian weaving texts. It is considered needlework fabric, used for counted thread work. *Rokas grāmata audējām* suggests a sett for basket-weave cloth of 20/2 cotton, doubled to give 90 working (180 single) ends/10 cm (22 doubled e.p.i.).

In the early nineteenth century Vidzeme farmhome weavers used basket weave for shawls, skirts, and

blankets. These items were often all made on the same warp to save loom setup time.

Canvas Weave
Kaneva sējums

Both canvas weave and lace weaves are considered to be derivations from plain weave in Latvia. However, canvas weave is classified separately from lace weaves because of the characteristics by which each weave is defined.

In canvas weave, texture is added all over the usual plain-weave surface by means of small floats or groups of floats which occur in close proximity to each other, as in fig. 4.26. These floats are usually over three, four, or five threads. Most commonly canvas-weave cloth has both warp and weft floats on both the front and back surfaces. Floats are evenly distributed and fully cover the surface so that no pattern is formed by the floats, just texture. There are no appreciable plain-weave areas between floats. Lace weave is characterized by areas of floats among areas of plain weave.

Comparing figs. 4.27 and 4.28 shows that the two fabrics share the same threading and treadling, but their different tie-ups lead to either canvas or lace, shown in the top and bottom respectively of fig. 4.29. The

canvas-weave fabric has weft-float spots between warp-float spots, while the lace fabric has plain-weave sections between warp-float spots.

A canvas-weave warp is often sleyed unevenly, grouped in dents or skipping dents of the reed to accentuate the small openings in the canvas fabric. In the weft direction, the open effect might be increased by using two shuttles, one with a single thread for picks that weave plain-weave sheds, and one with a doubled thread for picks that weave weft floats. The draft in fig. 4.30 shows groups of floats separated by two threads of plain weave. For increased texture the three warps of each grouped float section should be sleyed together in one dent of the reed, and the two plain-weave warps separating the groups should be sleyed individually in two separate dents. To further add texture to the

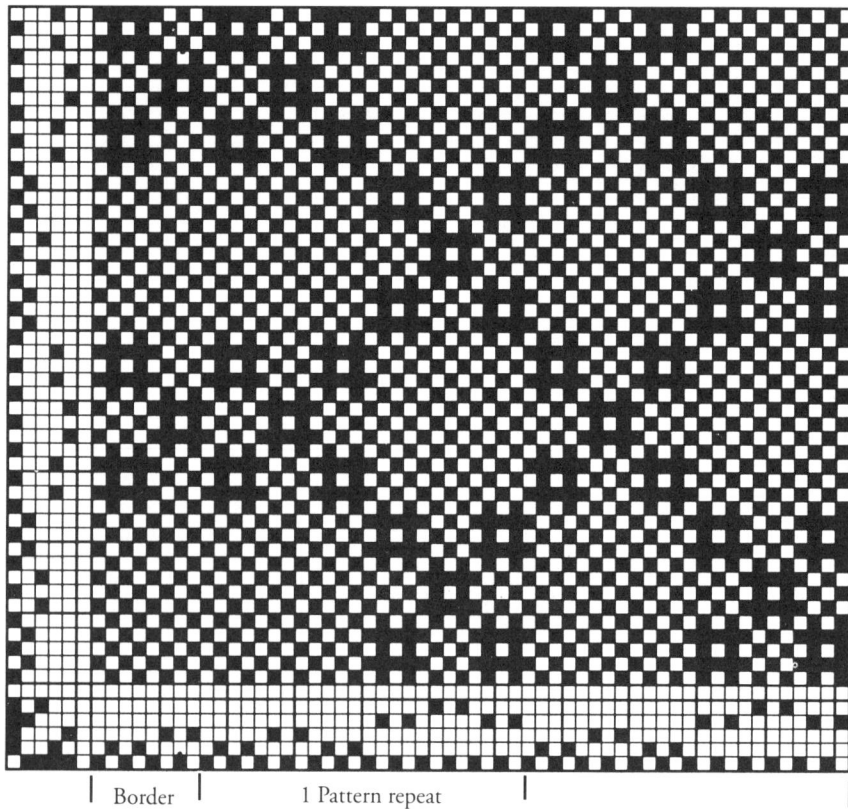

4.33. Border and two repeats of lace blocks, # 271 in Ltm.

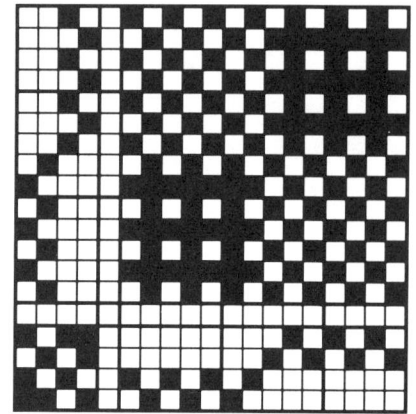

4.32. Lace weave, #141 in Ma.

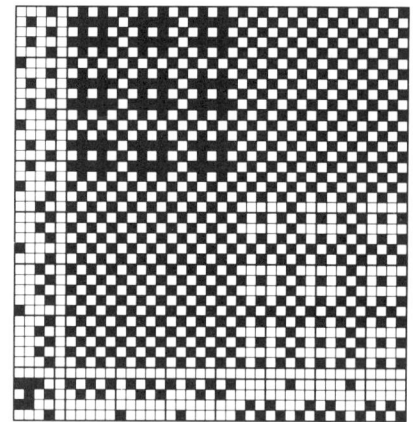

4.34. Four-shaft, two-block lace weave, #264 in Ltm.

weave, the center weft pick of each float group can be woven with a doubled weft, while all other picks are of single weft threads.

Another way to increase the texture of canvas-weave floats is shown in fig. 4.31. Here both warps and wefts are doubled in the center of each float group.

Figure 4.27 shows larger float groups, evenly adjoining over the cloth. This structure can prove a problem during weaving, as the warp ends that frequently float become less taut than those that regularly interlace as plain weave. For long pieces of fabric in this particular canvas weave, extra tension is needed on the warp ends that make floats.

Uses. Canvas weave was useful as a base cloth on which to count embroidery stitches. In twentieth-century Latvia it also was popular for dress fabric, window curtains, doilies, and runners. Cotton and linen were the most practical fibers for such uses.

Lace Weaves
Pubuļainie audumi

These decorative weaves, called *lace* or *spot weaves* in English, also derive from plain-weave interlacement. One set of warp threads and one set of weft threads interlace. The "lace" is formed by small floats of threads which produce textured areas amidst plain weave.

One example of what Latvian texts would call lace weave is shown in figs. 4.28 and 4.29. The floats and openings distort the fabric when off the loom, giving it a lacy quality that cannot be replicated by graphic representations.

Lace fabric differs from canvas weave by containing plain-weave areas. This plain-weave background allows for designing motifs in lace by using groups of floats as a foreground or focus of a design. Latvian texts warn that the lacy groups should not be too scattered because that would defeat the design visually.

Warp-floats, weft-floats, or both might be on one face of a lace-weave cloth, along with areas of plain weave. The opposite configuration of any float appears on the reverse of the cloth. Some drafts produce more undulation to the float areas than others do, either by forming longer float groupings or by combining warp groups in dents of the reed.

Around the world many versions of drafts arrive at similar lace-weave effects. Correspondingly, quite a few names are used for these weaves. *Pubuļainie audumi* is the Latvian term for fabrics with a bubbly surface like cobblestones. There was some difference among weaving texts as to just which weaves actually were classed as *pubuļainie*. In *Aušanas pašmācība* , lace, crepe, and honeycomb weaves were all listed under that title. Nonetheless, only the lace-weaves were called *pubuļainie*. These were drafts equivalent to the North American weaves known as *spot Bronson, Bronson lace, huck,* and *Swedish lace.* An attractive lace structure woven in an uncommon method is discussed in *Chapter Eleven.*

48

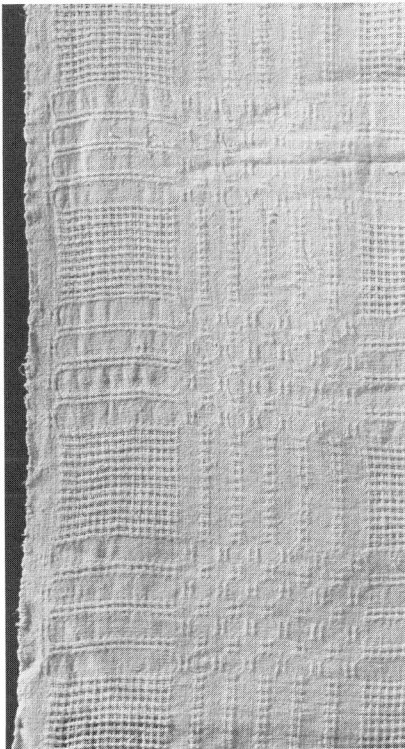

4.35. This towel, woven in Latgale in the early twentieth century, was bought in a farmers' market. The cloth must have proven serviceable, as this weave typically does for towels, because the linen is supple and burnished, and the piece has been so well used as to have a few holes worn in it. Probably from Latgale; 142 cm (60") L X 42 cm (16.5") W; warp and weft, linen, Z-twist, singles, bleached; 14 e/cm (35.5 epi); 14 p/cm. (35.5 ppi). ROM971.413.1. Gift of Mrs. Aleksandra Dzērvītis.

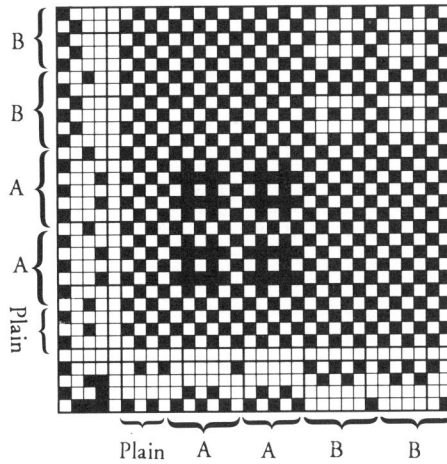

4.36. Threading blocks for towel in fig 4.35.

The length of a lace-weave float is usually three, five, or seven threads, limited by the cloth's function and warp sett. Figure 4.32 shows a four-shaft lace with plain-weave ground and warp floats over seven wefts, rather than the five-end floats of the previous example. In North America both these drafts would be called *huck weave*.

On three or more shafts it is possible to weave one kind of lace weave in designs of separate blocks. Warp floats or weft floats can appear on the same surface. Warp-float blocks alternate with weft-float blocks or plain weave. Otherwise, the combined floats would become so

long as to be unserviceable. Figure 4.33 is the draft of this type of weave, taken from a linen shawl woven in the first half of the nineteenth century in Zemgale. For some reason this type of draft, known as *spot Bronson weave* to North American weavers, was not presented in the general Latvian handweaving texts in the twentieth century.

It is often desirable in lace weaving to repeat a unit of threading so that patterning floats can occur next to each other, unlike in the previous draft. However, the floating threads (warp or weft) need to be separated by some interlacement with their opposite set of elements (weft or warp) to avoid overly long floats which are not practical. Figure 4.34 is one solution to long floats on four shafts, utilizing two separate blocks of lace for a design. Each of these two threading units can be repeated by adding to its end a warp from the other unit, used to bind the long weft-float. This structure is called *Swedish lace* in North America. Swedish lace drops the additional binding warp in the transition to the opposite unit, since the new unit begins on the same shaft as would be threaded for the previous unit's binder.

Figure 4.34 is a draft taken from a linen shawl in a four-shaft, two-block Swedish lace pattern, woven in the nineteenth century in Vidzeme. It shows how the blocks can be repeated, and how they can be positioned to form a design on a plain-weave background. One block is woven as weft floats and one as warp floats. This application with two types of floats on the surface is seen less commonly in North American lace weaves, which often have only one type of float per surface.

The towel pictured in fig. 4.35 is another example of Swedish Lace. Figure 4.36 gives the interlacement draft for it. Although the pattern is not symmetrical and the selvages are uneven, there is clever use of the weave structure and treadling for an overall design. Figure 4.37 gives the overall design for one repeat, showing how the warp-float areas (indicated by arrowheads), weft-float areas (in-

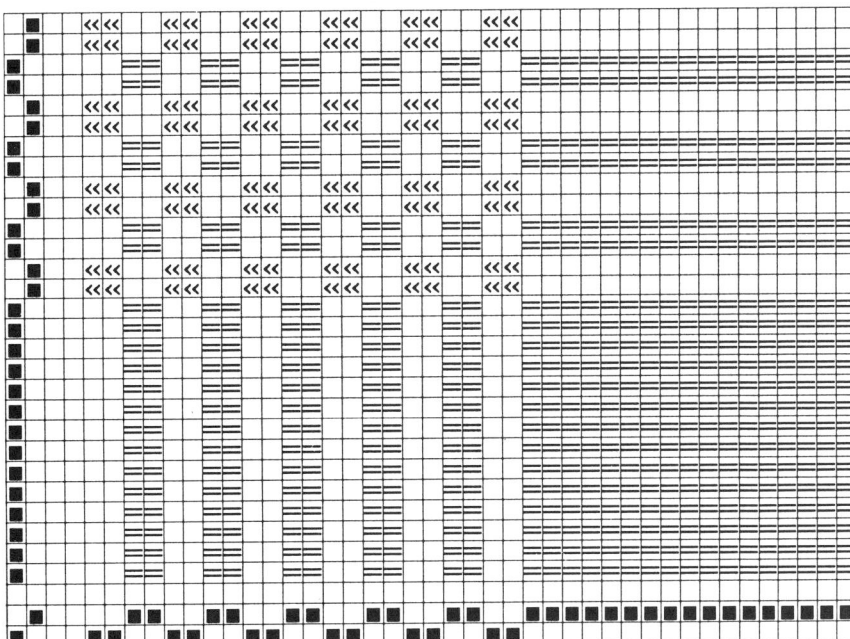

4.37. Overall design of three textures of towel in fig. 4.35.

49

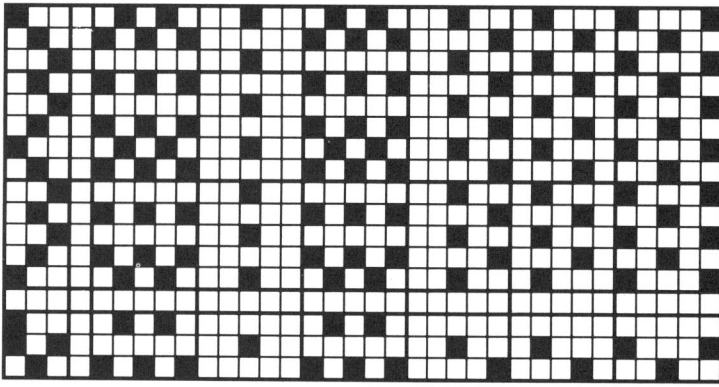

4.38. Curtain fabric draft in lace with spaced warp threads, #115 in Rga.

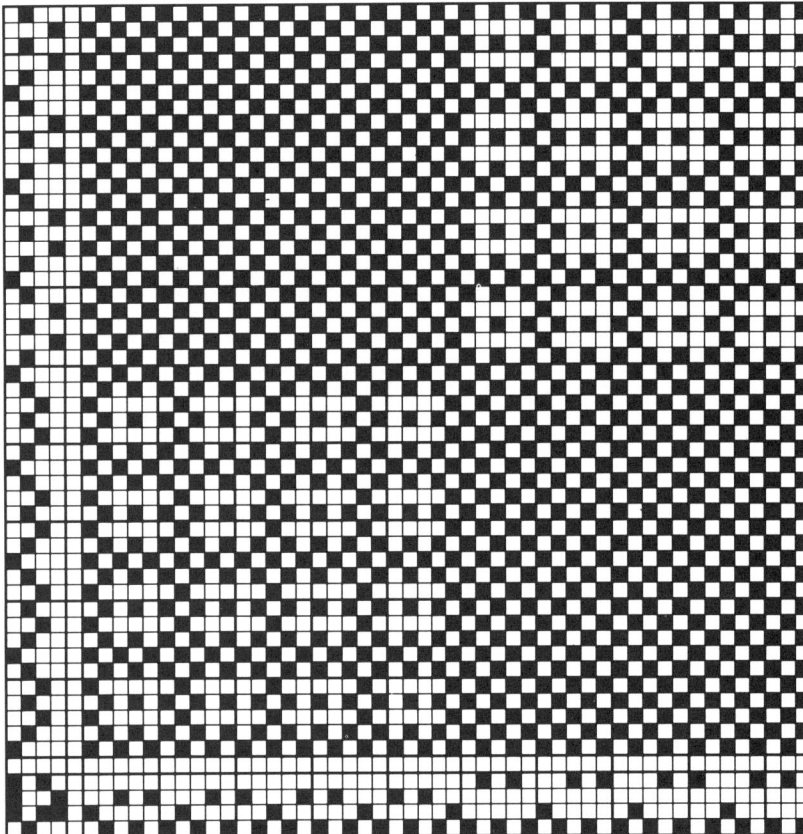

4.39. Two blocks of lace woven for an old shawl, #263 in Ltm.

4.40 Plain weave and two blocks of lace from old shawl, #265 in Ltm.

dicated by horizontal lines), and plain-weave areas (blank spaces) are all utilized to create an attractive textural design.

Another lace weave on three or more shafts uses repeated threadings of a block next to itself. It is called *Bronson lace* in North America, shown in fig. 4.38. Alternate threads are placed on shaft 1. The sixth thread (on shaft 2) is placed at the transition between pattern blocks to interlace with weft floats. This allows weft-faced blocks to appear side-by-side. The second and fourth threads are used to form warp or weft floats. They are threaded on the same shafts in each block. These are called *pattern shafts.*

Figure 4.39 shows a two-block Bronson lace pattern using four shafts. This fabric, from a linen shawl woven in the early 1800s in Latgale, has weft floats on one surface and warp floats on the opposite surface.

Like the Swedish lace shown in fig. 4.34, the Bronson lace blocks in fig. 4.40 use contrasting textures on the same surface, alternating one block of weft-floats and one block of warp-floats. This draft is also taken from a nineteenth-century linen shawl from Latgale, where float-type weaves had been popular for several hundred years.

Uses. Lace weaves do not get much attention in Latvian weaving books, although they undoubtedly were prevalent for centuries. Usually woven in line or tow linen, examples are found such as bed coverings, shawls, towels, women's head coverings, window or door curtains, neckerchiefs, tablecloths, and dress fabrics. Latvians favored this type of fabric when window curtains became part of farm house decor in the late nineteenth century.

Every household needed some of these attractive and functional fabrics. Lace weaves have tended to be preserved in present-day textile collections. Firmly-woven towels were likely to have been used as diapers or general cloths during the hasty emigration. Many of those examples still are in family collections.

Honeycomb or Gnarled Weave
Mezǧinaudums

The descriptive name of *honeycomb weave* identifies its main visual characteristic, namely its cellular appearance with a highly textured surface. Like lace-weaves, honeycomb weave has blocks of plain weave and floats. One set of warp elements is threaded in units. Two sizes of wefts, used at different times, function as a set of weft elements.

In its simplest form honeycomb weave uses two blocks, each threaded as a unit of plain weave, as in fig. 4.41. A unit contains an even number of warp threads, usually four to twelve. One unit is independently woven as plain weave with an even number of fine weft picks. The other unit does not interlace during these picks, producing warp floats on the surface of that block. After one unit is woven, two plain-weave picks of coarse wefts are entered. When beaten, these picks undulate around the two blocks' contrastingly rigid areas and form the characteristic wavy lines around the cells from selvage to selvage. The second block is woven in plain weave, followed by two more coarse wefts in full-width plain weave which undulate around the cells. Latvian texts always show two coarse picks used as a pair, unlike some European methods of using only one coarse pick between cells.

Honeycomb weave was most often used for four-block patterning. The four threading units' shafts were: A=1,2; B=3,2; C=3,4; D=1,4. Within a unit the pair of shafts could be repeatedly threaded for a total of four, six, eight, or ten warps. Figure 4.42 is a typical profile draft for the corner of a day-blanket woven in honeycomb weave. In fig. 4.43 the threading units are substituted for part of the profile draft. The tie-up is for lifting individual shafts and for the two plain-weave sheds. Treadles are paired to correspond to the threading units: 1,2; 3,2; 3,4; and 1,4. Alternately treadling a pair of treadles produces one block of plain weave, two blocks with half the warps floating, and one block with all the warps floating. Each block can be woven independently as in fig. 4.41.

4.41. *Two plain-weave units for honeycomb on four shafts.*

4.42. *Profile draft for four-block, honeycomb design, #136 in Rga.*

51

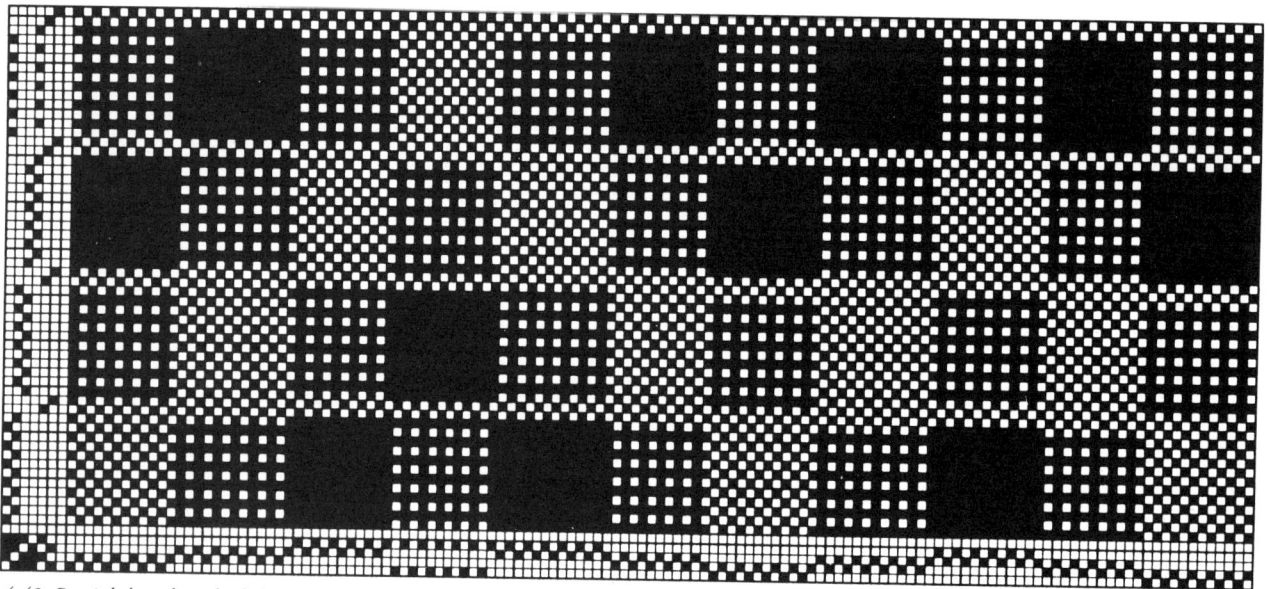

4.43. Partial threading draft for profile in fig. 4.42.

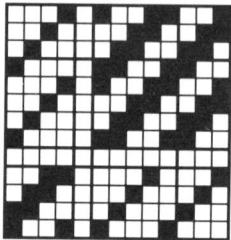

4.44. Four-shaft straight twill, two repeats.

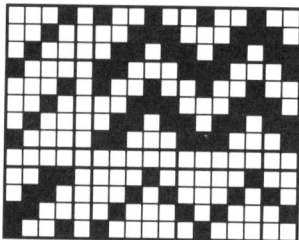

4.45. Twill with reversed threading, two repeats.

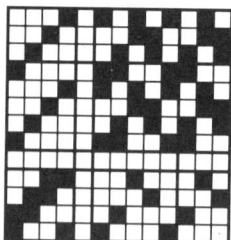

4.46. Twill with interruption in threading, two repeats.

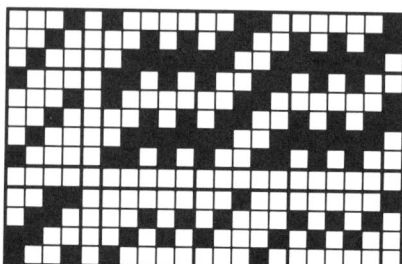

4.47. Twill with repeated section in threading, two repeats.

Uses. Honeycomb weave was unknown in Latvia until the early twentieth century, when it came into use in Vidzeme, through the Estonian weaving courses. Highly decorative, it became stylish for day-blankets, the covers that protected wool blankets from dust. Honeycomb day-blankets were usually woven of all cotton or of cotton combined with another fiber. As part of home decor, day-blankets were in subdued colors and frequently were of all bleached yarns or bleached warp yarn along with pale wefts. Absorbent towels in honeycomb construction also were woven in the early twentieth century. Cottage industry weavers in Vidzeme used both cotton and linen for these items.

The old pattern books recommend this weave in fine yarns, for example, 20/2 or 24/2 bleached cotton warp sleyed double in a 100 dent/10 cm (25/inch) reed. The fine weft is suggested to be a light-colored mercerized cotton of similar weight, and the coarse weft is four ends of the warp thread used together.

Derivations Based on Twills

Derived Twills

When the diagonal float line of a basic, straight twill is varied, the result is called a *derived twill* in Latvian texts. These twills can give attractive, intricate designs from drafts that are easy to record, thread, and treadle. Weaving may be done with one shuttle or with a variety of wefts. Derived twills are extremely versatile, useful, and attractive. By the twentieth century they were prevalent nation-wide in Latvian handweaving.

The pervasive nature of twills in handweaving makes them "everyone's child" with an accordingly excessive number of names. "Herringbone" to one weaver may be a "reverse twill" to another. This naming problem also occurred among Latvian weaving books and makes naming the following twills a lengthy exercise of little use. Therefore, descriptive terms and only a few colloquial names are used.

The following derived twill examples contain only one set of elements in each direction and display observable diagonals in warps and wefts. Their common starting point is the straight twill, previously discussed as a basic weave structure, fig. 4.44 and previous fig. 3.11.

Twill derivations are made by affecting length or placement of floats. This is done through varying one or more of the draft's three components: 1) the threading order, 2) the treadling order, 3) the tie-up. Any changes will affect both warp and weft floats of the fabric.

Some usual changes in any of these three draft components are *reversal* (fig. 4.45), *interruption* (fig.

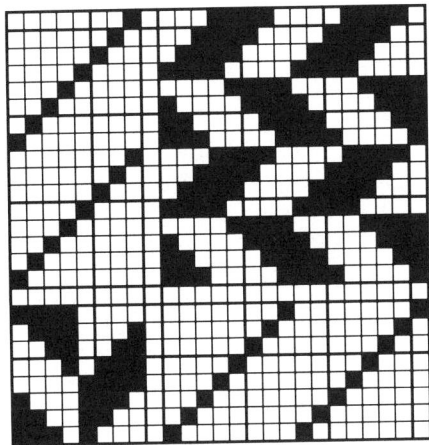

4.48. 4/4 twill draft for Plate 19, two repeats.

4.46), and/or *repetition* (fig. 4.47). Reversed sequences often are called *pointed*, and interrupted sequences may be called *broken*.

Uses. For years in Latvia sheets were woven of four shaft interrupted (broken) twill. Poor people often sewed two narrow widths together while richer people could buy sheets made on wider looms. Expensive sheets might have a design of several blocks of broken twill, each block requiring four shafts.

Until the mid-nineteenth century much patterned clothing material was straight twill and its derivatives. A single warp threaded to twill might provide, for example, skirt, shawl, and bedblanket cloth.

Thin blankets, meant to keep mosquitoes off horses, were woven of unbleached line or tow linen in four-shaft twills. Colored stripes or checks often patterned these horse blankets.

From the late nineteenth century onward, four- to eight-shaft twills were used in Vidzeme for soft "bed shawls." These had wool in various color combinations, the most common being two-colored checker-board designs. The eight-shaft blankets required more skill and complex equipment than had been previously available. Plate 19 shows an 8-shaft blanket using the straight twill threading and treadling order shown in fig. 4.48. The tie-up varies from the usual straight diagonal, giving a 4/4 derived twill in zig-zags.

Also in the late nineteenth century some towels and sacks were woven in reversed or "herringbone"

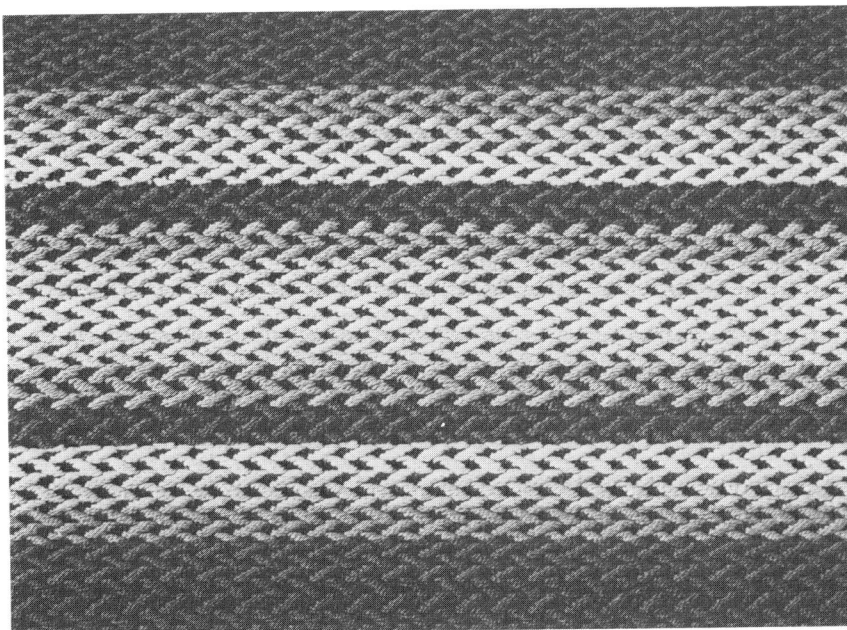

4.49. This treasured blanket was woven by Mrs. Emma Malta as a wedding gift to her niece. The black wool warp is a good foil to the multiply-colored wool weft stripes, among which brown predominates. Horizontal stripes shade through to yellow or green, separated by white. 1935; Vidzeme, County Madona, Township Saikava; 180 cm (71") L X 175 cm (69") W; warp, wool, Z-twist, 2-ply, S-ply, black; weft same as warp, multiple colors; 14 e/cm (35.5 epi); 16 p/cm (41 ppi). ROM972.25. Gift of Mrs. Olga Milmanis. See Plate 8.

twill, fig. 4.45. Coffin towels or grave towels which developed at this time were used to lower a coffin into the grave and were kept as family heirlooms. These narrow linen bands were woven in fine, dense reversed twill. Hand towels frequently were made in reversed twill. While sacks for carrying heavy, large items like potatoes were made in plain weave, those for cereals and flour were of four-shaft herringbone twill. Line linen warp and tow linen weft made a dense twill cloth of up to 16 by 12 threads/square cm (40 by 30/square inch). Bags which went to mills had colored threads woven in for identification.

An example of a derived twill blanket, woven in 1935, is pictured in Plate 8 and fig. 4.49. Figure 4.50 shows the 16-shaft drafting data. The compact nature of the weave avoids long floats in spite of the large-scale look of the latticework design. The combination of soft wool and twill construction produce a silky, supple fabric.

Latvians made extensive use of *point twills* with graduated float lengths for tonal blends within a design. When woven, the results

were far more interesting than a stark pattern made by hard-edge lines. This type of point twill effect, found in blankets of the late 1800s, was widely popularized about 1930 with the publication of designs by A. Skuja-Antēne, author of several weaving texts and pattern collections. Plate 20 shows a typical wool blanket woven with a light ocher wool warp and a dark ocher wool weft. The complex visual effect, shown close-up in fig. 4.51, appears to come from more shafts than the eight that are

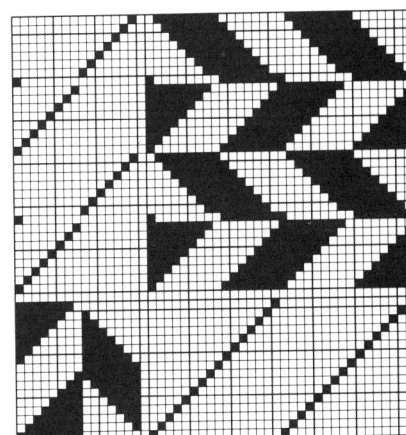

4.50. Two repeats of draft for blanket in fig. 4.49.

53

4.52. (above) Draft for blanket in fig 4.51. Border consists of the eight threads on the left repeated 27 times. The 14 right-hand threads are repeated 10 times, to fill out one repeat of the pattern. Woven to square.

4.51 (left) A professional weaver used a wide loom to produce this derived twill blanket without a center seam (detail shown). Ca. 1938; Zemgale, County Bauska, Township Vecumnieki; 177 cm (70") L X 142 cm (56") W; warp and weft, wool, 2-ply, S-ply, dark ocher warp, light ocher weft; 12 e/cm (30.5 epi); 12 p/cm (30.5ppi). ROM971.117.3. Gift of Mrs. Rita Mikelsteins. See Plate 20.

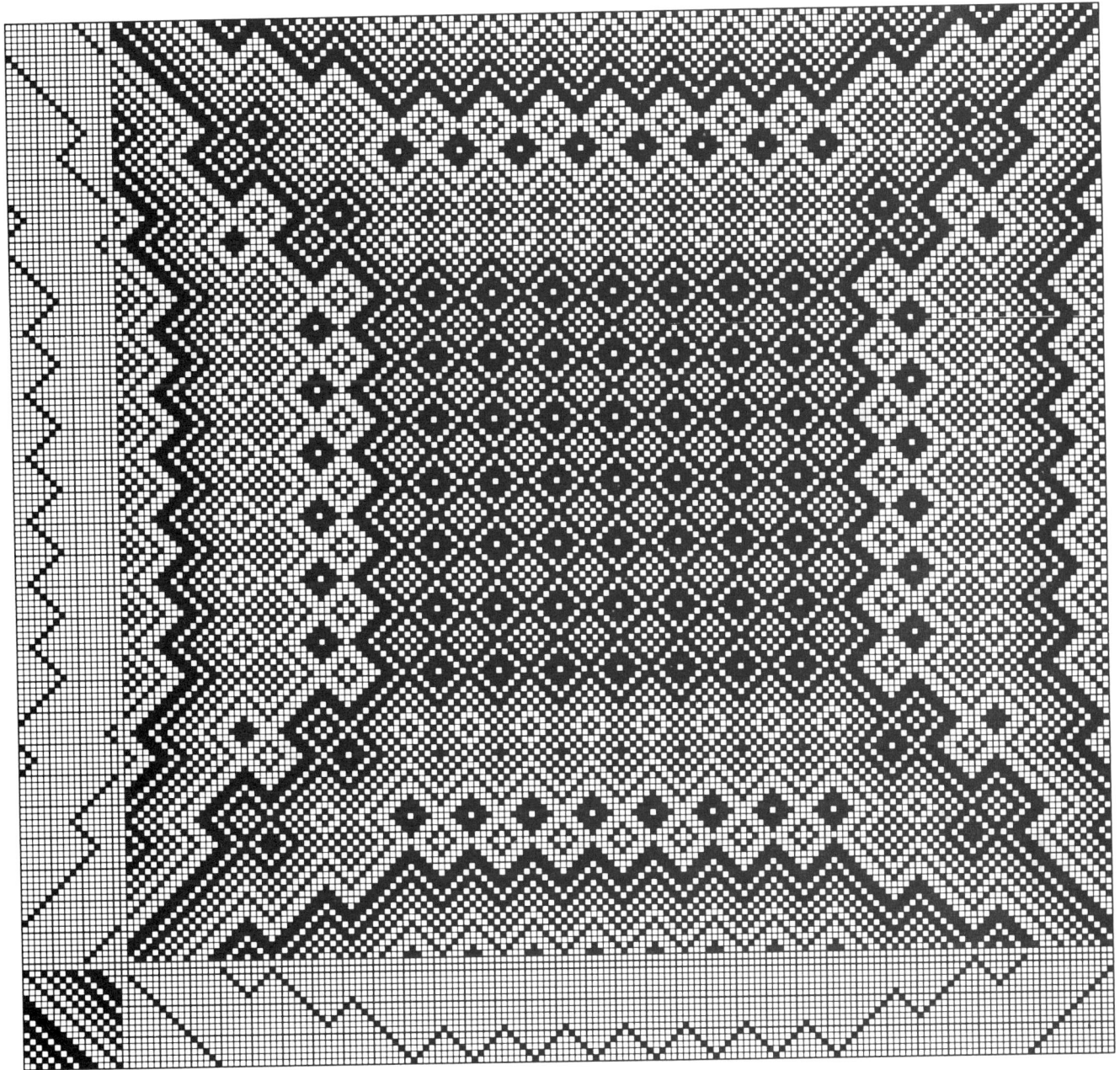

actually required. Its draft, fig. 4.52, shows that both the threading and treadling are interrupted and reversed. The tie-up is for a straight 1/1/3/3 twill.

The attractive tablecloth shown in Plate 10 and fig. 4.53 needed sixteen shafts to achieve the effect of tonal gradation in its pattern. Figure 4.54 gives drafting details of the reversing, diamond-like twill. The stiff, natural linen warp used in this cloth has some slight colour variations that give an effect of bands running down its length, which are contrasted with the bleached white of its fine cotton weft.

4.54. (above) Draft for tablecloth in fig. 4.53. Threading starts on shaft 15.

4.53 (right) Anna Bojazs (later Sizmais) wove this tablecloth for her hope chest about 1935 in Latgale province. She was a farm woman descended from generations of mothers who had taught their daughters how to weave. The slight banding effect is from variations in the linen's color. 188cm (74") L X 157 cm (62") W; warp, cotton, 2-ply, S-ply, natural, used doubled; weft, linen, singles, Z-twist, natural, 24 (12 working) e/cm (31 working epi); 14 p/cm (36 ppi). ROM976.272.3. Gift of Mr. Peter Alexandrovitch.

4.56. (above) One-half repeat of threading and treadling, to reversing points of pattern in fig. 4.55.

4.55. (left) This 32-shaft twill tablecloth was given by a local woman to a midwife in Livani, Kurzeme, in honor of the birth of her baby around 1940. In the turmoil of World War II, the midwife, Monika Alexandrovitch, died in prison. Her brother kept the cloth in good condition and brought it to North America. The piece has no center seam. 201 cm (79") L X 150 cm (59") W; warp, cotton, 2-ply, S-ply; weft, linen, Z-twist, singles; 24 double (12 working) e/cm (31 working epi); 12 p/cm (31 ppi). ROM990.20.1. Gift of Mr. Peter Alexandrovitch. See Plate 11.

Complicated design subtleties characterize the strikingly beautiful tablecloth shown in Plate 11 and figs. 4.55 and 4.56. This is a 32-shaft twill tablecloth that adeptly utilizes the contrasts of natural cotton warp with unbleached linen weft, producing delicate, subtly shaded patterning. Figure 4.56 gives the draft, which shows only one quadrant's pattern, due to the large scale of this threading. The warp is threaded from threads #1 to #206. This is followed by the reverse threading, # 205 to #2.

In weaving, weft picks #1 to #209 are treadled, then the treadling is reversed for picks #208 to #2, to produce one entire repeat of the pattern.

Complex twill designs. In the twentieth century, looms with more than four shafts were available for home use throughout Latvia. Correspondingly, the demand for attractive, easily managed designs increased. Frequently these were derived twill patterns on reversed (pointed) threading and treadling, which were simple to thread and treadle. Similar complex twill patterns had been known in Zemgale and Kurzeme for some time. Figures 4.57 and 4.58 are drafts from two nineteenth century shawls woven in Zemgale. Figure 4.57 is a ten-shaft point twill design in 2/2/1/3/2 interlacing, with treadling following the threading order exactly. Figure 4.58 is typical of a large body of 16-shaft twill designs threaded, and often treadled, in a simple point repeat. These drafts made fancy patterns of large or small scale through altered tie-ups. This draft reveals both how desirable efficiency was and how commonplace 16-shaft looms were. The same design could be woven on 13 shafts and 13 treadles but that threading and treadling would not be the regular, pointed progression available on the 16-shaft arrangement. Clearly, designs were made to fit the standard equipment and to weave up efficiently.

Uses. Wool bed blankets in complex twills became fashionable by the twentieth century. *Paraugi audumiem* gives instructions for a typical 12-shaft twill blanket, fig. 4.59. A reed of 40-50 dents/10 cm (10-12/inch) is sleyed two warps per dent. Directions recommend a white wool warp with mostly grey weft. Blue weft stripes are woven at each end. The border is threaded with section *A* three times and section *B* six times. The center of the blanket repeats only section *A*. It was a typical practice to use one color for warp and another for weft in blankets at the time, rather than using only one color for both.

4.57. One and one-half repeats of derived 10-shaft twill draft. #274 in Ltm.

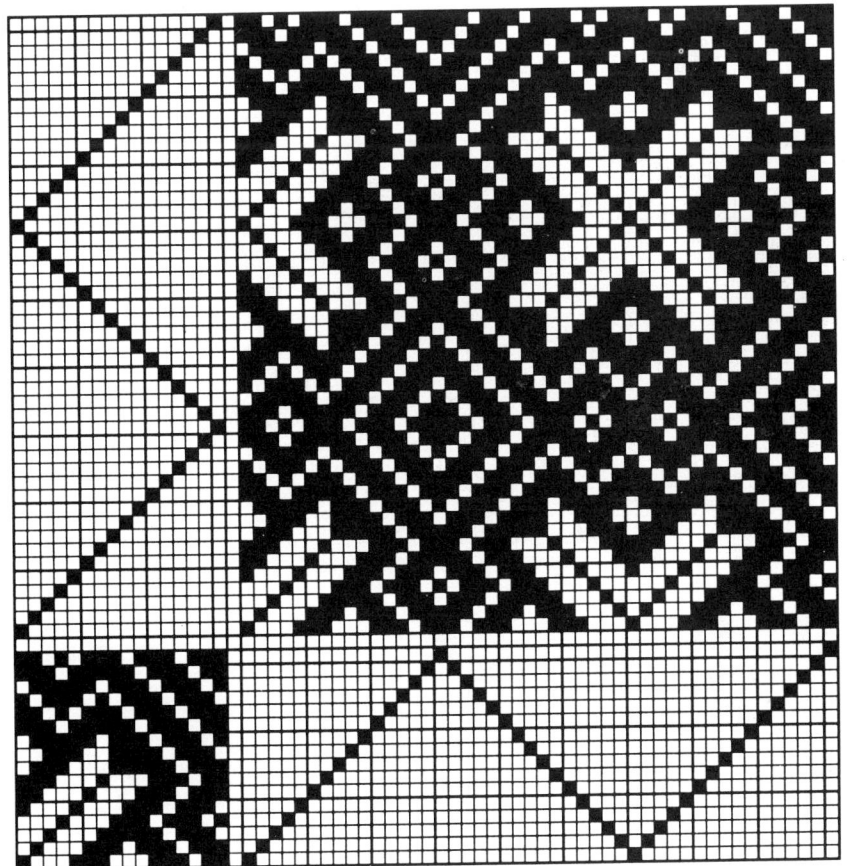

4.58. One and one-half repeats of derived twill draft from old shawl. #275 in Ltm.

57

4.59. One and one-half repeats of 12-shaft twill, #67 in Pa.

4.60. One and one-half repeats of pointed twill draft, #68 in Pa.

Another wool bed blanket pattern from *Paraugi audumiem*, for a fancy 16-shaft derived twill, is shown in fig. 4.60. A 40-50 dent/10cm (10-12/inch) reed is sleyed double. Suggested colors are grey warp with dark brown weft. Light red weft stripes the ends. The border is threaded with two repeats of section *A,* six repeats of section *B,* followed by a center of *A,* repeated for the desired width. This pattern is identical with #618 in Pēters Viļumsons' book, *Ceturtdienas rīts* (*Thursday Morning*). His books, featuring traditional motifs, were both popular and accessible throughout Latvia in the early twentieth century.

Pēters Viļumsons did a great deal to gather and spread such information through his classes and books. Figures 1.6, 1.7, 1.8, 1.17, 4.61, 4.62, 4.79, 7.13, 10.13 and 13.13 are reproductions of pages from his books. Many of the examples are of 16-shaft, pointed twill threadings. The tie-ups are found by rotating the design 90 degrees and tying the treadles to match the shaded squares. In most cases, only one half of the design need be tied

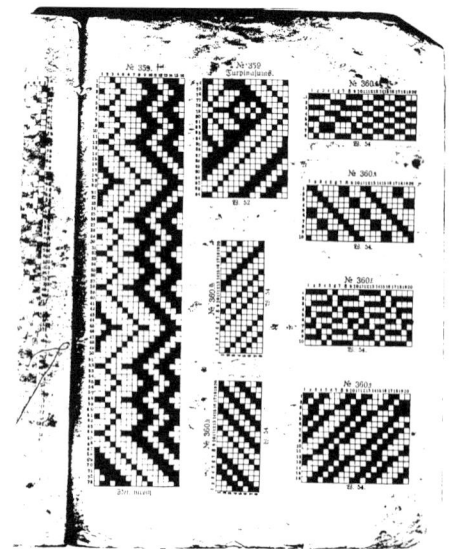

4.61. *Page of twill weaves from Viļumsons' third book.*

up to treadles because the second half is a reverse treadling of the first half. Many of the motifs used in these examples are typical Latvian geometric design symbols, representing variations on the sun, morning star, or other traditional figures, as in fig. 1.3.

One possible result of Pēters Viļumsons' pervasive influence is the blanket shown in fig. 4.63, which may have derived from his teaching. The blanket now resides in the Royal Ontario Museum's collection. The draft shown in fig. 4.64 is draft #603 in Viļumsons' book, *Ceturdienas rīts (Thursday Morning)*. Lavender wool is used for both warp and weft, except for two bands at either end, where a very dark blue weft shows off the twill pattern. The major portion of the blanket appears as an interesting texture, due to a single color used in an intricate structure. The lavender color has faded to grey on the surfaces, but can still be found in crevices between threads. The blanket drapes very well, with a silky touch. It is in good condition despite much use.

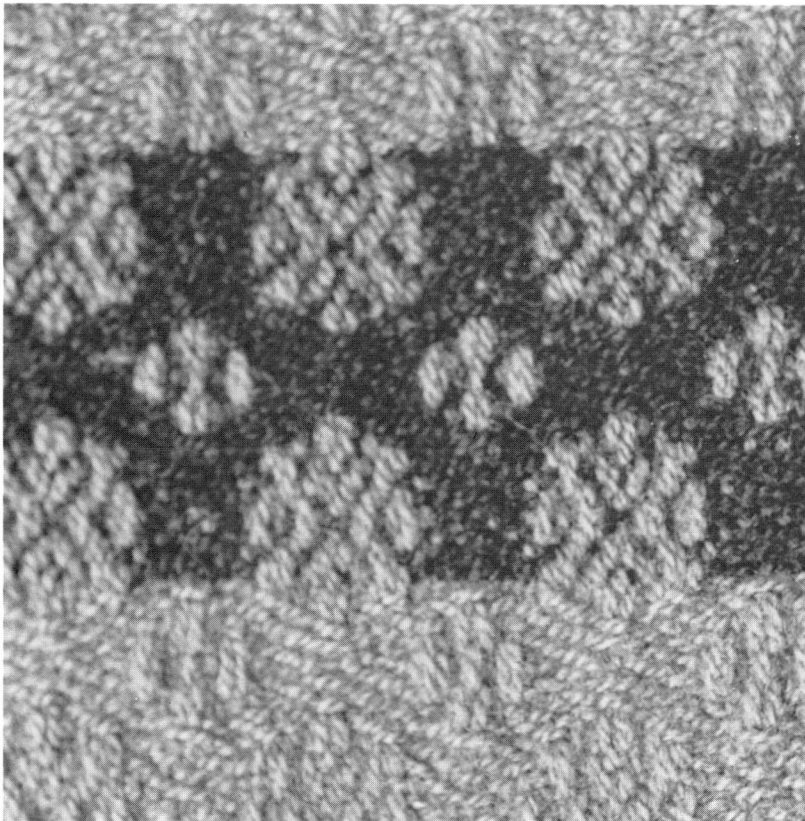

4.63. Detail, band in blanket woven about 1900 in Zemgale, at a time and in an area where Viļumsons taught. It was given to an 18-year old woman by her mother in the mid-1930s, and eventually it was brought to Canada. 175 cm (69") L X 145 cm (57") W; warp and weft, wool, 2-ply, S-ply,; 10 e/cm (25.5 epi); 10 p/cm (25.5 ppi). ROM971.321.2. Gift of Mr. and Mrs. Janis Ozolins.

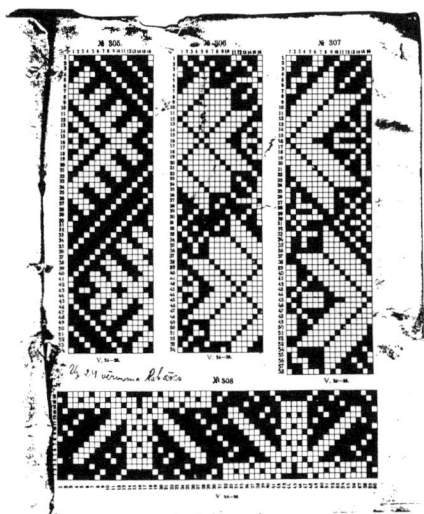

4.62. A page of fancy twills from Viļumsons' second book.

4.64. One and one-half repeats of draft from blanket in fig. 4.63.

4.66. (above) Design draft for 52-shaft pointed twill star pattern.

4.65. (left) Detail of a tablecloth in an extraordinary 52-shaft twill, part of a set of clothand napkins woven by Ansis Cirulis in the 1930s. Presumably a professional weaver's mechanical loom was used. 170cm (67") L X 167 cm (66") W, both plus fringes; warp, cotton, 2-ply, S-ply, natural; weft, linen, Z-twist, singles, used double, natural; 18 doubled (9 working) e/cm (23 working epi); 8 p/cm (20 ppi). ROM971.308a-c. Gift of Mrs. Dagny Wakfer-Vidiņš, in memory of her father, Lt.-Col. Kārlis Vidiņš.

The twill tablecloth pictured in fig. 4.65 uses 52 shafts to achieve a complex geometric design wherein one traditional morning star motif is framed by a second star. An identical design, from a late nineteenth-century wool blanket from Limbăzi, Vidzeme province, is shown in Latviešu tautas māksla, vol. 3. Figure 4.66 is the draw-down for the geometric morning star motif as woven on a pointed, 52-shaft twill draft, threaded shafts 1 to 52, then reversed from shaft 51 to shaft 2.

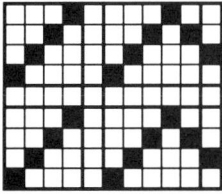

4.67 Typical twill draft for weft-faced rug, # 168 in Pa.

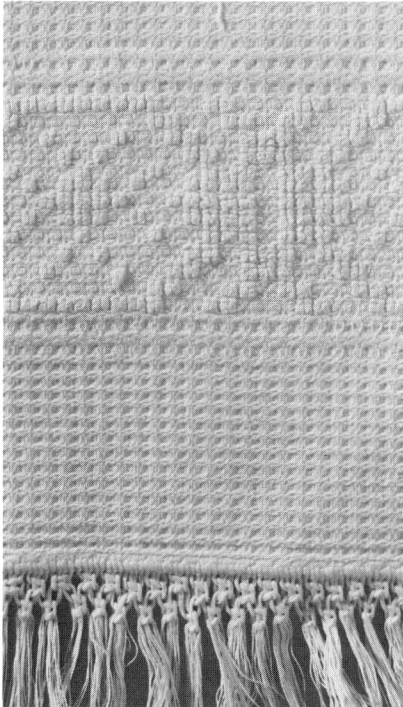

4.68. Four-shaft waffle weave draft, #113 in Ma. Two repeats.

Weft-Faced Twill

In the twentieth century, some weft-faced rugs were woven on derived twill drafts. The warp for these rugs was widely sett so the wefts gave full coverage. A standard twill threading, tie-up, and treadling order was used. Figure 4.67 is the draft for one such rug from *Paraugi audumiems*. The 8/3 tow linen warp is sett at 2.5 to 3 ends/cm (6 to 8 epi). Multiple colors of wool wefts were used in rotation to produce various diamond patterns on straight and reversed treadling of the twill sheds.

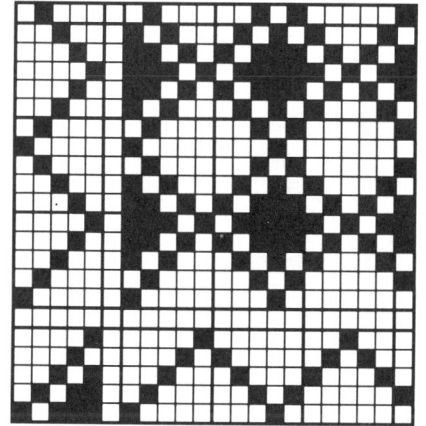

4.69. Five-shaft waffle weave draft, #114 in Ma, two repeats.

Waffle Weave
Šūniņaudumi

One derivation of reversed point twill on four or more shafts produces a surface of square hollows or "waffle" effect. One set of warp threads and one set of weft threads interlace with various lengths of floats.

Figure 4.68 is a basic waffle-weave draft. Figures 4.69, 4.70 and 4.72 are drafts for a number of possible waffle weave variations as presented in Latvian texts.

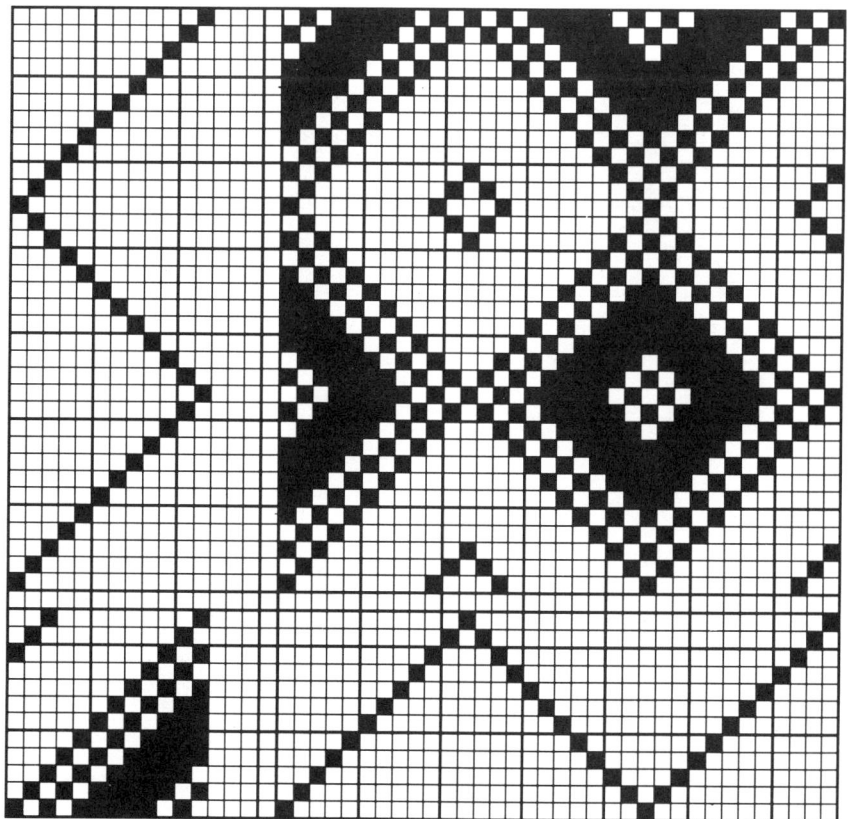

4.71 White linen towel in seven-shaft waffle weave. Added macrame fringes trim both ends of the towel. Pattern bands are formed by tufting with cotton weft, probably mercerized, similar to the yarn used for the fringe. 1935; Vidzeme, County Cesis, Township Lizume; 152 cm (60") (plus fringes) L X 39.5 cm (15.5") W; warp and weft, cotton, 2-ply, S-ply, bleached; 9 e/cm (23 epi); 12p/cm (30 ppi). ROM971.294.1. Gift of Mrs. Lucija Zvaigzne.

4.72. One and one-half repeats of seven-shaft waffle weave draft from towel in fig. 4.71.

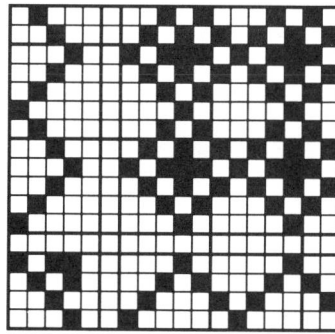

4.70. Twelve-shaft waffle weave draft, #117 in Ma, one and one-half repeats.

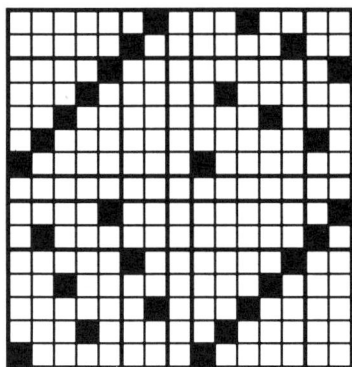

4.73. Basic seven-shaft satin interlacement, weft-faced.

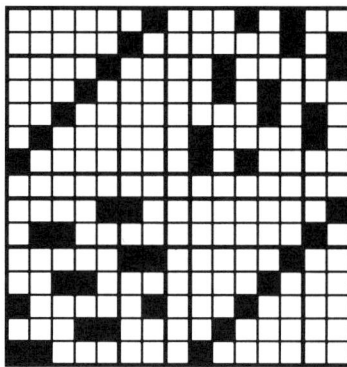

4.74. Reinforced satin draft, derived from fig 4.73. #70 in Ma.

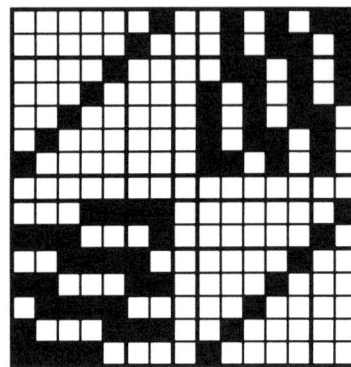

4.75. Diagonal repp based on fig. 4.73, #73 in Ma.

Uses. By the early twentieth century waffle weave was used for linen and cotton towels which absorbed moisture better than ones made of smoother weaves. Figure 4.71 is a white linen towel in seven-shaft waffle weave. Figure 4.72 gives the towel's draft. The pattern band of three extended crosses in hexagonal frames is formed by *tufting* (see *Chapter Eleven*).

The addition of a tufted band to a waffle-weave fabric was fairly common, perhaps because the waffle threading repeat makes the tufting easy to count and place. A five-shaft waffle-weave towel in *Paraugi audumiem* has a tufted border pattern. The draft is the same as fig. 4.69 Bleached 16/2 cotton is recommended for weft and warp, the latter sleyed double in an 80 dent/cm (20/inch) reed.

Besides being popular for towels, waffle weave also was used for wool bed covers in the twentieth century.

Derivations Based on Satin Weave

Reinforced Satin Weave
Pastiprinātie atlasa sējums

A weave that the Latvian books call *reinforced satin* can be derived from simple satin. In this new structure the long floats which characterize satin weave are held down by more than one binding thread. The added binding points are usually placed next to one or both sides of the

original satin binders, so the sheen and interlacement of the satin structure are retained. *Double-stitched satin* in English-language books is a related concept. (Tidball, 1962; Oelsner, 1952; Grosicki, 1975.)

Figure 4.73 shows a basic seven-shaft, weft-faced satin draft. In fig. 4.74, each binding point in the satin of the previous figure is extended warp-wise with one more binding point next to the original position, producing reinforced satin.

Uses. Reinforced satin was used in Latvia in the twentieth century for men's suiting or cotton fabrics. This weave required very fine yarns and multiple shafts, so it was not likely to be chosen often by handweavers.

Diagonal Repp
Diagonālripss

Diagonal repps were so named by the Latvians because diagonal ribs form on the weft-faced or warp-faced surface of the fabric. These differ from *diagonal ribs* in English-language texts in that Latvian ones are non-patterned fabrics, woven with one color showing on either surface.

Latvian diagonal repp is based on satins drafted on odd numbers of shafts (e.g., 5, 7, 9). Binding points are uniformly added on one side of the original binders. Total binding points usually are increased to equal one more than one-half the number of shafts. For example, fig. 4.73 is modified in fig. 4.75 into a diagonal repp in the warp direction.

Uses. Diagonal repps were of limited use by twentieth-century Latvian weavers for garment fabric.

4.76. Two repeats of a crepe draft, #119 in Ma.

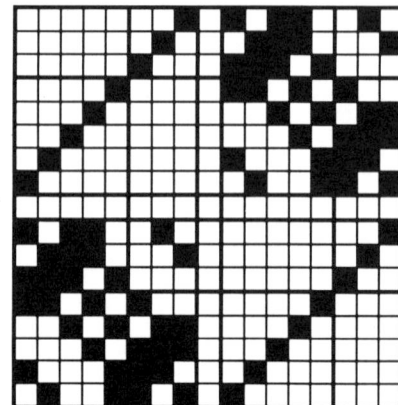

4.77. An eight-shaft crepe, #28b in Pa.

Derivations Based on Various Weaves

Crepe Weave
Krepa sējumi

Crepe fabric has an uneven, rough surface without a readily discernable pattern. It catches light so as to look grainy. It may be stretchy or firm, due to different constructions. While these effects could come from textured warps or wefts, or from mixing yarn twists in a cloth, true crepe weave results from an interlacement of warps and wefts. It may be a structure derived from either basic or derived weaves.

Figure 4.76 gives one idea of a crepe design. It is based on a straight four-shaft twill threading and treadling with a tie-up that uses two twill and two plain-weave sheds.

There are many other ways to form crepes through altering the threadings, treadlings, or tie-ups, or through combining structures. Figure 4.77 is an eight-shaft crepe which combines twill and plain-weave areas in four quadrants. This pattern was suggested in the twentieth century book *Paraugi audumiem* for dress fabric woven in very fine threads at nine ends per cm (36 epi). Both warp and weft are woven in a series of 12 threads of one color and then four of a second color.

Designing crepe on more than four shafts can become somewhat complicated for a home weaver, so in practice crepe weaving was probably done by rote from a limited number of drafts and seldom from designs originated by the weavers themselves. Crepe was not a common weave in Latvia until the twentieth century when it became known through classes and books.

Uses. Clothing fabric was a major use for crepes. *Paraugi audumiem* gave directions for several crepe clothing fabrics in wool patterned with stripes or simple plaids.

Blankets of crepe textured weaves were popular in Riga in the first half of the twentieth century. By their nature crepes were woven for functional fabrics emphasizing tex-

ture rather than pattern. Apparently in actual use there were limited variations woven in Latvia, although the lengthy and sometimes complicated theory behind crepe construction was discussed in the Latvian texts.*

Color-and-Weave Effects
Krāsu maiņas raksti audumā

Certain types of visual patterns in fabrics depend on the relationship of thread interlacement and placement of color in the warp and weft. Weave structure and colors interact to produce a visually cohesive piece. In Latvia these designs are called *color-shift patterns,* in English, *color-and-weave effects.*

Color-shift weaves are based on simple or derived weaves. Only one structure is present, developed with carefully placed color sequences in both warp and weft directions. The patterns often are called plaited or wickerwork designs in Latvian books. Many different designs may be possible on one warp, requiring precise planning and attentive weaving.

*Further crepe theory is in Oelsner, 1952; Cyrus, 1956; Grosicki, 1975.

The drawdown for a color-shift weave can be shown either as the structural interlacement or as the visual pattern. (Kurtz, 1981.)

In plain weave, the simplest color-shift effect is the alternation of dark and light warp and weft colors. This produces stripes either vertically or horizontally over the fabric, shown in fig. 4.78 which has color sequences noted along the sides of the drawdown. If these two effects are combined, the results are various checkerboard patterns of stripes.

Uses. Color-shift weaving was used in Latvia for some clothing fabrics and blankets but does not appear to have been very prevalent before the twentieth century. Patterns in this method are harder to record, prepare, and weave than weaves such as twill with one warp color and one weft color. Given the farmhome weavers' need for maximum productivity during brief time periods, a color-shift warp on the loom would have restricted applications. As most warps were of natural, hand-dyed, or commercially-dyed linen or cotton, a color-shift warp would have involved extra time, work, and perhaps cost.

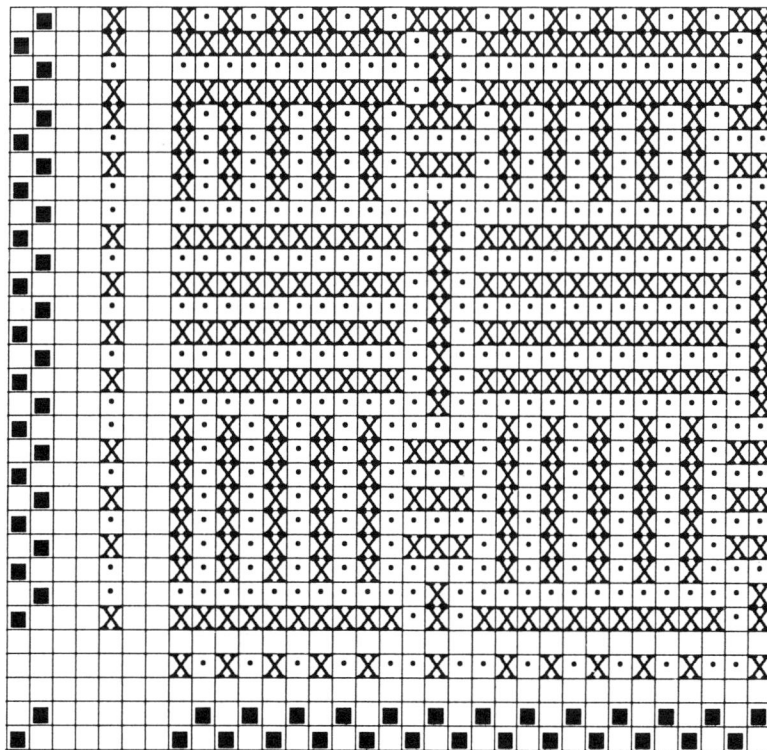

4.78. *Color-and-weave draft with warp and weft color sequences indicated along edges of drawdown.*

№ 602.   № 603.   № 604.   № 605.   № 606.   № 607.   № 608.

№ 609.   № 610.   № 611.   № 612.   № 613.   № 614.   № 615.

№ 616.   № 617.   № 618.   № 619.   № 620.   № 621.   № 622.

№ 623.   № 624.   № 625.   № 626.   № 627.   № 628.   № 629.

№ 630.   № 631.   № 632.   № 633.   № 634.   № 635.   № 636.

4.79. One page of "peg plans" for 16 shafts which are one-half the width of the total draw-downs, from P. Viļumsons' book, Thursday Morning.

Combined Simple Weaves

Two or more weave structures can be united to weave as concurrent independent areas within one fabric. In Latvia, as in some other Baltic and Scandinavian countries, such a synthesis is termed a *combined weave*, or *sakopotie sējumi*. In contrast to a *derived weave,* which derives from and varies one of the basic weaves, a combined weave preserves wholly distinct parts of its component weaves.

Combined weaves can join two basic weaves, two versions of the same basic weave, a basic and a derived weave, or two derived weaves. The combinations usually appear as horizontal stripes, vertical stripes, or rectangles composed of two weaves. Occasionally the visual result of combined weaves displays one weave filling in all around a second weave.

Combined Weaves of Two Dissimilar Structures

Stripes are a common way to combine two basic weaves. Figure 5.1 shows a twill and plain weave horizontal stripe combination. The maximum number of shafts necessary to weave a horizontal combination is equal to the minimum number required by the more complex of the weaves – four shafts in this example. Each stripe requires its own set of treadles; in this case four for twill plus two for plain weave equal a total of six treadles.

Vertical stripes combining plain weave and twill, as in fig. 5.2, require six shafts and four treadles. To allow independent vertical stripes of each weave, the total number of shafts equals the sum of the mini-mum number of shafts of both weaves. Fewer treadles are needed for vertical than for horizontal stripes, because the weaves are combined on each treadle's tie-up.

Rectangles of combined weaves require the most shafts and treadles because each rectangle must be

capable of weaving each structure. Rectangles of plain weave and four-shaft straight twill require eight shafts to produce, as in fig.5.3. At the edges of some combinations where two rectangles meet, there may be combined floats in the warp or weft, and the resultant structures will look slightly distorted from the original rectangles.

The farmhome weavers were limited in methods and structures of combined weaves because few shafts and treadles were available on their looms. Four shafts and two treadles could readily combine balanced plain weave *(A)* with warp-faced plain-weave "repp" *(B)* in vertical stripes. That combination is shown in the draft at fig. 5.4, from an old, ecru linen towel woven in Zemgale. The "repp" weave stripes have a sett twice as dense as in the plain-weave stripes. This towel was made for the hope chest of the weaver's daughter about 1835-1840, and was kept in the family until the weaver's great-granddaughter, Mrs. L. Roze, do-nated it to the Royal Ontario Museum in 1972.

Other configurations. These include *pusdrellis,* which literally means *half-block.* This four-shaft weave com-bines two dissimilar weave structures for block patterning and is called *M's and O's* in English. Areas of repp weave are combined with areas of

5.2. *Combined vertical stripes, #102 in Ap.*

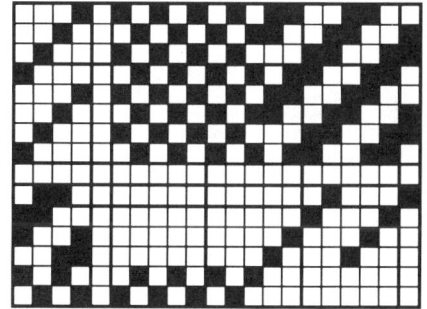

5.3. *Combined squares of two types of interlacements, plain weave and twill.*

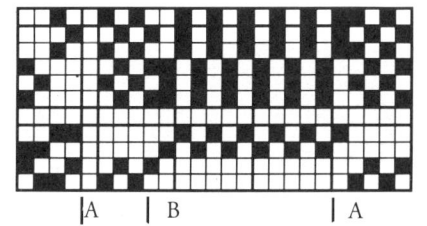

5.4. *Combined weave draft from singles linen towel, ROM 972.480.3.*

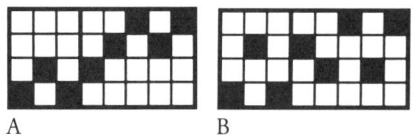

A   B

5.5. (above) A. One eight-thread unit for "half-blocks," to be repeated or followed by B, a second eight-thread unit. #245 in Ma.

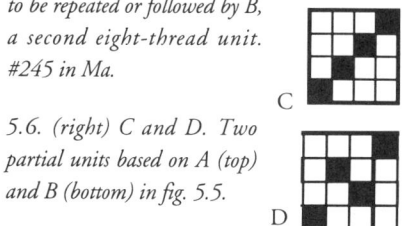

C

D

5.6. (right) C and D. Two partial units based on A (top) and B (bottom) in fig. 5.5.

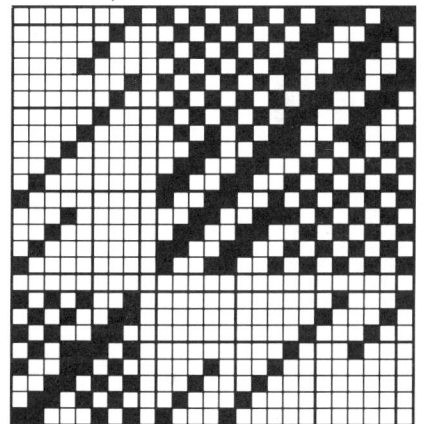

5.1. *Combined horizontal stripes, #101 in AP.*

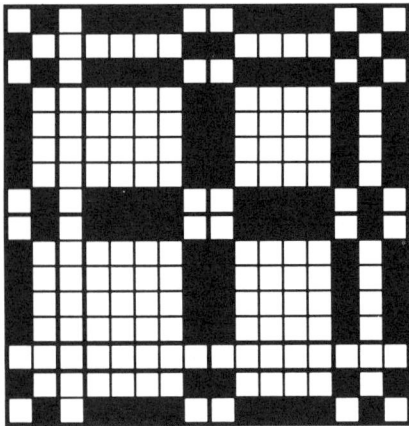

5.7. *Two-block profile draft, #244 in Ma.*

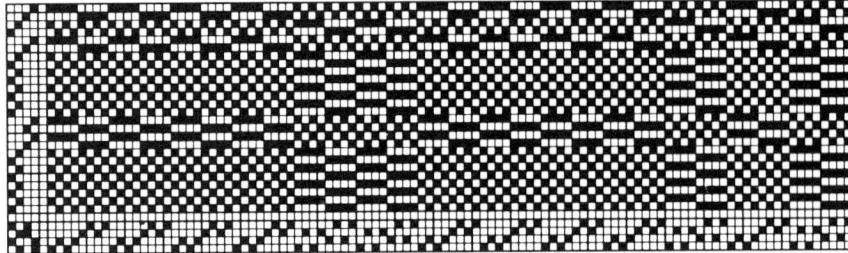

5.8. *"Half-block" interlacement of fig. 5.7, #245 in Ma.*

plain weave. The repp areas are weft-faced on both sides of the cloth. Each of the two areas is based on units which usually consist of eight threads, as shown at *A* and *B* in fig. 5.5. Partial units, shown in *C* and *D* (fig. 5.6), also can be used, but are less effective than the wider units when woven. Figure 5.7 is a profile design for this weave in two blocks, and fig. 5.8 shows the actual *half-block* threading for the design.

5.9. *Two derived twills were combined into this beautiful, 16-shaft tablecloths, woven in one width. This combination of discrete areas of point twill and of twill blocks was often woven by professional weavers of Kurzeme and Zemgale from the 1700s into the 1900s. Twentieth century; possibly from Zemgale; 146 cm (57") (plus fringes) L X 146 cm (57") W; warp, cotton, 2-ply, S-ply, natural; weft, linen, S-twist, singles, natural; 18 e/cm (46 epi); 15 p/cm (38 ppi). Collection of Ilga Jansons. See Plate 28.*

Generally motifs using smaller repp areas than plain-weave areas give a more stable cloth. In the twentieth century Latvian *half-block weave* was woven in very fine linen or cotton for tablecloths, napkins, towels, and upholstery.

Professional weavers with complex looms were able to make complex combined weaves. Two derived twills were combined into the beautiful, 16-shaft tablecloth pictured in Plate 28 and fig. 5.9. The design can be thought of as having three squares: two of four-shaft, broken, turned twill and one of eight-shaft,

point twill. The threading for the overall design is shown in fig. 5.10. In actuality the cloth's treadling has irregular numbers of picks within motifs, all the while retaining the broken twill ground. The draft shows one single, orderly repeat.

In this example's combination of point twill and twill blocks, the three parts of the design are never combined in the motif. Each part is woven individually at any one time. This is an old, somewhat limiting way of making motifs because it does not fully utilize the design possibilities within a draft. This simple, traditional designing changed with the spread of examples which combined separate components for fancier motifs. In Latvia this increase in complexity may have reflected artistic developments introduced by German masterweavers of linens in the 1700s. (Hilts, 1986.)

CONSIDERATIONS IN
PLANNING COMBINED WEAVES
Two difficulties in weaving combined weaves of separate areas should be considered when planning them. The first is uneven warp take-up between adjoining vertical stripes of different weaves. This occurs if one structure has more interlacements than its neighboring stripe, which weaves more loosely. Putting the two weaves on two warp beams or otherwise tensioning them unequally is the best solution for this problem.

The second difficulty may arise from using two fibers that have different stretch and shrinkage properties. For instance, wool and linen in the same fabric will shrink differently and cause distortion of the original weave. The simplest solution is to use compatible materials.

5.10. One repeat of combined weave in tablecloth in fig. 5.9.

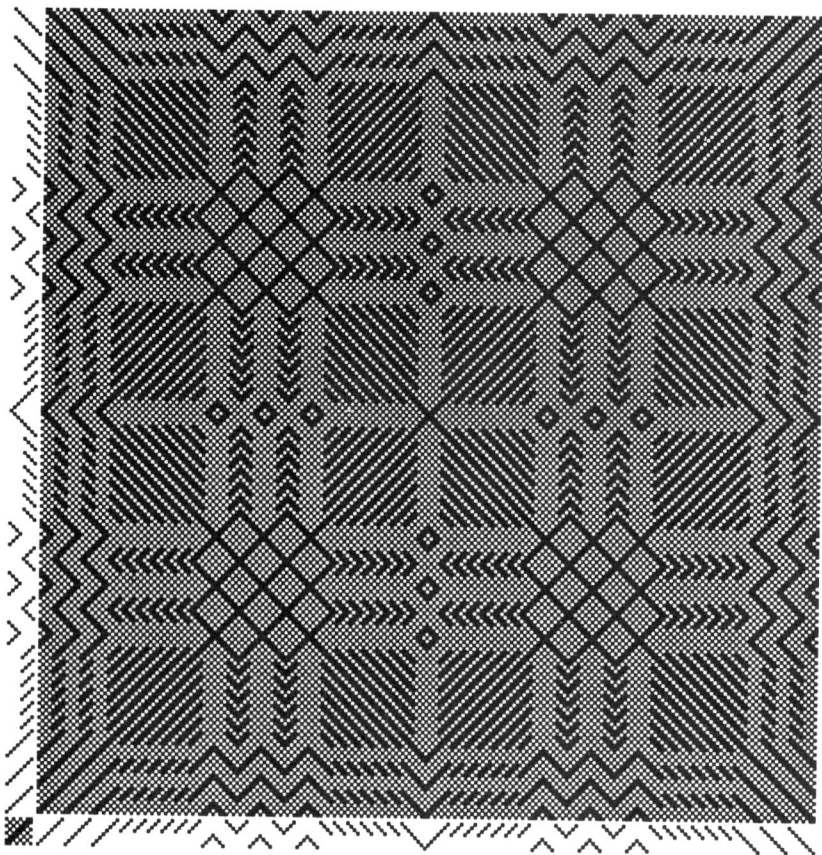

5.11. Draft combining twill and plain weave. Based on #114 in Rga.

5.12. Draft combining twill and plain weave, #44 in Ltm.

Integrated Areas

The draft in fig. 5.11 is an example of integrating two weave structures within a design.* A derived twill is combined with plain-weave to give an attractive eight-shaft weave for linen towels. A second example, from a wool blanket woven about 1920, also combines plain weave and twill in its draft, fig. 5.12. Such combinations give a firmer, stronger cloth than pure twill while offering pattern and texture to plain weave.

Uses. Stripes combining plain weave and four-shaft herringbone twill were woven in the nineteenth century for peasants' sheets. Dress and suit fabric, curtains, towels, upholstery, shawls, blankets, tablecloths – cloth for virtually any purpose might be in a combined draft. Multiple-shaft looms were more common by the twentieth century, making the weaving of complex combined weaves more feasible.

* The draft in Rga did not accurately produce its accompanying picture. The figure shown here is an enlarged design based on the Rga picture.

Combined Weaves of Turned Weave Structures

In some combined weaves two faces (warp-predominant face and weft-predominant face) of the same weave structure are juxtaposed in stripes or rectangles. Combining the two faces of a weave structure on the same surface of the cloth results in a turned weave. In fig. 5.13, both the warp face and the weft face of the same basic weave, five-shaft satin, are combined to form vertical stripes.

At the borders where two turned weave interlacements meet, it is desirable both visually and functionally to make "clean cut" joins. Figure 5.13 shows this type of join, with the edge thread of each square interlacing opposite to the edge thread of its neighboring square. This cleanly demarcates squares by preventing a warp or weft from floating beyond the edge of its square and giving a wavy edge. Previous fig. 5.3 shows an example where the edges of squares do not meet in a clean-cut fashion. Distortion to both structure and visual design is evident.

Some crepe weaves which could be considered combined weaves originate by arranging a clean-cut join between turned weave versions of one, small, textured interlacement. Figure 5.14 is the draft of a simple crepe weave. To enlarge the textured effect, yet avoid obvious pattern, a second interlacement, which is exactly opposite in floats to the first interlacement is added. The two interlacements alternate both vertically and horizontally, as in fig. 5.15. At the edges where each square of interlacement meets the opposite interlacement there is a clean-cut abutment.

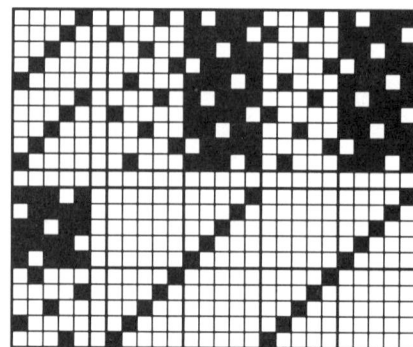

5.13. Two repeats of draft showing stripes of turned satin, from a late nineteenth-century linen towel woven in Zemgale. From ROM969.9.3.

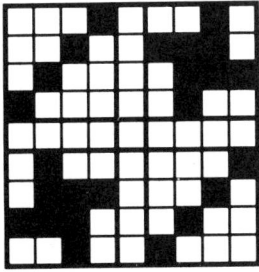

5.14. Draft for a four-shaft crepe interlacement.

5.15. Draft combining fig. 5.14 and its turned face, #126 in Ma.

Turned Weaves Combined for Block Weaves
Dreļļu audumi

A *block* is used in a design to represent each threading unit of a weave structure. In a design a block may be used alone, repeated horizontally or vertically next to itself, or joined with other blocks. The graphic representation of a design in blocks rather than as individual threads is called a *block draft* or a *profile draft* in English.

Block designs present a visual design without regard for the individual threads' interlacement within the cloth. Naturally the woven structure that will fit within the blocks must eventually be considered. Actual weaving is based on a *threading draft* which fills individual threads into each square of the block draft. While many weave structures may fill in a profile draft, the definitive block weaves in Latvia were *turned twill* or *turned satin*. When extremely complex designs were woven in these structures the cloth was no longer called simply a block weave, but was *damask*.

HISTORY AND TERMINOLOGY
The development of block weaves in northern Europe melds Flemish, German, Scandinavian, Dutch, Baltic and other influences. Block weaves have been known and used all around the rim of the Baltic Sea for centuries.

By the 1600s block weaving was so valued in Vidzeme province, which was under Swedish rule, that weavers of block cloths as well as the fabrics were being imported into Sweden. At the same time, Flemish master-weavers hired to supervise southern Latvian textile mills in Kurzeme, influenced the local skills and tastes there. In 1685, many Flemish weavers expert at linen damask weaving, fled religious persecution in their homeland. During the 1700s Flemish influence helped Saxony and eastern Germany become new centers for linen damask weaving. In that same era, Latvia entered another period of war and social upheaval, and its block weavers and their products faded from European prominence for 150 years.

In Vidzeme province in the 1700s and early 1800s, some estate weavers still wove pictorial damask of local scenes such as the manor's lord, a coachman, horses, or even a coach with wheels. (Alsupe, 1982.) These damasks probably were woven in the four-shaft broken-twill block construction familiar to Latvian weavers, rather than five-shaft satin blocks. Most skilled eighteenth century Latvian weavers used turned weaves in simple block designs rather than fancy damask ones. The repertoire of block designs grew in number and complexity over that century, reflecting the influence of Germany where linen weaving in blocks was flourishing.

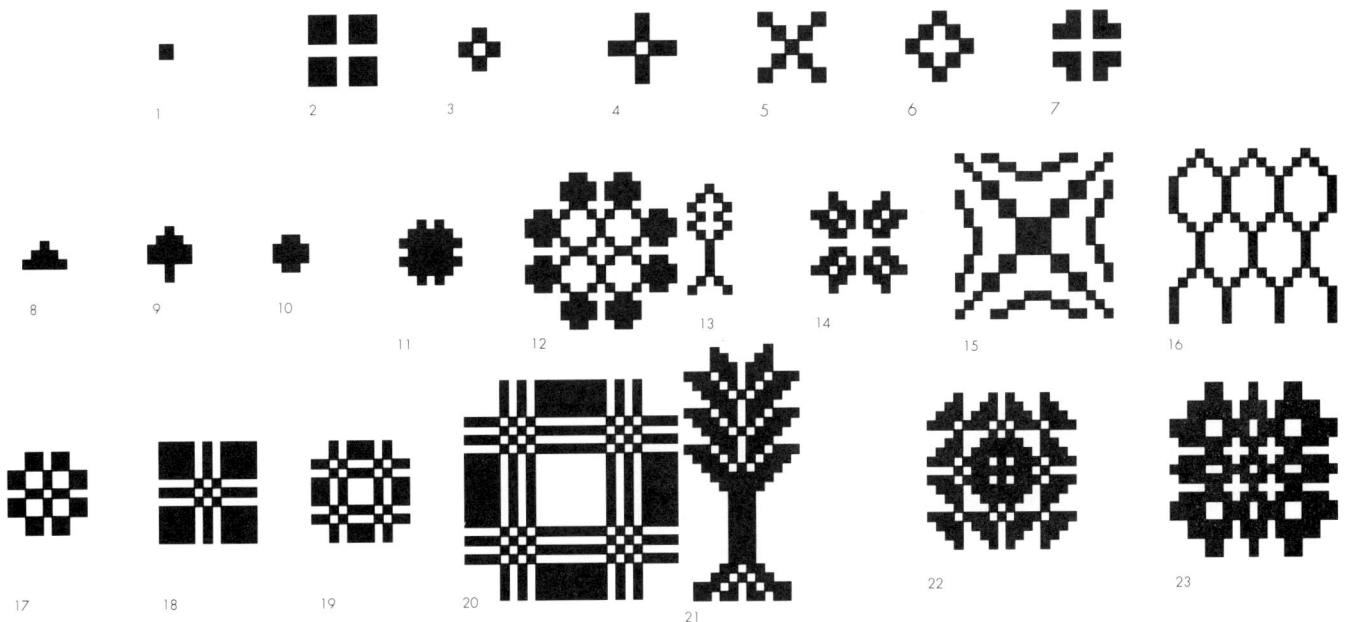

5.16. Popular Latvian block designs were depicted in Audēji Vidzemē. They include cross (4), fir tree (8 & 9), double star(14) rose (17), and Flemish rose (23).

In Germany, block weaves specifically developed in identity and name about 1700 and were quickly refined to a significant level of technical and artistic quality. (Hilts, 1986.) During that same time German weavers who traveled to Latvia to work on estates brought pattern notebooks written during training in Germany. From the 1600s onward, handwritten books of block patterns were copied among professional weavers in Latvia, as was the practice in Europe and Scandinavia. Many of the books shared the same patterns, designed to weave only one block of pattern at any one time, rather than combining blocks for more pattern variations. Under the eighteenth-century German influence, linen block weaving grew as a trade and printed books of patterns were circulated in Latvia.

One of the most adept works written on combined-block designs for linen weavers, Frickinger's *Weber Bild Buch*, entered Latvia from Germany soon after it was printed in 1740. It was used by weavers in both Vidzeme and Kurzeme, who applied four-shaft twill structures rather than satin ones within the blocks. Eventually patterns of seven or eight blocks were included in the professionals' books. In the late 1700s and first half of the 1800s many estate weavers still wove block cloth, but the bulk of it was woven by tradesmen and cottage industry weavers for commercial purposes. Block weaving was the most common patterning method of professional linen weavers. Looms with pulley mechanisms continued to be standard equipment for all these weavers.

As time went by, weavers of Kurzeme and Zemgale used satin construction for the block weaves. Weavers in Vidzeme and Latgale retained the older, twill-based structures for blocks. Barta in southwest Kurzeme was a well-established center for block-patterned linen weaving in the 1800s. In Vidzeme the Piebalga area became especially famous for block-patterned linens from the mid-1800s until World War I, supplying fabric to Latvia and parts of Lithuania, Poland,

Russia, Estonia, and Finland. In Kurzeme large blocks formed designs woven in two contrasting tones of linen for warp and weft. In Vidzeme designs were composed of small blocks and woven in natural linen. The cloth was bleached after weaving to produce a subtle surface design that depended on contrasts of light and shadow. Patterns for towels were different from those for tablecloths in Vidzeme, whereas in Kurzeme and Latgale the same patterns were used for both items.

Some Latvian terms used for block weaves appear to be based in German words and evolved as the German technical information was disseminated. (Alsupe, correspondence, 1987.) *Drell* in Low German, meant cloth used as "ticking," presumably cloth which covered mattresses and pillows. It was frequently a twill weave. Both the cloth's weave and use were implied by the name *Drell*. The Latvian name for a similar twill ticking was *triṇītis*, referring to "three-heddle," the simplest of the twill structures. By the 1700s the word *Drell* was adopted and modified in much of Latvia to specify cloth patterns of blocky, rectangular forms woven in turned-twill or turned-satin structures. *Triṇītis* came to mean any twills, although in general Latvian dictionaries even today it implies "ticking" rather than "twills."

Drellis, the Latvian word for blocks, never was used to describe unit weaves such as are used in float-patterned or tied-float weaves. (See *Chapter Six*.) In those cases the design units are called *parts (daļas)* rather than *blocks*. The term *drellis* had two specific applications. It could be used as a separate name for

turned-twill or turned-satin blocks, or it could be included in the name of several four-shaft weaves forming rectangular designs: *pārstaipu drellis*, overshot weave; *četrnīšu drellis*, crackle weave; *pusdrellis*, half-block or M's and O's weave; and *vagotais drellis*, ribbed block. Those four-shaft structures were the oldest types of interlacements for weaving motifs with large units of design. Versions of them were already used in the 1100s in parts of Latvia by home weavers.

When the word *drellis* was used alone, it did not include those four-shaft weaves. For many years the four-shaft arrangements were known to peasants as "pig" or "servant" blocks. The only "real," or "big" blocks were those woven by professional weavers using eight or more shafts for turned-twill or turned-satin weaves, a structural definition for *drellis* that continued into the mid-twentieth-century weaving texts. (Alsupe, 1982.)

BLOCK WEAVE STRUCTURE
Three-shaft and four-shaft straight twills were the oldest bases for "real" block weaves in Latvia. Satin blocks, preferred for their luster, came into use later when that interlacement was better known and looms were more developed. The twills and satins used for block weaves were arranged as *turned weaves*, juxtaposing the opposite faces of a weave. The most common Latvian turned weaves are shown in the drafts in figs. 5.17, 5.18, 5.19 and 5.20.

It apparently was accepted terminology in Latvia that four-shaft, broken twill formed a "four-shaft satin" interlacement, as in fig. 5.19. However, that name almost invariably

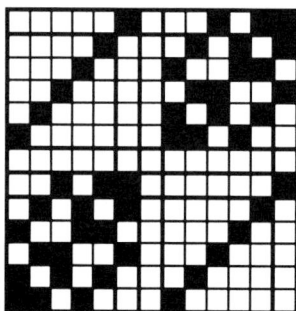

5.17. (left) Two blocks of three-shaft straight twill, turned.

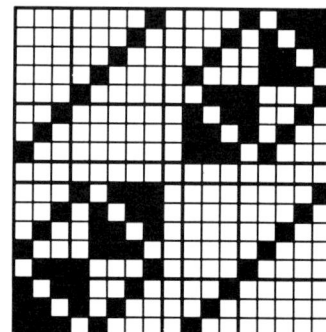

5.18. (right) Two blocks of four-shaft straight twill, turned.

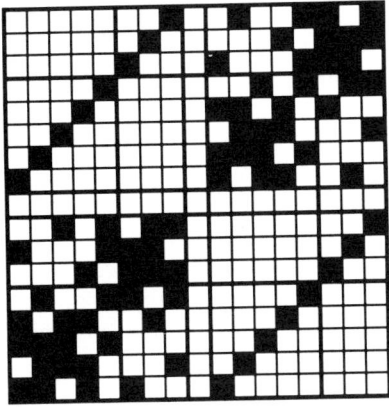

5.19. *Two blocks of four-shaft broken twill, turned.*

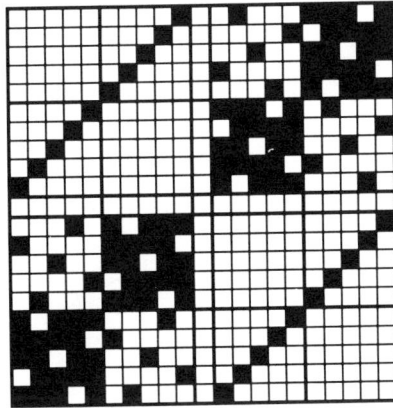

5.20. *Two blocks of five-shaft satin, turned.*

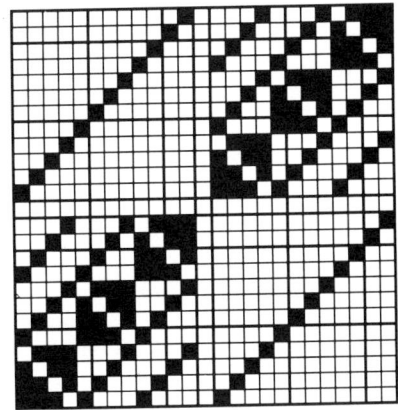

5.21. *Three blocks of four-shaft straight twill, turned.*

meant two or more blocks of the weave were used in the draft. If only one block was present, broken-twill weave was simply called a "twill." Reference to "satin" meant the draft had a base of five or more shafts per block as in fig. 5.20, and there might be one or several blocks present . Broken twill on four shafts simulated true satin's properties of reflecting light and of having no conspicuous diagonal, although neither quality was as strong as in true satin.

Turned-Twill and Turned-Satin Block Weaves

Block weaves of turned twill and turned satin all share a number of characteristics:

• There is a *weft-dominant* (called weft-faced) block opposed to a *warp-dominant* (called warp-faced) block, and it is possible to achieve both blocks simultaneously on the same surface of the fabric in both vertical and horizontal directions. Their textural contrast, accented by reflected light and/or by different colors, makes the pattern visible.

• Single sets of warp and weft threads form the cloth. Professional weavers preferred this because it saved materials, and was faster to weave. It was a more durable cloth than supplementary-weft pattern weaves.

• Each block's unit requires the same number of treadles as it has shafts within it. For example, a three-shaft unit needs three treadles as in fig. 5.17, and a five-shaft unit needs five treadles as in fig. 5.20.

• The units are relatively simple to plan, thread, and treadle to fit a block

design. Straight twill threading and treadling is repeated on an appropriate number of shafts and treadles for each of the blocks.

• The tie-up is arranged so opposite faces of component blocks are woven to fit the design. For example, on a three-block design with units of four-shaft straight twill, as in fig. 5.21, there are four treadles (1- 4) in a treadling unit which makes one row in the block design. Those four treadles (1-4) all need to be woven as a complete series before moving on to the next series of four treadles (5-8). After weaving treadles 5-8 in series, treadles 9-12 are woven (or 1-4 if the design calls for that row of blocks). Within a series of four treadles the shafts are tied so certain blocks weave weft-faced and the other blocks weave warp-faced, as necessary for the motif.

• The tie-up also is arranged so that the junctions of any blocks are clean-cut: at the edge of any block, each warp-float is stopped exactly at the border of that block by a weft-float in

the neighboring block, and each weft-float in the first block is similarly stopped by a warp-float. No floats extend into neighboring blocks. In each of figs. 5.17 through 5.21, clean cut-edges are visible where adjacent blocks meet: where black squares (warps) touch white squares (wefts) and vice versa.

5.22. *Tablecloth woven in a two-block pattern has a solid, satisfying hand which is rather weighty due to the thickness of its homespun linen weft threads. The eight-shaft design and generous amount of materials suggest a farmhome origin prior to World War II. Woven as one width. Twentieth century; Latgale; 206cm (81") L X 140cm (55") W; warp, cotton, 2-ply, S-ply, used double, natural; weft, linen, 2-ply, loose S-ply, used double, natural; 22 (11 working) e/cm (28 working epi); 11 p/cm (28 ppi). ROM990.20.5. Gift of Mr. Peter Alexandrovitch.*

5.23. *Two-block profile draft of design in cloth in fig. 5.22.*

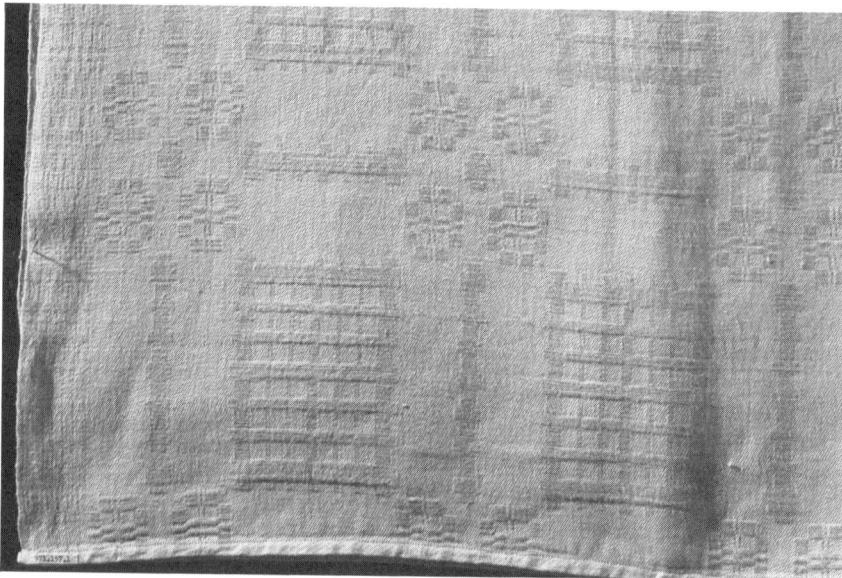

5.24. Twill block tablecloth woven by Mrs. Emma Skele in 1928, of cotton warp combined with a weft of linen home-grown in Latgale. The "rose" motif is placed in clusters between "window" squares. Latgale, Township Barkava; 188cm (74") L X 133cm (52") W; warp, cotton, 2-ply, S-ply, bleached; weft, linen, Z-twist, singles, natural; 28 e/cm (71 epi); 16 p/cm (41 ppi). ROM 971.157.1. Gift of Mrs. Emma Skele.

Uses. Block weaves of turned twill or turned satin originally were used in Latvia, as in much of Europe, for tablecloths and towels. In fact, turned twill and turned satin were the most common weave structures used for tablecloths in Latvia.

Tablecloths. Figure 5.22 shows a handsome linen tablecloth in a two-block pattern juxtaposing directions of twill lines. Its profile draft is shown in fig. 5.23. The threading draft for individual blocks is the same as that in fig. 5.18, each block containing four-shaft straight twill. Treadles are tied to give opposite twill angles in the two blocks.

The linen tablecloth pictured in fig. 5.24 uses four-shaft, straight twill blocks arranged in the rose design. Four blocks are arranged on 16 shafts. The rose and its permutations were the most popular of block patterns

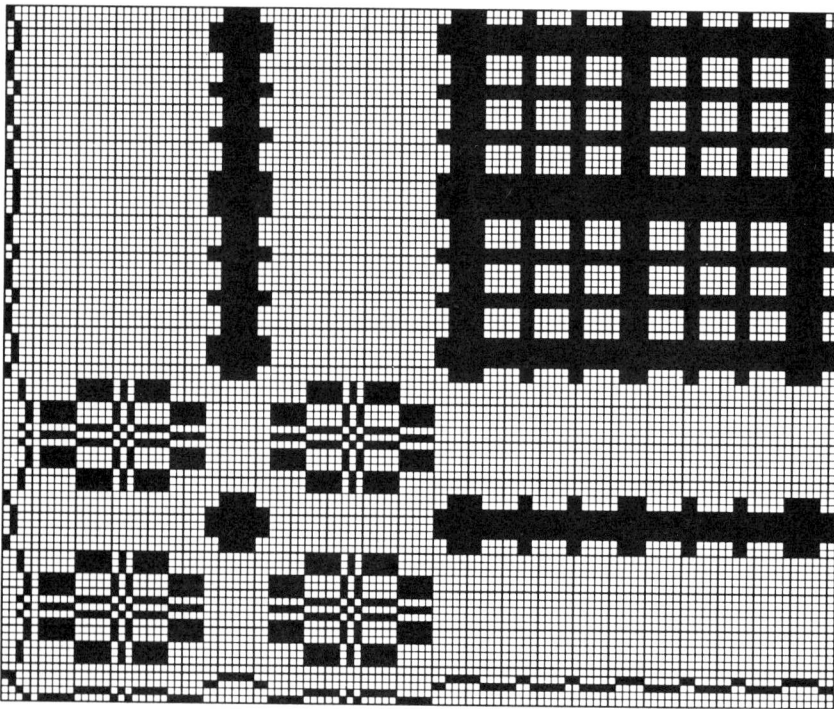

5.25. Profile draft of tablecloth in fig. 5.24.

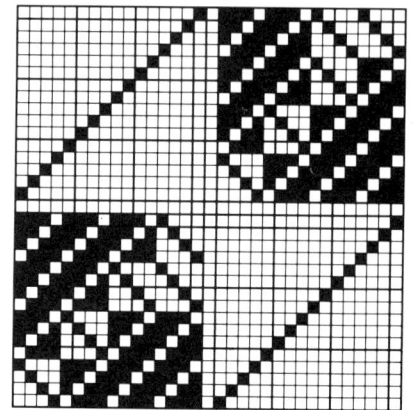

5.26. Draft for 16-shaft threading of four blocks of turned, straight twill, for fig. 5.25.

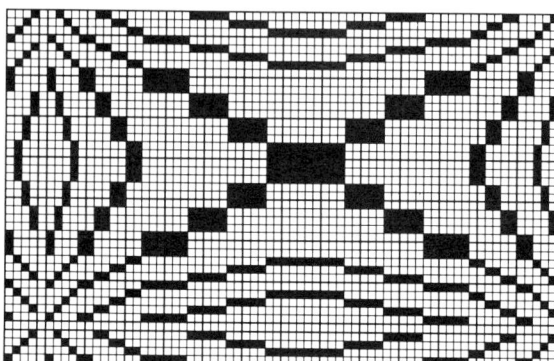

5.27. (left) Profile draft of four-block tablecloth design in Plate 15.

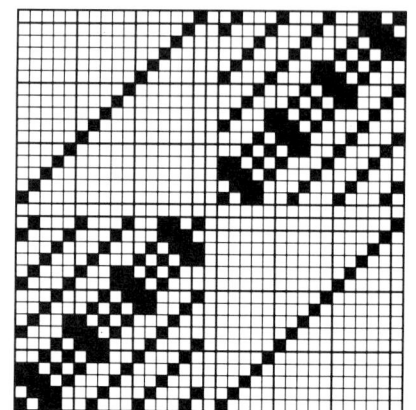

5.28. Sixteen-shaft threading of four blocks of turned twill in fig. 5.27 design. See Plate 15.

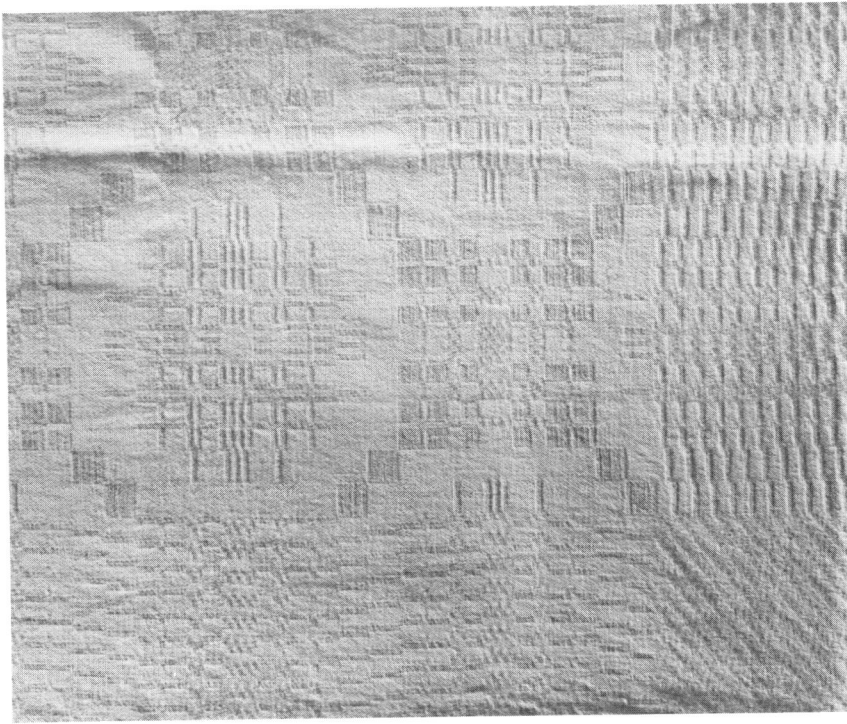

5.29. In the 1930s Matīs Zauers, a professional weaver, wove this tablecloth which is bordered on all four sides. Kurzeme, county Liepāja, Township Kateli; 170cm (67") L X 135cm (53") W; warp, cotton, 2-ply, S-ply, bleached; weft, linen, singles, Z-twist, natural; 18 e/cm (46 epi); 16p/cm (41 ppi). ROM971.224.2. Gift of Mrs. Made Brāzus, in memory of her father, Matīs Zauers.

5.30. Four-block profile draft of tablecloth in fig. 5.29.

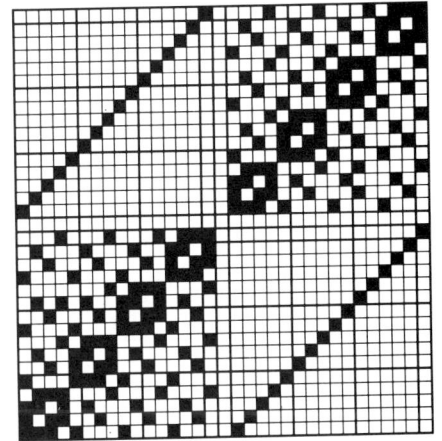

5.31. Sixteen-shaft threading draft of broken-twill blocks for profile draft in fig. 5.30.

used in Latvia. The profile draft is given in fig. 5.25. The unit threadings and tie-up combinations for the blocks are in fig. 5.26.

Another 16-shaft tablecloth, designed by arranging straight four-shaft twill blocks, can be seen in Plate 15. Its profile draft is shown in fig. 5.27. The block threadings for it are shown in fig. 5.28.

Twentieth-century Latvian weavers usually used one of two methods for tying up four-shaft blocks. The *straight twill tie-up* (typically with twill lines going in opposite directions as in the previous examples) or the *broken twill tie-up* were preferred. Figure 5.29 shows a fine linen tablecloth woven by a professional weaver. The broken twill tie-up was used in the rather extensive pattern which is profiled in fig. 5.30. The individual block threadings for this cloth are shown in fig. 5.31.

Blankets. Wool blankets were also woven in turned twill blocks. One such blanket from Kurzeme is shown in Plate 9. The profile draft for this attractive 16-shaft pattern is given in fig. 5.32. Four blocks of four-shaft broken twill are threaded as in fig. 5.33.

Towels. The 16-shaft towel in fig. 5.34 like the tablecloth in fig. 5.29, comes from the fly-shuttle loom of Matīs Zauers. Both items have four blocks of four-shaft, broken twill woven in fine cotton warp and linen

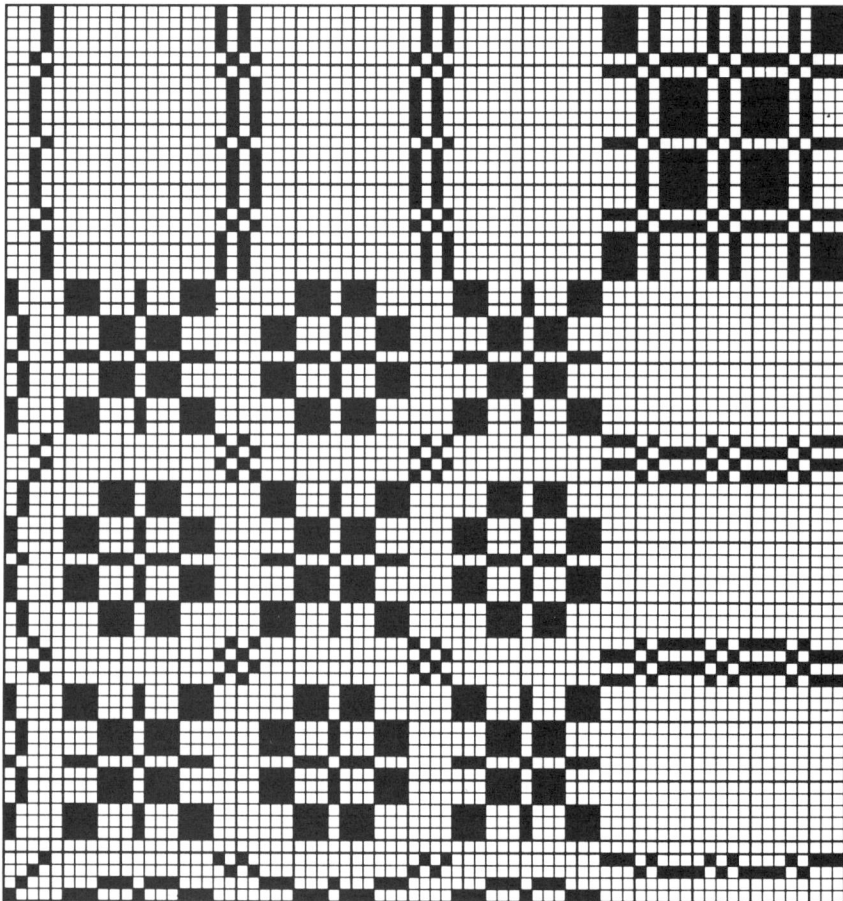

5.32. Roses and stars are featured in the profile draft of the blanket in Plate 9.

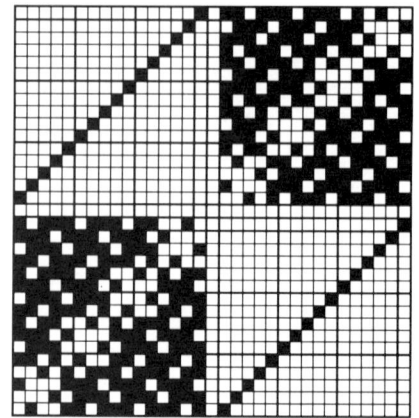

5.33. Sixteen-shaft threading of four blocks for fig. 5.32.

weft. The two pieces form an interesting contrast in block patterns because the tablecloth's large, intricate design seems to need more shafts than the towel's simple stripes and checks, when in fact both items require 16 shafts. Figure 5.35 shows the towel's four-block profile draft. Only eight treadles are in the towel's tie-up in fig. 5.36 because two of the blocks are always tied to weave as one face in a vertical stripe. By contrast

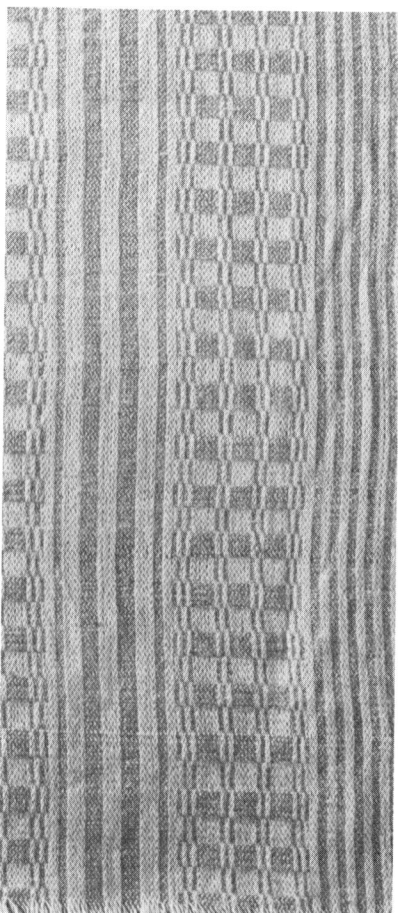

5.35. Profile draft for fig. 5.34.

5.34. This towel, woven in the 1930s, displays a subtle four-block design. Kurzeme, County Liepāja, Township Kateli; 74cm (29") L X 43.5 cm (17") W; warp, cotton, 2-ply, S-ply, natural; weft, linen, singles, Z-twist, natural; 24 e/cm (61 epi); 16 p/cm (41 ppi). ROM971.224.3. Gift of Mrs. Made Brāzus, in memory of her father, Matīs Zauers.

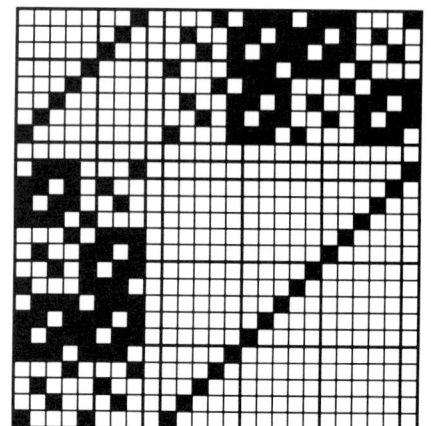

5.36. Threading of broken-twill blocks for profile in fig. 5.35.

the tablecloth needs 16 treadles to change all four blocks from warp-faced to weft-faced at different times.

The towel pictured in fig. 5.37 is rather uncommon in that it combines both tie-ups for four-shaft twill blocks within one piece. Similar to the previous towel's pattern of stripes and squares, this design also required 16 shafts for its four blocks. The profile draft is given in fig. 5.38. With the tie-up in fig. 5.39, the stripes are woven as straight twill lines in opposite directions, and the checks are woven as turned, broken twills.

Four-shaft blocks were the most common ones used for towels in Latvia. Nonetheless, satin blocks of five shafts each also were used by some weavers. One example mentioned above is a towel drafted in fig. 5.13. Two blocks of turned, five-shaft satin are woven as vertical stripes in that linen towel. Ten shafts are used, but only five treadles because each block is woven in only one of its "faces." There are narrow stripes of blocks for side borders but no end border patterns, suggesting the towel was cut from a long length

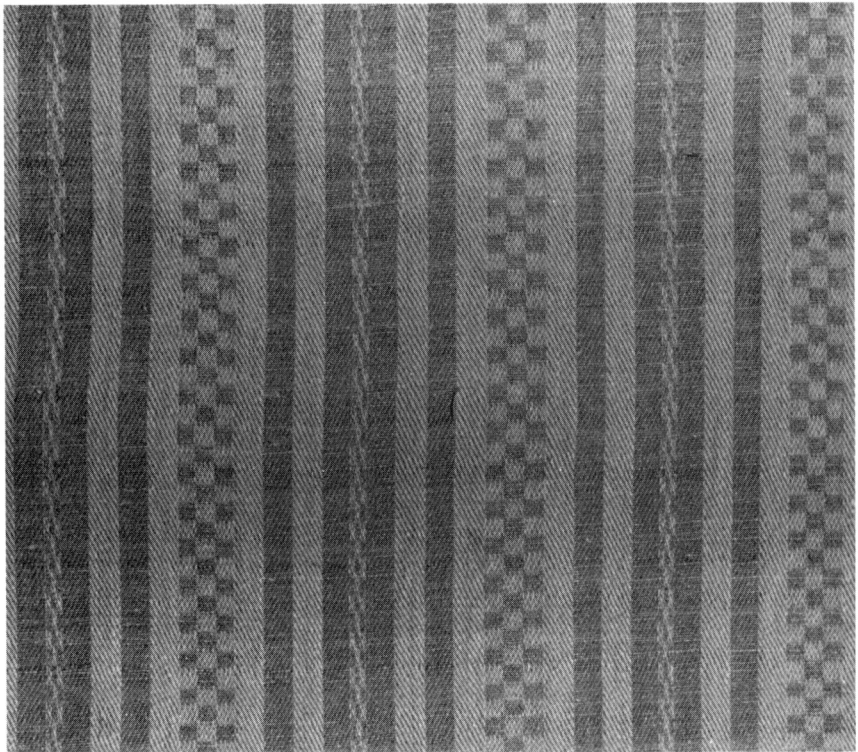

5.37. Mrs. Emma Skele skillfully wove fine threads to produce this soft towel which combines blocks of both broken and straight twill. 1928; Latgale, Township Barkava; 191 cm (36") L X 41 cm (16") W; warp cotton, 2-ply, S-ply, half-bleached; weft, linen, singles, Z-twist, natural; 28 e/cm (71 epi); 15 p/cm (38 ppi). ROM971.157.3. Gift of Mrs. Emma Skele.

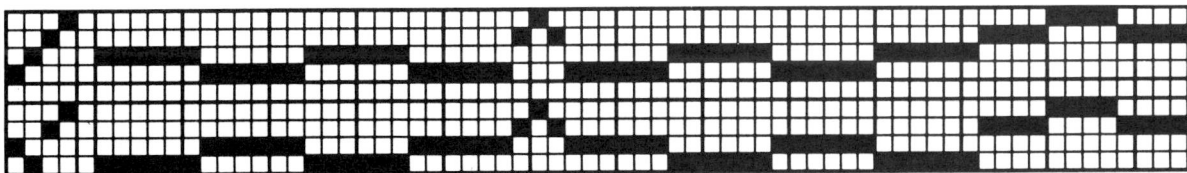

5.38. Profile draft for fig. 5.37.

of fabric. This draft is from a linen towel woven in the late nineteenth century in Zemgale.

Right into the twentieth century, home weavers in Vidzeme followed the professional weavers' lead and wove one type of block pattern for towels (usually long stripes with a few checks) and another for tablecloths (more elaborate patterns). In Latgale and Kurzeme, on the other hand, home weavers employed the same block patterns in towels, tablecloths, blankets, and clothing.

Uses. Block weaves were used throughout Latvia in the twentieth century for towels, tablecloths, napkins, upholstery, door curtains, blankets, bed covers, and some garment fabrics. Block weaves always were held in high regard due to the superior quality of materials, patterns, and skill they embodied.

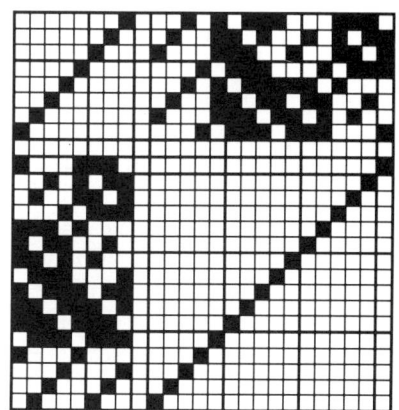

5.39. Sixteen-shaft threading draft using eight treadles, for four blocks of profile draft in fig. 5.38.

Twill Damask

When blocks of turned five-shaft satin are combined into an intricate pattern, usually in silk or linen, the resultant fabric is generally called *damask*. In its earliest years, starting with samples from 200 A.D., damask was woven in turned four-shaft broken twill or even straight twill blocks. (Becker, 1987.) The association of five-shaft satin structure with damask took centuries to develop. By the 1400s in Italy silk damask was woven in very elaborate designs based on blocks of turned satin. The turned-satin structure was adopted in the 1500s by Flemish master weavers for weaving ornate patterns in linen. Today in North America *damask* usually implies a complex patterning done in turned satin weave. Elaborate turned-twill patterns are called *twill damask* in North America, in contrast to *twill diaper* which implies few blocks in a simple, all-over pattern of turned-twill blocks.

Several admirable examples of early twentieth century twill damask from Latvian bed covers use wool rather than silk or linen. While the use of wool differs from the common concept of damask, the complicated patterning and use of four-shaft, turned broken-twill blocks ("four-shaft satin" in Latvia) in these examples certainly fall within twill damask's characteristics.

The coverlet shown in Plate 25 uses small blocks of turned, four-shaft broken twill, drafted in fig. 5.19. Due to the exceptionally involved nature of this pattern, no profile draft is given here.

A second twill damask bed cover is pictured in figs. 5.40 and 5.51.. It, too, is woven in small blocks of turned, four-shaft broken twill, fig. 5.19, to create traditional Latvian geometric symbols. An unusual three-color scheme of wool warp yarns - purple, pale orange, and a mixed purple-orange heather - is laced with ocher wool weft. The combination of soft colors on the wool has depth and is attractive. Except for the straight-twill borders which do not have the heather yarn, the three warp colors are

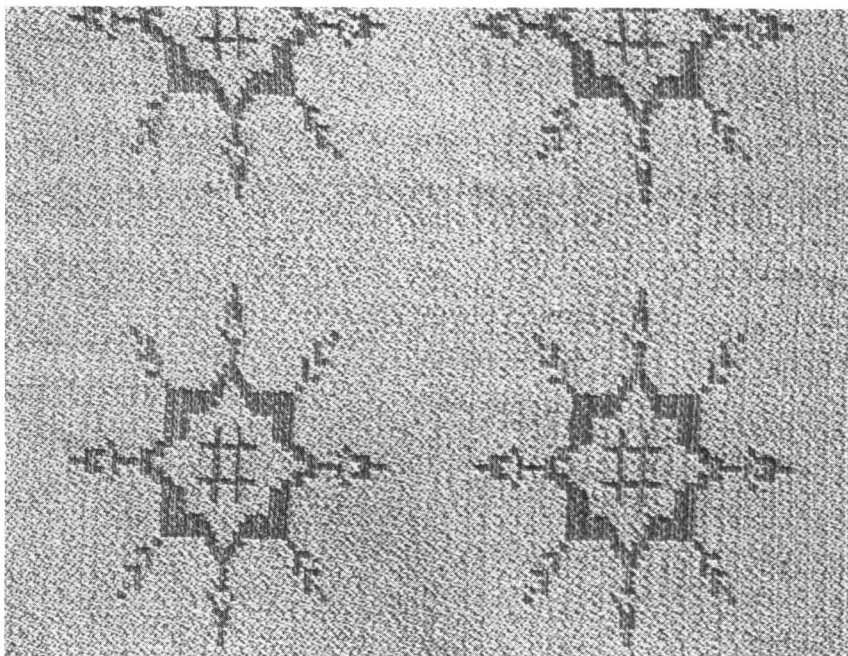

5.40. Twill damask bedcover adorned with traditional Latvian sun symbols in the center and the large "X" symbol for fire crosses. An un-traditional lightning bolt zig-zags between fire crosses. Its professional weaver, Mr. Gruvinš in Zemgale, was both skillful and daring. Ca. 1935; Zemgaale, Bauska; 207 cm (81.5") L X 149 cm (59") W. ROM971.46. Gift of Mr. Arnold Nulitis.

in regular sequence and add visual interest without disturbing the complex pattern. This blanket, heavier than the coverlet in Plate 25, also has good draping qualities. No profile draft is included due to the intricacy of the pattern.

Damask's extremely fancy patterns required many shafts, long-eyed heddles, and possibly a draw device on the loom, so it was almost always the domain of professional weavers. Damask is not mentioned in the twentieth-century Latvian texts for home weavers. The most complicated designs in those books were for float-weave structures or for several blocks of turned twill. Even those designs often were presented in long-eyed heddle drafts that in themselves required substantial knowledge and equipment to decipher and weave.

Block-weave Imitations

Home weavers prior to the twentieth century tried to imitate the block patterns produced by the professional weavers, but lacked the complex looms which could weave several four-shaft blocks. Instead, the farm women used weaves needing only four

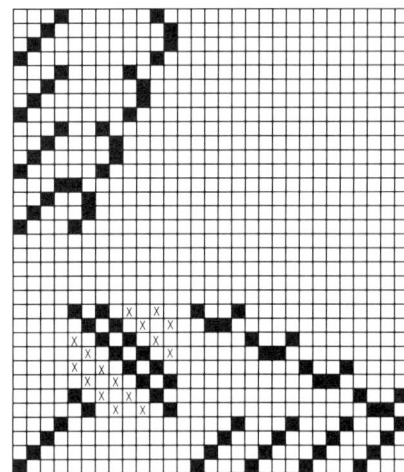

5.41. Straight-twill blocks as threaded on double-harness loom with counterbalanced front harness. Double-treadling is utilized. See text, Threading Type 1 for tie-up explanation, page 78.

shafts, such as *float-blocks*, *four-heddle blocks*, and *ribbed blocks*, which are discussed in *Chapter Six*. By the beginning of the twentieth century some non-professional weavers had 16-shaft looms which could accommodate four-block patterns. By the time texts and pattern books were printed in the early twentieth century, many directions were given for designs of two to four blocks. The books assumed that patterns needing more than 16 shafts would be woven on a double-harness loom with long-eyed heddles.

Turned Weaves on Double-harness Looms

In Latvia if a design in four-shaft turned twill needed more than 16 shafts a double-harness loom often was employed. (Double-harness loom systems are explained in *Chapter Two*.)

The typical double-harness loom setup had two rollers for mounting the four front shafts, as in fig. 2.11. Shaft 1 was linked to counterbalance shaft 4, and shaft 2 counterbalanced shaft 3. This was the *front* or *ground* harness, with long-eyed heddles on each shaft. In turned weaves the ground harness controlled the "grounding" structure of blocks. In Latvia this was either a straight or a broken four-shaft twill structure. Treadles controlled the shafts of this harness.

The *rear* harness of a double-harness loom used for turned weaves had counterbalanced shafts until those were largely replaced by countermarch shafts in the late 1800s. Shafts on this harness had short-eyed heddles and defined the pattern blocks. Additional treadles controlled the rear harness' shafts

DRAFTS

Two forms of threading and their drafts were used in Latvia for double-harness, turned-twill blocks. The form employing two pattern shafts for each block of design was preferred by twentieth-century Latvian weavers. By that time many double-harness looms had up to 16 shafts with countermarch action on the rear harness. Although it takes a bit longer to thread, this setup puts less strain on the warp threads during weaving. Each warp thread is moved only by either the front or the back harness, not both, during a shed. This avoids the strain placed on a warp thread from being in both a raised and a lowered heddle during a shed. See fig. 2.13, where warp 2 is strained. Two pattern treadles are used per block in the four-block draft with a straight-twill base, fig. 5.41, and the draft with a broken-twill base, fig.5.42.

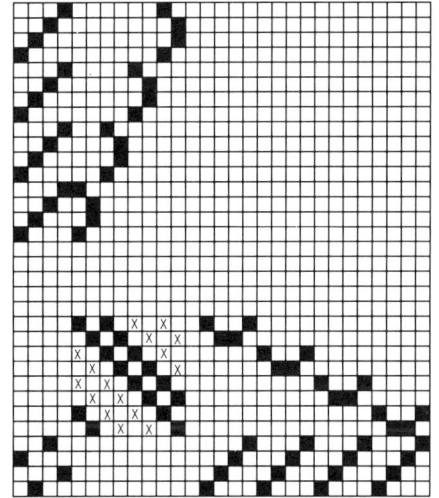

5.42. Broken-twill blocks as threaded on double-harness loom with counterbalanced front shafts. See text, Threading Type 1 for tie-up details, page 78. Double treadling is used.

5.43. Covers of pattern books by P. Viļumsons. On left is Pirmdienas rīts (Monday Morning). On right is Ceturdienas rīts (Thursday Morning). The medals are prizes he was awarded for his weavings.

TURNED FOUR-SHAFT TWILL WEAVES

THREADING TYPE I: PAIRS OF PATTERN SHAFTS PER UNIT

The structural derivation of this type of draft is based on the following analysis, using the popular base of broken twill. Fig. 5.44 shows the two possible faces (warp-dominant and weft-dominant) of four-shaft, turned, broken twill structure on two abutting units. Each unit is four warps wide and four picks high. Each is woven weft-faced once and warp-faced once vertically. Dark squares are warps, blank squares are wefts.

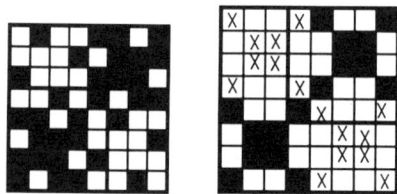

5.44. (left). Two blocks of turned, broken twill, each woven for warp-faced and weft-faced surface. This and the following four figures are based on #200 in Ma.

5.45. (above right) Grid with marks comparing warp positions in fig 5.44.

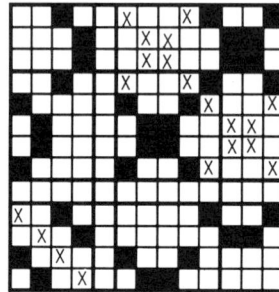

5.46. Threading draft on four shafts for structure in fig. 5.44. This interlacement is controlled by the rear, short-eyed heddle shafts. Its tie-up is for either a counterbalanced or countermarch loom.

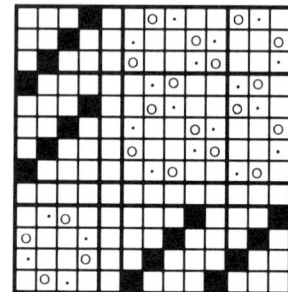

5.47. Grid with marks comparing warp positions in fig 5.44. Threading, tie-up, and treadling are added. See text below for symbols' definition. This draft gives broken-twill interlacement for the long-eyed-heddle, ground harness. Its tie-up is intended for a counterbalanced front roller system.

- On a new grid in fig. 5.45 mark a comparison of the places along each horizontal row of fig. 5.44 where one block's warps differ from the other block's in being raised or lowered. Use dark squares for raised warps, crosses for lowered warps, and blanks for warps sharing the same position.

For example, in the lowest horizontal pick of fig. 5.44, the first warp on the left side of the warp-faced block is raised, while the first warp on the left side of the weft-faced block (the fifth warp from the left) is lowered.

On fig. 5.45 mark a dark square in the left-hand block for the raised warp and in the right-hand block put a cross for a lowered warp in that block's comparable warp's square. The second warp thread in both of the blocks is lowered, and since the two blocks match in warp position make no mark on the new grid. Likewise, both blocks have their third threads in the same position (raised), so make no marks in the new grid. The fourth warps differ in position between the two blocks, so mark the raised one as a dark square and the lowered warp with a cross.
Repeat this process of comparing the positions of warps in the two blocks for each horizontal row of warps.

- Derive a threading draft, as shown in the lower rows of fig. 5.46. Give one shaft to each warp that has a wholly different interlacement from any other warp. Warps that interlace exactly alike share the same shaft. Two pattern shafts are needed for each block of design when they are compared in this manner.

- Tie-ups for the pattern shafts must indicate raised, lowered, and unmoved shafts for each pick in fig. 5.46. Dark squares (raised), crosses (lowered), and blanks (unmoved). Do this just as in the drawdown. Mark the first depressed treadle in the treadling position, then decide its tie-up: it must lower shaft 4, raise shaft 2, and leave shafts 1 and 3 at rest. The second row of the comparison needs a new treadle tie-up, so mark a new treadle in the treadling sequence and its tie-up. This process continues for all the rows of the comparison, resulting in the draft at fig. 5.46. This is the total information for the *rear* (pattern) shaft section of this double-harness weave.

- The interlacement information for the twill structures now must be established on the front harness. It is not necessary to consider the number of pattern blocks or the design to be formed. All that is sought is the long-eyed heddle threading, tie-up, and treadling of the two faces of turned twill.

- Return to fig. 5.44 and again analyze along horizontal rows for another new grid. This time, to contrast with the rear harness's symbols, use circles for raised warps, dots for lowered warps, and blanks for warps that share a position. Figure 5.47 is the resultant comparison of the warps' interlacement. It shows which of the four warps of both blocks, along each horizontal pick, are raised, lowered, or unmoved. It also shows that after four horizontal rows these first four rows repeat. So there are four unique columns of warps and rows of picks.

- Next, derive the ground harness threading as shown in the lower rows of fig. 5.47.

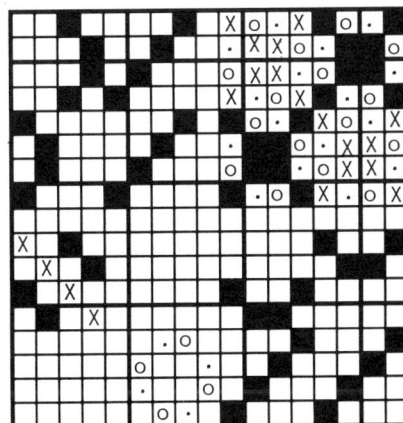

5.48. Synthesis of figs. 5.46 and 5.47 for two blocks of turned, broken twill, as set up on double-harness loom with counterbalanced front harness.

- The tie-up must take into consideration the counterbalancing of shafts 1 versus 4 and shafts 2 versus 3 over rollers. A direct tie-up is used with one shaft tied to each treadle and no lamms. The three symbols – circles, dots, and blanks – indicate possible positions of shafts in the tie-up. From its accompanying information the treadling is added. Figure 5.47 is the full draft for the *ground* shaft section of this double-harness weave.

- Figure 5.48 joins all the data from the drafts in fig. 5.46 and fig. 5.47, using the same symbols as those drafts. Fill empty spaces of each draft with marks from the other draft. When this draft is actually set up on a double- harness loom, the warp threads are only moved by one of the two harnesses during a shed. In final presentation in a Latvian weaving book, the marks for sinking shafts in the front harness's tie-up are omitted because there is an assumption of the counterbalanced roller system.

Exactly the same analysis method can be applied to turned-twill blocks with a straight-twill base, resulting in the two-block, double-harness draft in fig. 5.41. This draft, with two pattern shafts per design block, is preferable to a draft with one pattern shaft per block because it puts less strain on the warps. It was the most common one for double-harness block arrangements presented for non-"mechanical" looms in twentieth-century Latvia.

THREADING TYPE 2: SINGLE PATTERN SHAFTS PER UNIT

This form of threading, fig. 5.49, is only for designs involving more than eight pattern blocks, and thus is seldom included in Latvian home weavers' books. It has four ground shafts and one pattern shaft per block of the profile design. Similar drafts are frequently used by double-harness loom weavers in North America. However, Latvian home weavers' drafts assumed double-harness looms with a front harness of counterbalanced rollers and a rear harness of countermarch shafts.

- Compose a profile draft wherein each block represents a unit of four warp threads and four weft threads.

- Fill in threading of the pattern shafts on a grid, allowing one pattern shaft per block of design and four warps per unit, as shown in four blocks in fig. 5.49. Each warp also passes through a long-eyed heddle on the front harness in regular order of shafts 1, 2, 3, 4.

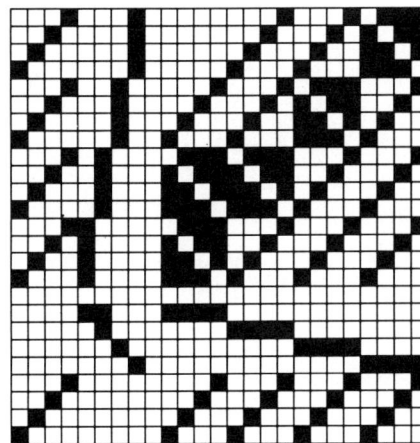

5.49. Straight-twill setup for four blocks of turned twill on double-harness loom, assuming a counterbalanced front harness. See text for derivation of draft, "Threading Type 2."

- Arrange a tie-up of pattern treadles so that the pattern shafts' blocks, which show as warp-faced are tied to rise, and all other pattern shafts sink.

- Ground shafts, hung from rollers that counterbalance, are tied up to allow for three positions: rising, sinking, or unmoved. In fig. 5.49 only the rising ground shaft is indicated because in Latvian books it was assumed that shaft 1 counterbalanced shaft 4 and shaft 2 counterbalanced shaft 3.

- The final draft in fig. 5.49 produces units of 1/3 or 3/1 twill with straight diagonal lines running in opposite directions between the two faces of the units.

Figure 5.50 is the double-harness draft for exactly the same profile design as the preceding example. The only difference in this second draft is that the ground treadles are placed in a different sequence from those in fig. 5.49, resulting in a broken twill base for the turned weave rather than a straight- twill base.

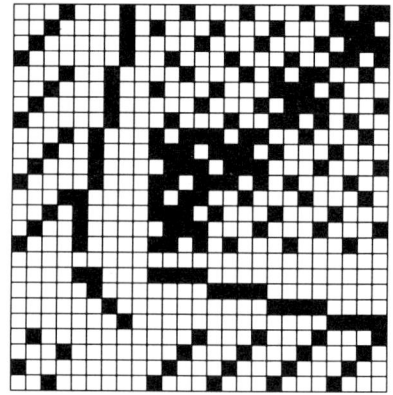

5.50. Broken-twill setup for four blocks of turned twill on double-harness loom, assuming a counterbalanced front harness. Only one pattern shaft is used per block and double-treadling is employed.

5.51. This blanket in turned blocks of four-shaft broken twill is the type of patterning possible on a double-harness loom with many pattern shafts. See page 76 in the text for details and draft.

CHAPTER SIX
Compound Weave Structures with Supplementary Wefts

Compound weaves interlace more than one set of warp and/or weft threads. Some compound weaves have added sets of elements which may function as: 1) supplementary wefts, 2) supplementary warps, 3) complementary wefts, and 4) complementary warps.

Other compound weaves combine whole weave structures. These compound weaves have at least two (or more) sets of warp threads and two (or more) sets of weft threads. Among this type of compound weaves the significant ones in Latvia are the double cloths.

Weft-patterned Cloth with Untied Floats

Audu rakstoti audumi

One of the easier methods of planning and weaving patterned fabric is to float a *supplementary weft* over a ground cloth. The supplementary weft, woven selvage-to-selvage, floats on either the front or back surface of the cloth, while its ground cloth interlaces in its own structure independently from the pattern floats. In early twentieth-century Latvian weft-patterned cloth the background fabric is usually plain weave, formed by one set of warp threads and one set of weft threads. Occasionally the ground cloth is

weft-faced plain weave, four-shaft straight twill, pointed twill, crepe, or other structures. Lengthy floats of supplementary weft render the fabric impractical, so Latvian designs avoided long weft floats over wide single blocks or over joined blocks, which in practice created one very wide block.

Two-block designs, like the one in fig. 6.1, were very common,

probably because only four shafts were needed. This design was called a *rose* and was one of the most long lasting, widespread designs known in Latvia. For several centuries *rose weaving* was used for blankets in Zemgale and Kurzeme. As shown in fig. 6.2, each block required two shafts so that plain-weave ground cloth could be woven under the supplementary weft floats. Two

6.1. *Typical two-block profile design used for patterning with supplementary weft.*

6.2. *Threading draft on four shafts for design in fig. 6.1.*

6.3. Detail, fabric for traditional costume skirt, patterned with supplementary weft. 1920's; fragment, 42cm (16.5") L X 56 cm (22") W; warp cotton, 2-ply, S-ply, black; weft, wool, singles, Z-twist, black tabby, purple, white, yellow, green, red pattern; 10 e/cm (25 epi); 32 p/cm (81 ppi). ROM971.209.163. Gift of Dr. K. Lesiņš. See Plate 2.

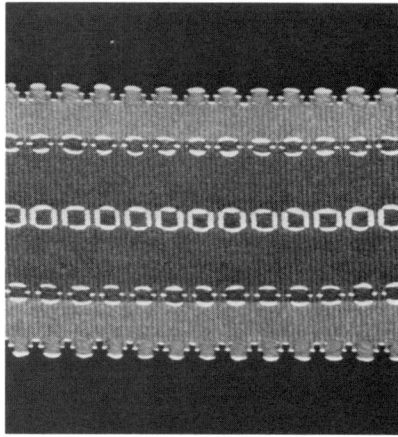

6.5. Mātis Zauers , a professional weaver , produced this wide seamless blanket in the 1930s. Kurzeme, Coutny Liepaja, Township Kateli; 160cm (63") L X 167 cm (66") W; warp, wool, singles, Z-twist, used doubled, dark grey; weft, wool, singles, Z-twist, black, two blues, white; 8 (4 working) e/cm (20,10 working epi); 38 p/cm (96ppi). ROM 971.224.1. Gift of Mrs. Made Brāzus, in memory of her father, Mātis Zauers. See Plate 3.

treadles are needed for plain-weave ground cloth, along with one pattern treadle per block of design. Two wefts are used, one for pattern and one for ground. Usually each pattern weft pick was followed by one of the alternated plain-weave weft picks, giving a 1:1 ratio of pattern to ground picks. If one weft thread was coarser than the other there may have been more pattern picks between ground picks or vice versa.

Combined widths of blocks could quickly increase the length of supplementary weft floats, so multi-shaft designs needed careful planning to tie down very long floats.

In Zemgale in southern Latvia, weaving tastes were influenced by intricate weaving done in factories there from as far back as the 1600s. Weft-patterned cloth became traditional for women's skirts of costumes in that area. Simpler methods of skirt decoration were used elsewhere. The fabric in Plate 2 and fig. 6.3 is an example of a Zemgale fabric. Its draft in fig. 6.4 shows the patterning interlacements on 16 shafts. A similar fabric is shown being woven in Plate 5.

Simple embellishments enhance the weft-faced blanket in Plate 3 and fig. 6.5. This blanket is an example of weft-faced plain weave with decorative supplementary wefts. The ground wefts are black wool with bands of light and medium blue. The colors evoke associations with the natural environment as did the weft-faced, plain-weave blankets of the 1800s. Within the bands are extra design features of weft color changes and floats of white wefts over three warps rather than just one. Fig. 6.6

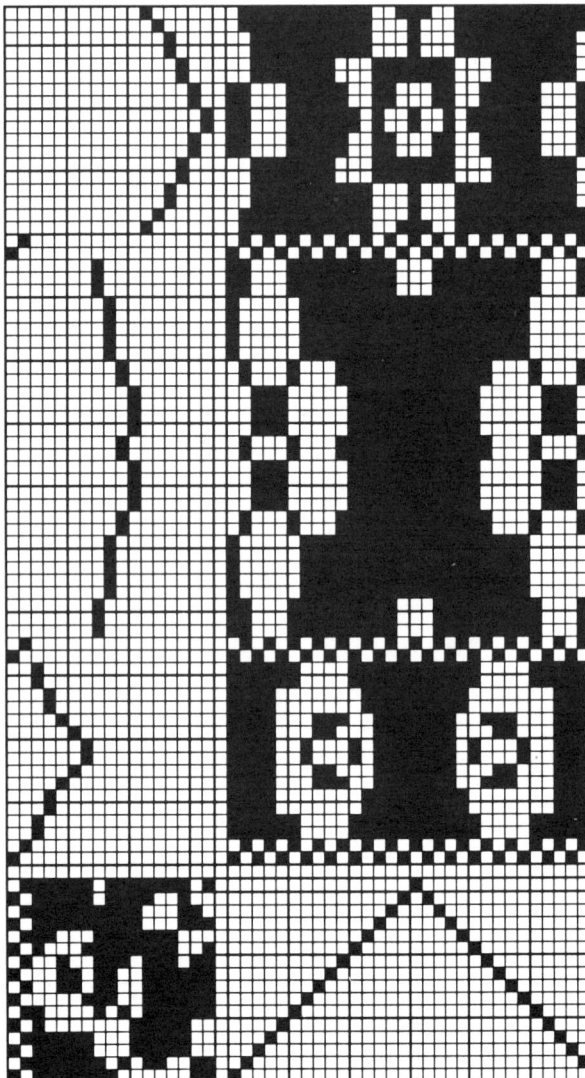

6.4. (left) Motifs from fig. 6.3. Use alternate tabby picks between pattern picks.

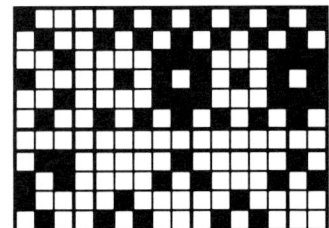

6.6. Two repeats of supplementary-weft design in fig. 6.5.

82

shows one of these rows of figures, involving a two-block draft with three warps per unit. The patterning is simple and of limited occurrence so that it could have been done by a home weaver selecting sheds by hand. However, there is a professional's authority in the strength of both color and design on this blanket.

Uses. In the twentieth century weft-float patterning became popular for decorating cotton aprons and garments, curtains, wool blankets and door curtains, and bedcovers. The latter were made either of unbleached linen and cotton or of a colored wool weft over a ground cloth of cotton.

Double-harness Weaving

Patterning via supplementary wefts was well-suited to very intricate designs based on traditional symbols which were in vogue in the 1900s. The complicated motifs adapted well to the increasingly popular double-harness weaving system, and especially to draw looms. There designs could be worked out with half the pattern shafts required by a single-harness loom.

Supplementary-weft patterning is one of the simplest weft-patterned cloth interlacements to arrange on a double-harness loom. Figure 6.7 shows a single-harness draft that needs 18 shafts. Figure 6.8 gives the double-harness threading, tie-up, and treadling for the same results on two ground and nine pattern shafts. Each warp passes through a rear, pattern shaft and a front, ground shaft. The ground cloth, under the supplementary-weft floats, is most often woven in plain weave or weft-faced plain weave. Treadling simply alternates a ground cloth weft pick with a pattern weft pick.

Patterned cloth woven on the draft in fig. 6.7 has a ground cloth of plain weave (or weft-faced plain weave) and supplementary pattern-

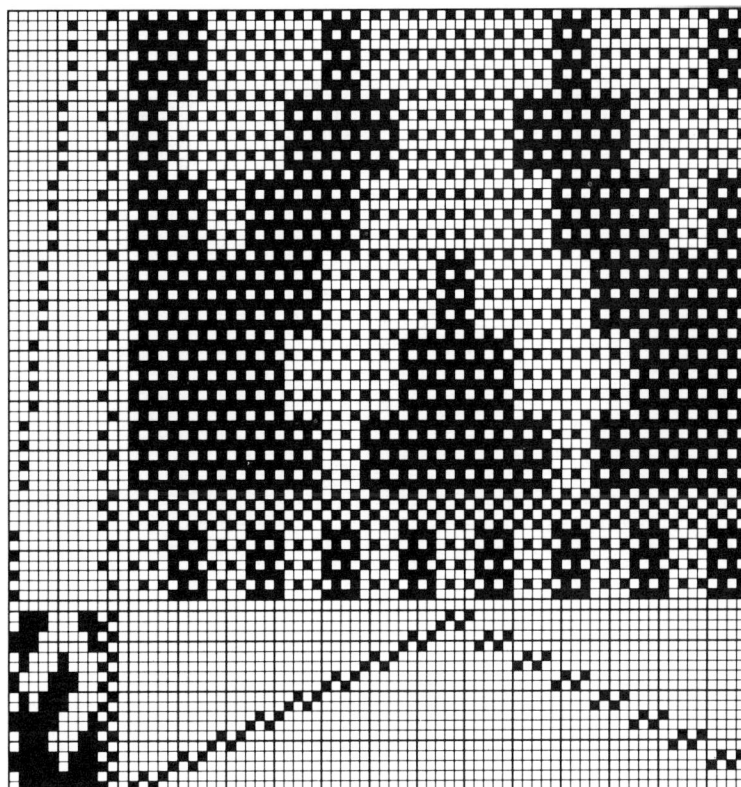

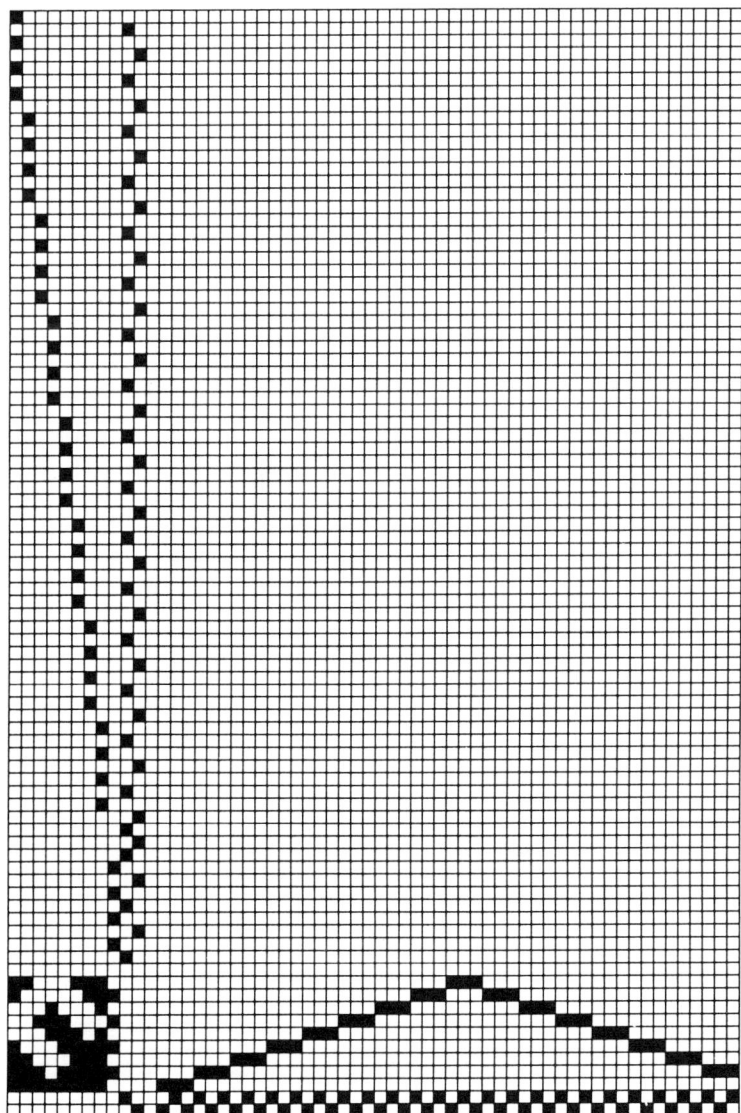

6.7. (above) Single-harness draft for supplementary -weft patterning on 18 shafts.

6.8. Double-harness version of draft in fig. 6.7.

UNTIED SUPPLEMENTARY-WEFT PATTERNING FOR DOUBLE-HARNESS LOOMS

THREADING

1) Plan the profile draft of the design, complete with "threading" and "treadling" orders of its component blocks as in fig. 6.9.

2) Count one short-eyed heddle (pattern) shaft for each independent block on the profile's "threading" design.

3) Decide how many warp threads wide each pattern block will be. On a graph paper grid, substitute a series of warps (*e.g.*, four in fig. 6.8) for each pattern block, putting the warps on their appropriate pattern shaft's row on the graph paper. These marked warps are in short-eyed heddles which actually can hold groups of warps.

4) The lower rows on the graph paper represent the front shafts with long- eyed heddles.

In order to weave plain weave there are two front shafts. Each warp thread must pass through one long-eyed heddle, alternating on front shafts 1 and 2. Figure 6.8 shows the double-harness threading draft for the beginning of fig. 6.9's design.

TIE-UP

• Tie up treadles so each pattern treadle (or draw cord) lifts those rear shafts whose warps are not to be covered by the pattern weft on that treadle's pick.

• Tie ground treadles as counterbalanced plain weave, shaft 1 versus shaft 2.

On both countermarch and draw loom drafts dark tie-up markings indicate where shafts are lifted. To weave the design on the upper surface of the cloth the dark tie-up marks are the same as the light marks of the design drawn on paper. A design may be woven with its face up or down.

SHED FORMATION

Shed 1: Raise front shaft 1. This opens one tabby shed. Weave a ground cloth weft. Close shed.

Shed 2: Raise all pattern shafts except # 6. The four warp ends in each heddle on rear shaft 6 will all remain down while all other warps will rise, as in fig. 6.10 on a draw loom.

The extra length of the heddle eyes on the front harness shafts allows a shed to pass through the eyes. Leave the front shafts in the neutral position. Weave in the shed formed in front of the reed with the pattern weft. Close shed.

Shed 3: Raise long-eyed heddle shaft 2, opposite to the first tabby shed. Weave ground cloth. Close shed.

Shed 4: Repeat shed 2. Weave pattern weft. Close shed.

Repeat the lifting cycle starting with tabby shed 1, followed by either the old pattern shed or a new one.

Usually the four-pick series of wefts is completed as a group before changing to a new pattern shed. The main criteria for treadling is that the design's blocks be woven to square as blocked out in the profile design, so pattern sheds may be used as often as needed (always alternating with tabby treadles) to achieve a squared design.

6.9. Profile draft for nine-block design patterned in untied supplementary weft, #218 in Ma.

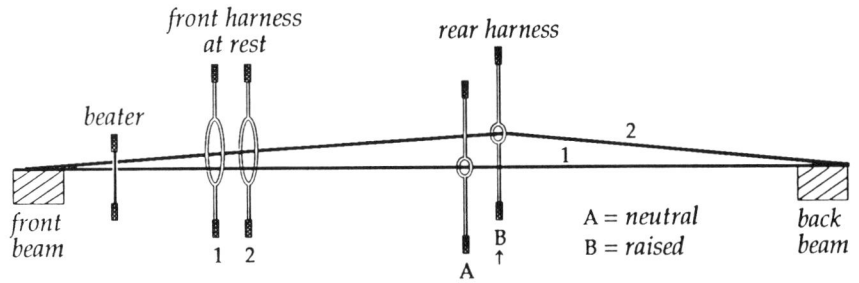

6.10. Untied supplementary weft's pattern shed, created only by rear shafts on a double-harness draw loom.

weft floats from selvage to selvage on both surfaces. With four front shafts, a ground cloth other than plain weave can be woven. One example of a draft for four-shaft, pointed-twill ground cloth is given in fig. 6.11.

It is relatively easy to draft the complete double-harness threading, tie-up, and treadling for a plain-weave ground cloth patterned by weft floats. The instructions on page 84 are for a loom with rear shafts that are not counterbalanced, *i.e.*, they move in-dividually. The front shafts have a counterbalanced action. On Latvian looms, those front shafts were often hung from cords over a roller, as in fig. 2.11.

Weft-patterned Cloth with Tied Floats

Audu rakstoti audumi saistītiem pārstaipiem

Weft-patterned cloth as described in the preceding section has a strong visual pattern and is relatively easy to plan, set up, and weave. It has a significant, practical limitation: the length of supplementary-weft floats. To avoid this restriction, cloth can be composed so certain warp ends regularly tie down pattern weft floats at short, functional intervals. These warps weave as part of the ground fabric and also tie the supplementary-weft floats. In Latvia the resultant fabric was called *weft-patterned cloth with tied floats*.

Warp threadings with tied floats usually placed the tie warps regularly

along two or more shafts at the front of the loom. Depending on the threading, each block of pattern used one or two pattern shafts. Designs of several pattern blocks often needed looms with more than four shafts to accommodate a tied-float weave threading. Therefore weft-patterned, tied-float drafts, like the block weaves, or *dreļļu audumi,* such as turned twill or turned satin, were beyond the capability of many Latvian looms until about 1900. Some weavers did produce tied-float structures in Latvia earlier than that, possibly using some hand control for pattern weft placement. Initial uses probably occurred sometime between the fourteenth and seventeenth centuries.*

* This estimated date of origin is based on the use of tied-float weaves by similar European countries, since no more definite date has yet been established. (A. Alsupe, correspondence, 1987.)

In the eastern province of Latgale, versions of weft-float patterning were traditional with home weavers long before multi-shaft looms were available. Early counterbalanced looms used by some professional weavers possibly were capable of producing multiple-block designs in tied-float weaves. When multi-shaft countermarch looms appeared, many levels of weavers throughout Latvia wove elaborate tied-float cloth.

For many tied-float weaves, double-harness loom systems were the most versatile equipment. These looms allowed more blocks of a design to be woven on fewer shafts and treadles than in a single-harness system. Ground fabrics in weaves

6.11. (below) Arrangement for fig. 6.9. with four-shaft twill ground cloth on double-harness loom, #220 in Ma.

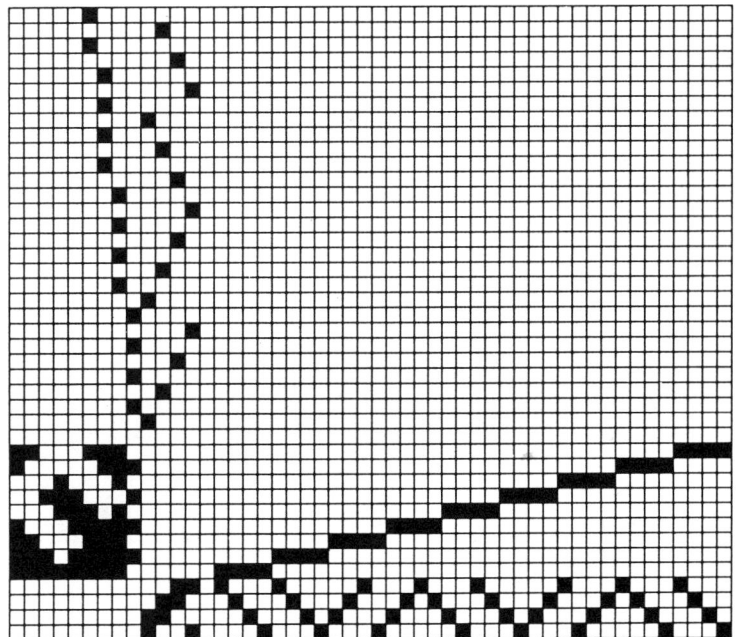

6.12. Draft with 2:1 ratio of pattern warps to tie warps, from #213 in Ma.

6.13. Draft with 3:1 ratio of pattern warps to tie warps, from #214 in Ma.

more complex than plain weave also were easier on a double-harness system. Tied-float drafts were woven on double-harness systems in Germany in the 1600s.* It is quite possible that the German master weavers and journeymen who came to Latvia brought this knowledge with them. Double-harness weaving methods for tied-float drafts are outlined on page 84.

* Marx Ziegler's *Weber kunst und Bild Buch* of 1677 give what was probably the first published instructions for setting up these weaves on a double-harness loom. (Hilts, 1987.)

Uses. Tied-float fabrics were initially used in Latvia for blankets. By the late 1800s the availability of tied-float weaves helped to meet the growing demand for decorative bed covers, tablecloths, rugs, and upholstery. Tied-float fabric also became an alternative to twills for clothing.

Drafting Systems

By the twentieth century there were a number of different drafts containing threading units with regular pattern ends and tie ends. These *unit drafts with ties* were woven in several methods, one of which formed a background cloth decorated by tied floats of supplementary weft.

Drafts with unit threadings that combine pattern warp ends and tie warp ends can be partially described with a ratio reflecting the number of warp ends serving each purpose within a single unit. For example, the occurrence of pattern warp ends compared to that of tie warp ends in the unit in fig. 6.12 is 2:1. This ratio differs among assorted types of tie drafts. Apparently the older drafts with ties had higher ratios of pattern warp ends to tie warp ends such as 4:1, 3:1, 2:1, 6:2, or 4:2. More recent drafts, in use since the late 1800s, had a 1:1 or even a 1:2 ratio. It was the older drafts, with several pattern ends between tie ends, which were used to create the classic Latvian examples of cloth patterned by tied-weft floats over a background cloth, such as fig. 6.29. By the early twentieth century 1:1 drafts were occasionally woven as weft-patterned cloth with tied floats. More often the 1:1 drafts and the 1:2 drafts were woven weft-faced with complementary wefts, a technique discussed in *Chapter Eight*.

2:1, 3:1, AND 4:1 TIED-FLOAT DRAFTS WITH PLAIN WEAVE

The most common of the old weaves with tied floats of supplementary weft had single tie warps adjoining groups of pattern warps. The pattern groups consisted of two, three, or four warp ends. The tie warps alternated between two tie shafts. The threading was usually arranged to allow plain weave as the ground cloth, which meant that the pattern warps needed two shafts per block of the design. Figures 6.12, 6.13, and 6.14 are examples of the three drafts based on threading units with two, three, or four pattern ends. Their pattern warp:tie warp ratios are 2:1, 3:1, and 4:1 respectively.

Within Latvian profile drafts for this weave structure, regardless of the ratio used, each block of design represents one tie warp end and one group of pattern warp ends. Thus the threading unit of these weaves required that both tie warps (on shafts 1 and 2) be used alternately between two sets of pattern warps, but those two sets of pattern warps could be threaded on different pattern shafts to

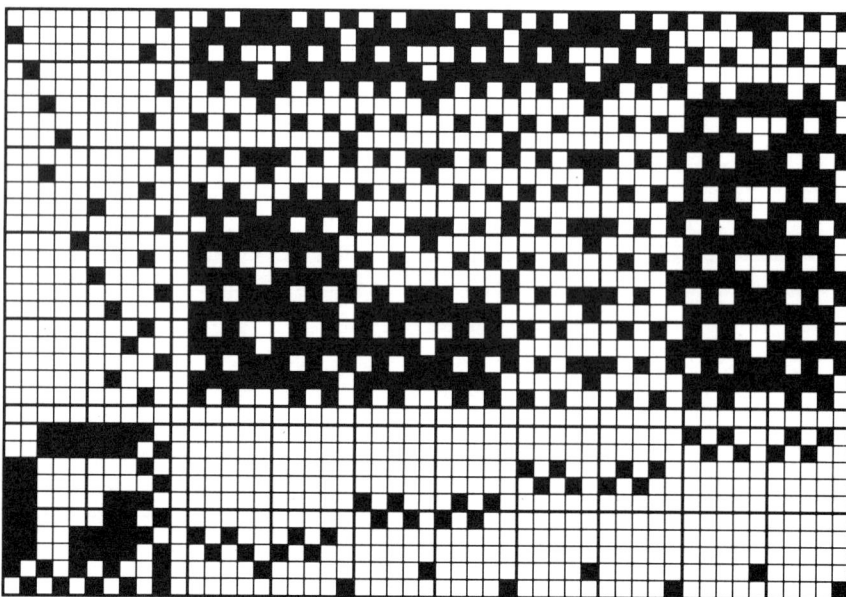

6.14. Draft with 4:1 ratio of pattern warps to tie warps, from #215 in Ma.

create different pattern blocks as required by the design.

To retain the plain-weave interlacement within 2:1 and 4:1 ratios, pattern warps might be in odd-even or even-odd order within their block, depending on which tie warp (even or odd) they followed. The drafts at figs. 6.12 and 6.14 show both options for threadings. In the 3:1 ratio threading in fig. 6.13, each group of pattern warp threads are always on the even-odd-even shafts, therefore when combined with the two tie shafts the warps all together form plain weave.

Figure 6.15 shows a small, twentieth-century table cover woven of fine cotton warp and linen weft in a 2:1 version of the structure's draft. A profile draft of the corner is given in fig. 6.16, and in 6.17, units of the 12-shaft threading are shown. This piece exemplifies how a single design block of the weave consists of one tie thread plus its pattern threads (two in this case) and also how the pattern warps are in odd-even or even-odd order within their unit, depending on which tie warp (even or odd) they follow.

Due to the spacing of the ties along the draft, supplementary-weft floats of pattern are as long as twice the width of pattern ends plus one tie end. The 2:1 draft has floats over five warps, the 3:1's are over seven, and the 4:1's are over nine warps. At the edge of a design block, alternate long floats are halved in width, giving relatively straight vertical edges to the design block.

Uses. In North America this draft consisting of two alternating ties and a pattern ends, with a pattern:tie ends ratio greater than 1:1, is sometimes called *tied-Beiderwand*. In Latvia it simply was known as a *weft-patterned, tied-float* arrangement. Historically it was used for bed blankets. In more recent times it has been applied to table covers, blankets, bed covers, wall covers, and upholstery.

An early twentieth-century profile design for upholstery woven on the 3:1 version of this draft is in fig. 6.18. To reduce the number of treadles needed, double treadling is

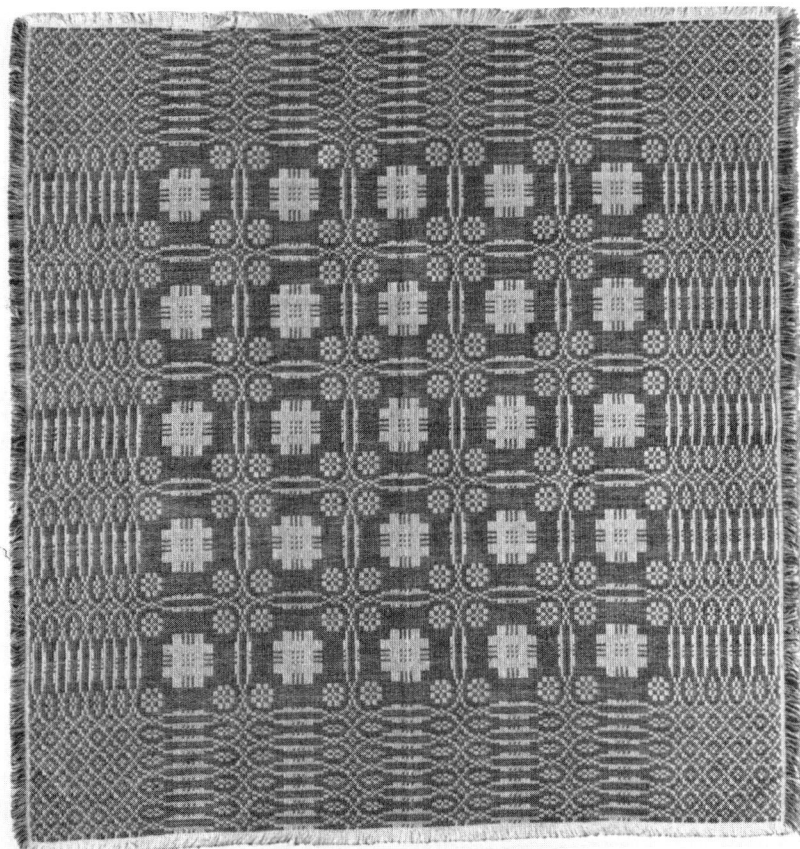

6.15. *Decorative table cover. Twentieth century; 60 cm (24.75") L X 57cm (22.5") W, both plus fringes; warp, cotton, 2-ply, S-ply, natural; pattern weft, linen, singles, S-twist, used double, natural; tabby weft like warp; 16 e/cm (41 epi); 20 p/cm (51 ppi). ROM 990.20.2. Gift of Mr. Peter Alexandrovitch.*

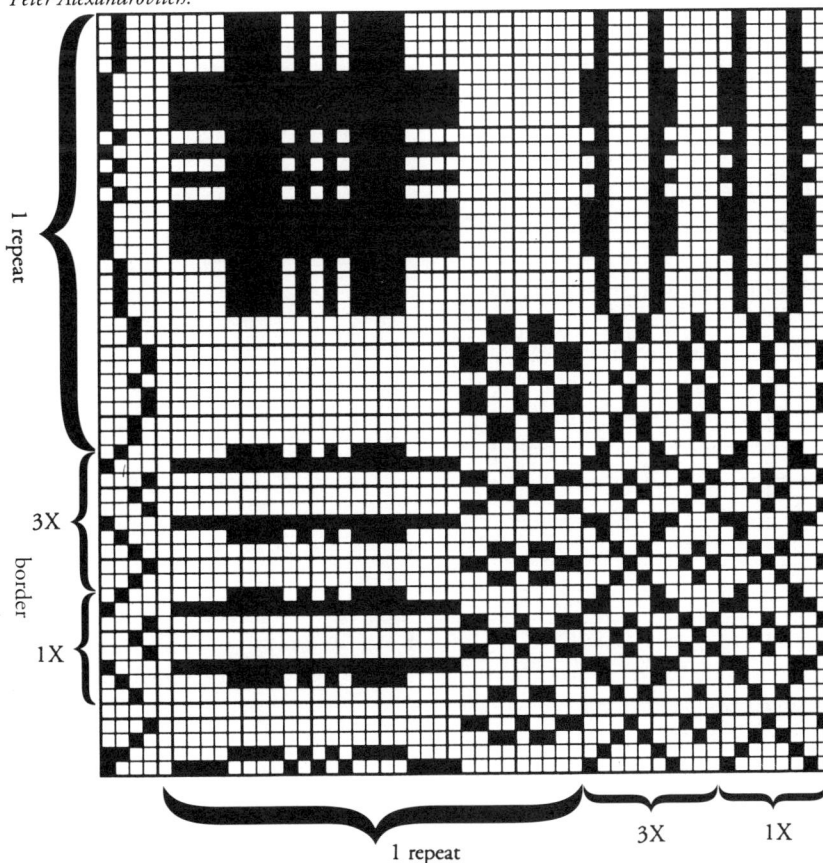

6.16. *Four-block profile draft of lower, right corner of piece in fig. 6.15.*

87

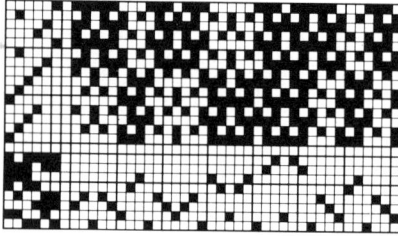

6.17. Partial section of threading of 2:1 units for fig. 6.15. Two pattern warps plus one tie warp constitute one block. A selvage of plain weave can be threaded on shafts 1 and 2.

6.18. (right) One and one-half repeats of profile draft for four-block design, #169 in Rīga.

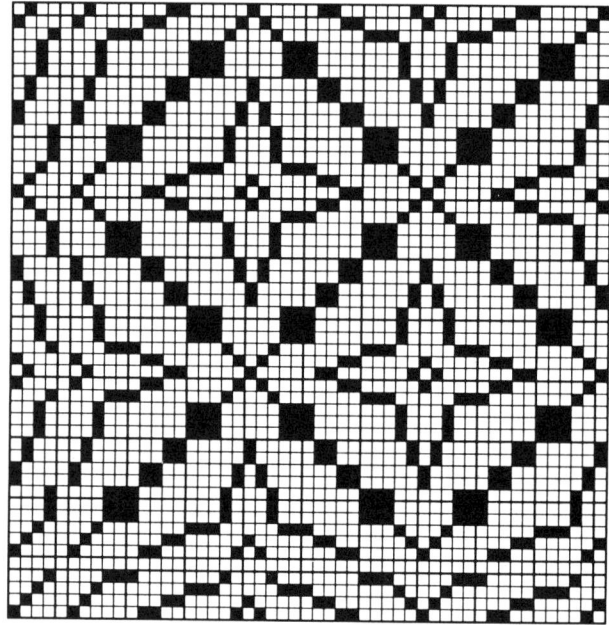

6.20. Two repeats in profile draft for pattern band components in fig.6.19.

6.19. Detail of a novel 8-block blanket, showing pattern bands with false center seam, reflects the talents of its creator, Mrs. Kļaviņs, a graduate of a Latvian home economics institute .1938; Kurzeme, Ventspils; 240 cm (94.5") L X 131 cm (51.5") W; warp, cotton, 2-ply, S-ply, black; weft, wool, 2-ply, S-ply, maroon, green, red, beige, yellow, tan, rust; 18 e/cm (45 epi); 14 p/cm (36 ppi). ROM972.130. Gift of Mrs. Laima Kerans. See Plate 21.

utilized; that is, two treadles are depressed at once. Double treadling was typical on tied-float drafts. Fibers for this upholstery fabric, as suggested in the instruction book, *Rokas grāmata audējām,* could be 30/2 cotton warp, with a ground weft like the warp, and pattern weft of wool. The sett was to be two threads per heddle, four per dent, in a 65 dent/10 cm (16 dent/inch) reed.

Twice the number of tied-Beiderwand pattern blocks can be woven on a double-harness loom equipped with a similar number of pattern shafts as can be arranged on a single-harness loom. Some examples of double-harness drafts are given on pages 94-96.

REARRANGED 2:1 DRAFT
The fascinating blanket shown in fig. 6.19 and Plate 21 is based on a block weave threading which curiously approximates a 2:1 draft. There are no double-weave areas in this cloth, as in true *Beiderwand* cloth (page 129), nor any true plain-weave picks as in the tied-Beiderwand weaves pre-

viously discussed. The threading uses three sizes of warp groupings – single, double, and triple – which are often re-assembled into triple-ended groups that function as single ends in plain-weave sheds. This atypical interlacement is conveniently controlled by a double-harness loom. The threading draft does not allow for true plain weave sheds.

The eight-block profile draft is given in fig. 6.20. Various pattern bands use different parts of the profile design. Figure 6.21 shows the full drafting of four pattern units as if woven on a single-harness loom.

Each block's unit of threading includes both tie shafts and their pattern shafts.

1:1 TIED-FLOAT DRAFTS
Weft-patterned cloth with tied floats based on a 1:1 ratio of pattern:tie warps were apparently adopted into Latvian weaving by the early 1900s. Figure 6.22 shows this structure. It has the advantage of needing only one pattern shaft per block of pattern. A 1:1 ratio produces very short patterning floats of weft which go over three warps before being tied down. Short floats may be desirable for

designs with narrow horizontal lines. In designs with wide areas of pattern, blocks can be repeated next to themselves so that the weft floats combine visually to form a broad horizontal band of pattern.

Before the early part of the twentieth century 1:1 structures evidently were not widely used in Latvia. One draft which did come into use there is known in North America as the *summer/winter* draft. In that draft, each four-end unit of the threading alternates one of its two tie warp ends between one of two pattern warp ends. Both pattern ends are threaded on one pattern shaft, as in fig. 6.22. Threading units can be repeated next to themselves. The threading diagram in fig. 6.22 is the

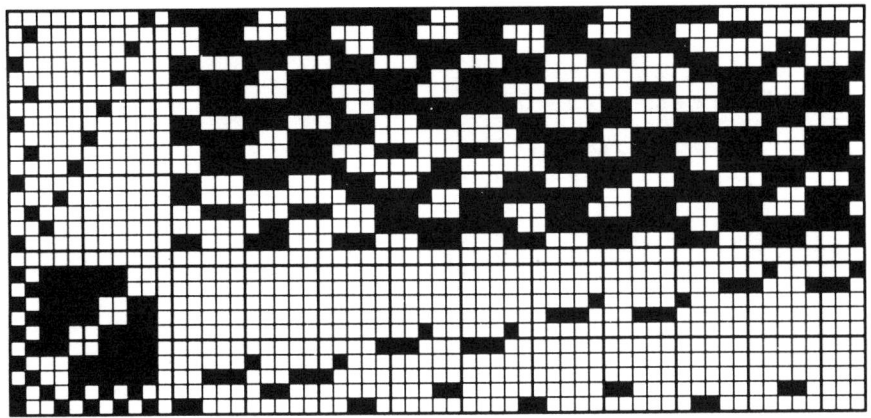

6.21. Four units of 12 threads each, showing how four blocks in fig. 6.19 weave on single-harness loom. Note the arranging of warp groupings in "tabby" sheds (2 left-side treadles) versus pattern sheds.

beginning of the design profile given in fig. 6.23. Four warp threads are substituted in the threading unit for each square block in the profile draft.

Tie-ups in this weave often are for double treadling, which reduces the treadle numbers. In double treadling only pattern shafts are tied

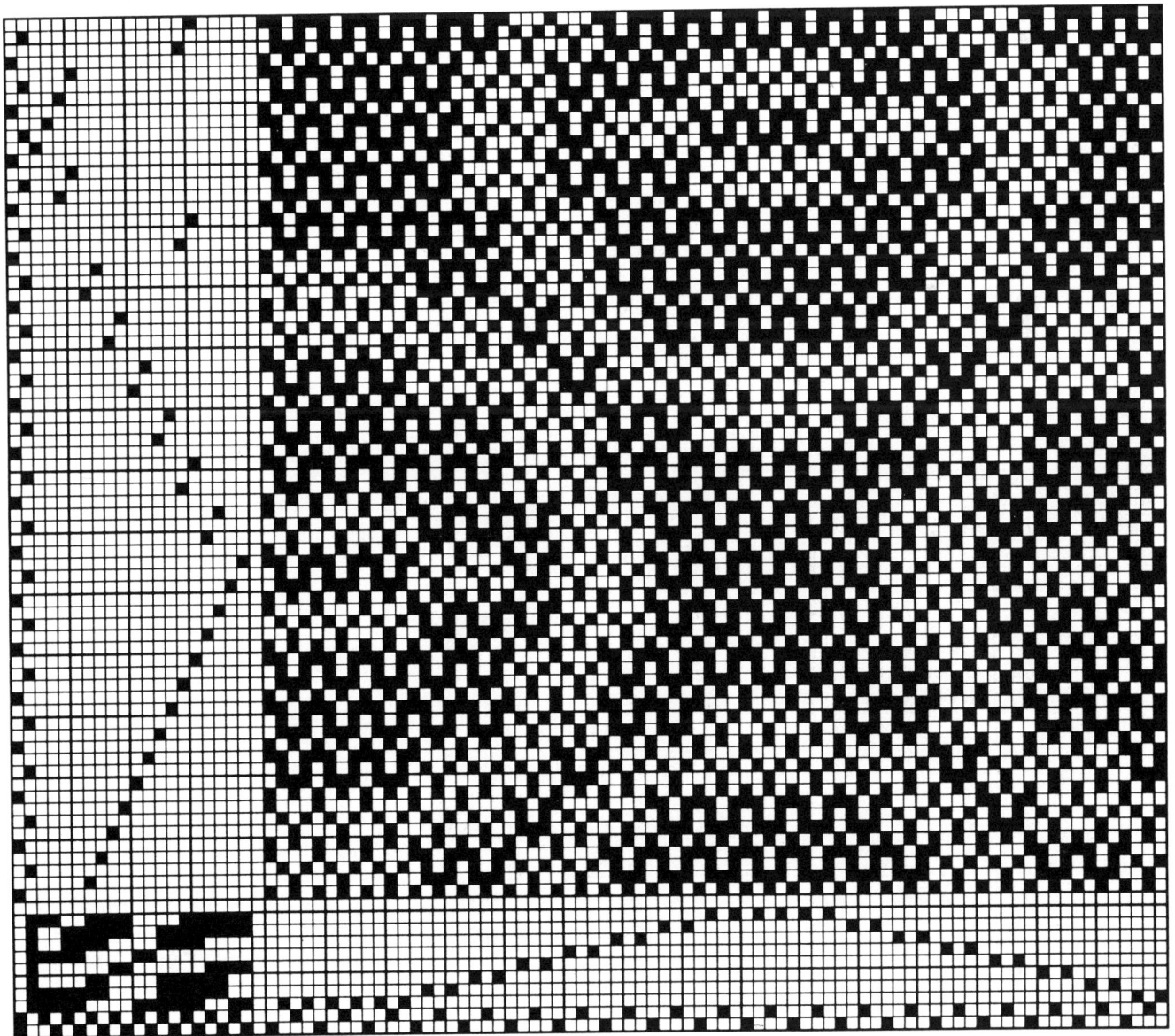

6.22. Draft with 1:1 ratio of pattern warps to tie warps. Single- treadling version of #217 in Ma.

6.23. Profile draft suitable for 1:1 tie draft shown in fig. 6.22, #216 in Ma.

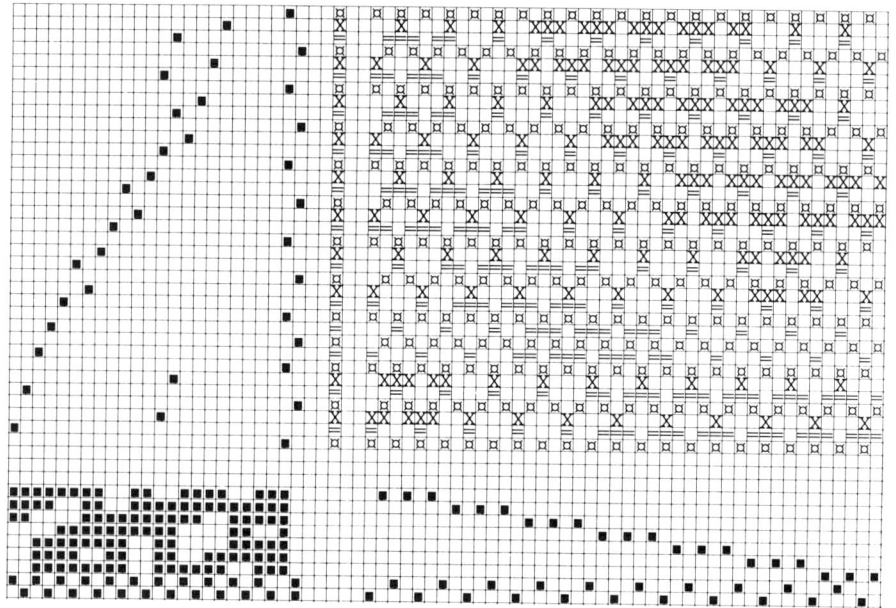

6.24. Draft with 1:1 ratio of pattern:tie warps, with uneven number of pattern ends per design block, based on #227 in Ma. Weft color order indicated beside treadling and described on p.93.

to pattern treadles, and the two tie shafts each have a treadle of their own. Actual treadling for the pattern weft pick combines one tie shaft's treadle along with the appropriate treadle tied to the background's pattern shafts. Underneath the supplementary-weft floats, the ground cloth is woven in plain weave by alternating one shed consisting of all tie warps against one shed made up of all pattern warps. One plain weave pick precedes each pattern pick.

Variations from the above 1:1 draft with four warp ends per unit *(summer/winter)* may have an uneven number of pattern warp ends within each design block. Tie warp ends are threaded to maintain odd-even order on alternating shafts, as in fig. 6.24.

4:2 AND RELATED TIED-FLOAT DRAFTS

Blocks in the profile draft given in fig. 6.25 can be threaded to tied-float units with a different assemblage of the tie and pattern warps, as indicated in fig. 6.26. Here, the tie warps are paired, rather than occurring singly across the threading. Two shafts hold the tie ends and, as in the preceding weaves, two shafts are needed for each pattern block. A plain-weave ground lies under the supplementary pattern wefts and is woven by following each pattern pick with one of the alternating tabby picks. Pattern weft picks are tied alternately by the two tie warp ends. This particular treadling of the draft seems to be almost exclusive to Latvia. In neighboring Lithuania, the customary treadling raises only one of the tie ends for all pattern picks. This weave was also used in Estonia, to the north of Latvia, in the twentieth century. This versatile draft's origins are obscure and seemingly it is limited in distribution to only a few Baltic countries. See pages 162-163.

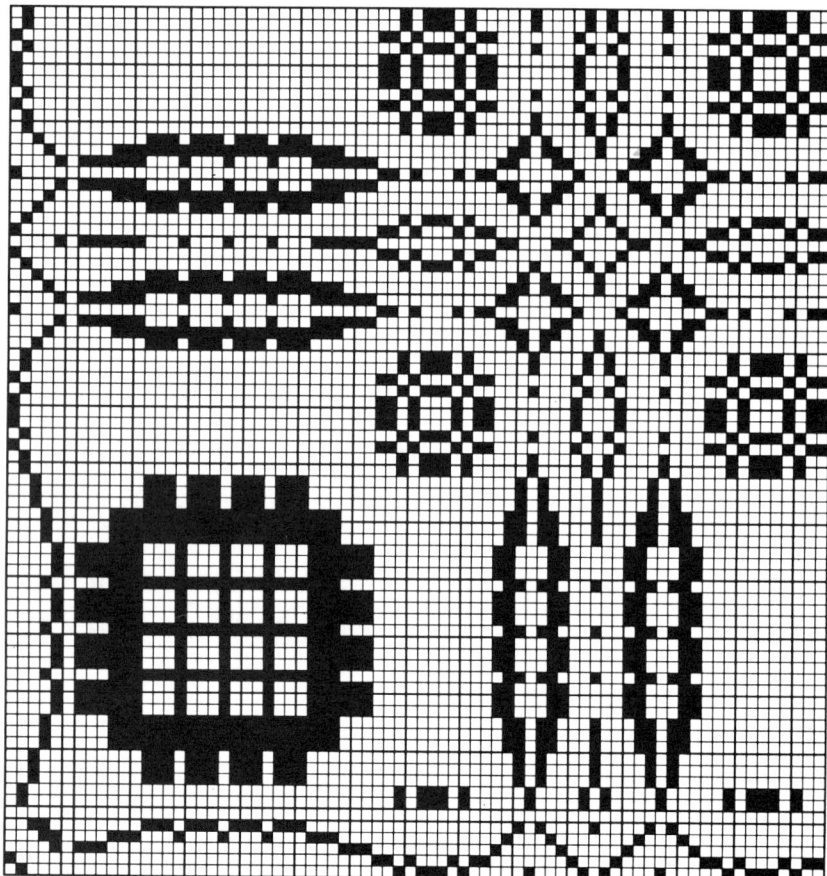

6.25. Five-block profile draft for bedcover in 4:2 units, based on #72 in Pa. Note that some blocks are combined in tie-up.

Uses. This paired-tie draft historically was used in western Latvia. (A. Alsupe, correspondence, 1987.) It often occurred with a 4:2 ratio of pattern warps to tie warps. Like the previous tied-float drafts, this one requires more than four shafts to produce designs of two or more blocks, so it was not readily used by home weavers. Most designs in the 4:2, 6:2, or larger-ratio drafts would require multi-shaft or double-harness looms.

Several blankets shown in *Latviešu tautas māksla,* a survey of old Latvian textiles, were woven in the traditional manner with wool pattern wefts floating over linen or cotton ground fabric. Figure 6.27 is the profile of a blanket from about 1900, woven in Bikava, a county of Latgale in eastern Latvia. The design was called *Leafy* or *Lapainis* design and was very popular not only in Latgale but also in southern Zemgale, Lithuania, and Poland. Threading units for the four-block draft are given in fig. 6.26.

In the twentieth century this paired-tie, weft-float weave was being used for bed coverings and blankets, usually in the 4:2 ratio draft. The pattern book *Paraugi audumiem* included several single-harness loom designs such as the one in fig. 6.28. Its units for four blocks are shown in fig. 6.26. Materials recommended for it were a warp of 40/2 linen with 18/1 linen weft, used single as tabby weft and double for pattern weft. If the weaver preferred cotton, a 20/2 warp, with a tabby weft of 8/1 linen, and a pattern weft of 18/1 linen could be used. In either case the warp was to be sleyed at two warps/dent in an 85 dent/10 cm (22 dent/inch) reed.

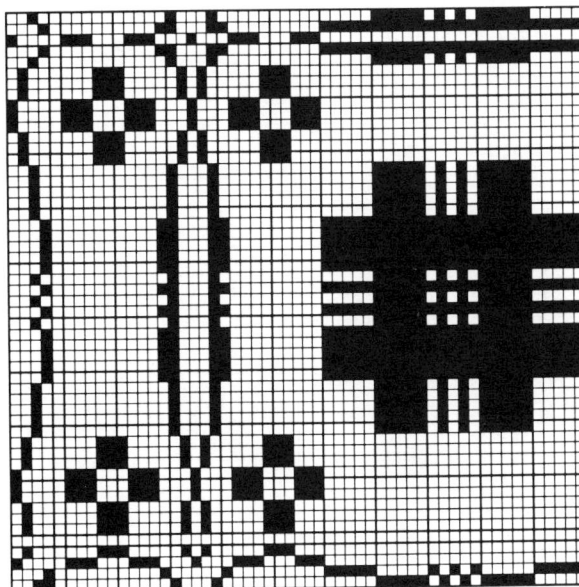

6.26. *Five threading units for blocks of profile draft in fig. 6.25.*

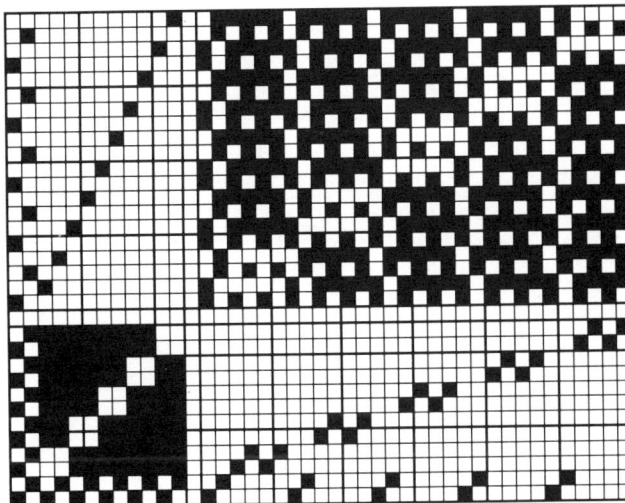

6.27. *Four-block profile draft of old blanket, #25 in Ltm. Blanket with the "Leafy" design, woven in Latgale, Latvia, circa 1900. In the Ltm photo, linen forms the ground cloth under blue wool supplementary weft floats.*

6.28. *Four-block profile draft for bed blanket, #73 in Pa.*

6.29. Blanket in intricate sun and morning-star block design with supplementary weft patterning. ca. 1930s; Latgale; 196 cm (77") L X 152 cm (60") W; warp, cotton, 3-ply, S-ply, black, used double; pattern weft, wool, 2-ply, S-ply, orange; tabby weft, same as warp, used single; 20 (10 double) and 4 single e/cm (25 double and 10 single epi); 6 pattern and 6 tabby p/cm (15 ppi). Collection of Mr. Peter Alexandrovitch. See Plate 23.

Pictured in fig. 6.29 and Plate 23 is a spectacular blanket woven on a 6:2 paired-tie draft. It was treadled in the Lithuanian traditional method, described on page 162. The geometric patterns are elaborately detailed, necessitating 88 blocks of the paired-tie draft. One full repeat of the design extends from the side border to the center of the blanket. There are borders along the sides only. One border is two blocks wider than the other. The end hems were woven without supplementary wefts, so they fold more neatly. Figure 6.30 shows one repeat of the central design and border. Figure 6.31 demonstrates how two individual blocks interlace. The black cotton warp is arranged so that single ends form the tie warps and doubled ends are the pattern warps.

6.30. Design of right border and one design repeat of fig. 6.29.

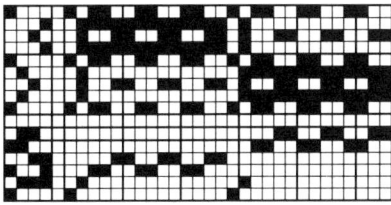

6.31. Two 6:2 units as woven for blocks in blanket, fig. 6.29.

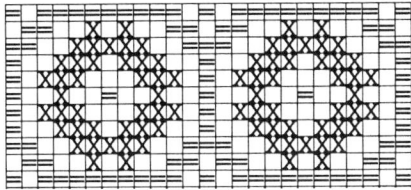

6.32. Design for blocks in three colors, combining supplementary weft and background colors. Based on #226 in Ma.

6.33. Table cover or sample of three-color design. 1939; Riga; 46 cm (18") L X 53 cm (21") W; 20 e/cm (50 epi); 40 p/cm (100 ppi); woven by Zenta Zvidris. Collection of Latvian Canadian Cultural Centre, Toronto, Ontario.

Tied-float Weaves with Two or More Supplementary Wefts

It is possible to weave more than one pattern weft between each pick of ground weft, thus adding further color components to a supplementary-weft design. While this technique could be applied to simple weft-patterned float structures, Latvian texts only discussed it in relation to tied-float drafts with pattern:tie ratios of 1:1, 2:1, and 3:1.

A block design in three colors – the warp color plus two others – is given in fig. 6.32. A warp and weft of one color form a plain-weave background, while the two patterning colors produce tied floats of supplementary wefts.

Figure 6.24 is a partial draft of one tied-float weave that can be used for the desired results. It is in a 1:1 pattern:tie warp ratio, with each block of the design threaded as three tie and three pattern warps. In treadling, the two plain-weave picks are used alternately between a cycle of two pattern picks. The pattern picks must

be treadled as a cycle to complete one horizontal design row. One pattern pick produces floats in certain areas of the design. The second pattern pick is treadled to give floats in other sections. Both pattern picks use the same tie warp within one cycle. If a horizontal row only has one pattern weft showing, the second color is not part of that cycle.

Uses. Most of the uses suggested in Latvian texts for weft patterning in two or more colors are on the *tied-Beiderwand* drafts with ratios of 2:1 or 3:1. Figure 6.33 shows such a cloth, woven in 1939 in Riga. The profile draft is given in fig. 6.34. Two repeats of each of its 2:1 units are given in fig. 6.35. The warp and tabby weft are 2-ply natural cotton. Throughout the piece the two pattern wefts that complete each cycle are selected from three different colors. The ground is tabby. This small item might have been a table cover or a sample woven in a craft school.

In the pattern book *Paraugi audumiem*, this weave in three colors is used for upholstery woven of 24/2 cotton warp and tabby weft, with

6.34. Five-block profile draft for fig. 6.33.

wool pattern wefts. The warp is sleyed two per dent in an 80 dent/cm (20/inch) reed.

Apparently weaving tied-float drafts with a ground cloth under pattern weft floats in two or more colors was a twentieth-century innovation in Latvia. This structure lent itself to the same uses as other tied-float drafts, namely, tablecloths, blankets, bed covers, and upholstery.

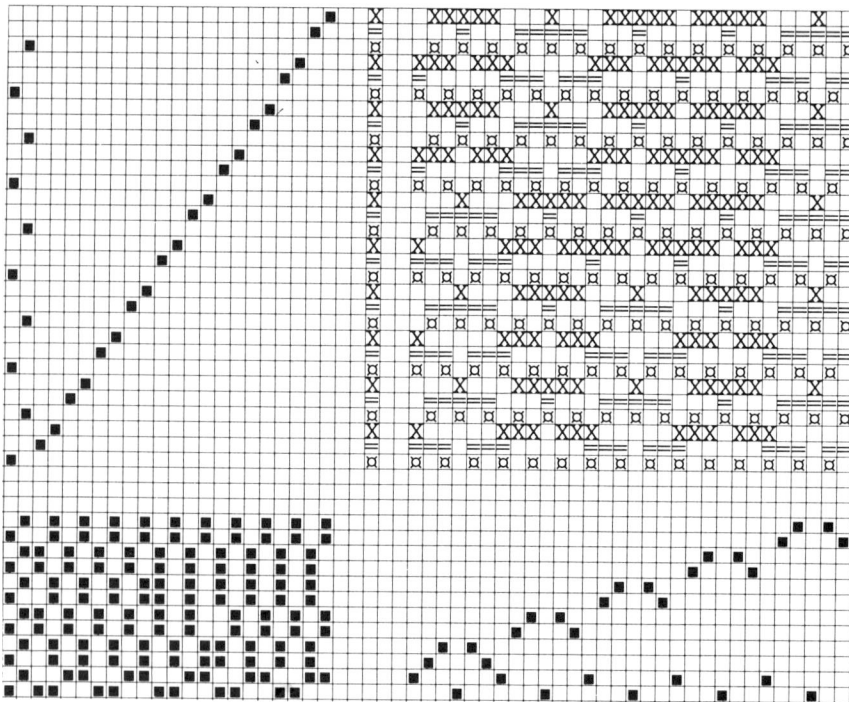

6.35. *Ten three-end units for the blocks of profile draft, fig. 6.34. Weft color order noted beside treadling.*

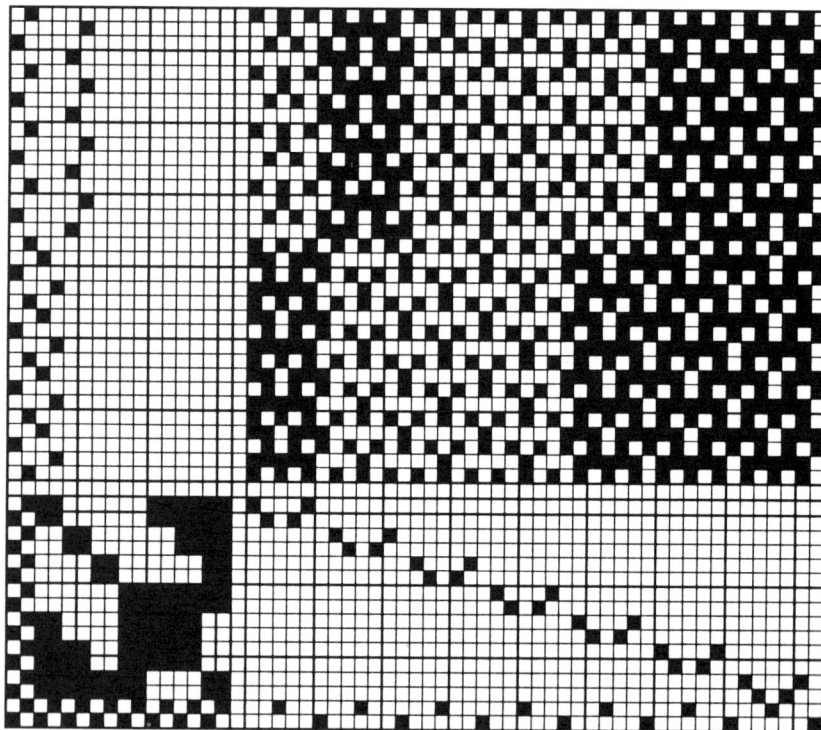

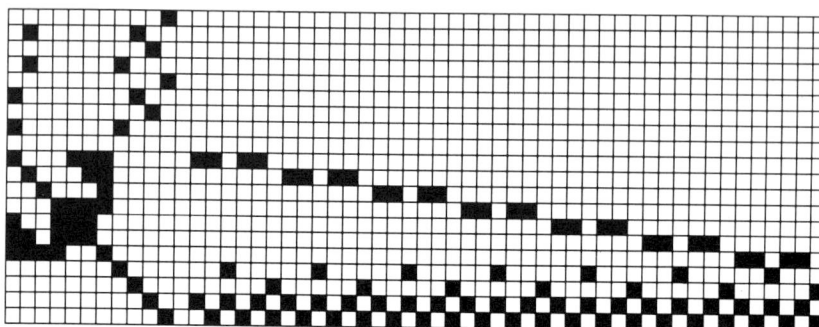

Tied-float Weaves on Double-Harness Looms

Tied-float structures have a variety of numeric relationships between the pattern warp ends and tie warp ends. These ratios determine whether or not to weave a particular structure on a double-harness loom. For certain drafts, that loom system can reduce the number of shafts and treadles needed for patterns. If the ratio of pattern ends to tie ends is 1:1, that is, one pattern end followed by one tie end, the weave is not practical to put on a double-harness loom. It will use just as many shafts for pattern blocks on the double-harness threading as on a single-harness threading. An example of this type of draft is the threading in fig. 6.24.

A double-harness loom is more desirable for weave structures of ratios such as 2:1, 3:1, 4:1, 4:2, or 6:2. In these ratios the group of pattern warp ends which adjoin each other and form a pattern block can all be threaded on one pattern shaft. Besides the front harness, a double-harness loom needs only one rear shaft for each block of pattern. The double-harness threading thus reduces the total number of shafts needed for a draft.

On a single-harness loom, each pattern block requires at least two or more shafts, depending on its ground weave structure. Most tied-float weaves in Latvia had a plain-weave ground cloth which meant that two pattern shafts were needed for each pattern block. For example, fig. 6.36 is a draft for 2:1 *tied-Beiderwand* weave, which has a plain-weave ground. There are two shafts for each pattern block so that the two plain-weave sheds can be formed, and there are two shafts for the tie warps of each block.

6.36. *(above left) 2:1 tied-Beiderwand draft for single-harness loom, with six warps per unit, based on #222-b in Ma.*

6.37. *(left) 2:1 tied-Beiderwand draft for double-harness loom, with six warps per unit. Tie warps are threaded through both harnesses. #222-b in Ma.*

TIED-FLOAT WEAVE

Directions are for a loom whose rear shafts have an unbalanced, rising shed action. This weave was usually drafted for countermarch or perhaps a dobby-type pattern harness. The front, ground shafts have counterbalanced action (from a roller system) of shaft 1 versus shaft 2. Ground cloth is in plain weave.

1) Make a profile design using blocks, including the "threading," "tie-up,"and "treadling" orders, as in fig. 6.39.
2) Choose a tied-float weave structure with a pattern-to-tie warp ratio greater than 1:1 for the actual cloth, for example 2:1 tied-Beiderwand.
3) Draw out the threading draft on graph paper. The lower two rows represent the long-eyed heddle shafts for plain-weave ground cloth. Two of these produce plain weave. In this example, fig. 6.37, they are marked so that all warps pass through the shafts alternately on 1 and 2.
4) Indicate tie shafts on next rows above the long-eyed heddle shafts. These have short-eyed heddles and are part of the rear harness. Most Latvian tied-float weaves used two tie shafts, as in tied-Beiderwand. Enter marks for the tie warps on the appropriate shafts, leaving spaces between the ties for the pattern warps. In fig. 6.37, two spaces are needed for each group of pattern warps between tie ends.
5) Indicate pattern shafts. The upper rows are the rear, pattern shafts with short-eyed heddles. One rear shaft is needed for each independent block of pattern in the design. Substitute a series of warps (in this example, two) for each pattern block, putting the warps on their appropriate pattern shaft's row on the graph paper. Figure 6.37 indicates this. When actually threaded, each block's adjoining warps can all pass together through one pattern heddle and thus time is saved in threading.
6) Check that each warp passes through one short-eyed heddle shaft and one long-eyed heddle shaft, and that pattern warps have separate vertical columns from tie warps.
7) Arrange the tie-up of shafts to treadles.

  a) Tie *pattern treadles* (rear harness) so dark blocks of the profile's design mean pattern wefts show over sunken warps, and white blocks are raised warps. There is one pattern treadle per horizontal row of pattern.
  b) Tie *tie-treadles* (rear harness) to the two tie shafts, treadles 8 and 9 from left in fig. 6.37.
  c) Tie *ground treadles* (front harness) to the two front, long-eyed heddle shafts for plain weave. These two shafts include all warps, even the ties. They are on the two right-hand treadles, 10 and 11 from left, in fig. 6.37.

8) Arrange the *treadling order,* which follows the design's block combinations, by substituting:
  a) pattern treadle A + one tie shaft's treadle - use pattern weft.
  b) front, ground shafts' tabby treadle 1 - use ground weft.
  c) pattern treadle A + the alternative tie shaft's treadle - use pattern weft.
  d) front, ground shafts' tabby treadle 2 - use ground weft.

This treadling series should weave one block in height with appropriate warp sett and weft sizes. The series may be repeated with the same or with a new pattern treadle. All four picks of the series should be completed before changing to a new pattern treadle.

ALTERNATE THREADING

An alternative, standard threading in Latvia for the double-harness loom placed the tie warps through only short-eyed heddles rather than both short-eyed heddles and long-eyed heddles. Figure 6.37 shows such a draft with the tie-up and treadling accommodating the new threading. This threading reduced the number of times the tie warps were threaded through a heddle, and therefore saved set-up time. Plain-weave ground was formed by two treadles tied to combine the tie shafts with the long-eyed heddle shafts (third and fourth treadles from right in fig. 6.38).

It is unclear from Latvian drafts whether in this set-up the tie shafts with short-eyed heddles were typically part of the front or rear harness. Either association would work, as long as the tie shafts could move independently of each other and of any other shafts. The texts vaguely imply that only ground shafts were on the front harness.

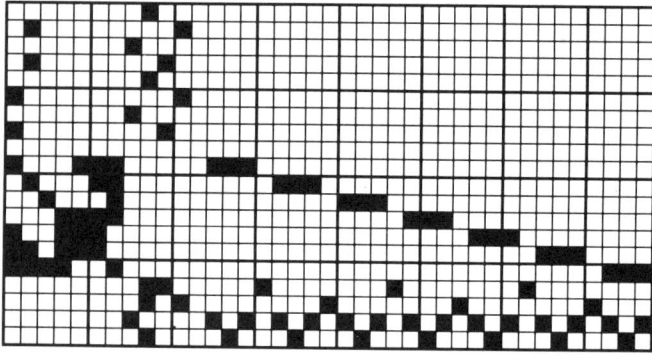

6.38. 3:1 tied-Beiderwand draft for double-harness loom, with four warps per unit. Tie warps are threaded through one harness. #223 in Ma.

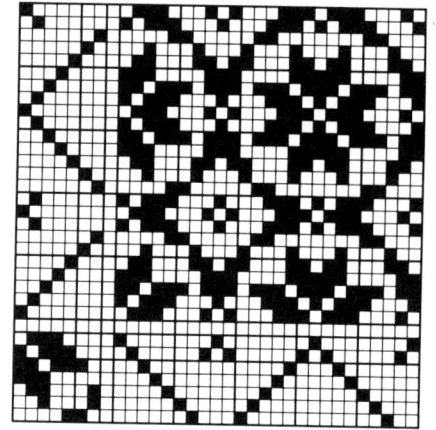

6.39. Profile draft for double-harness pattern, #221 in Ma.

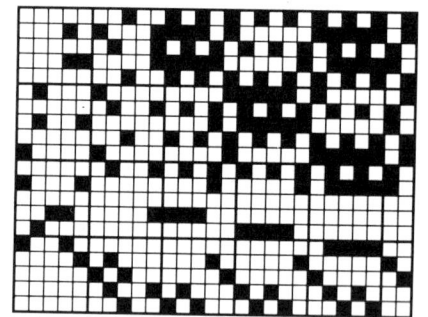

6.40. 4:2 paired-tie draft for double-harness loom, #173 in Ap.

The same 2:1 draft threaded on a double-harness loom uses only one rear shaft per block of pattern, plus two shafts for tie warps, and two ground harness shafts in front. The tie warps may or may not be threaded through the long-eyed heddle shafts, as in figs. 6.37 and 6.38. Both of these drafts show double-harness tie-ups and threadings of the single-harness units given figure 6.36. Figure 6.38 also shows a 3:1 ratio which, due to the wider pattern units, uses only one threading unit per block for the same block pattern as served by fig. 6.37.

As the number of pattern blocks in a tied-float weave structure rises there is a corresponding increase in advantages of the double-harness system. When weaving with a low total of pattern blocks, the reduction of pattern shaft numbers may not be necessary or beneficial for the following reasons:

• a single-harness, multi-shaft loom is generally less difficult to thread than a double-harness loom;

• a single-harness loom puts less strain on the warp threads than a double-harness loom;

• in either system there always are two or more shafts used for the tie warps, and a double-harness loom needs shafts for the ground harness, so only pattern shaft numbers are reduced by a double-harness system;

• the double-harness system may involve modifying up the loom to handle both harnesses.

Eventually there comes a point where multi-block designs requiring a large number of shafts and/or treadles on a regular loom may only be practical to weave on a double-harness loom.

Uses. There were mainly two kinds of structures used in Latvia for double-harness weaving of cloth with tied floats of supplementary weft. The first is *tied-Beiderwand,* commonly used in ratios of 2:1, 3:1, and 4:1.

One unusual example of tied-Beiderwand from the late 1800s has mixed ratios, featuring morning star motifs in a border of 3:1 blocks and a round central design of 7:1 blocks. (Stepermanis, No. 59, 1961-67.)

The second supplementary-weft draft often used on double-harness looms is the *paired-tie weave* with even number ratios of 4:2 as in fig. 6.40, 6:2, 8:2, or even 10:2.

Occasionally tied-float drafts were modified to give a ground structure other than plain weave, such as in fig. 6.41. Here the ground weave structure is 2/2 twill controlled by the four front shafts with long-eyed heddles. If hung on rollers, these shafts would be arranged so that shafts 1 and 3 were counterbalanced and shafts 2 and 4 were counter-balanced. In the rear harness are two shafts for ties and seven pattern shafts, all with short-eyed heddles. On a single-harness loom 80 shafts would be required to produce this design in tied-float, weft-patterned cloth on twill ground. A ground cloth woven in other than plain weave was somewhat out-of-the-ordinary in Latvia, so a draft such as this one was seldom seen.

Cloth with Supplementary-Weft Floats in Twill

By the 1930s, Latvian weavers were applying the supplementary-weft methods to twill threadings, also. The basic ground cloth of plain weave was woven on a twill draft. A supplementary weft was added on twill sheds, alternating with the tabby sheds of the ground weave.

A twill threading causes certain warps to be lifted on shafts currently being treadled, although those warps are secondary to the pattern itself at that point. The supplementary weft gets tied down incidentally by those warps, and the result avoids extremely long floats.

This interlacement apparently was of limited use in Latvia, showing up in a few ornamented fabrics such as aprons or blankets. One such blanket is the brightly-colored piece in Plate 4 and fig. 6.42. There are wide plain-weave bands of weft-faced

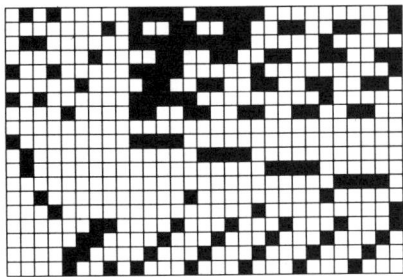

6.41. Double-harness draft with twill ground, based on #225 in Ma.

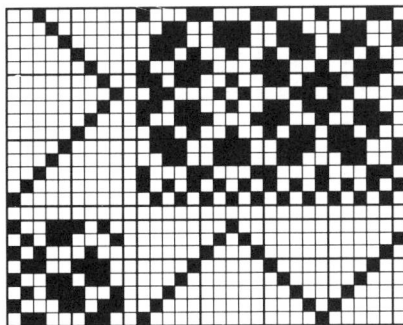

6.43. One and one-half repeats of eight-harness twill woven weft-faced with tabby picks and bands of tabby, as in fig. 6.41.

ribs, or repp, in either grey or lime green wool wefts. Narrower pattern bands are woven weft-faced on an eight-shaft twill threading as shown in fig. 6.43. Each pattern pick alternates with the two plain-weave sheds.

Four-shaft Blocks with Bound Floats

A four-shaft loom is not capable of loom-controlled turned-satin and turned-twill block interlacements which give fancy, attractive patterns. Yet Latvian homeweavers with four-shaft looms frequently desired showy block designs. Three solutions to that problem are based on weaves with a ground cloth patterned by floats of supplementary weft. All three can be thought of as block weaves because a pattern block can be repeated next to itself within the design. In actual threading, one or two warps intervene between blocks to catch the pattern weft floats and bind them down into the ground cloth. Unlike tied-unit weaves, these four-shaft weaves have no specific shafts serving only tie warps within each threading unit. Instead, repeats of one unit are separated by binding warps threaded on shafts borrowed from other units.

6.42. Mrs. Marija Upenieks wove this twill-patterned blanket of cotton warp and home-processed wool wefts. A detail is shown here. There is a center seam. ca. 1930; Latgale, County Daugavpils, Township Varkava; 208 cm (82") L x 131 cm (51.5") W; warp, cotton, 2-ply, S-ply, used double, black; weft, wool, 2-ply, S-ply, green, grey, yellows, browns; 8 (4 working) e/cm (10 working epi); 16 p/cm (41 ppi). ROM971.342.2. Gift of Mrs. Monika Gabrans, donated in memory of Marija Upenieks, donor's mother and the weaver. See Plate 4.

These weaves all are named with a descriptive word modifying the word for block, *drelli*: ribbed block weave, *vagotais drellis*; float block weave, *pārstaipu drellis*; and four-heddle block weave, *četrnīsu drellis*.

Ribbed Block Weave
Vagotais drellis

One choice for a Latvian weaver wanting to produce loom-controlled block patterns on four shafts was *vagotais drellis*, meaning "ribbed" or "furrowed" blocks. The name literally refers to the rows formed vertically by the interlacement of a warp, a tabby weft, and a supplementary weft for pattern. The cloth's texture looks like a neatly plowed field of parallel ribs.

Two design blocks are available in this four-shaft construction. Each block is a unit on two shafts. The threading is *on opposites*, with each unit's two shafts always threaded in a pair opposite to the other unit's two shafts. This is similar to *monk's belt* weave in English.

Figure. 6.44 shows a typical draft and its resulting interlacement. This example comes from directions for a tablecloth and napkins with weft of 20/2 cotton and warp of 40/2 cotton sett at 240 ends/10cm (60 epi). Threading of the first unit is on shafts 1 and 2 for eight warps, then two binding warps on shafts 3 and 4. This unit on shafts 1 and 2 can be repeated as often as necessary for the pattern as long as there are two binding threads after every eighth thread. Then the second unit of eight warps on shafts 3 and 4 is threaded, followed by two binding warps on shafts 1 and 2. Again this unit, and two binding warps, is repeated to the design block's width. Where the two units meet, the two warps that bind one unit's threading are part of the eight warps which form the new unit.

Four treadles are tied-up. Two tabby treadles weave plain-weave background. One pattern treadle is tied to shafts 1 and 2 and the other pattern treadle is connected to shafts 3 and 4. Depending on the sizes of threads used and the effect desired,

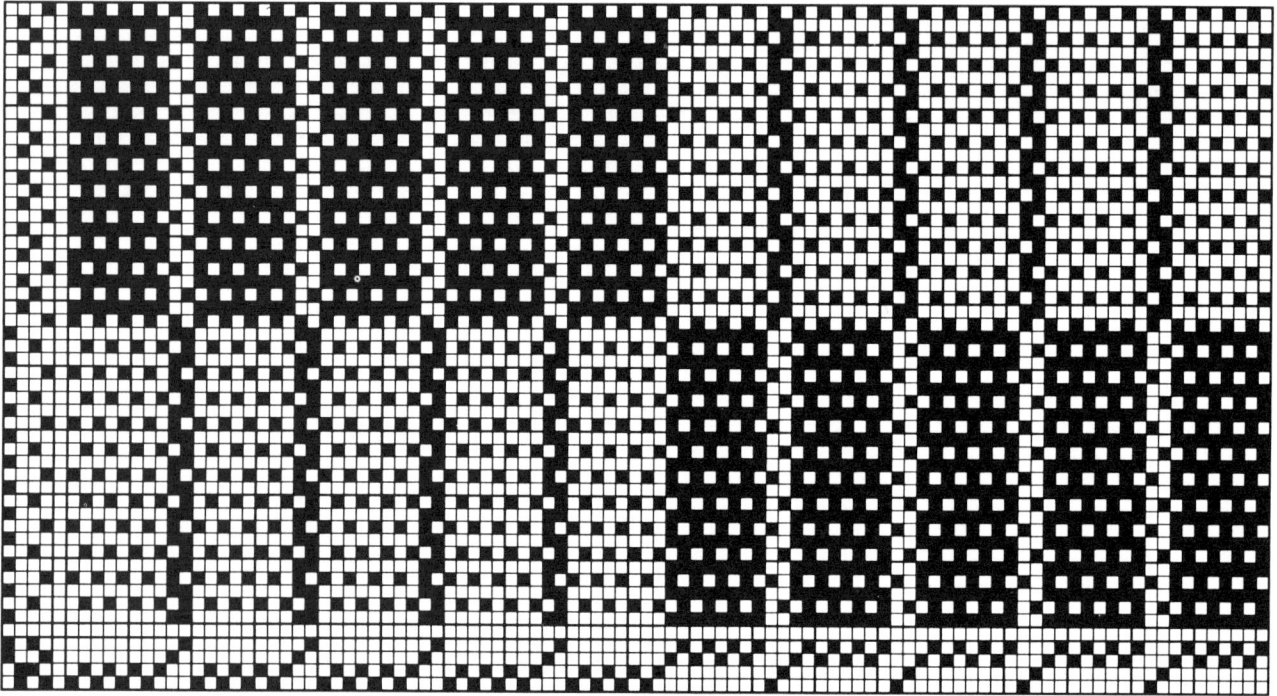

6.44. *Five repeats of each unit in ribbed blocks, #125 in Rga.*

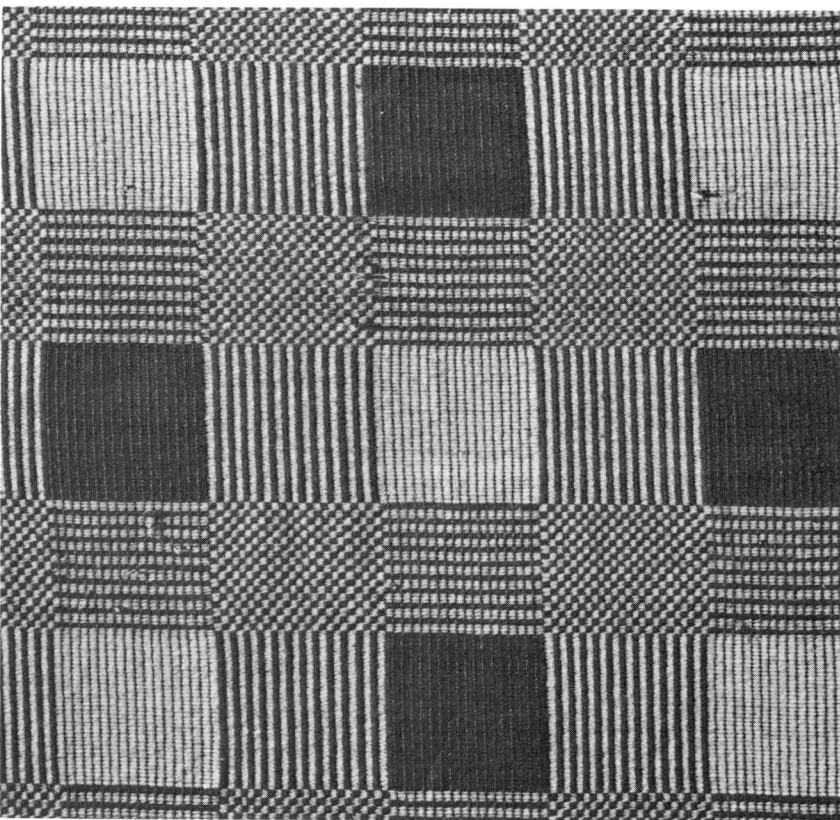

6.45. *Mrs. Lizete Zulerons created a stunning variation of a ribbed-block blanket for her hope chest when a girl of 17 in 1892. She spun wool from her father's farm in Zemgale, dying it pale orange. Lizete, who passed away just before her 100th birthday, was justifiably proud of her efforts. Her daughter-in-law was often told of how the blanket originated, and in turn she passed the information on to her daughter-in-law. Zemgale, County Bauska, Township Rundāle, farm Plavenieki; 160cm (63") L X 137cm (54") W; warp, cotton, 2-ply, S-ply, black; pattern weft, wool, singles, Z-twist, orange; tabby weft, same as warp; 24 e/cm (61 epi); 14 each tabby and pattern p/cm (36 each ppi). ROM972.57.1. Gift of Mrs. Lizete Zulerons. See Plate 14.*

either one or both tabby picks may follow a single pattern pick. A design block can be woven vertically as tall as desired by repeating the same pattern treadle between ground weave picks.

The twentieth century Latvian pattern books recommend avoiding narrow blocks or few repeats, which can make too busy a design. It is acceptable to use a number other than eight warp ends in the pattern ribs' threading, but the number used should be even and usually should apply to both units to maintain equal widths of blocks. The binding warps always total two.

The piece designed and woven by Lizete Zulerons in fig. 6.45 and Plate 14 is deceptively simple in appearance. Examination of the draft and treadling in fig. 6.46 shows her clever juxtaposing of blocks. Two unbound units alternate in wide stripes for half of the design's areas, while the other half is threaded to the usual ribs with tiny dividing stripes of binders. This creates four separate areas to thread horizontally and four to treadle vertically before the pattern repeats itself. The construction does not have a true tabby available due to skips in the odd-even order of warp threading. The finished design has a contemporary boldness and fascinating intricacy. The blanket drapes well and it shows years of service.

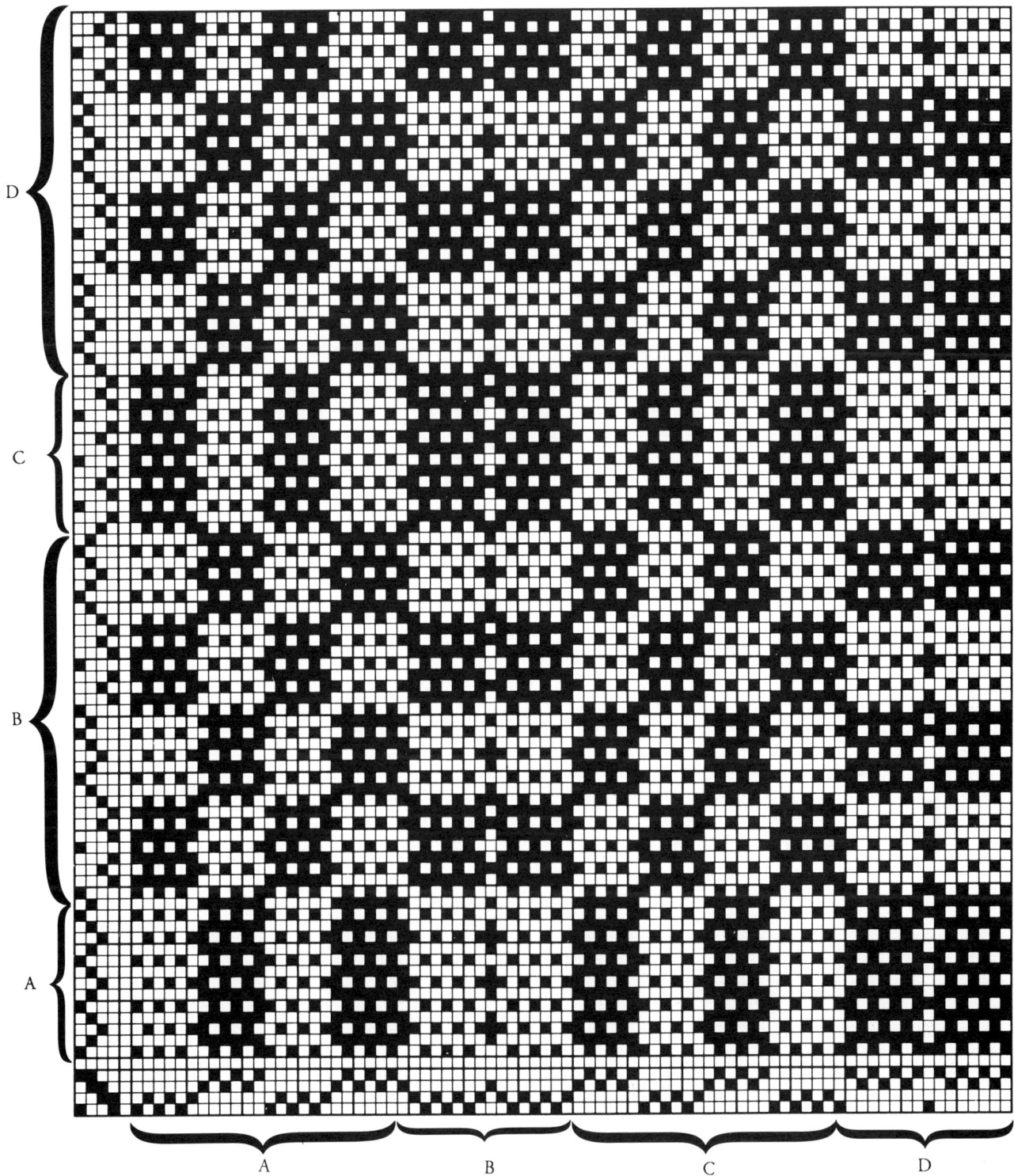

6.46. Four threading areas and four treadling areas of blanket in fig .6.45.

Blankets of ribbed blocks could also be woven weft-faced, with multicolored wool pattern and tabby wefts covering a linen or cotton warp. Ribbed blocks on four shafts were very popular over many years for blankets, tablecloths, napkins, towels, couch throws, and other simple patterned pieces.

Float-block Weave
Parstaipu drellis

Float-block structure allows the weaver with a four-shaft loom to design in up to four blocks of pattern. There are three threads in the interlacement: a warp, a ground weft of the same thread as the warp, and a supplementary weft that is usually colored and larger than the other threads. The supplementary weft floats on the surface in pattern areas and in non-pattern areas it either passes behind the cloth or interlaces in the ground weave. The ground weft interlaces in tabby order. A variant of this weave is called *overshot* in North America, where it is drafted differently from the Latvian system of blocks.

99

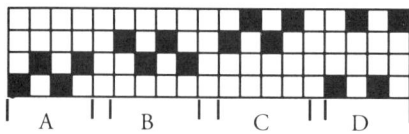

6.47. Four units for threading four-shaft float blocks, # 236 a-d in Ma.

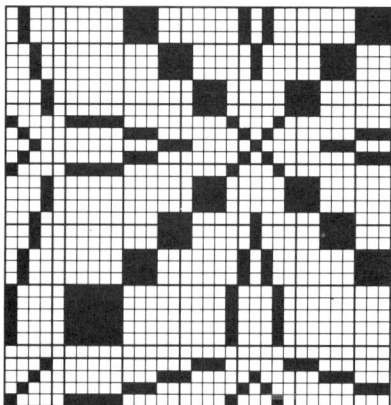

6.48. Profile draft for four-shaft float blocks, based on #237 in Ma.

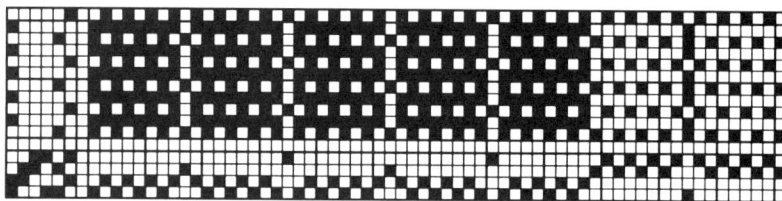

6.49. Beginning threading for fig 6.48 in float blocks with one binding warp between blocks.

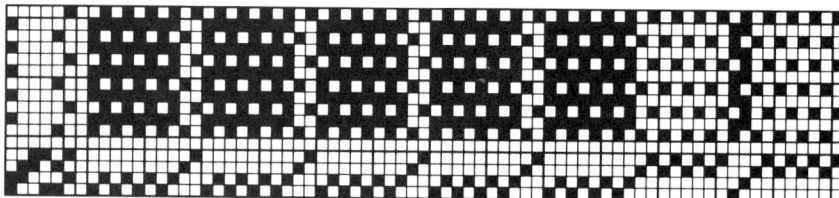

6.50 Beginning threading for fig 6.48 in float blocks with two binding warps between blocks.

6.51. Two placemats as cut from loom in the 1950's. 80 cm (31.5") L X 40 cm (16") W; warp, cotton, 2-ply, S-ply, natural; weft, linen, singles, Z-spun, natural; 18 e/cm (46 epi); 16 each tabby and pattern p/cm (41 each ppi). ROM973.37.8. Gift of Mr. Olgerts Grikis.

Threading retains an odd-even shaft sequence throughout the draft. Units are threaded as an even number of warps on two shafts per unit. Each unit starts on an odd numbered shafts: block A = 1,2; block B = 3,2; block C = 3,4; block D= 1,4. Frequently the units consist of four warp threads, as in fig. 6.47. If a design requires a larger pattern area than is practical for a weft float to cover, the pattern weft is bound down by one or two warps threaded on shafts not in the pattern unit. For example, when units of four warps are substituted in the blocks of fig. 6.48 there is an interruption in the float if it is longer than two A units (eight warps). The float may be bound with one or two warps. If with one warp, as in fig. 6.49, one shaft not in unit A is used. If further binders are needed, the other shaft not part of unit A alternates with the first binder's shaft. To retain the odd-even threading order, the units of A reverse their shaft sequence after each binding warp. This reversal is not necessary if two binding warps are added to the structure, as in fig. 6.50. The two shafts not used in the A unit are both used between A units. Binding warps are not inserted at the end of a block's threading, nor are they counted as part of the number of ends within a unit.

The regularity of float lengths can make float-block cloth look like a tied-unit weave, due to an equal base number in all threading units. There are two main threading differences between the two structures.

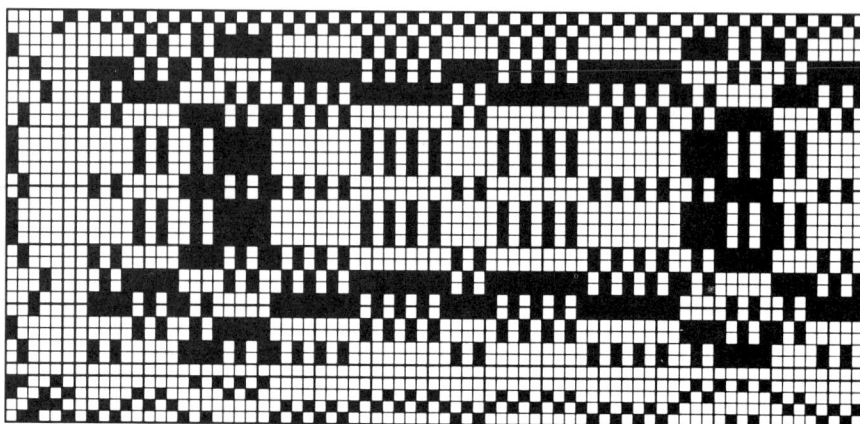

6.52. Typical units of four-shaft float blocks and their resulting visual asymmetry, from fig. 6.51.

• A tied-unit system reserves certain shafts only for tie warps while the float-block system uses all shafts as both pattern and binder shafts.

• The tied-unit system always includes the tie warps as part of each threading unit whereas the float-block system does not. It is possible to combine different blocks in a tied-unit design, e..g. A+B, while in the float-block structure only one block of design, e.g. A or B, can be woven at any one time.

Float blocks have six different sheds, four for pattern and two for tabby. The pattern treadles are tied up as in 2/2 twill weave. Treadle order depends on the desired design. One tabby weft pick always alternates with one pattern weft pick.

Each threading unit starts on an odd numbered shaft, so it is easy to make a draft for a float-block threading. In actual weaving the equal length of units becomes altered by the way some units incorporate one or two binding warps from neighboring units. This leads to asymmetry in a pointed pattern.

Figure 6.51 shows a pair of placemats as taken from the loom. Their draft in fig. 6.52 typifies regular units of float blocks. Asymmetrical lengths of floats occur between all mirror-image blocks beyond the single one on either side of the *rose's* center block. There also can be seen a narrow vertical band along only one side of the dividing area between roses, caused by a two-thread unit forming where two units threaded on opposite shafts meet. These aberrations were acceptable in Latvia because they were a natural part of a uniform drafting system.

Figure 6.53 pictures a float-block fabric wholly threaded on opposites. This threading accents the tonal contrast between neighboring blocks and reduces the number of imbalances present in a threading like the preceding one. In the profile draft, fig. 6.54, there are few places where adjacent units will share warp threads.

Uses. Float blocks have been popular in middle and Eastern Europe for a very long time. Weavers of Kurzeme, southern Zemgale, and Latgale made block patterns in untied, supplementary-weft float weaves for centuries. Simple versions were known in Latgale in the 1100s. Loom-controlled, float-block weave was within the realm of a farmhome weaver's four-shaft, counterbalanced loom. Over ensuing centuries the home weavers of Latvia often used float blocks to emulate the professional weavers' block patterns, which were woven in turned weaves on many shafts. Those early turned-weave patterns could be copied in float-block weave because blocks were not combined within a design.

In the late nineteenth century, float-block weave became very popular for day-blankets which covered the regular bed-blanket. In Vidzeme the blankets were of natural cotton ground cloth with pale linen pattern wefts. In all other areas of Latvia they were of dark colors in wool over a cotton or linen ground. Motifs alluding to leaves and flowers were often chosen.

For generations showy towels such as the one in fig. 6.55 were hung, often horizontally, on the walls of homes during special occasions. Natural colored, fine cotton warps, and singles linen pattern wefts were frequently chosen to give formality to the towels. In the towel pictured, there is a very slight deviation from maintaining regular units in the warp threading, making no tabby available.

6.53. *Half of coverlet in four-shaft float blocks of star pattern. 1922; Vidzeme, County Cēsis, Township Priekuli; 187 cm (73") L X 88 cm (34.5") W; warp linen, singles, Z-twist, partially bleached; pattern weft, linen, singles, Z-twist, natural; tabby weft like warp; 20 e/cm (51 epi); 14 each tabby and pattern p/cm (36 each ppi); woven by Julija Plucis. ROM 971.460.1. Gift of Mrs. Voldemars Brods, niece of weaver.*

6.54. *Profile draft for fig 6.53, threaded on opposites for weaving.*

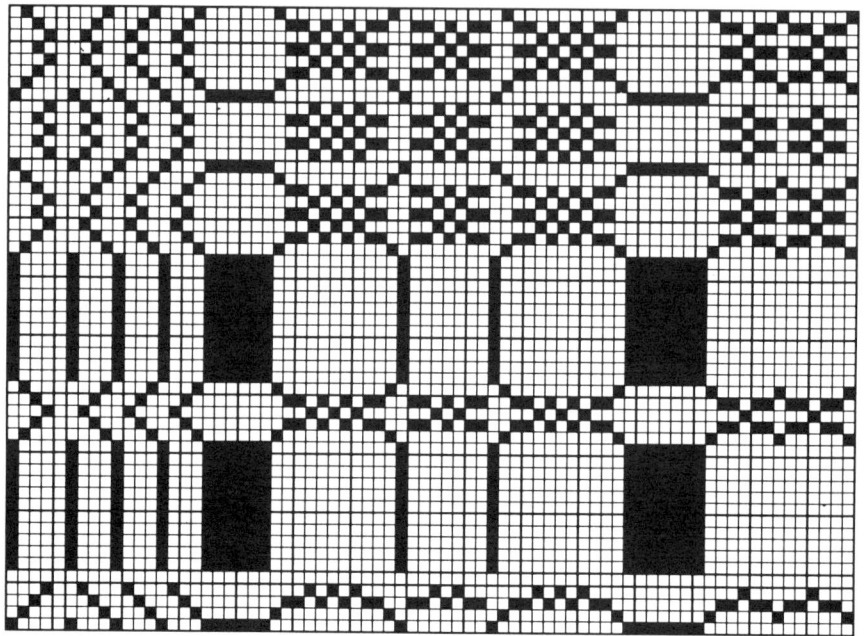

6.56. Profile draft for towel in fig. 6.55.

6.55. Towels were made in fancy patterns of four-shaft, float-block weaving by home weavers like Monika Alexandrovitch, who wove this one in the early 1930s. She trimmed it with complementing bands of crocheted lace as was characteristic in her home region of Latgale in the east of Latvia. 229cm (90") L X 33cm (13") W; warp, cotton, 2-ply, S-ply, natural; pattern weft, linen, singles, Z-twist, natural; tabby weft like warp; 24 e/cm (61 epi); 14 each pattern and tabby p/cm (36 each ppi). ROM990.20.3. Gift of Mr. Peter Alexandrovitch.

The change is so minor, however, that the profile draft in fig. 6.56 could be threaded with the units of fig. 6.47 for virtually an identical fabric. This profile is given to the center of the towel's design, and each unit is woven with four pattern and four tabby picks in alternation.

Another application of float-block weave appeared in the twentieth century. It can be seen in fig. 6.57. In their search for a nationalistic folk art, weavers revived the old peasants' *siena*, a straw mat hung on the wall for warmth. In its new form the decorative possibilities of the mat were emphasized. Figure 6.58 shows the draft for the mat in fig. 6.57, wherein the unit threadings are modified for symmetry in design.

Another minor change from traditional float-block weave in this piece is that both tabby picks intervene between the pattern wefts of straw, the straw weft being considerably larger than the fine cotton warp and tabby threads.

Four-heddle Block Weave
Cetrnīšu drellis
On first glance this appears to be the weave known as *crackle* in North America or *jamtlandsdräll* in Sweden. However, the Latvian version has a unique threading, treadling, and resultant structure. The weave uses

6.57. Wefts of straw were woven into fine cotton warps for pieces like this table runner/wall hanging. Ca. 1969; Kurzeme, Saldus; 140 cm (55") L X 60 cm (23.5") W; warp, cotton, 2-ply, S-ply, black; pattern weft, dried grass stalks, green and yellow; tabby weft same as warp; 6 e/cm (15 epi); 4 each pattern and tabby p/cm (10 each ppi); woven by Mrs. Hilda Kupes. ROM971.109a. Gift of Mrs. Velta Uiska, sister of the weaver.

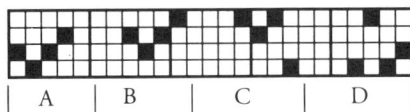

6.59 Four threading units of four-heddle block weave, #247 a-d in Ma.

two wefts, one like the warp for tabby picks and one which is coarser and of contrasting color for supplementary-weft floats of pattern. The Latvian threading units produce floats over one, three, or four warps. In North American *crackle weave* and Swedish *jamtlandsdräll* there are floats over one, two, or three warps. These different constructions result from contrasting methods of joining blocks during threading.

Figure 6.59 shows all four threading units. In fig. 6.60, the units are combined to form a motif.

6.58. One repeat of pattern in fig. 6.57.

Uses. The two-block version of this weave, fig. 6.61, was frequently used for towels, tablecloths, and napkins in stripe or checkerboard patterns.

A four-block towel of fine linen is shown in fig. 6.62. Its profile draft is given in fig. 6.63.

DRAFTING AND WEAVING

FOUR-HEDDLE BLOCKS

THREADING

- Four design blocks are possible, seen in fig. 6.59. Use at least two repeats of a block to have observable pattern-weft floats when woven.
- Use all four blocks, A-D, for a four-block design, as in fig. 6.60.
- Use blocks A, B, and C for a three-block design.
- Use the C block and a slightly altered D block as in fig. 6.61 for a two-block design.
- Always alternate threads between odd and even numbered shafts. Any four-thread unit can be repeated next to itself as often as desired, using all four warps of the unit.
- Within a unit the fourth warp is a *binder* for the patterning weft float.
- At the transition from one threading unit to the next one, drop the last warp end from the concluding unit's four warps. Dropping that warp maintains the odd-even shaft sequence between units.

Latvian books did not have examples of skipping a block, *e.g.* A to C without B in between. This could be done and the odd-even sequence still be retained if the last warp of the unit before the transition is not dropped. If only two blocks are threaded, the units in fig. 6.61 make an adjustment to the D units threading so no warps need be dropped at any transition.

TIE-UP

- Tie-up as for 2/2 twill with two tabby treadles included.

WEAVING

- Alternate tabby picks after each supplementary weft pick. See fig. 6.60.
- Pattern wefts float over three warps and are tied by a fourth warp within blocks.
- At the transition of one block to the next (for example, A to B) there is a four-end weft float, shown in fig. 6.60. The two-block units automatically make a regular weft float length at the transition from one block to the other, fig. 6.61.
- In any horizontal row two pattern blocks will both appear due to being inescapably linked via how the blocks are threaded and treadled. Blocks A+D, B+A, C+B, and D+C work together.

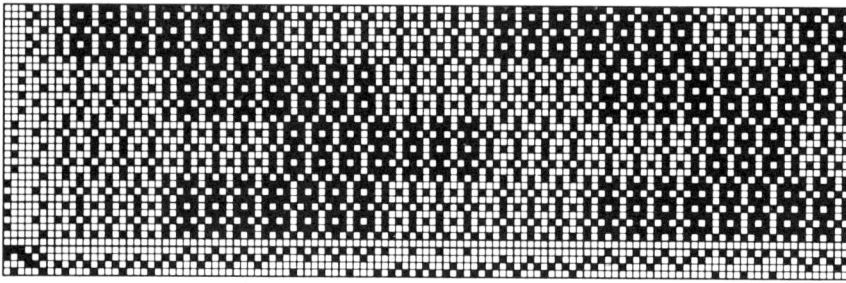

6.60. Four blocks threaded as four-heddle block weave.

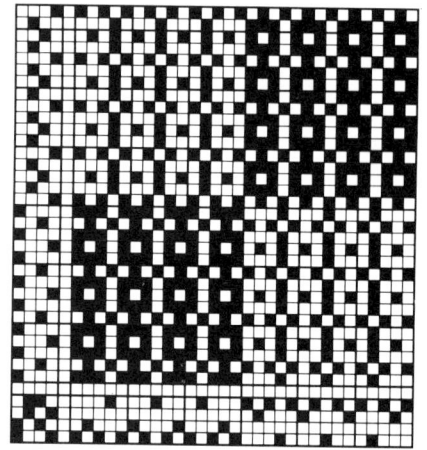

6.61. Threading for two units of four-heddle block weave, #150 in Ap.

Four-heddle block weave was somewhat limited in use in Latvia, being applied mostly in towels and tablecloths since the nineteenth century. Two-block patterns were the most usual, followed by four-block patterns. Three-block pattern designs were not often woven, possibly because planning good examples of such patterns is very difficult due to the way blocks work together.

Eight-shaft Float Blocks

The blanket pictured in figs. 6.64 and 6.68, woven about 1920 in Riga, is based on a structure evidently introduced to Latvia in the twentieth century. There is a ground cloth in tabby weave patterned by bound supplementary wefts. There are a number of threading and treadling errors in this piece, which apparently was an attempt to learn an unfamiliar weave.

6.63. Profile draft for towel in fig. 6.62.

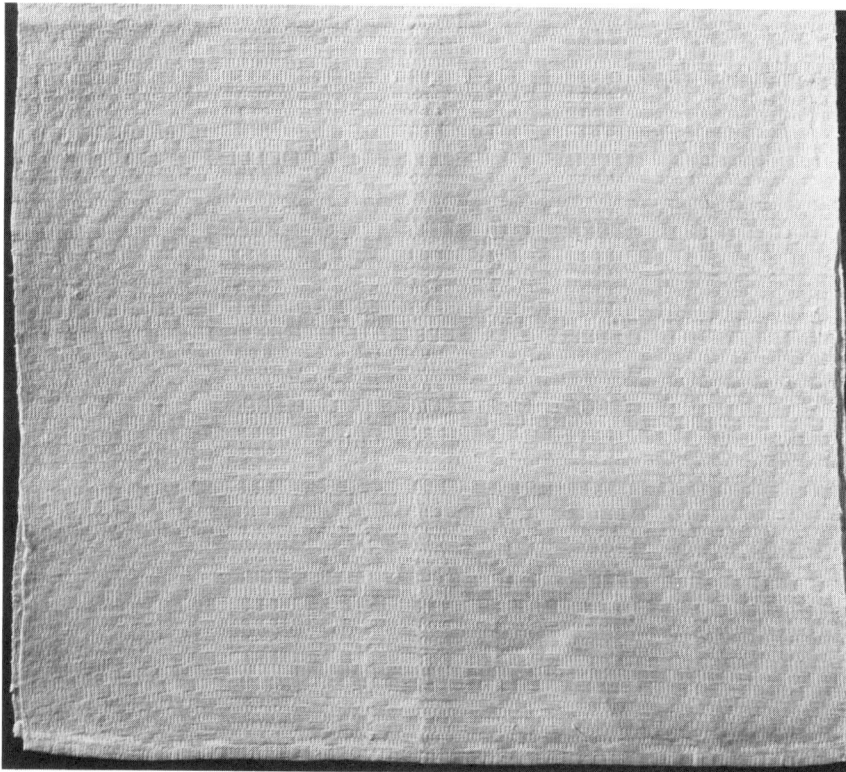

6.62. Four blocks were used for this linen towel, purchased in Kurzeme in 1938. The bleached white ground cloth originally displayed weft floats of a blue-green color, now faded to silver-grey, from bean flowers. It is woven with the knowledge of good patterning and the skillful control that distinguish an especially attractive fabric. Kurzeme, County Ventspils, Township Dundaga, farm Gabzbe; 130.5cm (51") L X 37 cm (14.5") W; warp, linen, singles, S-twist, bleached white; pattern weft, linen, singles, blue-green faded to silver; tabby weft same as warp; 24 e/cm (61 epi); 10 each pattern and tabby p/cm (25 each ppi). ROM971.333.5. Gift of Mrs. Elza Gustaus.

6.64. Blanket woven in two panels on eight shafts with float blocks. 190 cm (80") L X 128 cm (50") W; warp cotton, black; pattern weft, wool, singles, Z-twist, dark purple faded to tan; tabby weft like pattern weft, black; 14 e/cm (36 epi); 12 each pattern and tabby /cm (30 each ppi). Collection of Latvian Canadian Cultural Centre, Toronto, Ontario. Another view is shown in fig. 6.68.

Figure 6.65 is the profile draft for one repeat, and fig. 6.66 is a partial threading draft of how the units should be treated. Examples and drafts for this weave are rare in pre-World War II Latvia. The piece shown probably reflects how weaving information was disseminating within the Baltics at that time.

Float blocks of this nature were woven in neighboring Lithuania and the rules for their formation are described on page 106. (Čepelyté, 1960. Researched by M. Kati Meek.)

Cloth Reinforced with Supplementary Wefts

Apakšaudi

Reinforced weave, or *pastiprinātie audumi*, evidently was uncommon enough among early twentieth century Latvian handweavers so that definitions of what constituted that type of cloth vary in their textbooks. Generally in Latvia, reinforced cloth could be described as a fabric with an extra set of elements (warp or weft) added for strength. These extra threads are held in place by occasional interlacements with the front fabric and are inconspicuous from the front. There is also some reference to reinforced fabric with two sets of elements in both warp and weft, which in North American terms is a true double cloth.

As a functional fabric structure without patterning beyond stripes, the cloth apparently was of very limited interest to Latvian handweavers. There also was the drawback that it required more treadles, frequently twice as many as the original structure's number.

Reinforced weaves wove a main cloth in a simple structure such as four-shaft straight or broken twills of 2/2 or 3/1 interlacements. The supplementary weft used as reinforcement was usually coarser than the yarns used as main warp and weft. Figure 6.67 is one of the few reinforced cloth examples from handweavers' pattern books. It is a 1930s draft for a bed blanket, with a 12/2 cotton warp and two or more colored wool wefts. The warp is

6.65. Four-block profile draft for blanket in fig. 6.64.

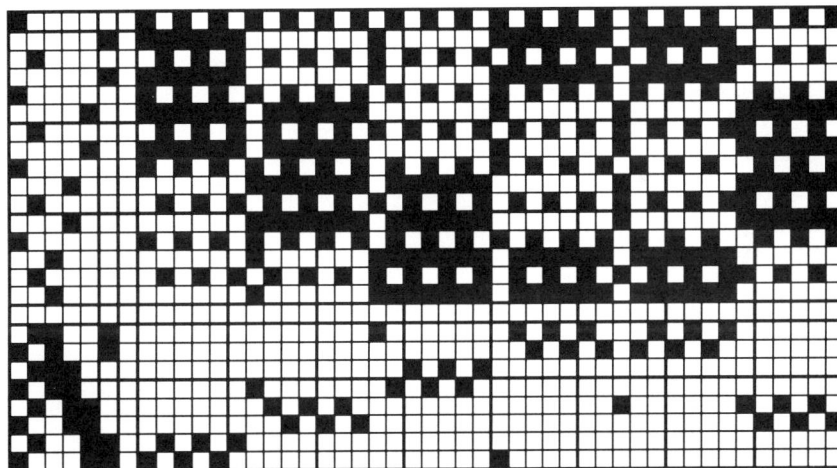

6.66. Example of threading of single and repeated units in blanket in fig. 6.64.

threaded single in the heddles and double in a 60 dent/10cm (15/inch) reed. When woven weft-faced in alternating picks of two colors the fabric has differently colored sides, each in satin weave. The original satin's five shafts are sufficient for the reinforced cloth and twice the treadle numbers are needed.

Uses. The additional threads in this weave contributed weight and density, characteristics desirable in fabric for heavy garments like capes or coats, for upholstery, and for bed blankets.

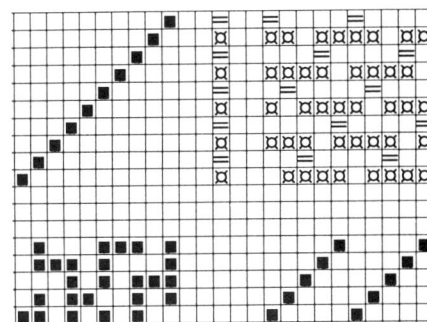

6.67. Draft for satin cloth reinforced with supplementary weft also in satin weave. Different weft colors indicated by symbols beside treadling order. #117 in Rīga.

LITHUANIAN-STYLE EIGHT-SHAFT FLOAT BLOCKS

THREADING

- Two separate shafts form threading units for each of four blocks:
  block A = shafts 1 and 2;
  block B = shafts 3 and 4;
  block C = shafts 5 and 6;
  block D =shafts 7 and 8.

- Repeat these two shafts for a given number of times, e.g., a total of six or eight or 10 warp threads, for one threading unit.
- Blocks A and C are opposites and blocks B and D are opposites.
- Retain the odd-even shaft sequence for plain weave in the threading.
- Use binding warp ends to prevent long floats of supplementary wefts when a threading unit is repeated next to itself. The binder in any block is one warp from the opposite block's pair of shafts, whichever shaft retains the odd-even shaft sequence. See fig. 6.6.
- Place a binding warp after each block unless the block sequence has adjacent, opposite blocks, in which case no binder is used.
- A threading unit may have an odd or even number of warp ends.

If there are an even number of units in a pattern repeat, the units may have odd or even numbers of warps (not counting binding warps).

If there is an odd number of units to a pattern repeat, each unit should have an odd number of warps (not counting binding warps)

WEAVING

- Tie treadles as in fig. 6.6. .
- Use two wefts, a ground weft for plain weave and a supplementary weft for patterning. Treadle as in fig. 6.6.
- Blocks weave in pairs: A+B, B+C, C+D, D+A. Weave blocks to square the pattern.

6.68. Eight-shaft float block weave for a blanket in the popular "Leafy" pattern. See fig. 6.64 for details.

CHAPTER SEVEN

Compound Weaves
with Supplementary Warps

Just as in the supplementary-weft weaves described in *Chapter Six*, the following supplementary-warp interlacements contain three sets of elements. Two form the ground warp and ground weft of the main cloth. In this case, the third set is an extra set of warp threads added for the purpose of either patterning or strengthening the main cloth.

Warp-patterned Cloth
Velku rakstoti audumi

If an interlacement of warp and weft threads becomes background to a second, supplementary set of warp elements, the floats of the extra warp threads can be used to add pattern. The fabric looks as if cloth patterned with supplementary wefts has been turned 90 degrees.

Looms. Multi-shaft looms are required to reproduce any but the simplest patterns in supplementary-warp weaves. It appears that these weaves came into use in Latvia along with multi-shaft looms in the late 1800s. The weaving method lends itself to either countermarch or draw looms, because the same supplementary-warp pattern shafts are raised for several picks in succession. Since supplementary-warp patterning requires the use of two warp beams and many shafts, it was of limited occurrence in Latvia. This type of fabric was more likely produced by professional weavers. It might also have appealed to them because only one shuttle is needed during weaving, producing a pattern in a time-saving manner.

Uses. Elaborately-patterned wool blankets were a frequent use of this weave. One particularly elaborate pattern can be seen in fig. 7.1 and Plate 16. The 32-block profile draft from this handsome blanket can be seen in fig. 7.2. It has a plain-weave base. Doubled threads function as single pattern-warp ends. Figure 7.3 shows fourteen of the units as threaded. Rather than having repeated pattern shafts, each pattern unit has one pattern shaft with two threads in it. The doubled pattern warp ends emphasize the traditional

7.1. Warp-patterned wool blanket with moon cross design, one of two woven around 1910-1920 and owned by a family from Ventspils, Kurzeme. During World War II the family was sent to Siberia and gave the blankets to a friend before leaving. After the war that friend gave one of the blankets to her homeless cousin. This blanket shows little wear and retains its silky hand. Its main sign of age is that the brown pattern is now on a background of beige rather than the original salmon color. 157 cm (62") L X 171 cm (67") W; warp, wool, 2-ply, S-ply, brown (used double), light beige; weft, same as light beige warp (used double); 6 light and 12 brown (12 working) warps/cm (30 working epi); 12 p/cm (30 ppi). ROM972.64.1. Gift of Mrs. Velta Mednis. See Plate 16.

7.2. *Profile draft for one and one-half repeats of moon cross design in fig. 7.1.*

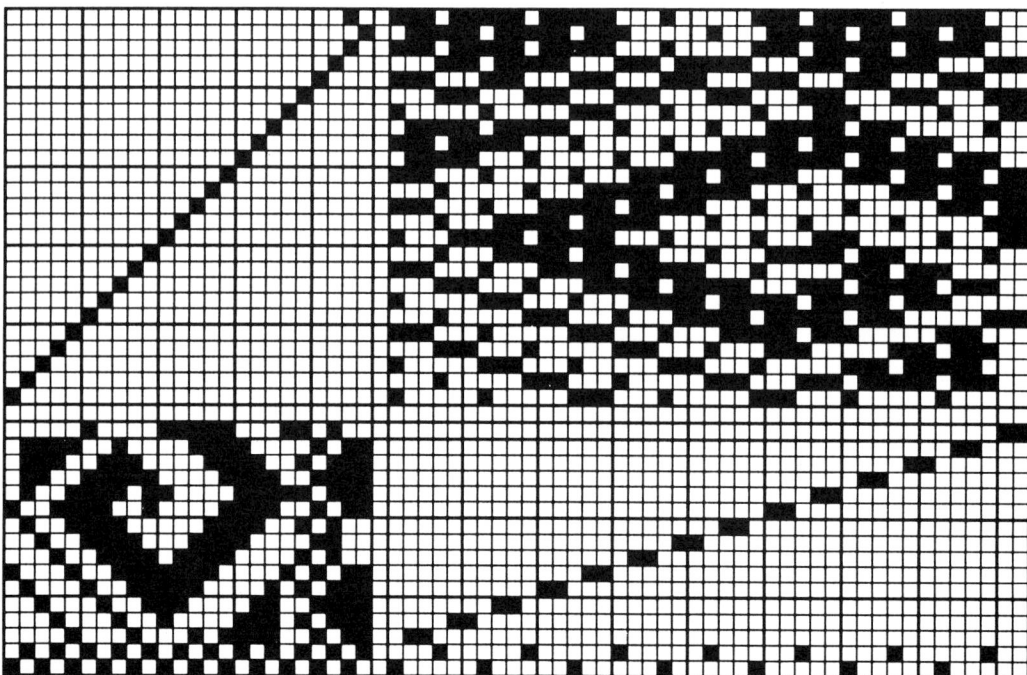

7.3. *(left) Threading draft for 14 units in profile draft, fig. 7.2.*

SUPPLEMENTARY-WARP PATTERNING

DRAFTING

• Make a design such as the profile draft in fig. 7.4, representing a fabric's pattern blocks. There are as many pattern shafts as the total number of design blocks.

• Decide on the ground cloth. It is often plain weave, for which two ground shafts are needed. If the warp is sett very closely, plain weave may be put on four shafts to reduce friction. Place the ground warp on the front shafts of the loom, the pattern warp on the rear shafts.

7.4. Profile draft suitable for supplementary-warp patterning, #233 in Ma.

THREADING

• In a threading draft, substitute several warp threads for each block of design.

In fig. 7.5, each design block from the beginning of fig. 7.4 is replaced with an eight-thread unit in which pattern and ground warps alternate 1:1. It is also a common practice to thread units with uneven numbers of pattern ends, always retaining the 1:1 pattern:ground warp ratio. Pattern warp ends may be single or multiple threads.

• Use two colors of threads, one for ground warp and ground weft, a second for pattern warp.

Make the two warps separately and wind onto two warp beams or, for looms with one beam, weight the pattern warp independently. The pattern warp interlaces less frequently than the ground warp and there is unequal take-up between the two.

TREADLING

The treadling combines pattern shafts and ground shafts on each pick.

• If plain weave forms the ground cloth, use each of the two sheds alternately with the current pattern shed as in fig. 7.5. Keep pattern shafts up for several picks in succession to create visible floats on the surface of the fabric. Avoid long floats.

7.5. Threading draft for fig. 7.4, using four patterning warp ends per unit.

7.6. *Profile draft of blanket patterned with supplementary warp, #41 in Ltm, Vol. II.*

motif of moon crosses. The fine wool threads pack in firmly to create sharply defined patterning.

Using sixteen blocks for its design, the wool blanket profiled in fig. 7.6 originated in Zemgale in 1920. Figure 7.7 shows one repeat of the 18-shaft threading. This blanket might have been woven on a 16-shaft loom equipped with a second harness attachment in front of the pattern shafts. Regular, short-eyed heddles would have served on the two tie shafts.

Long-eyed heddles are not necessary for supplementary-warp weaving because the advantages of combined sheds are not applicable to this technique.

Figure 7.8 pictures an open weave doily from a twentieth-century pattern book. Supplementary-warp patterns and canvas weave alternate in vertical stripes. In fig. 7.9, a partial draft is given, showing the threading for each band. Double treadling would be an efficient method to use for this fabric.

Combinations

Twentieth-century Latvian weavers occasionally wove dramatic combinations of supplementary-weft patterning with supplementary-warp patterning. Figure 7.10 is a design draft from one such example, intended for use at the corners of a tablecloth and napkins. The *Paraugi audumiem* pattern book recommends using a ground warp and weft of 40/2 linen (used double), with a supplementary warp and weft of 40/2 linen or cotton. Warps are dented 2/dent for ground areas and 4/dent in pattern areas, in a 100 dent/10cm (25 dent/inch) reed. The threading and partial treadling are noted in fig. 7.11. Double treadling would be helpful in executing this weave.

7.8. *Detail of doily with vertical bands of canvas and plain weaves between bands patterned with supplementary warps. Warp, 20/2 cotton and 16/2 viscose (used double for pattern); weft, 20/2 cotton, 12 ends and picks/cm (30 epi and ppi). Based on #128 in Pa, woven by Jane Evans.*

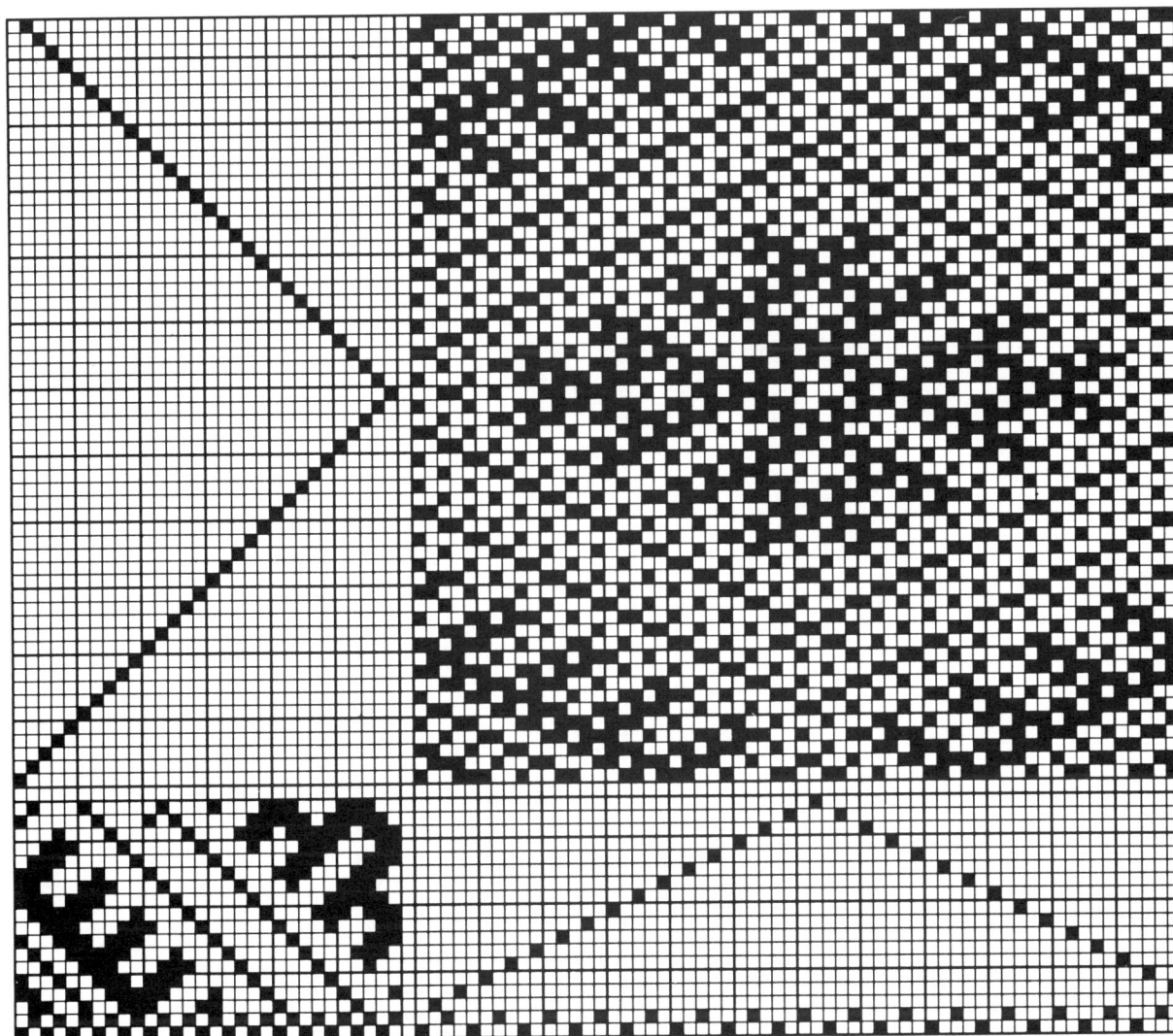

7.7. Threading draft of one repeat of units in design of fig. 7.6.

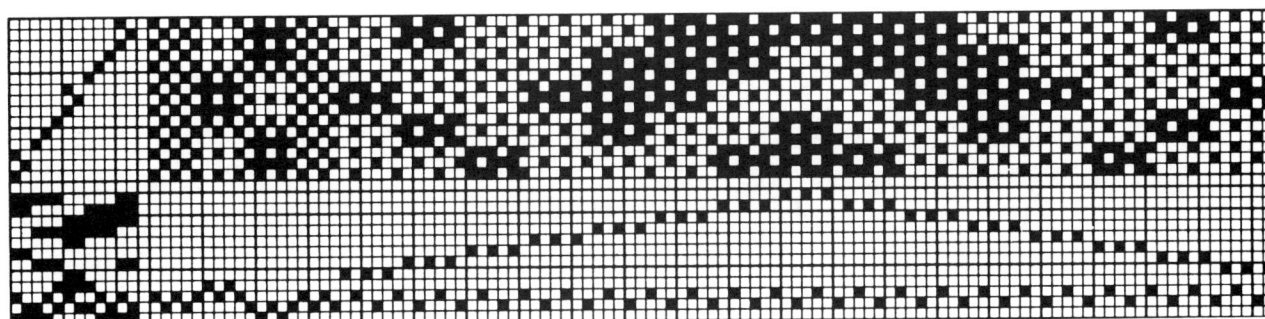

7.9. Threading draft on 12 shafts for vertical bands of plain weave, canvas weave and supplementary-warp patterning in fig. 7.8. An overplaid could also be added by including colored warp and weft stripes, as suggested in Pa.

Cloth Reinforced with Supplementary Warps
Apakšvelki

Cloth reinforced with the addition of supplementary warps shares many characteristics and uses with cloth reinforced with supplementary wefts. An extra set of elements interlaces at the back of a non-patterned, simple weave such as twill. The supplementary, reinforcing threads add weight and durability without distorting the appearance of the front surface.

Figure 7.12 shows the draft for a warp-faced fabric in 3/1 straight twill, backed with a supplementary warp woven in 1/3 twill.

The large number of shafts which may be needed, along with the lack of pattern showing on the cloth and the possible need for two warp beams, diminishes the attraction of thiscloth for home weavers. Certainly in Latvia it was of limited appeal and even in the twentieth century was only found in text books rather than pattern books for home weavers.

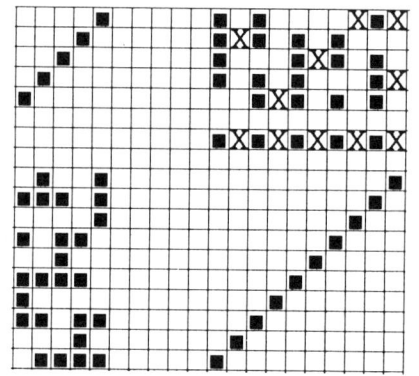

7.12. Supplementary warp used as reinforcing warp. Both warps indicated by symbols above threading, #169 in Ma.

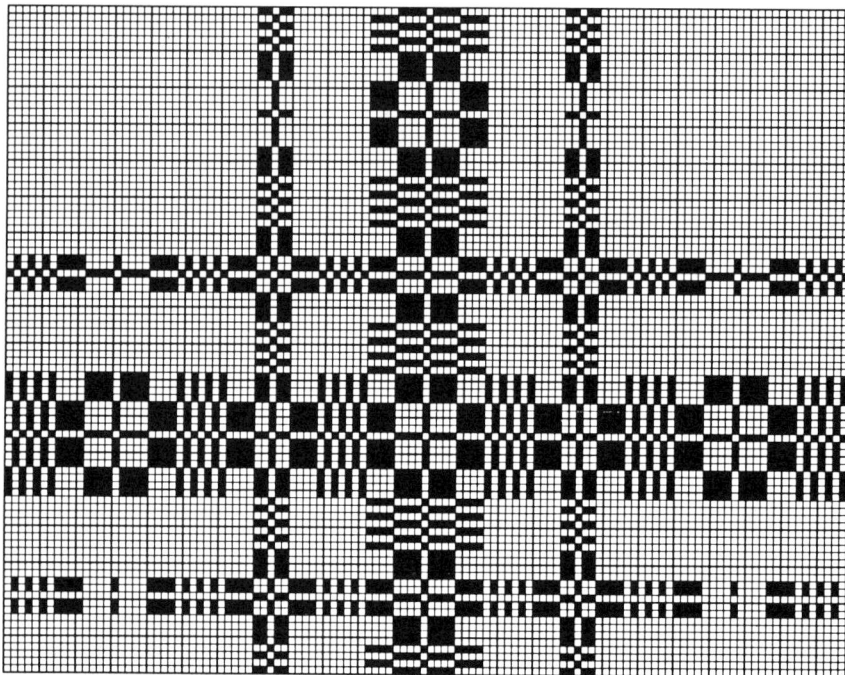

7.10. Corner of design which combines supplementary warp and supplementary weft patterning, based on #76 in Pa.

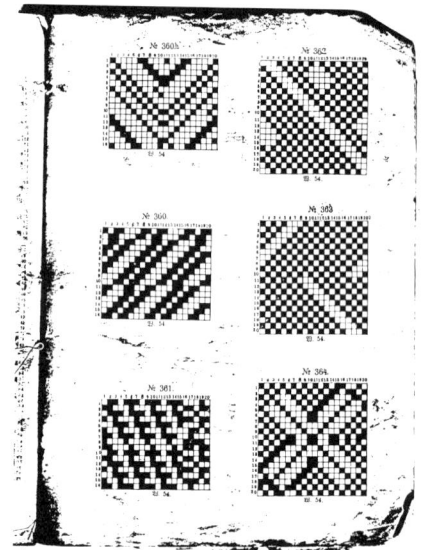

7.13. Page of drafts from Latvian weaving text, Wednesday Morning, by P. Viļumsons.

7.11 Partial threading draft for design in fig. 7.10.

CHAPTER EIGHT

Compound Weaves
with Complementary Wefts

The following compound weaves have three or more sets of threads. There are two or more weft sets, called *complementary* because they are co-equal in the construction of the cloth. All of the complementary wefts are needed to complete the weave's interlacement. No one weft is supplementary to a ground weave in this construction.

Complementary wefts weave in a cycle known as a *pass,* within which each weft pick is called a *lat.* Fabrics woven with complementary wefts often have two, three, or more wefts (lats) per cycle (pass). The reciprocal movements of the wefts usually form a *double-faced* fabric on which the front and back surfaces have the same structure. Wefts which show in areas on one surface of the fabric will appear in the opposite areas on the reverse surface.

These weaves are based on twill or tied-unit threadings. Unless otherwise noted, the following threading drafts indicate color of weft threads by the use of several symbols placed between the threading and treadling. Weft color alternation is indicated by symbols beside the treadling. Warp threads are indicated by a blank square, as in fig. 8.1.

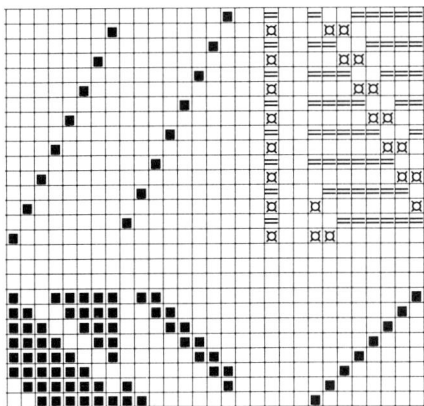

8.1. Corkscrew weave draft treadled "on opposites." Two wefts are indicated by symbols beside treadling.

Weaves Based on Twills
Weft-faced "Corkscrew" Weave
Slīpais ripss

Slīpais ripss or *sloped repps* are a type of compound weave derived from twills. There are two sets of wefts, usually in different colors, and one set of warp threads in this weft-faced structure. Using two colors accentuates the all-over twill design. The twill lines form ribs on the cloth, hence the name *repp*. In English this weave is called *corkscrew twill.*

Designs for corkscrew twills contain twill progressions of threading rather than blocks. The single set of warp threads is threaded to a straight or pointed twill which most frequently is based on an odd numbers of shafts.

There are several possible relationships between the two weft interlacements. They may be treadled wholly *on opposites,* as is shown in fig. 8.1. They also may be treadled to slightly offset their junctions. One example of this is shown in fig. 8.2. In all cases, both wefts are co-equal in the construction, and neither weft forms an independent ground weave with the warp.

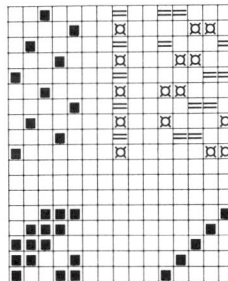

8.2. Corkscrew weave draft treadled with one warp raised on two consecutive sheds.

Uses. Corkscrew twills require multishaft looms for most applications. In twentieth century Latvia these weaves were generally only used for fine woolen suiting and coat fabrics. Although they produce quite attractive and functional fabrics, these twills were of limited appeal to the majority of home weavers.

Weft-faced Patterned Repps
Rakstoti ripsaudumi

Handweavers in Latvia often sought weaves with which pattern motifs could be developed. One particular type of corkscrew twill attracted the attention of home weavers for this reason. Called a *patterned repp derived from twill,* it has complementary wefts in two colors woven weft-faced over a single set of warp threads. The hidden element remains as single threads throughout, therefore excluding it as a true repp weave by Latvian textbook definition. See *Chapter Four.* A ribbed surface does result from this weave, however, so it was commonly called a *repp.*

These "repps" have a pointed twill threading draft and tie-up, usually on an even number of shafts. Each weft follows a twill sequence along diagonal lines. The twill treadling order for the first weft (normally in the dominant color) determines the motif. A second weft (background color) alternates with the first weft, always in the shed exactly opposite to that of the first weft.

8.3. Detail, weft-faced patterned repp rug woven from draft in fig. 8.4. Warp of singles tow linen used triple, sleyed three working ends per cm (8 working epi). Wool wefts (or rags) in two colors cover the warp. Designed and woven by Jane Evans.

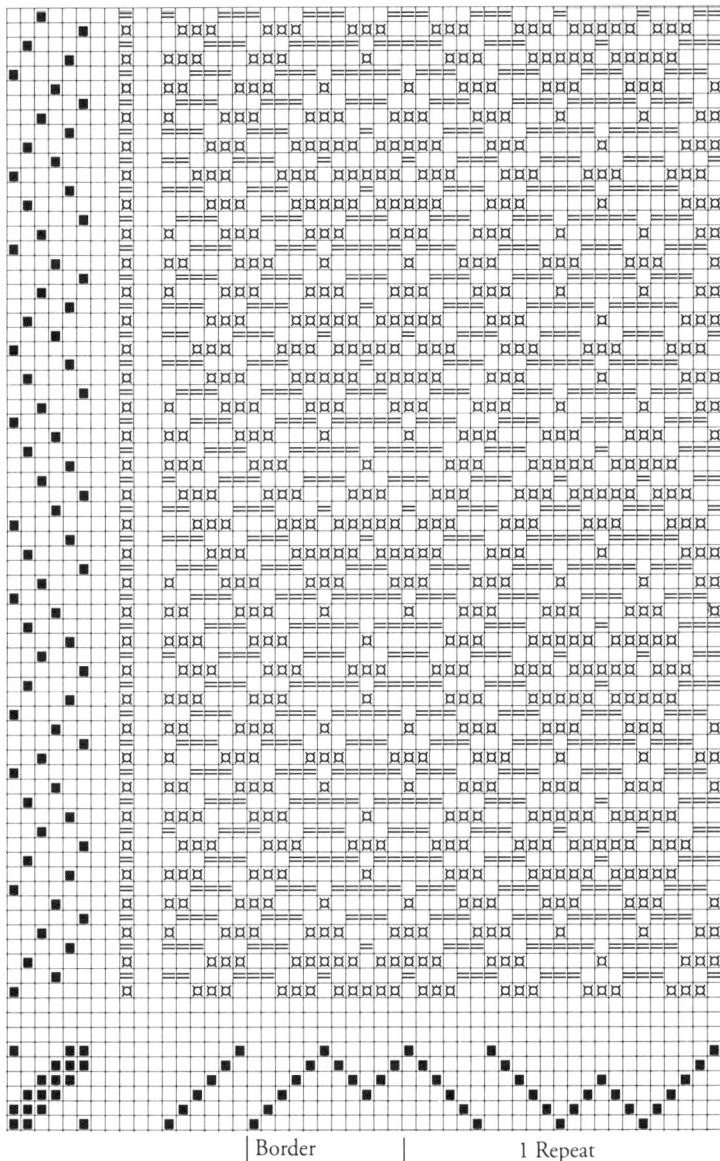

8.4. *A twill threading draft from the 1930s for border and one repeat of weft-faced patterned repp rug, #143 in Rīga. Alternate weft colors indicated by symbols beside treadling.*

8.5. *Detail of a blanket woven in the late 1920's of linen and wool on a family farm in Latgale. Wool processing and dyeing were done on the self-contained 25 hectare (60 acre) farm. Marija Upenieks, the weaver, learned to weave from her mother. The pattern, a four-shaft pointed twill treadled on opposites, probably was chosen through discussions with other women who came to confer in the evenings. They did not use books, but shared their own array of information. Mrs. Gabrāns, the weaver's daughter, recalls the piece serving as a bedspread as well as a blanket. 213 cm (84") L X 128 cm (50") W; warp, linen, 2-ply, S-ply, mixed natural and partially bleached threads; weft, wool, singles, Z-twist, green, yellow, red, blue; 5 e/cm (13 epi); 36 p/cm (91 ppi). ROM971.342.1. Gift of Mrs. Monika Gabrāns, in memory of Marija Upenieks. See Plate 12.*

DRAFTING AND WEAVING

WEFT-FACED PATTERNED "REPP"

- Begin with a point twill motif, for example fig. 8.4. The weft-patterned "repp" threading is the same as the original twill threading, with the warps spaced in the reed to allow the weft to pack in and cover the warp threads.
- Retain the original twill tie-up.
- Treadle the original twill treadling as the first pick of weft, which is in the pattern color.
- Treadle a second weft pick in a contrasting color on the treadle tied up exactly opposite to the first pick. This is *weaving on opposites*, one possible interlacement of weft-faced corkscrew twill.
- Continue to treadle the original twill's sequence as the first pick of each opposite pair of wefts.
- If part of the pattern needs vertical elongation, repeat any pair of picks several times.

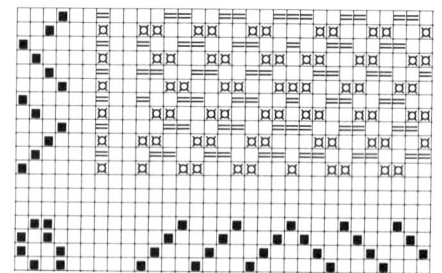

8.6. *One threading repeat of point-twill draft for fig. 8.5. Symbols beside treadling indicate alternate weft colors.*

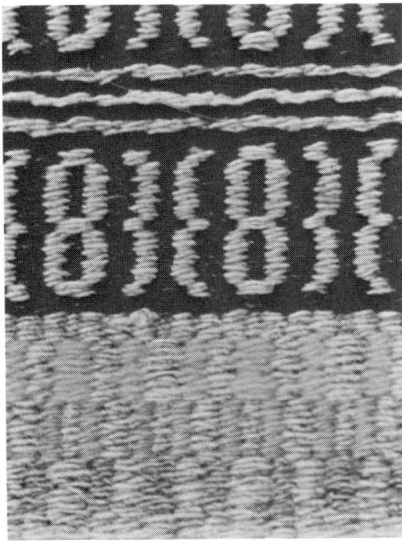

8.7. Detail, pattern band of blanket on opposites, woven in Estonia with Latvian designs and colors by Mrs. Juuli Lammertson. Estonia, Tartumaa, Kambja County; 132 cm (52") L X 127 cm (50") W; warp, cotton, 3-ply, Z-ply, natural; weft, wool, singles, Z-twist, blue (now grey), black, yellow, orange, salmon, white, lavender, heather white/red/green; 6 e/cm (15 epi); 32 p/cm (81 ppi). ROM972.179. Gift of Mr. August Laansoo, the weaver's son. See Plate 13.

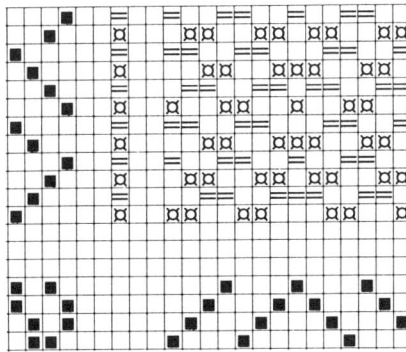

8.8. Threading draft for fig. 8.7. Alternate weft colors indicated beside treadling. Each pair of opposite picks is repeated to make a large diamond, as in Plate 13.

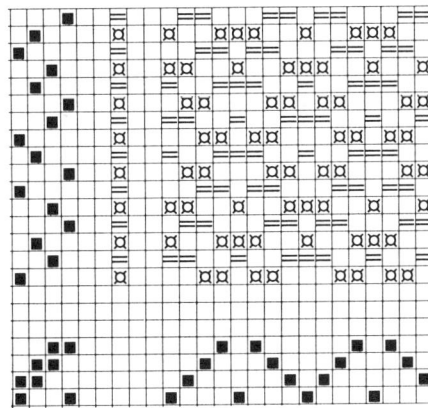

8.9. Two repeats of the popular "rosepath" twill draft, woven on opposites. Alternate weft colors indicated beside treadling order.

8.10. Detail of a blanket woven before serfdom was abolished, when four-shaft looms were still used by both home and professional weavers. Its skillful patterning might indicate the work of a professional weaver, or the hand-controlled weft patterning of the twisted rows and float areas might indicate a home weaver's care. 157 cm (62") L X 158 cm (62") W; warp, linen, singles, Z-twist, natural, used double in plain weave sheds; wefts, wool, singles, Z-twist, green, natural grey, brown, black, white; pattern weft, wool, 4-ply, S-twist, white; 3 e/cm (7.5 epi); 20 p/cm (51 ppi). ROM971.274. Gift of Mrs. A. Dzērvitis. See Plate 17.

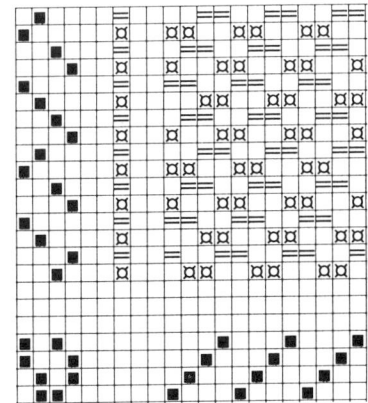

8.11. Several repeats of draft for fig. 8.10, which combines bands of twill, plain weave over doubled warp ends, and patterning floats. Color sequence noted beside treadling order.

A twill design is easily converted to a weft-faced, patterned "repp" structure. The rug in fig. 8.3 is from a Latvian pattern book which recommends a warp of tripled coarse tow linen. Three-ply wool (or rag) wefts are in two colors. A 30 dent/10 cm (8/inch) reed is single sleyed. Treadling should repeat every pair of treadles at least twice, alternating light and dark wefts.

Uses. Rugs and blankets were popular uses for this weave. The blanket shown in fig. 8.5 and Plate 12 is an excellent example of a twill- based, weft-faced patterned "repp." It has a center seam due to the narrow home loom width. The ends of this piece are bound by a narrow cotton band which is turned as the hem and machine stitched to the blanket. Fig. 8.6 gives the draft information for the main ground pattern, in which some solid colored bands are also woven on the same treadling.

Figs. 8.7 and 8.8 show another lovely blanket based on a twill draft woven weft-faced and treadled on opposites. This blanket is an example of regional weaving characteristics. Although the blanket is recognizably Latvian in design and color selection, it was woven in Estonia by the Estonian daughter-in-law of a Latvian. (See anecdote, page vi)

From the 1880s onward, one of the most popular patterned repps in the Vidzeme area was based on the *rosepath* twill, fig. 8.9. Weaving teachers of the time, influenced by Finnish work, helped bring both the draft and the weaving method into favor in Latvia.

It was common to weave blankets with plain-weave bands horizontally between rows of weft-faced repp patterns. These plain-weave bands usually were weft-faced but might be sett so that the warp and weft both showed.

The blanket pictured in fig. 8.10 and in Plate 17 is from Kurzeme in the early 1800s. A convoluted eight-shaft draft would be needed for the blanket if its patterns were fully loom-controlled. It is most likely that a four-shaft twill was the base, and that the few non-twill pattern wefts were woven by a hand-controlled method. The draft in fig. 8.11 shows the likely straight four-shaft twill threading and a standard 2/2 tie-up. The chevron in the colored pattern band is woven with two colors of complementary wefts alternated on opposite sheds. After the chevron pattern area, weft-faced, regular repp is formed over doubled warp ends. Then a center decorative accent of two rows of hand-twisted black and white wefts is woven, after which the sequence reverses to finish the band symmetrically. All those interlacements could be easily controlled on the four-shaft draft. At the outer edge of the pattern band is a square motif of alternate weft picks that go 1) in floats over six warps then under six warps, and 2) in weft-faced, regular repp over doubled warp ends.

The sheds of these few floating pattern wefts probably were made with a pick-up stick in front of the reed, or with a stick behind the heddles which was turned on its side when needed to form the single pattern shed. (Old looms had string heddles whose eyes were usually longer than the normal heddle eye of twentieth century looms. A small shed could be transferred forward easily from behind the heddles.)

In the twentieth century, small table covers, called *table blankets,* became fashionable. Some of these had plain-weave bands between weft-faced bands of point twill woven with complementary wefts. Rosepath, fig. 8.9, was a particularly popular draft for this purpose. See also fig. 12.3.

Twill-units Weave

For advanced weavers the Latvian text *Mācies aust* dealt with a technical problem in "repp" cloth derived from plain weave. The weft floats in a "repp" fabric might become so long as to allow the group of hidden elements to draw together. To avoid such grouping, the hidden warps can be woven to bind inconspicuously behind a float, held flat and in order. A stiffer, stronger cloth results. Figure 8.12 displays both sides of an enlarged, weft-faced example of this stabilized interlacing.

Although the sample's surface looks like columns of two-shaft, weft-faced "repp" weave, extra shafts and treadles have been used to accommodate the hidden, stabilizing structure. In the draft for this structure, fig. 8.13, two units of 3-shaft twill are threaded alternately. They are woven with two complementary wefts interlacing alternately in 2/1 twill with one unit, and floating over the other unit. Each weft is a separate color and weaves with a separate unit. The warp is sett so that wefts compress into a closely woven weft-faced surface.

Weaves Based on Tied Units

The use of two or more complementary wefts to complete a cycle (pass) of weft picks (lats) also was applied in Latvia to tied-unit threadings. These are the same tied-unit threading drafts that were previously discussed for cloth woven with a ground weave patterned by supplementary weft(s) described in *Chapter Six*. Patterns from twill-based drafts are all-over designs related to twill lines, whereas tied-unit drafts give designs based on blocks.

For most Latvian applications, weft-faced items woven with a tied-units draft have two sets of warp in two sizes. One set is a fine tie warp and one is a coarse pattern warp. These drafts are not woven fully weft-faced, tie warp ends are visible on the surface. Fine tie ends are less conspicuous than large ones. All pattern warp ends are fully hidden by wefts. Greater diameter in the pattern warp causes more weft to be visible on the surface, strengthening the clarity of the design. Twentieth century Latvian books called the result *weft-patterned cloth with a double warp arrangement.*

Tie warp ends bind complementary weft floats on both front and back of the cloth, and pattern warp ends control the wefts' presence on the cloth's top or bottom surface within each pattern block. This gives a double-faced cloth whose weft elements play equivalent and reciprocal parts on opposite faces of the fabric.

8.12. *Weft fabric with columns of floats on the surface, stabilized by extra warp/weft interlacements on back, #64 in Ma. Woven by Jane Evans.*

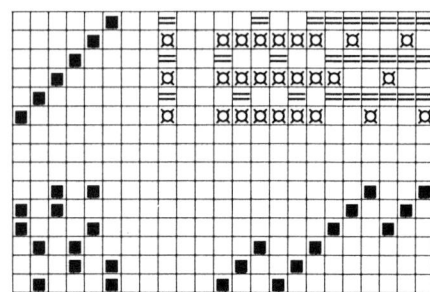

8.13. *Draft for two units of stabilized "repp" as in fig. 8.12. Alternate weft colors are indicated beside treadling.*

TIED-UNIT WEAVES

The usual threadings for tied-unit weaves have pattern:tie warp thread ratios of 1:1 or 1:2, with drafts such as figures 8.14, 8.15 and 8.16. On these drafts, weave two or more colored wefts in a regular cycle, from selvage to selvage.

THREADING

Two tie shafts alternate across the threading (fig. 8.14).

• Thread a pattern warp after each tie warp thread. Pattern shafts correspond to design blocks, one shaft per block.

Four tie shafts across the threading in a straight twill sequence (fig. 8.15).

• Thread one pattern warp end after each tie warp end. Eight warp ends compose one threading unit.

• Each pattern shaft corresponds to one design block. Other twill bases, such as those with three or five warp ends, could be used as the tie warps' threading, with units based on one repeat of the twill.

Two tie warp ends threaded in a pair between single pattern warp ends (fig. 8.16).

• Thread one pattern shaft for each design block.

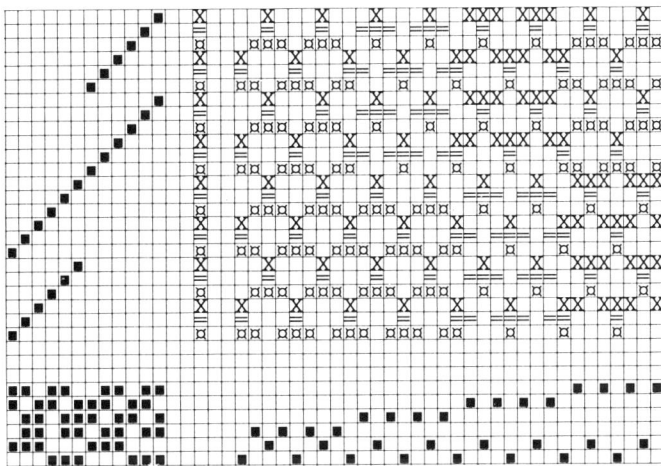

8.14. Four-end units in 1:1 pattern: tie end ratio, based on #232a in Ma. Three weft colors, indicated by symbols beside treadling sequence, form each row of pattern. In North American texts, this is known as a summer/ winter draft. This interlacement is sometimes called taqueté.

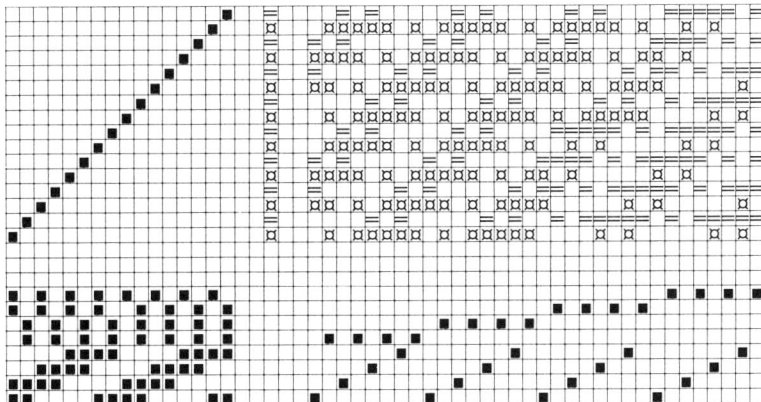

8.15. 1:1, eight-end units with tie warps in four-shaft twill order, based on #230 in Ma. Two weft colors, indicated by symbols beside treadling sequence, form each row of pattern. This interlacement is sometimes called samitum.

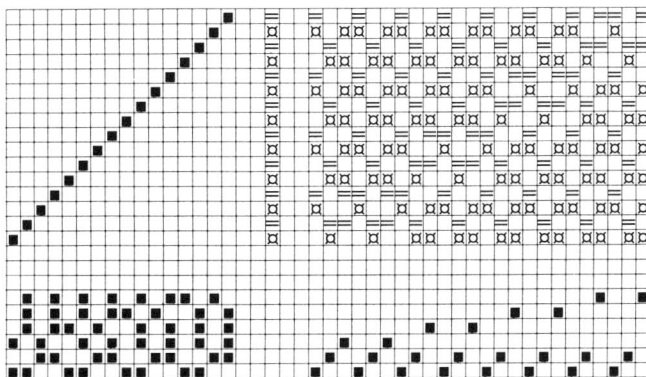

8.16. 1:2, three-end units, shown with two repeats of each of four units. Two weft colors, indicated by symbols beside treadling sequence, form each row of pattern.

continued

8.18. Border and two repeats of profile draft for weft-faced rug. Based on #174 in Pa, a 1930s pattern.

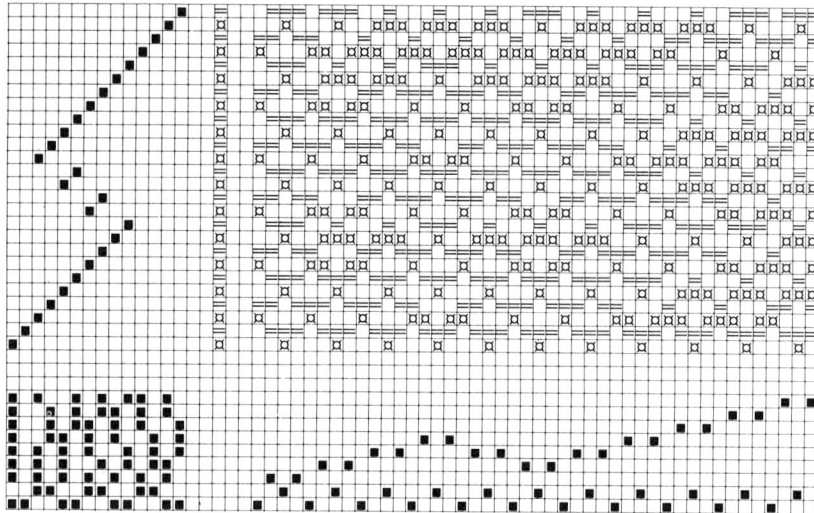

8.17. 1:1 draft for beginning of design in profile draft shown in fig 8.18. Single treadling with two weft colors, as indicated by symbols beside treadling order.

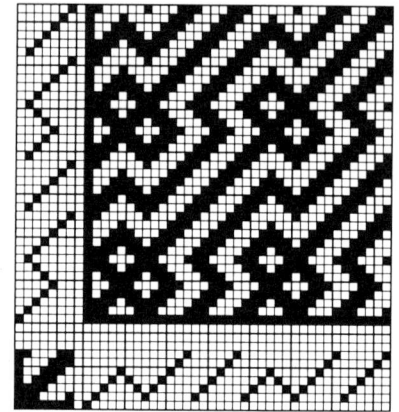

TIE-UPS

Each tie-up for the preceding drafts has two sections, pattern shafts (upper) and tie shafts (lower).

Tie shafts so that at every pick only those design blocks which are *not* to show on the top surface are tied to the treadle. In fig. 8.17 treadle 3 is tied to lift pattern shafts 3, 4, 5, 9. Thus pattern blocks D, E, F will be left down and covered by the weft pick which will show on the top of the fabric. Blocks A, B, C, G will show that weft's color on the back of the cloth because those blocks' warp ends are raised and cover the weft pick going underneath them.

The profile draft in fig. 8.18 pictures the full, two-color design for the threading units in fig. 8.17.

TREADLING

Double treadling is frequently the best way to obtain all the tie-up permutations on complementary-weft drafts.
- Place tie shaft combinations on one set of treadles.
- Place pattern shaft combinations on another set of treadles.
- Depress one treadle from each set for each weft pick, as in fig. 8.19.
- Raise one tie shaft during both lats' pattern picks, raise the other tie shaft for the next two lats.
- When all four wefts have been woven one pass is complete.

Double treadling for fig. 8.18 is shown in fig. 8.19. This 1930s carpet has pattern shafts tied on opposites on pairs of treadles. As a general rule there are four picks (lats) within one cycle (pass). In this particular example the pattern book's directions note that pairs of pattern treadles may be changed when ties are changed (i.e., after two lats), if that is necessary to square the pattern.

TREADLING FOR TWILL BASE

Four-shaft twill base for the tie warp threading. Fig. 8.15 puts the tie warps in a 2/2 straight twill construction. This combines with the pattern shafts that are tied up opposite to each other on pairs of treadles.
- Treadle through the straight twill sequence for each block of weaving with both colors for a total of eight lats per pass.
- Select a new pair of pattern shafts.

Treadling the tie warps in a 2/2 twill sequence changes the 1:1 pattern:tie warp ratio. Some weft floats go over five warp ends and thus are very clearly visible. The ties form a twill diagonal rib line.

If three weft colors are used, lift the pattern shafts so that for each color pick only the parts of the design to show as that pick's color are left down. Figure. 8.14 shows a *summer/winter* example. In any given block one color pick shows as the block at the front of the fabric, and the two other weft picks are both at the back of that block. With two tie shafts there are six lats in one pass. Figure 8.20 shows three colors of weft progresions in treadling when the tie base for the draft is a four-shaft twill. There are 12 lats in one pass.

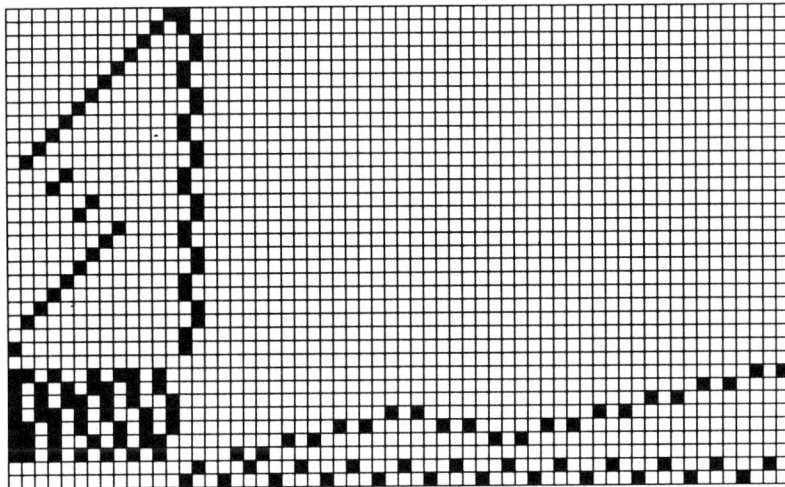

8.19. Double-treadling draft for fig. 8.18, which uses alternating picks of two colors.

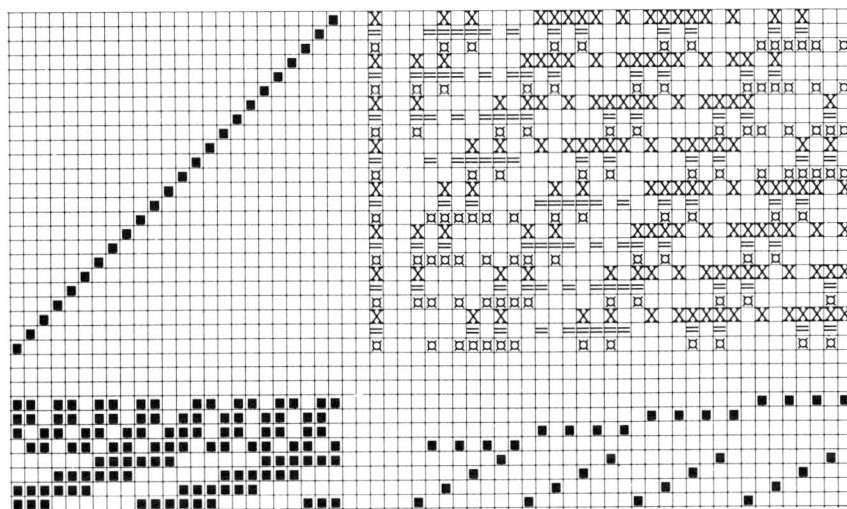

8.20. Three-color weft order, noted by symbols beside treadling, for twill-based draft, #232 in Ma.

Items woven on multi-shaft and mechanical looms could have extremely fancy, large designs that were forcefully individual in character. Naturally the "rules" of treadling were modified by adept weavers, usually so that one pass consisted of one tie's lats, as in fig. 8.19. Apparently the draft of fig. 8.16, with two ties in a pattern:tie warp ratio of 1:2, was a favorite among skilled weavers. It could be used for endless, creative designs, as seen in the following examples. Besides sharing the same basic threading unit, these items all also have two-sized warps.

A relatively old example of a weft-faced, complementary-weft blanket in a 1:2 pattern:tie warp ratio is shown in fig. 8.21 and Plate 18. The very fine black cotton warp is arranged to give single tie ends and three-strand pattern ends. Only the fine tie warps show over the handspun wool wefts. Sun motifs form an all-over pattern and borders, requiring 11 shafts for nine 1:2 units. The nine-block profile draft is in fig. 8.22. Each block is six working warps wide, or two threading repeats of the basic three-end unit. Six wefts equal one block in height, indicating the weaver considered the two lats treadled under one warp to comprise a pass.

From late in the nineteenth century comes a blanket woven in the surprisingly non-traditional design, shown in its graphic profile draft, fig. 8.23. Only 13 shafts were needed by the Zemgale weaver who obviously was a gifted designer. Each block of design is one threading unit wide and four wefts high.

A somewhat atypical design appears on the blanket pictured in fig. 8.24, from Ventspils on the western coast of Kurzeme. Woven about 1920, this piece contains both geometric motifs and a four-sided border of stylized trees. Its profile draft, fig. 8.25, can be found in Pēteris Viļumsons' book, *Thursday Morning*. The flexibility of this unit draft allows this blanket to have two threading units per block like in fig. 8.21, and also to have four lats per pass like the blanket in fig. 8.23.

The two warps – tie and pattern – need to be under different tensions. Tie warp ends bend around wefts while pattern warp ends pass straight through the center of the cloth. To keep the pattern warp ends straight and the tie warp ends free to bend during weaving, there is strong tension on the former and less tension on the latter. The two sizes of warps also relate to their contrasting tensions. If the pattern warp ends are heavier they can handle the tight tensioning better, while the tie warp ends can be finer because they are under less tension.

The differing interlacing of warps with wefts also means that the total length of tie warp is longer than that of pattern warp. Tie warp ends, bending around wefts, traverse a longer distance between ends of the cloth than the pattern warp ends which pass straight through the center of the cloth. These differences in tensions and lengths of warps require two warp beams, one for the looser, longer tie warp elements and one for the tighter, shorter pattern warp elements.*

Uses. Weaving both with tied-unit drafts and with complementary wefts apparently became common in Latvia after the mid-1800s, but only in certain parts of the country. The products most often were tablecloths, upholstery, rugs, bedcovers, or other

* In North America a system with two sets of warps used under two tensions has sometimes been called a *stuffer warp* method. (Atwater, 1973; Tidball, 1966)

8.21. Blanket in weft-faced, 1:2 units, woven full-width. ca. 1870; Zemgale, Tukums County, Sniķeri Township; 182 cm (71.5") L X 144 cm (57") W; warp cotton, 2-ply, S- twist, black, used single for tie ends, triple for pattern ends; weft, wool, singles, Z-twist, black, variegated blue; 6 ties and 3 working pattern ends/cm (23 epi); 15 p/cm (38 ppi); woven by great-grandmother of donor. ROM972.480.1. Gift of Mrs. Lidija Roze. See Plate 18.

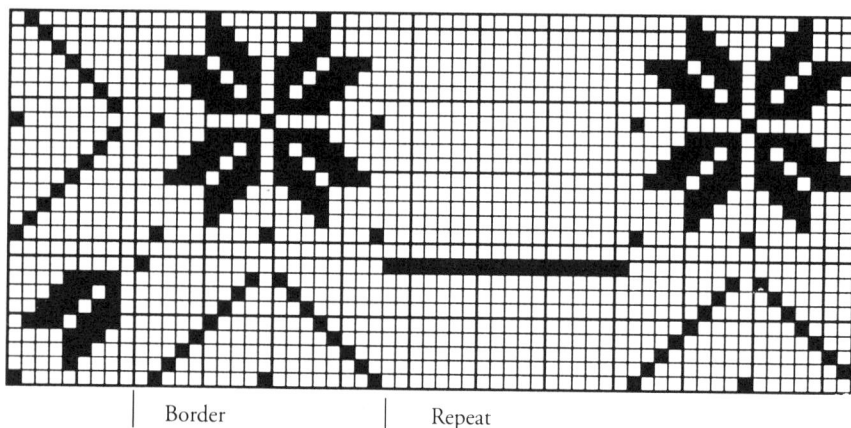

| Border | | Repeat |

8.22. Left border and one repeat of morning stars profile draft for fig. 8.21.

Both of the following pieces were designed by masters in their fields and were probably woven by their students at craft schools around 1930.

The piece in fig. 8.26. is by Mr. A. Dzērvītis, an authority on Latvian folk arts. Fig. 8.27 is the 12-block profile draft. Each block is two threading units wide and six weft picks high. Generally two wefts comprise a lat, although there are randomly split pairs of lats. The

8.24. Trees and sun symbols cover this blanket, woven in 1:2 units. 180 cm (71") L X 137 cm (53.5") W; warp, cotton, 2-ply, S-twist, black, single for tie ends and quadrupled for pattern ends; weft, wool, 2-ply, S-ply, gray, red, used doubled; 9 working e/cm (23 epi); 8 p/cm (20 ppi). Collection of Liena Kaugars.

8.23. Profile draft for blanket woven in 1:2 units threading, #92 in Ltm, vol. II.

8.26. Mr. A. Dzērvītis cleverly arranged traditional sun symbols in reversing colors across this large, one-piece carpet or wall hanging. Ocher and deep blue wool wefts interlace with linen warps of two sizes - large pattern and small tie warps. Occassional, brocaded wefts of red are added by hand, replacing the blue in specific sun motifs. Riga; 208 cm (82") L X 188 cm (74") W; pattern warp, linen, 4-ply, S-ply, natural; tie warp, linen, fine 3-ply, S-ply, dark brown; weft, wool, 2-ply, S-ply, blue, ochre, red; 4 tie and 2 pattern e/cm (10 tie and 5 pattern epi); 16 weft/cm (41 ppi). ROM 971.167. Gift of Mrs. Aleksandra Dzērvītis.

handsome, sturdy piece is 208 cm (82") long by 188 cm (74") wide and has no seams.

A large wall blanket designed by Mr. Ansis Cīrulis is shown in fig. 8.28. This piece is rather exceptional due to the use of three complementary wefts throughout its design. The draft in fig. 8.29 gives an example of weaving in units of three colored wefts.

8.25. (right) Twenty-four-block profile draft for border and one repeat of pattern on blanket in fig. 8.24.

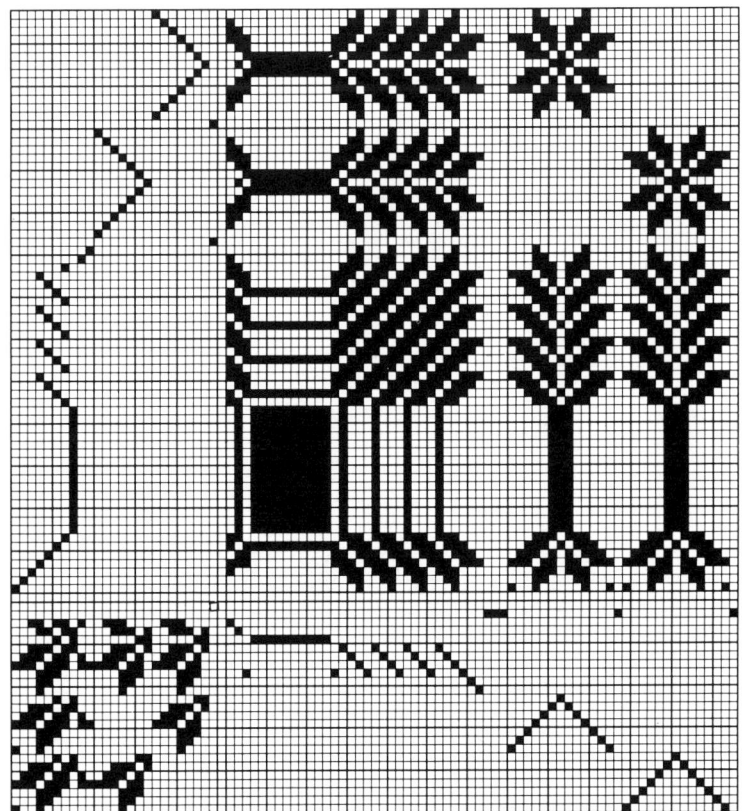

| Border | Repeat |

8.27. Profile draft for carpet in fig . 8.26, to be threaded to 1:2 units of fig 8.16.

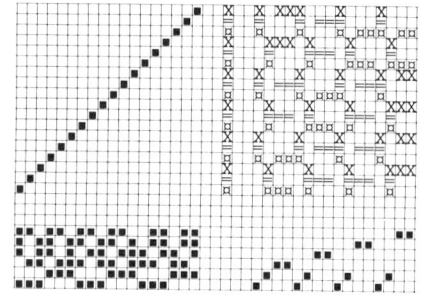

8.29. Four units as woven with three complementary wefts in fig 8.28 wall blanket. Weft colors indicated by symbols beside treadling.

8.28. (below) Wall blanket, designed by Mr. A. Cīrulis as a gift for Mr. P. Dindonim. Two dissimilar sizes of warp threads are used under three colors of wefts which run selvage-to-selvage. The piece, featuring morning stars, exhibits expert planning and execution. Pre-1943; Latvia; pattern warp, cotton, 2-ply, grey, black, brown, used in groups of 8; tie warp, cotton (?), 2-ply, brown; weft, wool, 2-ply, S-ply, dark brown, green, orange; 3 tie and 2 pattern e/cm (7.5 tie and 5 pattern epi); 3.5 p/cm (9 ppi); woven by A. Cīrulis or his students. Collection of Garezera tautas mākslas musejs, Three Rivers, Michigan. Gift of grandaughter of A. Cīrulis.

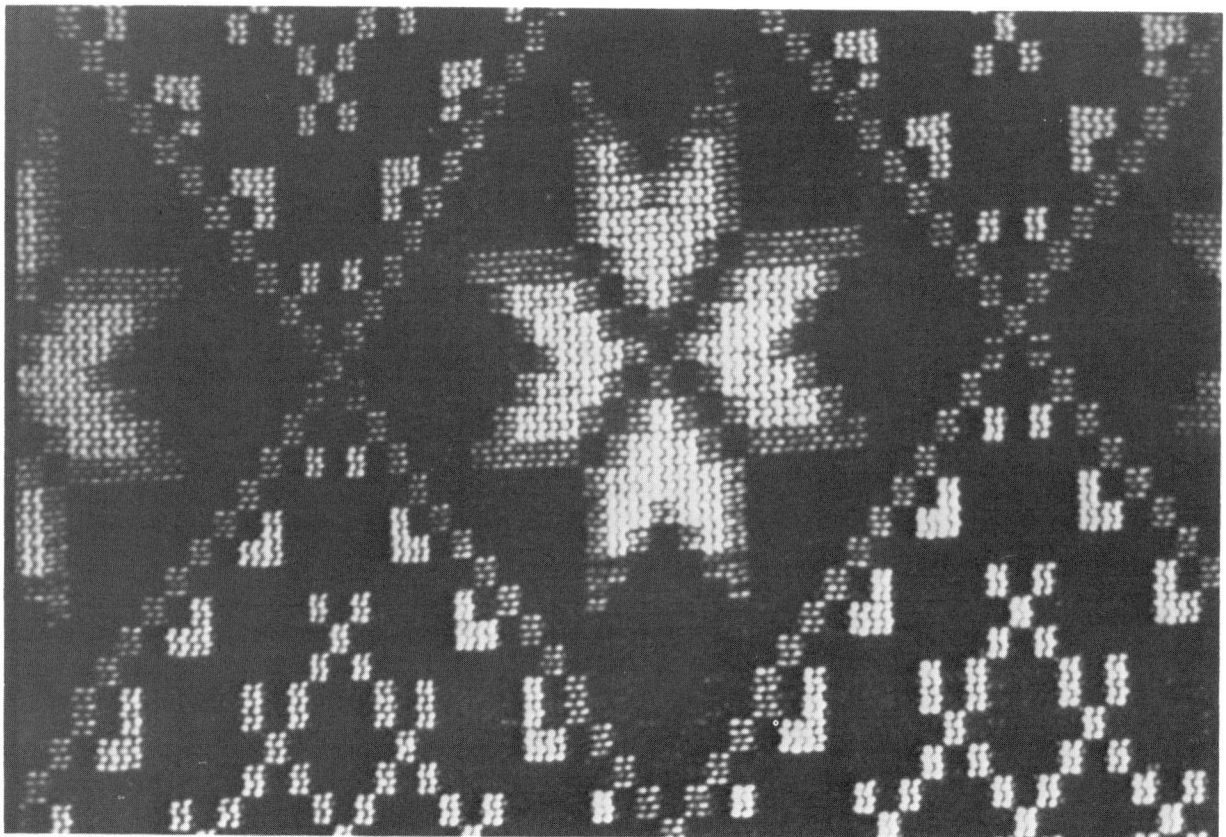

CHAPTER NINE
Compound Weaves
with Complementary Warps

These interesting compound weaves have three or more sets of threads, of which at least two sets are warps that function co-equally in the structure. Usually a double-faced fabric is formed, with front and back surfaces woven in the same structure.

One major difference between weft-faced and warp-faced weaves with complementary sets of elements is that all of the complementary-warp weaves discussed previously are based on twills. Tied-unit-weave drafts, frequently woven weft-faced, were not woven warp-faced in pre-World War II Latvia.

Warp-faced Corkscrew Weave
Slīpais ripss

This weave is the warp-faced version of the previously discussed *weft-faced corkscrew twill*. In Latvian it was called a *slīpais ripss* or *sloped repp*. It uses two complementary warps of two colors, and one set of weft threads which is covered. The all-over twill motif forms angled ribs on the cloth. A draft for a warp-faced corkscrew twill is given in fig. 9.1. A version woven *on opposites* appears in fig. 9.2.

Uses. In twentieth-century Latvia warp-faced corkscrew weave was used somewhat more widely than weft-faced corkscrew weave for coat and suiting fabrics made of fine wool threads. Both weaves evidently were used infrequently by handweavers.

Warp-faced Patterned Repps
Rakstoti ripsaudumi

One four-shaft twill variation which became very popular after the mid-1800s in Latvia was called *patterned repp derived from twill*. Two complementary warps and one weft were woven in pointed twill patterns. An example is in fig. 9.3. A twill, fig. 9.4, is the profile draft for fig. 9.3, and is partially drafted in fig. 9.5.

On first glance this weave is reminiscent of the warp-faced corkscrew twills which had warps in exactly opposite interlacements, as drafted in fig. 9.2. Rather than use a doubled number of shafts for the two twill drafts, a patterned repp threading interlocks both the drafts on only one twill's set of four shafts. In the resultant interlacement, the wefts' twill structure is replaced by rows of 1/1 plain weave with occasional floats

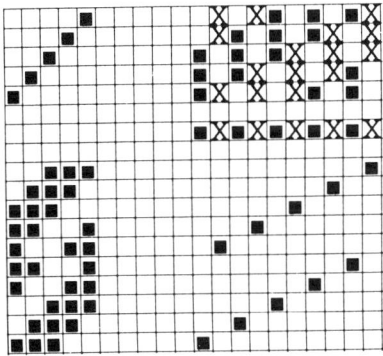

9.1. Two-colored, warp-faced corkscrew twill draft on 10 shafts, #205 in Ap. Different warp colors are indicated by symbols above threading draft.

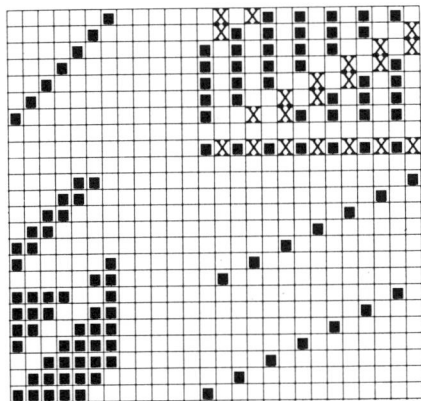

9.2. Warp-faced corkscrew twill woven on opposites, #206 in Ap. Different warp colors are indicated by symbols above threading draft.

DRAFTING AND WEAVING

WARP-FACED CORKSCREW THREADING

- Begin with a straight or pointed twill threading which usually contains an odd number of shafts.
- Place one repeat of the basic twill draft along the threading draft, with one empty square left after each warp end.
- Add a second, identical twill in the threading draft, on a second set of shafts parallel to the first draft. See fig. 9.1.
- Use a single color of warp threads for each set of shafts.
- Double the sett for warp-faced density.

WEAVING

- Use the same number of treadles as for the original twill draft, with the second twill's tie-up added above the first twill's tie-up. Fig.9.1 tie-up is for offset lifts. Fig. 9.2 has opposite lifts.
- If the warp floats become too long for practical functions, binding points may be added such that the floats hide the ties while being limited by them. This also adds firmness to the fabric.

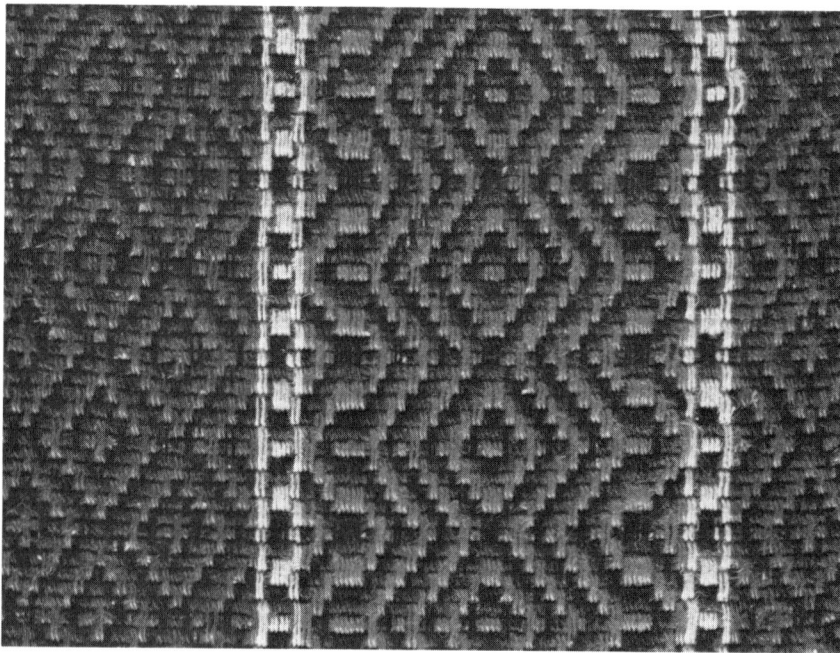

9.3. Woven example from border through part of the center band of a warp-faced, patterned repp rug , based on #185 in Ma. Woven by Jane Evans.

over two warp ends. The warps' twill structure is maintained, albeit as two twills on alternate threads. The sett is condensed to be warp-faced, and the cloth has diagonal ribs of warp floats on the surface in a twill motif. The two warps are complementary in that they are co-equal in the construction. If either warp were removed, a single, standard twill interlacement would re-emerge, because it is the starting point for drafting this weave.

Uses. Warp-faced patterned repps were very popular in the late nineteenth and early twentieth centuries for rugs. Wooden floors in new farm homes added comfort, raised interest in decors, and required upkeep, so there was a demand for floor coverings. Looms could accommodate scatter rug sizes. Several strips of rugs might be sewn together for a larger, room-sized carpet. Warp-faced structures became known through contemporary teachers, many of whom learned those weaves during training in Estonia.

Rugs often used multi-colored tow linen or wool warps over rag or tow linen wefts. Eventually the predominant designs of warp-faced patterned repp rugs consisted of a border along each edge and an overall pattern in the center.

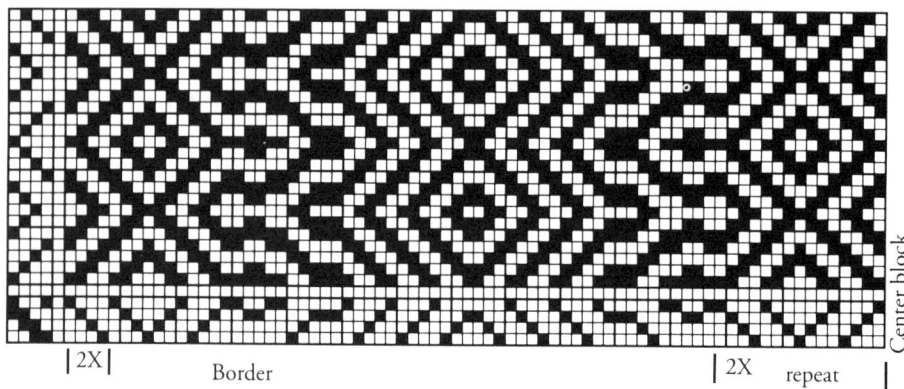

|2X| Border |2X| repeat | Center block

9.4. Twill design used as basis for blocks of warp-faced patterned repp interlacement, as in fig. 9.3.

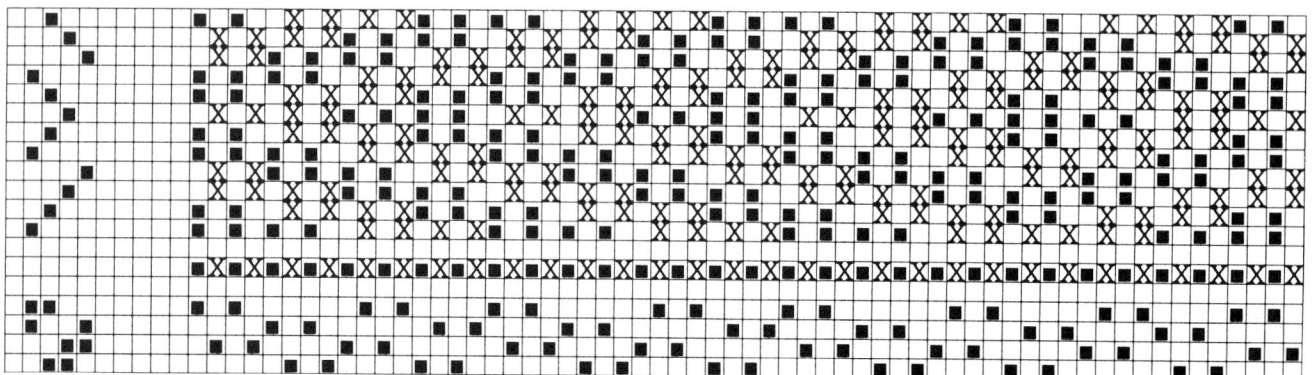

9.5. Partial threading draft for converting fig. 9.4 into warp-faced patterned repp, based on #186 in Ma. Different warp colors are indicated by symbols above threading draft.

124

WARP-FACED PATTERNED REPP

THREADING

- Begin with the original twill's threading order, fig. 9.4, which becomes the dominant color's threading order in the new fabric.

- Thread at least two warp threads in place of each single warp in the original twill. The two warp threads are of alternating colors, one dominant (usually dark, D) and one background color (usually light, L), throughout the whole new draft.

- These two threads need to be on shafts that will not weave on the same weft shot (e.g., 1 vs. 3, or 2 vs. 4 in a normal 2/2 twill tie-up such as in fig. 9.5). Usually it is best to replace each original warp with four or even more new warp threads, to allow for the condensed width of a warp-faced threading.

Figure 9.6 shows the four units of dark/light warps to substitute for single warps on shafts 1, 2, 3, and 4 in a point-twill draft.

- For shaft 1's warps substitute D on shaft 1 and L on shaft 3.
- For shaft 2's warps substitute D on shaft 2 and L on shaft 4.
- For shaft 3's warps substitute D on shaft 3 and L on shaft 1.
- For shaft 4's warps substitute D on shaft 4 and L on shaft 2.

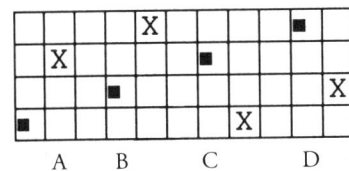

9.6. *The four shortest units for threading warp-faced patterned repp. Alternate warp colors are indicated by different symbols.*

Vertical stripes are possible by threading both shafts of a unit with the same color.

- After substituting those units into the previous twill design, a new draft like at fig. 9.5 emerges. (The units are arbitrarily of four warp ends each.) Each row of weft now interlaces in near plain-weave order of 1/1, with a short float over two warps where one threading unit meets a different unit. Each warp maintains its own twill interlacement.

- Fig. 9.3 shows the same pattern as it would appear when compressed to be a Latvian weaver's *warp-faced patterned repp derived from twill.*

TIE-UP

- Use a 2/2 twill tieup, fig. 9.5, which assures the two shafts of a threading unit never are lifted together.

WEAVING

- Use one size weft. It is completely hidden by the warps so that the characteristic twill diagonal of floats is displayed as a ribbed pattern on the surface.

- The original treadling order for the twill pattern may remain the same or it can be altered providing no long warp floats occur.

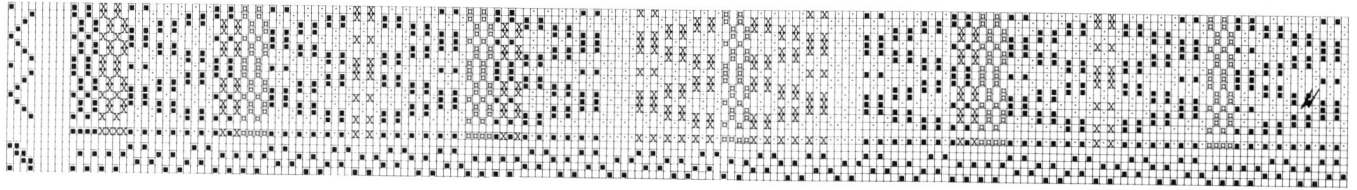

One such warp-faced rug found in a pattern book from that era is partially drafted in fig. 9.7. This pattern uses four warp colors, always alternating two within each unit of four warp ends, and repeating many units to obtain the desired width for the rug.

Warp-faced patterned repp cloth was used in upholstery, door curtains, carpets, and other sturdy fabrics, in addition to rugs. Throughout most of Latvia it was normal for blankets to be in weft-faced patterned repps, but in some districts along the Daugava River blankets were also made in warp-faced patterned repp.

9.7. Partial draft for 1930s warp-faced, patterned repp rug, #165 in Pa. Four different warp colors are indicated by symbols above the threading. Draft is shown below in enlarged segments labelled with number of repeats for each unit. Begin threading with upper left segment, from left to right.

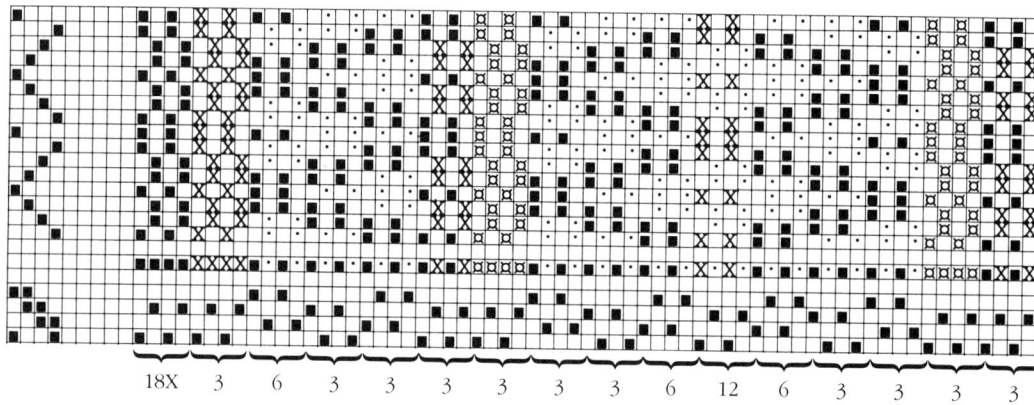

18X 3 6 3 3 3 3 3 3 6 12 6 3 3 3 3 3

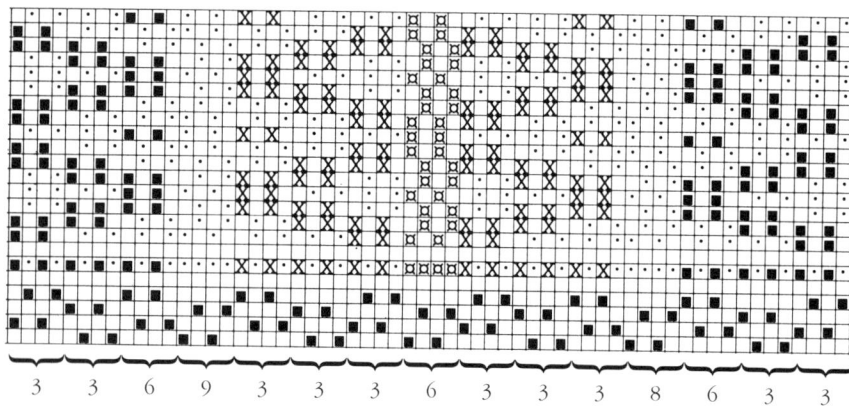

3 3 6 9 3 3 3 6 3 3 3 8 6 3 3

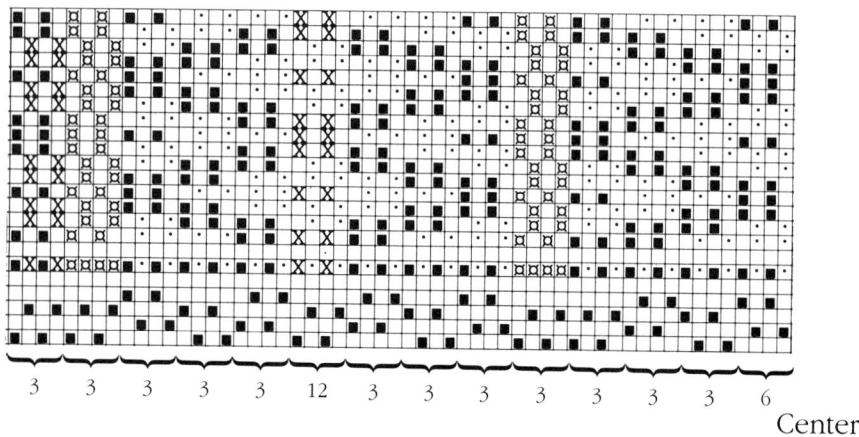

3 3 3 3 3 3 12 3 3 3 3 3 3 3 6

Center

CHAPTER TEN

Double-cloth Weaves

It was noted earlier that compound weaves interlace with three or more sets of threads or elements. All the compound weaves previously discussed interwove their elements into a single layer of cloth. The following examples of compound weaves have at least two sets of warp threads and two sets of weft threads occuring in two independent layers that are combined during weaving. The two separate cloths are woven simultaneously, one over the other, forming *double cloth*, or *divkāršie audumi*. The two layers of double cloth can be linked by one of several systems. The four which are most commonly found in Latvian textiles follow.

Stitched Double Cloth

In this interlacement the two layers of cloth are joined intermittently by a thread from one layer weaving into the other layer. As with backed cloths in Latvia, this weave was used to add weight and density to a fabric. Unlike backed cloth, second sets of both warp and weft elements are added. This double-cloth fabric – with two sets of both warp and weft elements – was usually woven for men's suiting fabric. Figure 10.1 is a stitched double-cloth draft, showing two weft threads.

Tubular Double Cloth

A system Latvians called double cloth joins two layers at both edges to form a tube when off the loom. This fabric had such limited applications that, although it is mentioned in twentieth-century Latvian texts, no tubular projects are suggested in those books.

The draft in fig. 10.2 gives the set-up for a tubular fabric. Its two plain-weave layers are connected on both edges during weaving. One weft passes through all sheds producing a tube of single cloth from a double weave technique.

Patterned Double Cloth

Double cloth interlacements in Latvia were used primarily for block patterning. In this system, two differently colored cloth layers interchange in rectangular sections, producing a geometric pattern on each layer. Within each pattern area, the two fabric layers are separate and they cross through each other only at the edge of each area. The pattern is identical in design on both front and back sides of the completed fabric, with the colors reversed.

Most drafts for patterned double cloth are in blocks of plain weave. Each layer of cloth is constructed by two shafts, therefore four shafts are needed to weave a block of pattern in two layers.

The two drafts in figs 10.3 and 10.4 show how to exchange the two layers to front or back of the fabric. Figure 10.3 shows a surface layer made by all odd-numbered warp and weft threads, while the back layer is made by all even-numbered warp and weft threads. In fig. 10.4 the surfaces are changed so that the even-numbered threads are on top and the odd-numbered threads are on the back. The only difference between these two drafts is their tie-ups, each of which uses four treadles. With eight treadles it is possible to weave either set of threads as top or back layer.

If the odd-numbered threads are all one color and the even-numbered threads are all another color, two differently colored surfaces are possible. A design of blocks such as fig. 10.5 can exploit this. In the draft in fig. 10.6 each of the two blocks has its own four shafts. In actual weaving both the warp and weft threads are alternately light and dark throughout, and the treadling determines which color is on the surface of each block.

Uses. Patterned double cloth was popular for bed blankets in Kurzeme

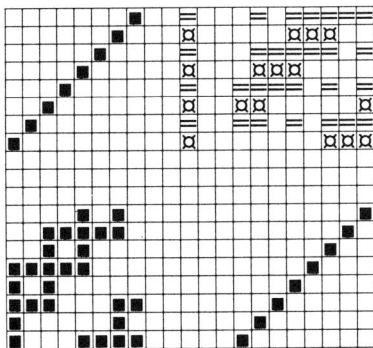

10.1. Eight-shaft draft for suiting fabric of double cloth, #228 in Ap. Different weft colors are indicated by symbols beside treadling.

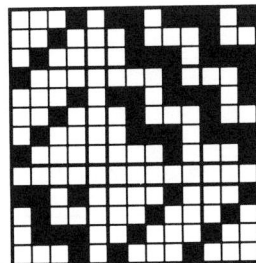

10.2. Draft for tubular double cloth, #179 in Ap. One weft is used throughout.

10.3. Upper fabric woven of odd-numbered threads in double-cloth setup, #203a in Ma.

Fig. 10.4. Upper fabric woven of even-numbered threads in double-cloth setup, #203b in Ma

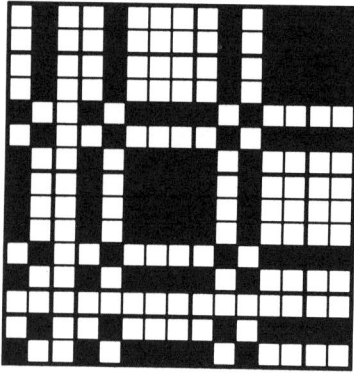

10.5. Two-block profile draft for double-cloth woven on four shafts, #203c in Ma.

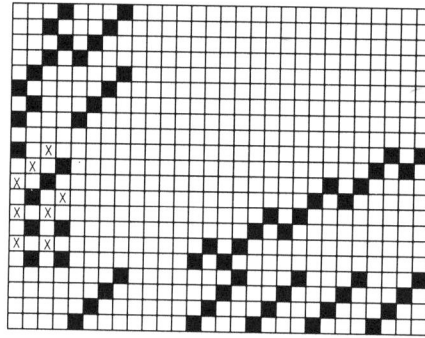

10.7. Double-cloth setup on double-harness loom threaded and woven in light/dark order. Based on #206 in Ma.

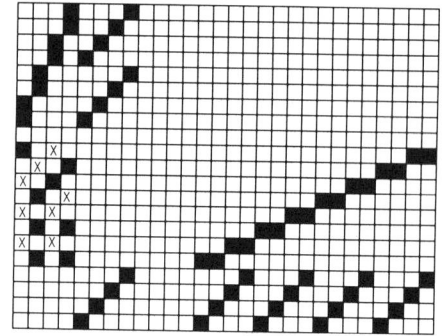

10.8. Double-cloth setup on double-harness loom threaded and woven in two light/two dark order. Based on #207 in Ma.

and Vidzeme. In Vidzeme in the late nineteenth and early twentieth century *table blankets* of double cloth began to appear, possibly inspired by Scandinavian teachers. These were in block patterns of colored threads, a change from the traditional white linen and cotton tablecloths.

Patterned Double Cloth on Double-harness Looms

On single-harness looms the two-layer system of pattern blocks in plain-weave double cloth uses four times the number of shafts and treadles as the number of blocks in the pattern. Within limits this is a need best served by multi-shaft looms if designs use up to four blocks. In Latvia, double-cloth designs using over 16 shafts were adapted to be woven on double-harness looms.

A double-harness loom reduces the number of pattern shafts and treadles from four to two per block. There are also four ground shafts and

treadles. Four long-eyed heddle shafts are hung for counterbalanced action from the two front rollers, as in fig. 2.11. There are two ways of drafting a motif in double cloth for the same woven result from a double-harness loom, shown in figs. 10.7 and 10.8. These drafts assume a countermarch system for the pattern harness. In the tie-ups, dark squares indicate rising shafts, *x* denotes sinking shafts, and blank squares are unmoved shafts.

There are two differences readily noticeable between the drafts: the pairs of pattern shafts are threaded and treadled in different sequences. Figure 10.7 is warped and woven in

an order of one light thread, one dark thread. Figure 10.8, on the other hand, follows the order of two light, two dark threads in both warp and weft sequences. To compensate for the different color orders, and therefore the need to move shafts differently to obtain similar double-layered results, the two drafts also require another significant change. The treadling order of pattern shafts is altered in conjunction with the color order of wefts. Tie-ups of pattern shafts remain alike between the two approaches to the same pattern, as do treadling sequences of the front harness.

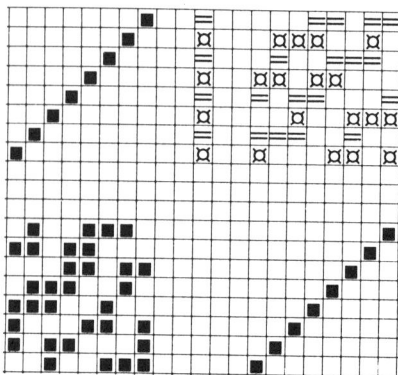

10.6. Double-cloth setup for two blocks, showing alternating weft colors only, as indicated by symbols beside treadling, #203d in Ma.

10.9. Eight-shaft, 2:1 Beiderwand draft, based on #156 in Ap.

Although both drafts look alike in their front harness tie-ups, in fact they have a crucial difference. In fig. 10.7 shafts 1 and 3 counterbalance, and shafts 2 and 4 counterbalance. In fig. 10.8, shafts 1 and 2 counterbalance, and shafts 3 and 4 counterbalance. The pattern shafts' threading and the treadling would tell a Latvian weaver which way to arrange the front harness.

2:1 and 4:1 Drafts
for Double Weave

An unusual weave structure is available from a draft which is often called *Beiderwand*. It was used intensely in a very few parts of northern Germany in the 1700s and 1800s. Evidently in Latvia examples of Beiderwand weave were rather rare. The Beiderwand threading draft relates to the threading draft called *tied-Beiderwand* in *Chapter Six*. Structurally, the two fabrics are unrelated, the former producing a double cloth, the latter weaving a single cloth with tied floats. Latvian texts scarcely included Beiderwand, and did not give it that name, simply calling it a *weft-patterned weave with tied floats*.

Figure 10.9 is an example of a 2:1 ratio draft in this weave.

In Beiderwand there are two warps of similar size: a *main warp* that forms balanced plain weave with a fine weft, and a *binding warp* that interlaces with a coarser weft. The fine plain weave can be called the main structure, and the coarser weave can be called the secondary structure. Traditionally the main structure (plain weave) in Beiderwand formed the pattern and the coarser secondary structure formed the background in a design. When this draft is woven the traditional way, as in fig. 10.9, there are areas of free double cloth and areas where the two structures are woven together. Both of the warps and the plain weave weft traditionally were of linen, later of cotton; and the coarse weft was of wool.

One of the few Latvian representatives of *Beiderwand* fabric is shown in fig. 10.10. This piece has

10.10. A soft, drapeable blanket in 4:1 Beiderwand, woven with borders all around. 1920; Vidzeme, County Cesis, Township Ranke; 204 cm (80") L X 136 cm (53.5") W; warp, cotton, 2-ply, S-twist, black; weft, wool, singles, Z-twist, white, grey; 26 e/cm (66 epi); 16 p/cm (41 ppi); woven by Edwards Nuzis, the donor's cousin. ROM971.294.4. Gift of Mrs. Lucija Zvaigzne.

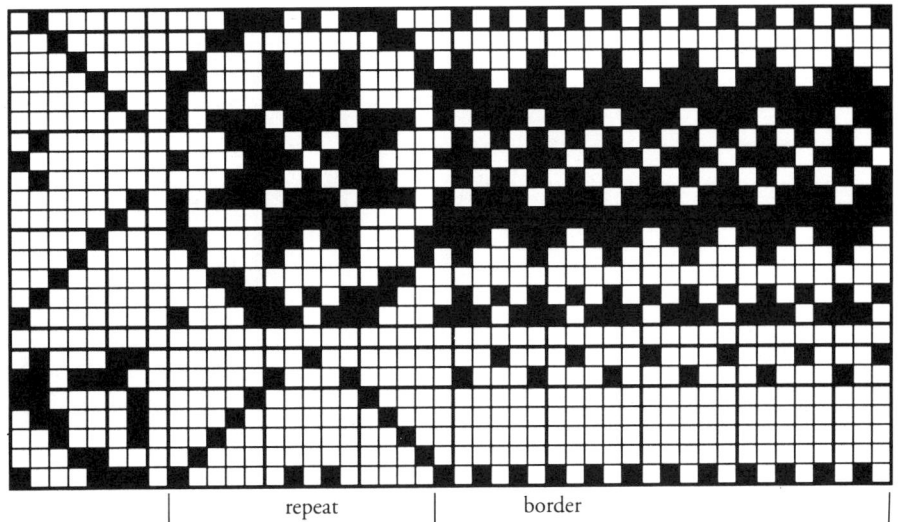

repeat   border

10.11. Profile draft for blanket in fig 10.10. The pattern has eight morning star motifs between its borders.

129

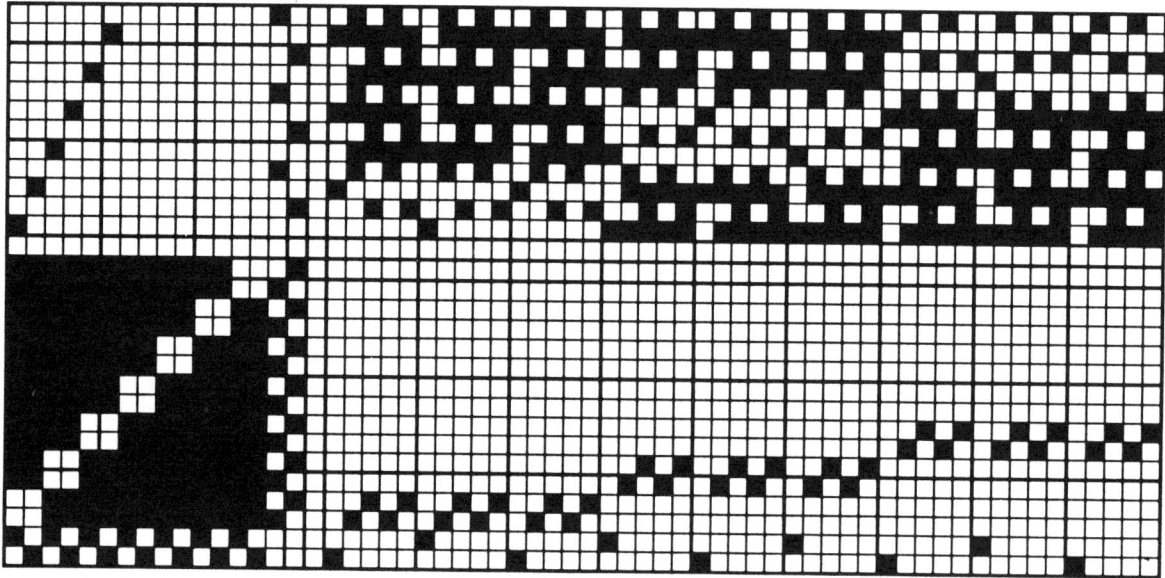

10.12. Threading units for blanket in fig. 10.10. See text for how to substitute into profile draft in fig. 10.11.

an especially interesting honeycomb effect in the non-double-cloth areas. The relationship between yarn sizes and sett causes a wavy, cellular effect by the weft floats, an attractive addition to the blankets' visual character. Figure 10.11 is a profile draft of the right border and one design repeat, which require 16 shafts for seven blocks of pattern. In fig. 10.12, 12 threading units (three blocks) are shown. In this particular blanket each block of the design uses 15 very fine cotton warp ends per block of the profile draft - three binder ends and 12 pattern warps. Binder ends alternate across the draft. Six picks of alternating grey (secondary) and white (plain weave) wool wefts constitute a block in height. The ground picks follow in regular alternation, regardless of which pattern block's units are woven.

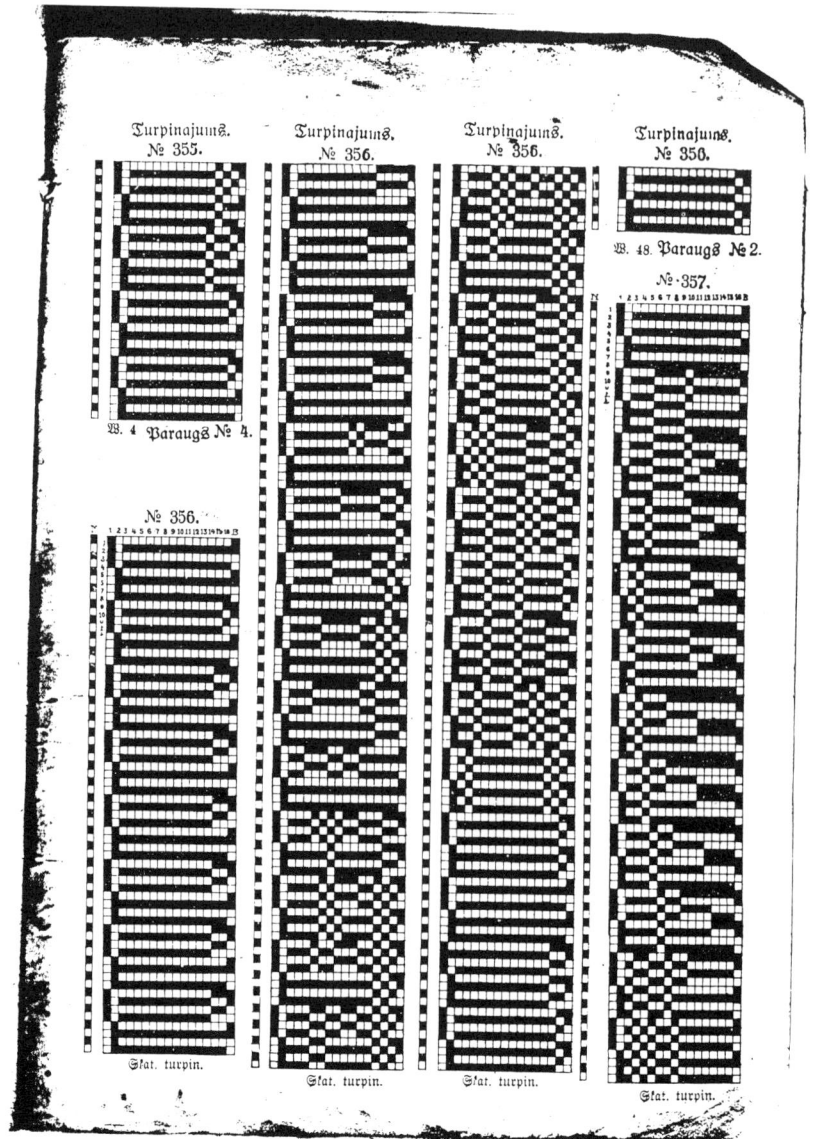

10.13. Page of double-cloth drafts from Vilumsons' book, Wednesday Morning.

CHAPTER ELEVEN

Hand-controlled Pattern Weaves

The love of patterned fabrics led Latvian home weavers to use several techniques to achieve motifs more intricate than their looms could control. These methods were usually worked on a loom threaded to plain weave or other simple structure. Shafts, treadles, and reed all contributed speed and control during weaving, while the weaver manipulated weft and/or warp threads to achieve the pattern. Working this way is time-consuming, so most hand-controlled patterning was done by home weavers rather than by professionals. Three types of structures – "stick weave" lace, tufts, and *inlaid floats of supplementary wefts* - were the traditional hand-patterning methods for home weavers. These three were supplemented by several other formations by the late 1800s.

Both simple and compound weave structures served as bases for hand-controlled patterning.

Simple Weaves with Continuous Wefts

Stick Weave

Skalu audums

One of the oldest methods of decorating simple plain weave was to alter the structure slightly with warp and/or weft floats, like the lace weaves in *Chapter Four*. Shed sticks were used on two-shaft looms to create a particular lace weave interlacement. The stick-woven structure became so popular that it was re-drafted for looms with more shafts in the twentieth century.

Latvian stick weaving, or *skalu audums*, is not *pick-up weaving* as known in North America, where a stick is used to lift warps between the web and the shafts. It is somewhat like the Swedish s*word weaving*. (Johansson, 1982.) It differs by retaining the sticks in place throughout the whole weaving. A stick is up to 10 cm (4 inches) wide and slightly longer than the warp's width. Two people, one in front doing the weaving and one in back managing the sticks, add speed and comfort to weaving of the Latvian version. For this reason *skalu audums* or *stick weaving* was also called the *honeymoon weave.* *

The draft in fig. 11.1 shows one repeat of a two-shaft loom's threading, on sticks, and fig. 11.2 diagrams the actual setup. All warps initially are threaded through two shafts to form plain weave. Five sticks are carefully inserted across the warp behind the shafts. Each successive stick, represented by rows starting at the top of the draft, picks up threads indicated by dark squares. Each stick always lifts all the threads on all preceding sticks (higher rows on the draft), plus its own new blocks of pattern. In one repeat there are two or three units of each block

*Much of the information on this weave, including the pictured sample, is thanks to the knowledge, skill, and generosity of Mrs. D. Šefers of Toronto, Ontario, who graduated from the Home Economics Institute in Riga prior to World War II.

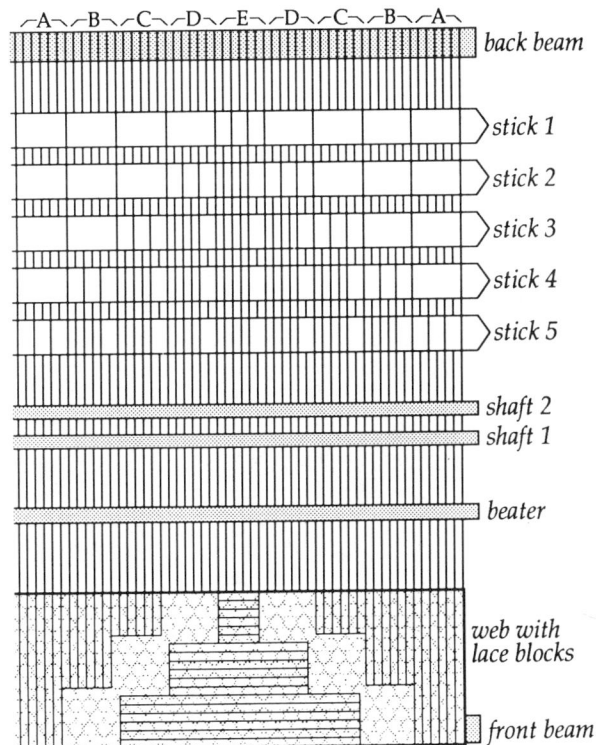

11.2. Stick-weave lace arrangement on two-shaft loom. Fabric woven at front of loom has areas of plain weave, warp-float lace, and weft-float lace.

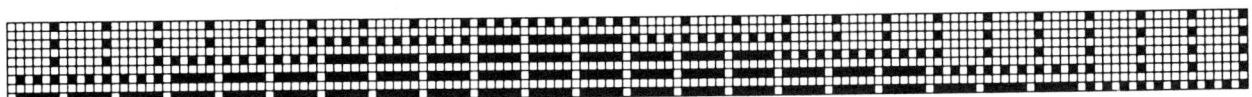

11.1. Draft presentation for arranging warp over five sticks for one repeat of lace pattern, #71b in Pa. See "Stick Weave" in text.

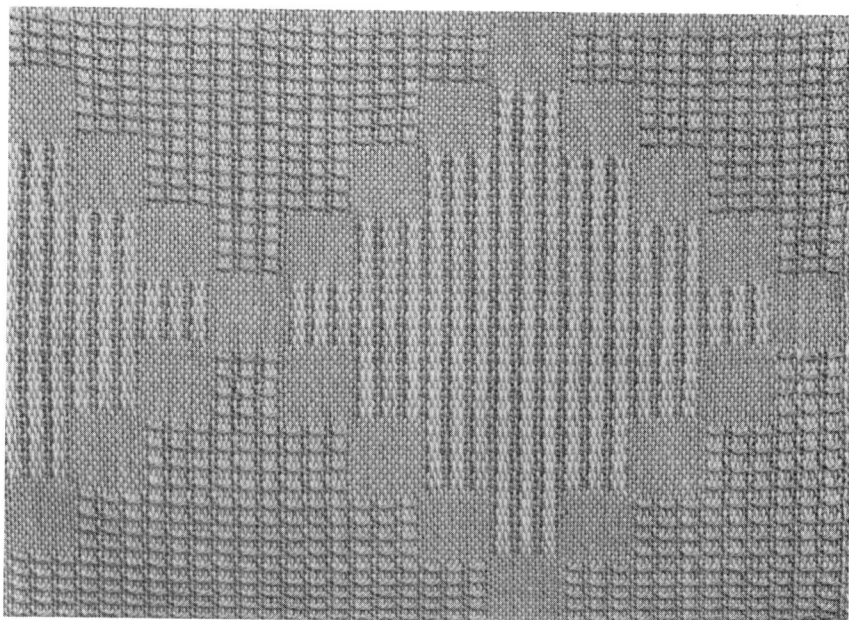

11.3. Ancient motif woven on two-shaft loom with stick-weave lace setup. Knowledge of this once-standard method has become rare since WWII. Arranged and woven by Mrs. Dzidra Šefers.

WEAVING
STICK LACE

- Set up warp as described in text.

- Move a stick forward, very close to the shafts, turning it on its side.

Due to the length of the heddle eyes a low shed will form all the way from the stick to the web's edge.

- Choose sticks in any order to give different blocks of patterns.

- After a pattern shed is woven, allow the stick to fall flat again, and move it back.

- Treadle three tabby picks (odd, even, odd).

- Repeat for the next pattern shed by turning another stick, then weave three tabby sheds (odd, even, odd).

threaded in width, as in the draft. (In fig. 11.2, only one unit of each block is shown for clarity). When all five sticks are threaded, they are pulled to the back beam and stacked on top of each other. The stick at the top of the draft is on the top of the pile.

The old looms were well-suited to the stick-weaving of lace. The hand-tied string heddles had eyes of around 2 cm (.75 inch) in length. The shafts, which consisted of two parallel wooden sticks which held the flexible heddles, could accommodate some shed distortions.

The most frequent old examples of stick lace patterning have large diamonds, as in fig. 11.3. The stick method of weaving a pattern is slow but effective.

Uses. Stick-woven lace was particularly widespread in Latgale and Vidzeme. It was used for shawls and bed covers since sometime between the eighth and twelfth centuries.

The draft in fig. 11.4 is for a twentieth century bed cover made of fine, white cotton or linen warp with linen weft. It is treadled slightly differently from fig. 11.3's example in that each treadling unit contains two pattern picks rather than one.

Stick-woven lace is aptly described in the Latvian name *pubuļainais sējums,* which implies a "bubble" or "cobblestone" effect. Puckers emerge from blocks of plain weave, warp floats, and weft floats, distorting the cloth's surface. Besides being decorative these blocks' threadings were very practical. When floats occur only on certain selected warp threads, slack floating warps

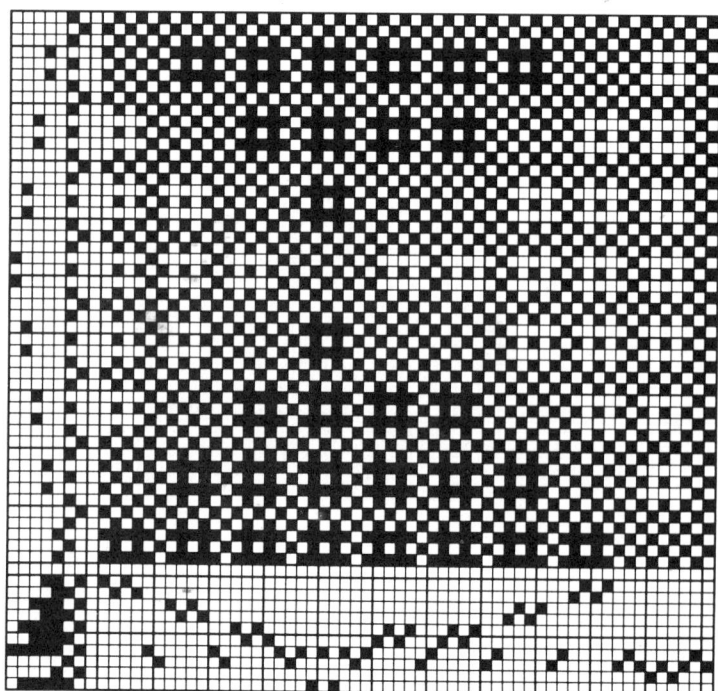

11.4. Setup for stick-weave lace if woven using regular loom shafts. Ten shafts imitate the old setup's five sticks, although nine shafts actually would be sufficient. #71a in Pa.

result because the plain-woven areas have greater take-up in length than the float areas. The stick-lace structure varies the interlacements of floating warp ends, so they remain reasonably taut during weaving.

Loom-controlled Stick-lace

Loom-controlled stick-lace was very popular into the twentieth century in Latvia. When multi-shaft looms became available, the draft in fig. 11.4 was designed to duplicate the popular stick-woven lace.

This now-traditional draft is apparently based on the stick set-up rather than on more regular, logical unit threadings. Each pattern treadle of the new draft is tied to emulate one stick in the old draft, and two treadles form the tabby sheds. In fact, this customary draft would use one less shaft if reduced to its minimal number of required shafts and treadles.

Leno
Caurumotais raksts
Leno weave is a method of patterning via open spaces in plain weave. The spaces form when adjacent warp threads are twisted around each other and held in place with the regular weft, fig. 11.5. Each twist may involve two, four, or even six warp ends to give a lacy openwork effect. In Latvian this was called *pierced patterning* or *twisted plain weave*.

Leno decoration, like true lace, was very popular in the province of Latgale. The Latgalian towel shown in fig. 3.6, uses leno for decoration in vertical stripes. Other more elaborate openwork motifs are also possible in leno patterning.

By the 1930s some leno was being woven with the use of *doups*, which are partial heddles of thread loops that twist warps through loom control rather than hand manipulation. Doup leno was of limited interest to home weavers, and only briefly mentioned in Latvian weaving books.

Uses. In the twentieth century leno ornamented tablecloths, napkins, window curtains, and towels.

Simple Weaves
with Discontinuous Wefts

Simple weaves using one set of warp threads and one set of weft threads can be patterned by using several discontinuous wefts which weave within narrow sections of the web. Latvian books called this technique *cloth with folded-in patterning,* or *audumi ar ielocītiem rakstiem.*

Gobelin Weave
Gobēlena audums
Gobelin weave is a weft-faced, plain-weave interlacement with discontinuous wefts. Finite areas of colored wefts form a pattern on the smooth surface of the weaving. The

11.5. The twisted warps of leno patterning on plain weave.

name comes from the French Gobelin tapestries.

One way the wefts may meet when they change across a shed is by forming slits vertically at their junction in the cloth. This technique was used for *kilim,* or *kelima,* rugs in Latvia until the late nineteenth century. It is a very labor-intensive method and became undesirable when it could not be commercially justified by craftsmen. A few home weavers continued to use it into the first half of the twentieth century, weaving carpets or wall blankets of wool weft over linen warp. At that time some professional artist-weavers in Latvia also adopted the technique for their work.

Spaced Plain Weave
Retinātā vienkārtņa audums
An interesting variation on the gobelin patterning method using discontinuous wefts is shown in fig. 11.6. Warps are spaced in the reed so that, for example, two dents each hold three warp threads, then five dents are skipped. During weaving the individual wefts of different colors weave back and forth within their pattern areas. Two wefts overlap in the same shed where the colors meet. Due to the spaced warp, pleats form naturally when the cloth is removed from the loom.

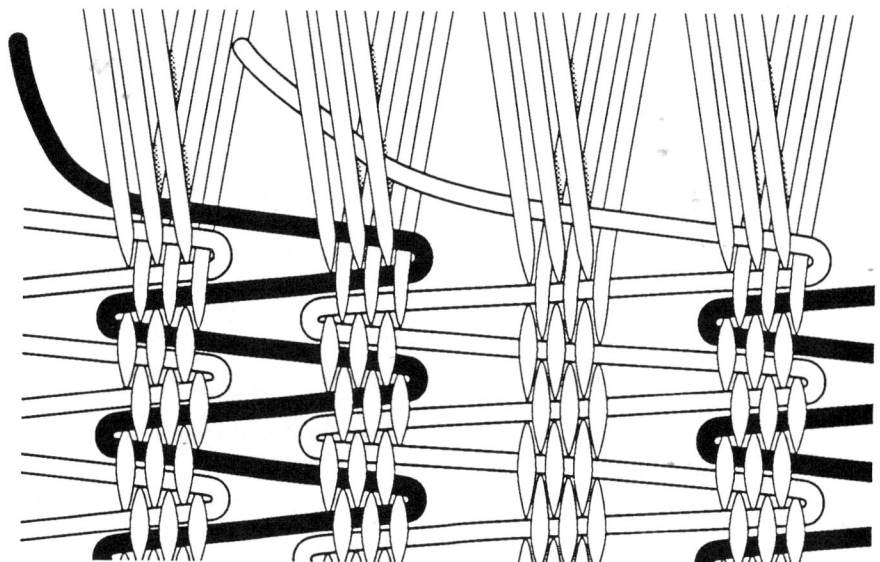

11.6 Two weft colors interlaced in spaced plain-weave cloth. Based on #252 in Ma.

This spaced weaving technique was popular in the twentieth century for bed covers, door curtains, blankets, cushions, and other heavy fabrics. Patterning was frequently in the form of slanted lines.

Compound Weaves with Supplementary Wefts

Compound weaves contain more than one set of warp and/or weft threads. Ancient Latvian methods of decorating fabrics often placed supplementary wefts in discrete areas for pattern motifs on a ground cloth of plain weave or some other structure. Sometimes sheds for supplementary wefts were formed with the help of sticks behind the shafts, somewhat like the old stick weaving described above, without tie-down warp threads. In other instances the inlay wefts were guided by a youngster who sat under the loom. Several Latvian techniques use discontinuous, supplementary, pattern wefts.

Measured Plaiting
Dalītais pinums
Plain weave, weft-faced plain weave, basket weave, crepe weave, or similar structures are the ground fabric for *measured plaiting*, called *inlay patterning* in North America. The length of pattern-weft floats is variable, measured by the weaver.

Whatever ground cloth is woven, two separate sheds are treadled for the laid-in supplementary wefts. Pattern wefts are followed by one or more ground picks. Pattern motifs may cover the whole cloth or only finite areas on a background cloth.

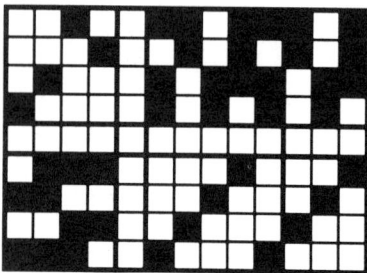

11.7. Supplementary weft (treadles 2 and 4) inlaid over a ground of plain weave (treadles 1 and 3), #255 in Ma.

In fig. 11.7, a simple plain weave forms the ground cloth, alternating with picks of supplementary wefts. In fig. 11.8, a crepe ground cloth is formed by the alternate wefts.

Since only two-shaft looms are necessary for the simplest versions of these weaves, Latvian peasants began weaving them sometime between the eighth and twelfth centuries.

Uses. Until the late nineteenth century many fabrics in eastern Vidzeme and Latgale were decorated with laid-in patterning, frequently in red. Towels, pillows, sheets, tablecloths, shirts, and aprons had motifs woven directly into the cloth or into a band which was sewn on the item. Little wear was given to the ornamented area, so it might be cut off and re-used.

Professional weavers seldom had the time required for laid-in patterning. Twentieth-century home weavers used the technique for window curtains, blankets, cushions, wall blankets, upholstery, and other decorative fabrics.

Ribbed Plaiting
Vagotais pinums
A favorite method of laid-in patterning in Latvia gave a ribbed surface appearance, resulting from a set of tie warps holding the

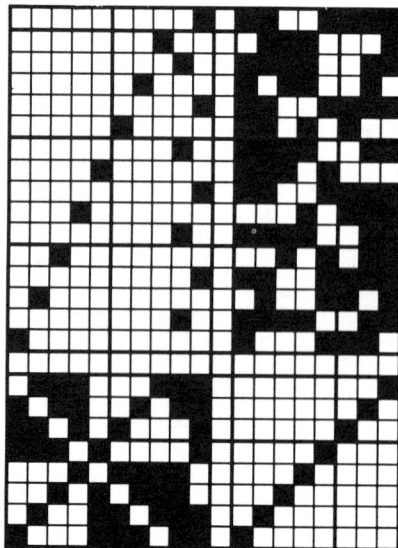

11.8. Supplementary weft (treadles 9 and 10) inlaid over a ground weave of crepe (treadles 1-8), #256 in Ma.

supplementary wefts. The pattern could be formed either as an overall ribbed surface, or as a ribbed area on a smooth background of plain weave or weft-faced plain weave.

The draft in fig. 11.9 has eight pattern warp ends, over which the supplementary weft floats to form a rib, and two tie warp ends, which tie the floats. Ribs of 10 or 12 warp ends are also possible, depending on the size of warp. *Paraugi audumien* gave many patterns for this sort of ribbed inlay with varying widths of ribs. Usually the recommended background cloth was linen or cotton and the pattern wefts were wool.

This cloth is woven with the back side up, and each pattern weft is laid in by hand within its pattern area. Each pattern shed is followed by two plain-weave picks (four picks if woven weft-faced). Any ends of pattern wefts fasten in a plain-weave shed. All ribs are of one width in a piece.

This structure is similar to the Swedish dukagång weave, with one significant difference. Dukagång inlay patterns have one warp end between columns of weft floats, while in ribbed plaiting there are two warp ends between columns of weft floats. Both techniques may be done to cover all or parts of the surface.

Uses. Ribbed plaiting originated in the 1800s in Vidzeme and Kurzeme, where it decorated blankets. The pillow in Plate 22 and fig. 11.10 illustrates a popular application of ribbed plaiting in twentieth- century Latvia. By then cushions were a significant addition to home decor.

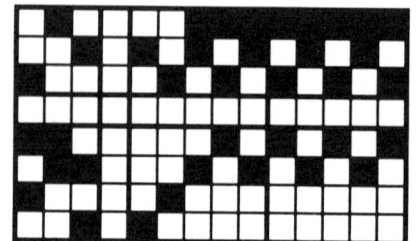

11.9. One repeat of draft for ribbed plaiting, with ground weft woven on picks 1 and 2, and supplementary weft on pick 3. Borders or bands of plain weave can be threaded by repeating shafts 1 and 2 only. #254 in Ma.

Knotted Pile of Fringes
Bārksts

Knotting short lengths of supplementary threads into a ground cloth, fig. 11.11, was of limited application in Latvian textiles. The technique is known in Finland as *ryijy,* and in Sweden as *flossa* and *rya.* It was used in Estonia and in its neighboring Latvian province of Vidzeme.

Uses. In the second half of the nineteenth century, knotted pile of wool was added to horse and sleigh blankets for warmth and decoration. A slow method of weaving which gives great freedom of design, knotting came to be used most by twentieth-century artist-weavers in Latvia.

Tufting or Loop Weave
Cilpainais pinums
or pērlīšu raksts

One weave was an exception that used a continuous supplementary weft for patterning, rather than a discontinuous one. *Tufting* or *loop weave* has been a favored technique among Latvian home weavers since the early twentieth century. Its name is taken from the textured surface of small, raised loops which define a pattern above a ground cloth, fig. 11.12.

The simplest threading for tufting requires only two shafts for the ground weave, with the weaver raising the pattern wefts into tufts. To make the tufts, a small rod like a knitting needle is used to selectively pick up a supplementary weft which passes over, for example, two warps, then under two warps, across the fabric. Two rows of plain weave ground are then woven to secure the pattern weft. The supplementary weft is usually a thicker yarn with a tighter twist than the ground cloth's threads.

With looms of more than two shafts it is possible to use threadings other than plain weave for the ground cloth. Basket, lace, and waffle weaves can facilitate counting and placement of loops. For instance, the towel in previous fig. 4.71 has a seven-shaft waffle-weave draft. The threading

established the supplementary weft's path as under three warps, then over one, as in fig. 11.12.

Occasionally tufts are formed by raised supplementary warps rather than wefts. This necessitates two sizes of warp threads, each wound on a separate back beam, with the pattern warp longer than the ground warp. A standard supplementary-warp draft is threaded on four shafts. The tufting warp ends are selected and held up by a rod, then the ground warps are woven with several picks of weft to stabilize the cloth.

Uses. Tufting was used on blankets in Latgale for centuries. It became a preferred option for decorating towels, cushions, blankets, and bed covers, especially in eastern Latvia. Typically towels had a band of tufted pattern across the end, as in fig. 11.13. Cushions and bed covers had designs upon their whole surface.

11.11. Method of adding knotted lengths of thread for pile over a ground cloth.

11.12. Supplementary weft used for tufting on plain-weave ground fabric.

11.10. Detail, typical cushion patterning in ribbed inlays, for which many patterns were given in books in the 1900s. Ca. 1870?; Latvia?; 43 cm. (17") L x 48 cm. 179") W; warp, cotton, 2-ply, Z-ply, natural; tabby weft, same as warp; pattern weft, wool, mostly 4-ply, S-ply, some 2-ply used double, assorted colors; 20 e/cm (50 epi); 8 pattern p/cm (20 ppi) and 14 tabby p/cm (36 ppi). ROM 972.355.2. Gift of Mrs. Lonija Brivkalns. See Plate 22.

Double Cloth

Pick-up Patterned Cloth

Rakstots divkāršais skalu audums

Double cloth (page 119) can be weaver-manipulated to produce designs. A four-shaft loom is used, with a stick selectively picking up particular sheds to supplement the loom's shedding action. This slow, precise technique can produce very intricate patterns. It was of limited use in twentieth-century Latvia for decorative cushions, wall blankets, or couch blankets.

11.13. A typical design for a band of tufting loops to border the ends of a towel, based on #10 in Pa.

11.14. (below) Double-weave pick-up was used in the twentieth century for patterning pillow tops with traditional symbols. This design of 117 blocks per side is based on #162 in Pa.

PART THREE

The Weaves

CONTEMPORARY AND MODIFIED USES

In *Part Two: The Weaves, Theory and Traditional Applications*, almost every item discussed was woven in Latvia prior to World War II. After 1940 the prominence of weaving and handwoven textile production diminished in Latvia.

The following chapters examine various aspects of the legacy of the old Latvian weavings. Work by contemporary artisans of Latvian descent who have been living outside of Latvia is surveyed in *Chapter Twelve*. These weavers have used their rich heritage of handweaving patterns to produce items ranging from straight reproductions to powerful works of art.

I enjoy weaving Latvian national costumes. The old colorways and patterns continually inspire me to try new combinations while still staying within the boundaries prescribed by tradition for the region. The beautifully woven skirts, intricately patterned sashes and colorful mittens make me aware of tradition and history. They create an appreciation for the old crafts and admiration for the women who, after long days of hard work, still enjoyed creating such beauty in woven, embroidered or knitted garments.

LIENA KAUGARS

Some contemporary applications of the Latvian weave structures are explored in *Chapters Thirteen* and *Fourteen*, especially as they apply to the weaving of rugs with graphic or pictorial designs.

These chapters are for weavers who seek design freedom within structural parameters. Particular emphasis is given to heavy-duty items like rugs, with loom-controllled patterning for geometric designs, and the freeform method of weaving pictorial designs. Ideally, the exploration of options based on traditional textiles will stimulate even more ideas for creative uses of these drafts.

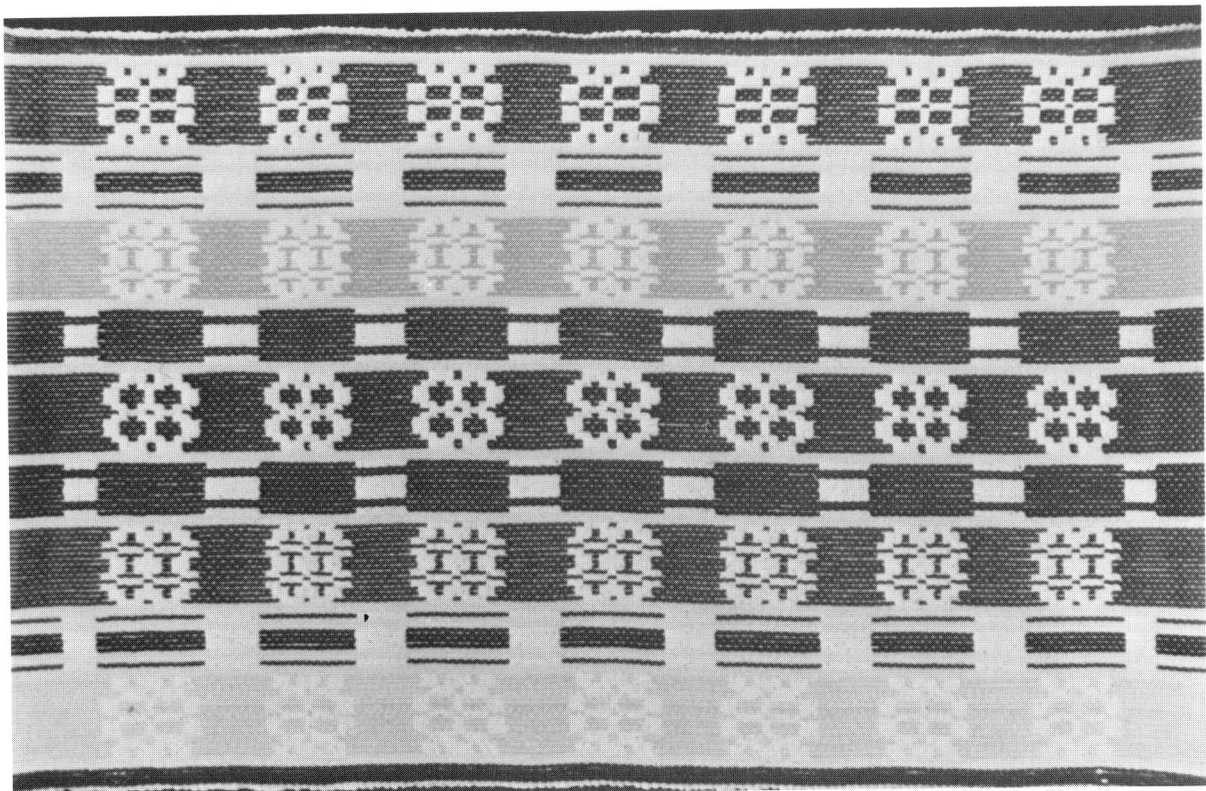

12.A. "Majolica Rug" of 4:1 tied-Beiderwand units arranged for warp-faced and weft-faced pattern. 1990; 113cm (44.5")L X 69 cm (27.25"W; warp, cotton, 8/4. white, blue, rose, yellow, violet, green; tabby weft, cotton, 8/4, white; pattern weft, cotton flannel, 1.3cm (.5") strips, white print; 10 e/cm (24 epi); 6 p/cm (14 ppi). Designed and woven by Jane Evans. See page 153 for weaving information.

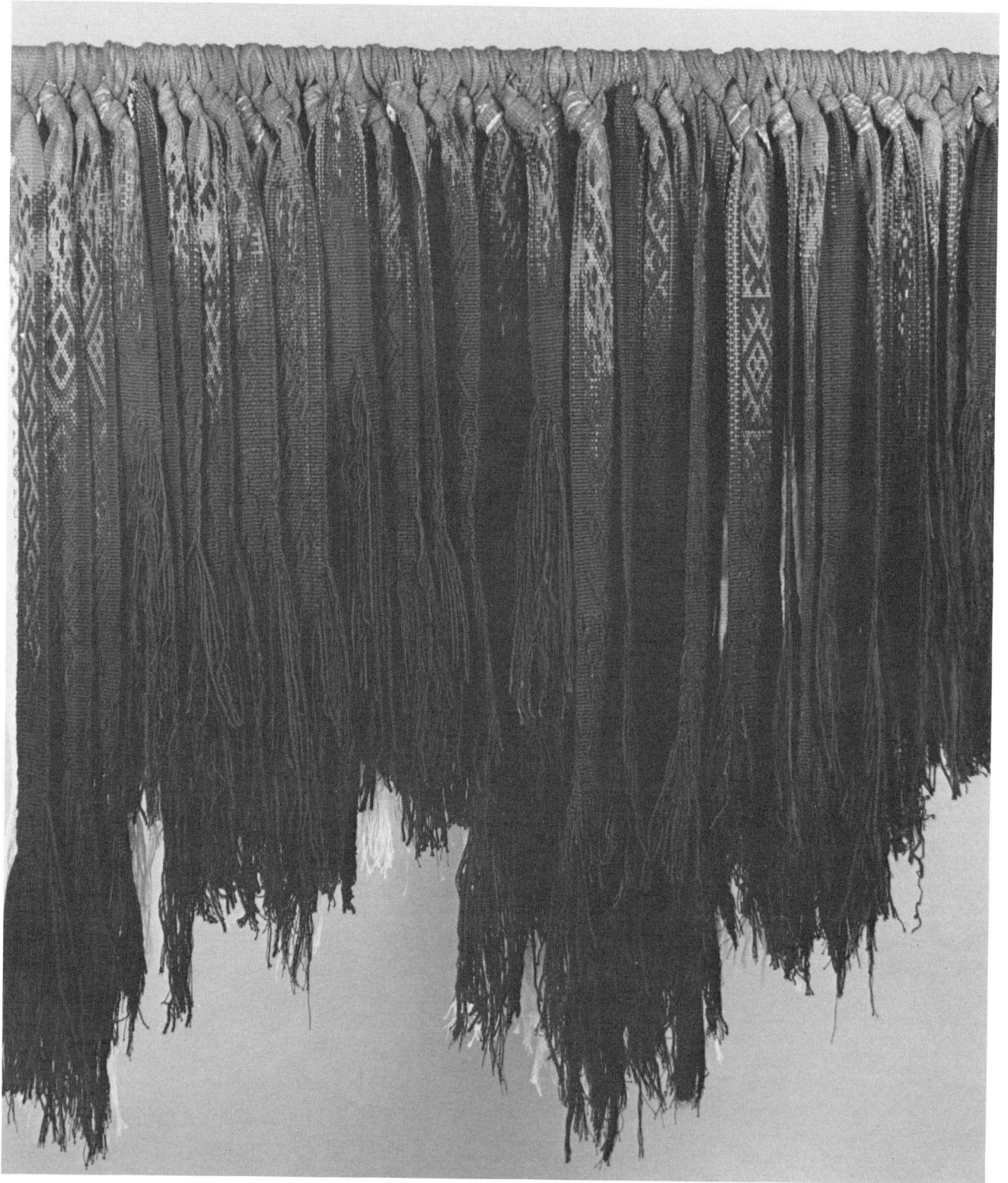

12.B. "Divided We Stand/Dvēsele kas negrib zust," woven by Vita Plūme in 1987. Red and white sashes woven in a traditional pick-up weaving method on an ikat ground cover one side of this piece; red and black sashes fill the other side. Plūme uses both traditional belt motifs and the destruction of those traditional symbols to express the wounds of assimilation. See page 142 for additional information.

CHAPTER TWELVE

Contemporary Ethnic Weaves

12.1. Tablecover by Mirdza Strauss. Her choices of structure, colors, and materials reflect her background. Subdued hues are used in float-block weave (see Chapter Six) for this tablepiece. Warp, 24/3 cotton, mercerized, beige, brown, grey-blue; tabby weft, same as warp; pattern weft, wool, 12/2, white, gold, brown, rust, green; 9.5 e/cm (24 epi); 11 p/cm (28 ppi). Collection of Liena Kaugars. See Plate 29.

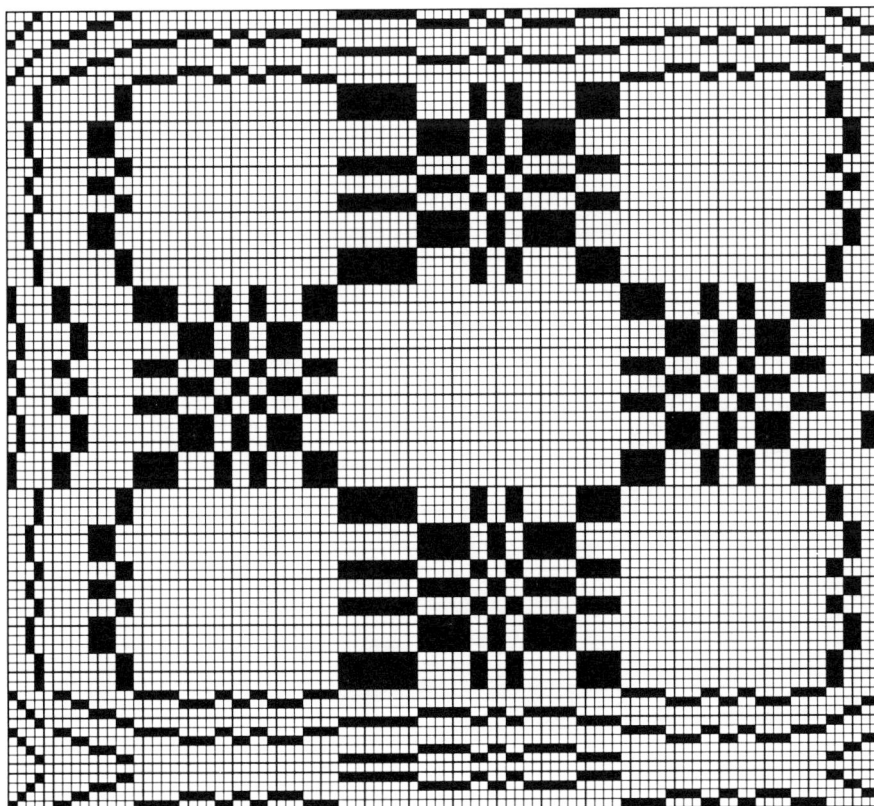

12.2. One repeat of profile draft for band in fig 12.1. Design is slightly assymetrical. Profile blocks' threading units: 1 = shafts 1,2; 2 = shafts 3,2; 3 = shafts 3,4; 4 = shafts 1,4.

Contemporary weavers of Latvian descent living in North America use the traditional design elements and weave structures of Latvia in a wide spectrum of applications, from reproductions of traditional textiles to strong expressions of feelings about displacement.

Works such as the small table-covers, figs. 12.1 and 12.3, also shown in Plates 29 and 30, woven in 4-shaft weaves, exemplify traditional Latvian weaves. Both tablecovers are by *Mirdza Strauss*, who learned to be a skillful weaver in the Latvian school, *Kaucmindes majturibas instituts*, prior

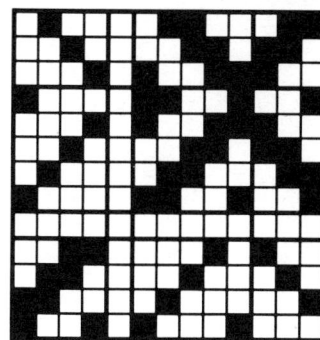

12.3. (above) Runner in classic rosepath design woven by Mirdza Strauss. 47 cm (18.5") plus fringes L X 35 cm (13.75") W; warp and tabby weft, cotton, 24/3, beige; pattern weft, wool, 12/3, grey, black, white, brown, green, rust, ochre; same sett and picks as fig. 12.1 above. Collection of Liena Kaugars. See Plate 30.

12.4. Traditional rosepath draft, as in fig. 12.3.

139

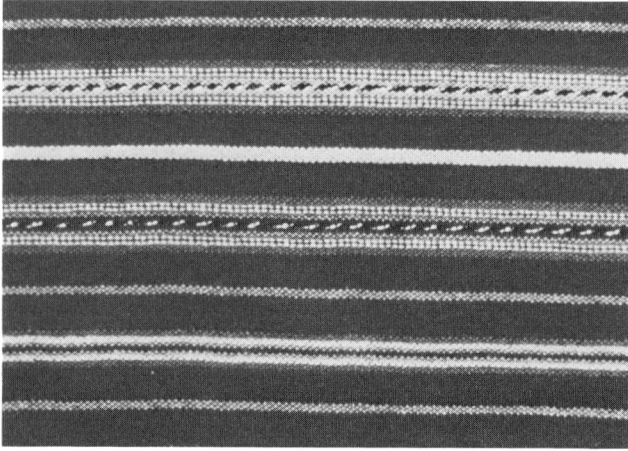

12.5a. Reproduction of traditional skirt fabric from Vidzeme, in plain weave with typical accents of twisted wefts. 1987; warp, 20/2 cotton, green; weft, wool, 18/2 and 20/2, blue, red, yellow, white, green, black; 9.5 e/cm (24 epi); 8.5 p/cm (22 ppi). Woven by Liena Kaugars. See Plate 26.

12.5b. Reproduction of traditional skirt fabric from Zemgale. 1985; warp, cotton, 20/2, brown; weft, wool, 18/2 and 20/2, black, white, red, yellow, green, brown; 9.5 e/cm (24 epi); 9.5 p/cm (24 ppi). Woven by Liena Kaugars. See Plate 27.

12.6. Wallhanging woven by Mr. Dzidra Šefers on a double-harness loom. Several different interlacements form pattern bands. 1987; ca. 165 cm (65") plus fringes L X ca. 91 cm (36") W; warp, linen, 40/2, natural; tabby weft, linen, finer than warp; pattern weft, wool, used triple; 9 e/cm (23 epi).

to World War II. She and her students have continued the traditions of home weavers in Latvia. Figure 12.2 is the traditional 4-shaft float-block draft for the tablecloth in Plate 29 and fig 12.1. The runner in fig. 12.3 and Plate 30 is drafted in classic rosepath, fig. 12.4. While both these weavings were done in 1982 in New Jersey, U.S.A., they are examples of transplanted early twentieth century Latvian work.

A contemporary weaver of Latvian descent, *Liena Kaugars* of Kalamazoo, Michigan, was a student of Mirdza Strauss. In the 1980s Liena Kaugars wove the skirt fabrics shown in figs. 12.5a and b, and Plates 26 and 27. These are adept reproductions of old costume fabrics from Vidzeme and Zemgale. The latter fabric is based on the rosepath draft in fig. 12.4, and is the oldest twill type of skirt patterning still in use in Latvia. Both skirts are made of pure wool in colors faithful to their prototypes.

Another weaver originally from Latvia, Mrs. *Dzidra Šefers* weaves in Toronto, Ontario, Canada, on a traditional-style double-harness loom. She uses a drawloom with roller pulleys and long-eyed heddles for the front harnesses. The decorative and functional fabrics she produces are very similar to those she learned to weave prior to World War II at the home economics school in Riga (the same school attended by Mrs. Strauss). The wall hanging shown in

12.7. *Double-harness threading draft for one and one-half repeats, showing two pattern bands from fig. 12.6. See text for how each is woven.*

fig 12.6 includes the age-old supplementary-weft structure of wool weft floats over a plain-weave ground cloth of linen. Its draft in fig 12.7 requires 16 regular pattern shafts and two long-eyed heddle shafts for weaving units without ties. Two of the motifs in this piece are shown in fig. 12.7). The lower motif is woven with supplementary wefts over a ground of tabby (made by alternating the long-eyed heddle shafts), and the upper one is woven with two complementary wefts treadled *on opposites*.

Mrs. Šefers also works in the relatively old structure of *tied-Beiderwand,* as seen in the tablecloth in fig. 12.8. Figure 12.9 is the profile draft for the border and one and one-half motifs of the tablecloth. The threadings for each unit are given in fig. 6.12.

Other contemporary weavers of Latvian descent reflect their heritage in less traditional forms. Mrs. *Velta Vilsons* wove the large, decorative works shown in Plates 31 and 33 which are installed in public buildings in Toronto, Ontario, Canada. Plate

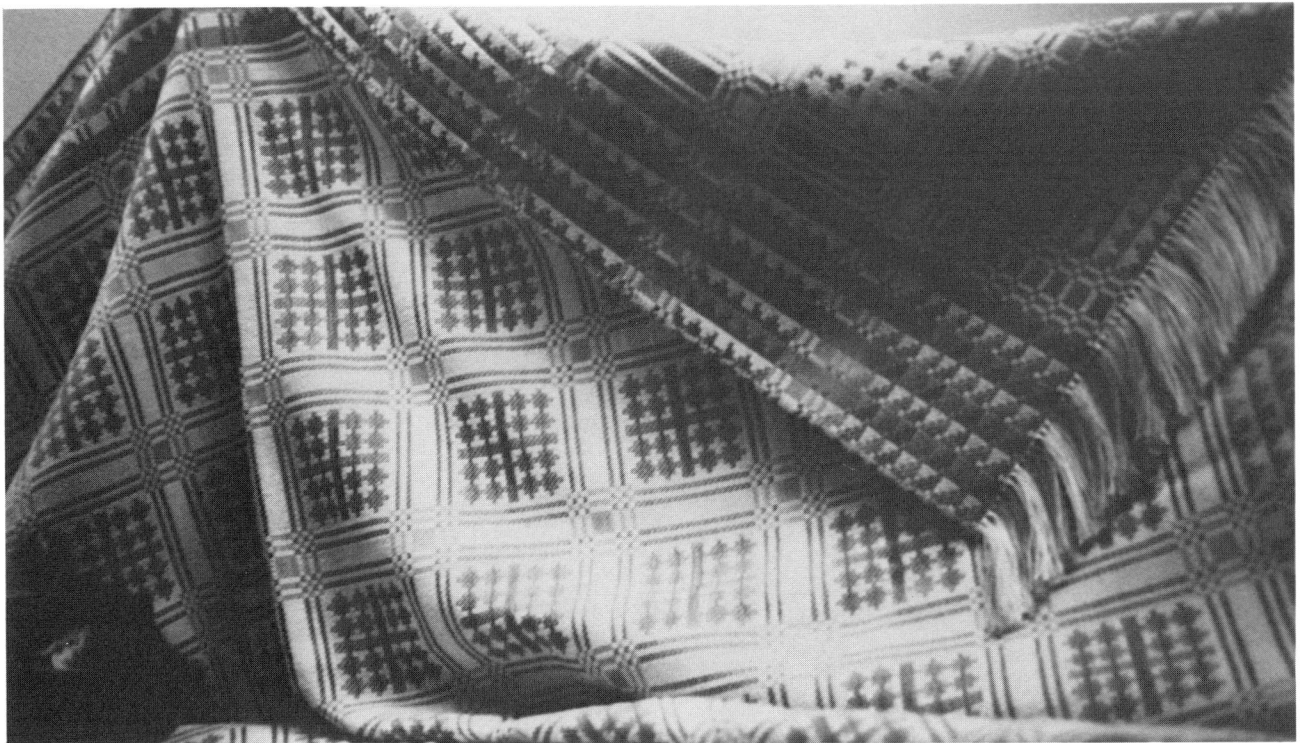

12.8. *Tied-Beiderwand tablcloth similar to traditional cloths from Latvia, woven in 1986 by Mrs. Dzidra Šefers. Two widths, each 96cm (38"), are joined. 130 cm (51") plus fringes L X 190 cm (76"); warp, cotton, 16/2, bleached white; weft, cotton sewing thread, used quadrupled, ecru; 18 e/cm (46 epi).*

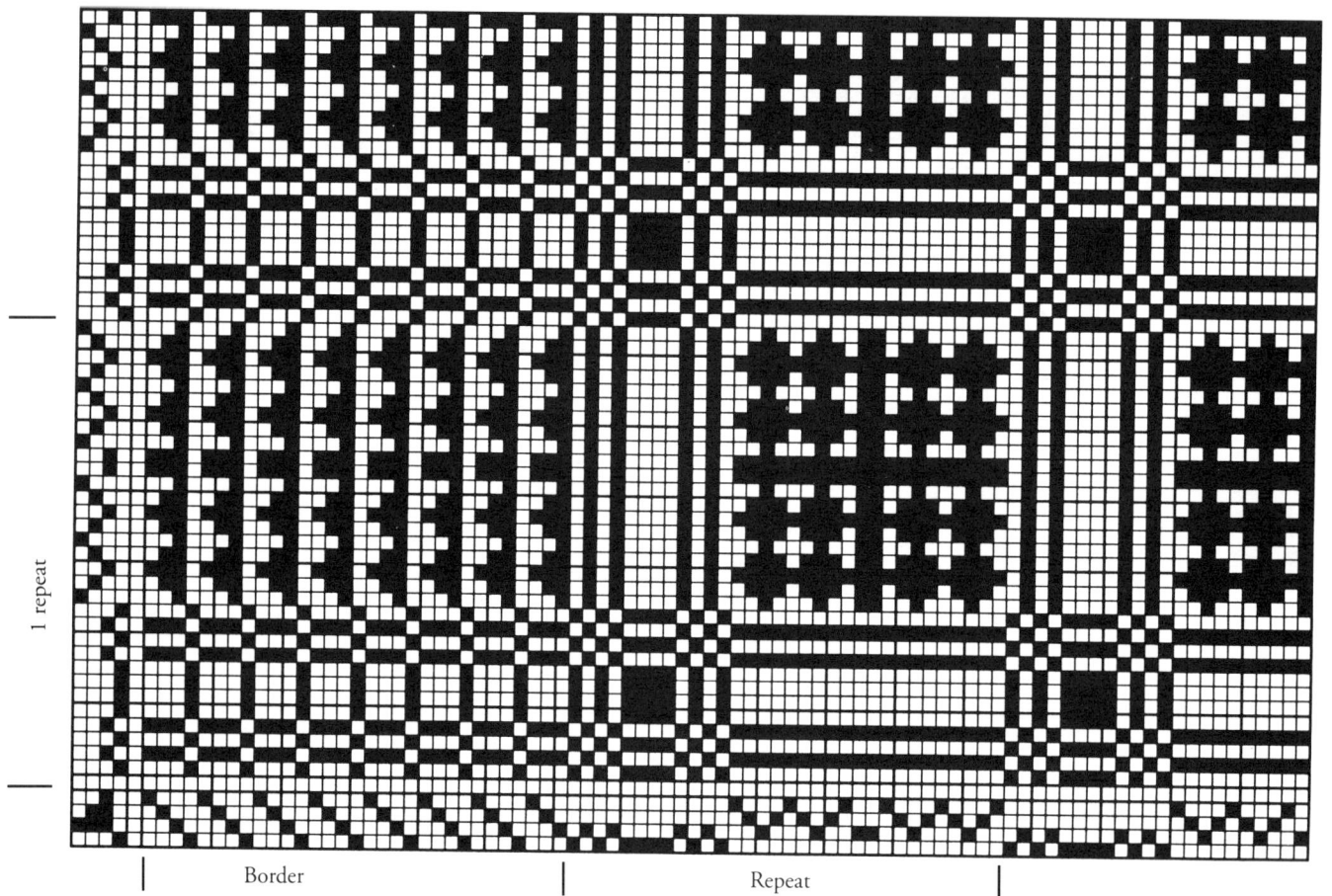

12.9. Profile draft for border and one and one-half threading repeats of pattern area for 2:1 tied-Beiderwand tablecloth in fig. 12.8.

33 shows three panels in a weft-faced four-shaft twill. The draft is in fig. 12.10.

Vita Plūme intends that her works carry strong messages through their amalgamation of traditional Latvian woven forms and colors with universal images. Each work is titled for further emphasis. Born after World War II and living outside of Latvia, Plūme weaves to express several generations' feelings of displacement, sorrow, resentment, and determination.

"Back to the Wall/...*kur tauta lai ietu?,*" shown in Plate 32 and fig. 12.11, uses dark red and white, the colors of Latvia's flag, contrasted with black. Another piece by Plūme in

this color scheme, *Latvian Flag II/Dievs, Tava zeme deg,* is shown in Plate 34.

One of two surfaces of sashes which form Vita Plūme's free-hanging *Divided We Stand / Dvēsele kas negrib zust* is shown in fig. 12.B (page 138).

Somber red and black belts fill one side, in contrast with white and red on the reverse side. Each sash is ikat dyed and woven in traditional pick-up methods. Other works by Plūme arrange sashes in the many colors of the old costumes.

12.10. Draft for hanging in Plate 31.

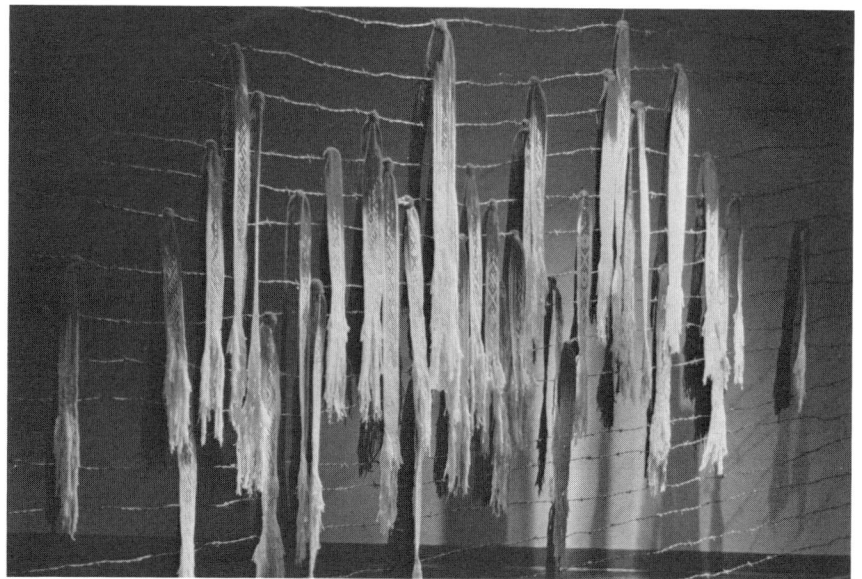

12.11. Detail, "Back to the Wall/ ... Kur tauta lai ietu?" Forty fragments of traditional Latvian sashes, all woven in pick-up techniques as of old, hang from the barbed wire fence in this work by Vita Plūme, Halifax, Nova Scotia. See Plate 32.

CHAPTER THIRTEEN

Modified Simple Weaves

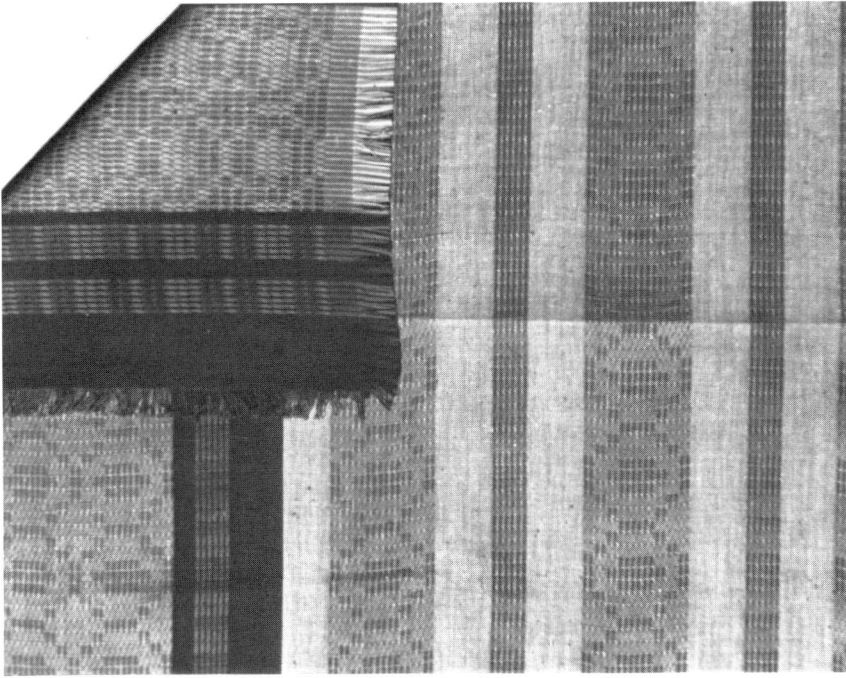

13.1. Cotton runner with atypical colors, reflecting changes in materials available after World War II. Precisely woven with very fine threads, it very likely has been produced for sale by a Latvian craftsman who had access to such materials and still wove after the war years. Latgale; 88 cm (34.5") plus fringes L X 44.5 cm (17.5") plus fringes W; warp, cotton, 2-ply, S- ply, rust red; weft, cotton, 2-ply, Z-ply, olive green, light green, white; 15 e/cm (38 epi); 21 p/cm (53 ppi). ROM990.20.11. Gift of Mr. Peter Alexandrovitch.

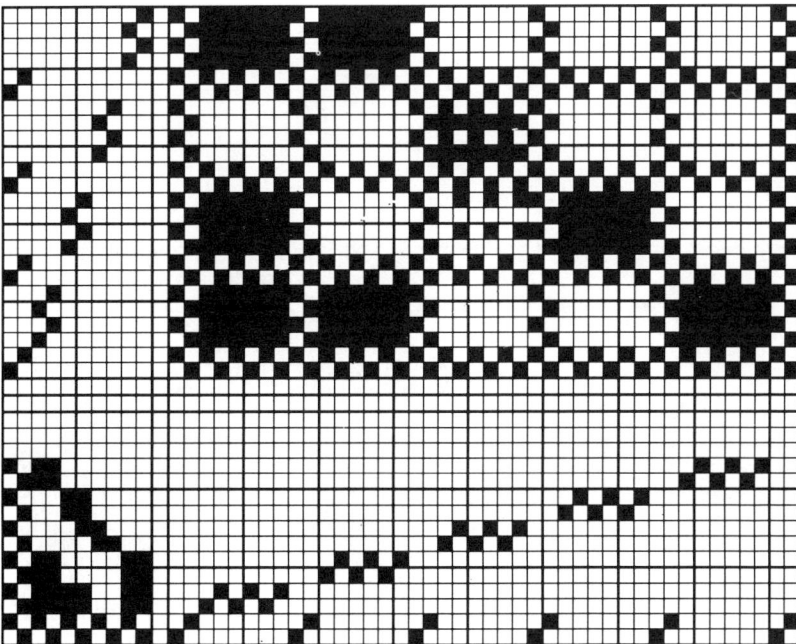

13.2. Twelve-shaft threading draft for paired-tie units as used in runner in fig. 13.1. A tie-up error changes the interlacement of the third unit.

In the following pages, drafts which have been used in traditional Latvian textiles, especially threadings which weave tied units, have been modified for some contemporary applications. Numerous other adaptations are possible as well.

All of the following weaves are based in plain weave with one set of threads in each element, warp and weft. Interlacements are loom-controlled.

Lace Weaves on Tie Drafts

Lace weaves are derived from plain weave and have floats in their warp and/or weft directions. See *Chapter Four*.

Threadings with tie-down threads placed within units of threading lend themselves to lace weave adaptations. The decorative runner in fig. 13.1 is one example of a lace *paired-tie* weave with some rather interesting characteristics. The paired-tie draft, fig. 13.2, has a 6:2 ratio of pattern to tie warps, rather than a more traditional 4:2 relationship. Surprisingly, there is a significant, uncorrected tie-up error in the woven piece. The block controlled by shafts 7 and 8 does not weave a proper float group throughout. In general, though, it is a cleverly designed and carefully woven item.

Further lace possibliities on both the *paired-tie* and *tied-Beiderwand* drafts are shown in fig. 13.3. Units of 2:1 tied-Beiderwand (right side of picture) are threaded in a point order, followed by a plain-weave band. Paired-tie units then are threaded in mirror-image order (left side of picture). Each unit (six picks) is woven as weft floats, warp floats, and combined floats, for a total of eighteen picks which are then repeated one time. Then the three structures are woven repeating each unit three times (upper section on

13.3. Sampler of tied-Beiderwand and paired-tie drafts woven for lace effects. 8/2 cotton, 9 e/cm (22.5 epi), woven to square. Woven by Alison Philips.

Unbalanced, Turned Plain Weave

When one surface of a weave structure and its opposite surface both show on one face of a fabric, the combination is called a *turned weave*. *Unbalanced plain weave* has either a warp-faced or weft-faced surface (colloquially "repps"). Combining blocks of these two ribbed effects can give sturdy fabrics with unusual visual characteristics in loom-controlled patterns, as in the "Blue Shadows" rug pictured in fig. 13.5 and Plate 41.

One way of weaving turned interlacements is to alternate two sizes of elements in both warp and weft directions. Short floats over two threads occur in certain places, while for the most part the fabric is in plain weave, as shown in fig. 13.5. An alternation of thick and thin warps and wefts allows for clear design blocks and avoids unbound floats in warps or wefts. This weave can use fine yarns of two sizes for sturdy garment fabrics, and it particularly lends itself to heavy items like rugs. Only one warp beam is necessary to maintain an even tension. Drafts for this weave are related to the drafts in *Chapter Four*.

Two-shaft Drafts
One type of draft for unbalanced, turned plain weave is based on units controlled by two shafts per unit, fig. 13.6. Clear-cut designs are easy to plan and execute in this system. Its

picture), for a total of 54 picks. This extended treadling is repeated at the top of the picture.

Lace woven on tie drafts offers interesting design potential. Few traditional lace weaves can weave warp and weft units simultaneously in both the horizontal and vertical directions. Designs with tied units are countless because the units may be repeated next to themselves or may skip for any profile draft sequence as long as the tie-down warps remain in order.

13.4. Draft for the sampler in fig. 13.3. Each six-pick unit may be treadled once or repeatedly. See text for explanation.

UNBALANCED, TURNED PLAIN WEAVE IN TWO-SHAFT UNITS

DRAFTING

• Use a balanced plain-weave sett.

• Decide how many warp ends will compose the wide part of a unit (four in fig. 13.6). The unit's width is limited only by how long a weft float is acceptable. The second shaft in a unit is threaded with one warp end.

• Make a profile draft for one-half the number of shafts available. Two shafts are needed for each unit, fig. 13.6.

TIE-UP

Arrange each unit's two shafts to weave opposite each other on successive picks, forming plain weave. See fig. 13.6.

Blocks may be combined on a treadle. Tie up each section of pattern on two treadles, opposite to each other's tie-up, rather than try to double treadle.

WEAVING

Alternate two sizes of wefts, wide and narrow. Use one large element, such as several threads of yarn or a cloth strip, for the wide weft. Use one strand of warp thread for the narrow weft.

The thin weft closely binds warps and adds flexibility to the fabric. Where a weft-faced block meets a warp-faced block, two adjoining shafts move alike and break the plain-weave order. This join is inconspicuous.

main limitation is the need for numerous shafts to control any designs beyond very simple ones. Directions for drafting and weaving this method are above.

Shadow Weave Drafts

This drafting method allows four shafts to weave four design blocks, as in the rug in Plate 41 and fig. 13.5. Fig 13.7 shows four units of the draft, called *shadow weave* in North America. Although similar to the previous two-shaft units, it cannot weave independent blocks because each shaft is used both for single warps and wide groups. A balanced twill tie-up is treadled on opposites,

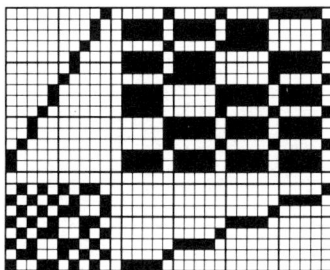

so blocks always weave in combination - A+B, B+C, C+D, D+A. A psuedo-tabby is available.

This type of draft could be used on any even number of shafts to get as many blocks as shafts. Figure 13.8 is an example of an eight-shaft draft for shadow weave. Complete drafting and weaving directions for shadow weave are on pages 146-147.

13.5. Detail, "Blue Shadows" rug, woven in unbalanced, turned plain weave, showing thick-and thin weft alternation. Warps alternate a single white thread with groups of four blue. Hems of 8/4 cotton are woven by treadling shafts 1 and 3 versus shafts 2 and 4. 1986; 107 cm (42") L X 61 cm (24") W; warp, cotton, 8/4, blue and white; thick weft, cotton fabric strips; thin weft, cotton, 8/4, blue; 9.5 e/cm (24 epi); 3 p/cm (8 ppi). Designed and woven by Jane Evans. See Plate 41.

13.6. Eight-shaft draft for four two-shaft units, each shaft used only in one block's threading.

SHADOW WEAVE

DRAFTING

1. Make a profile design of as many blocks as there are available shafts (four in this case). Either block or twill motifs are viable. Figure 13.9 is a sample profile draft.

2. Transfer the profile draft to alternate squares of graph paper, as begun in fig. 13.10. These are the primary warps which will determine the pattern, and in threading each will be a wide group of warps.

3. Follow each primary warp by a shadowing warp, indicated with different symbols or colors in the blank squares. Opposite shafts are "shadows."

   • To determine which shafts are opposites, draw a circle and place the four shaft numbers around it at equal intervals. Shafts 1 and 3 are opposite each other, and shafts 2 and 4 are opposite, as in fig. 13.11. (A similar circle of opposites can be drawn to find the shadows for any even number of shafts.)

   • To achieve symmetry, if the primary warps are being threaded in a clockwise order around the circle (1 to 2, 2 to 3, 3 to 4, 4 to 1), write in the shadowing warp *after* the primary warp. On fig. 13.12 the left side of the draft has a primary warp on shaft 1 followed by a shadow warp on shaft 3, then the primary warp on shaft 2 is followed by a shadow warp on shaft 4.

   • At the point where a draft reverses, begin to work counterclockwise around the circle (from 1 to 4, 4 to 3, 3 to 2, 2 to 1). *Drop* the shadowing warp from the reversing warp, and thereafter all shadow warps will *precede* their primary warps.

   In fig. 13.12, there is no shadow warp on shaft 2 after the second primary warp on shaft 4. Instead, the shadow is on shaft 1 and is thought of as linked with the primary warp on shaft 3. When the primary warps reverse later to once again go clockwise around the circle, shadow warps both precede and follow the reversing primary warp. Also seen in fig. 13.12 is a repeated unit of threading where a primary warp and its shadow are repeated. There is no problem of too long a weft float here because the tie-up provides plain weave in this area.

4. When the threading draft is filled in, check to see that all turning points of primary warps have a mirror image of shadow warps around them.

TIE-UP

5. Add the 2/2 tie-up as in fig 13.7. Tie two extra treadles to 1,3 and 2,4 to weave a near-tabby, which is useful for hems. (A balanced, straight twill tie-up is used for however many shafts are drafted.)

WEAVING

Alternate two sizes of wefts (thick and thin) between two treadles tied opposite to each other. Use the circle diagram in fig. 13.11 for determining shadows here, too. Treadles 1 and 3 are opposites, and 2 and 4 are opposites, as in fig. 13.12.

   • Weave a thick weft on the primary treadle of a pair and the thin weft on the opposite treadle.

   • Treadling order can be *as drawn in* or any other choice, as long as each primary treadle is followed by its opposite treadle.

   • Just as with threading, treadling order has the principle of dropping shadows at reversing points, shown in fig. 13.12.

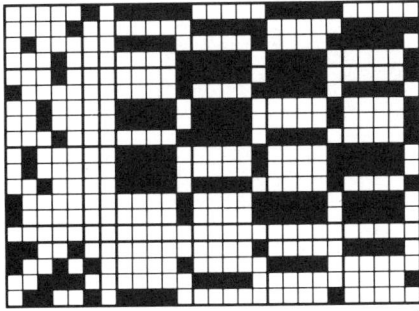

13.7. (left) Four-shaft draft for four two-shaft units, each shaft used in two different blocks' threadings.

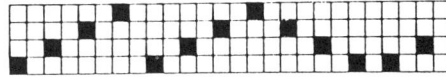

13.10. (above) Beginning notation of primary warps for shadow weave draft, showing first 13 warps from left side of profile draft in fig. 13.9.

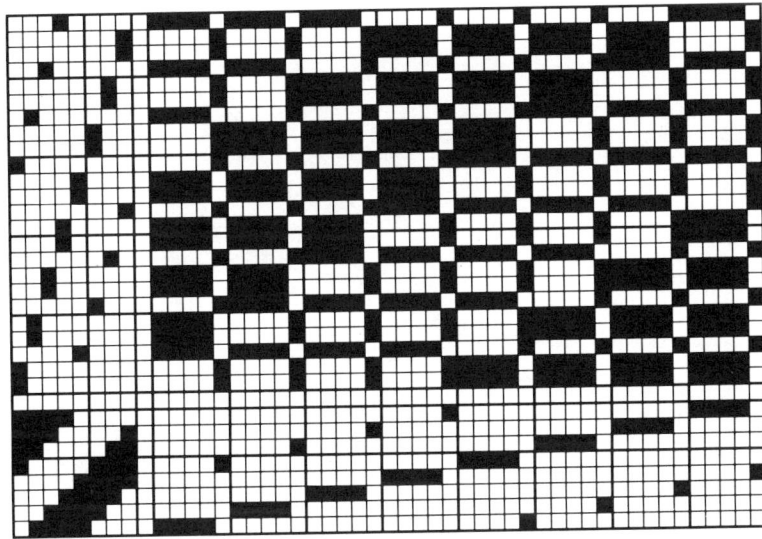

13.11. Circle diagram placing a loom's four shafts in opposite orientation.

13.8. Eight-shaft draft for eight two-shaft units.

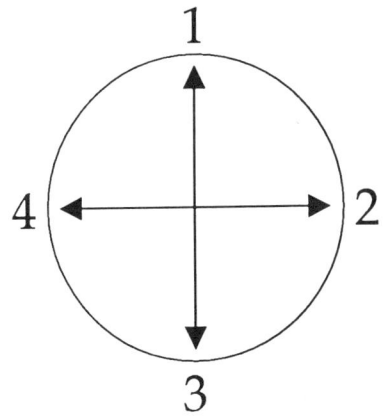

13.12. Draft for shadow weave version of left side of profile draft in fig. 13.9.

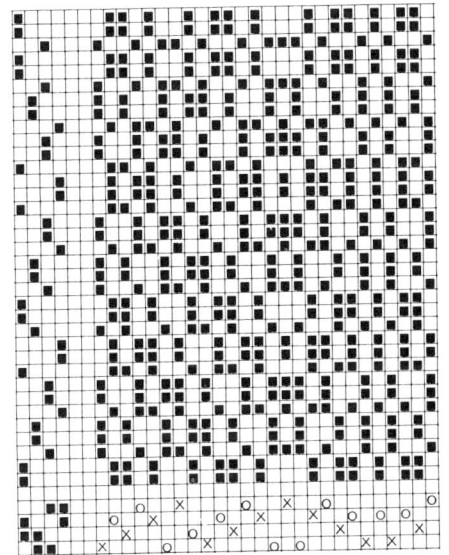

13.9. Profile draft for four-shaft shadow weave fabric.

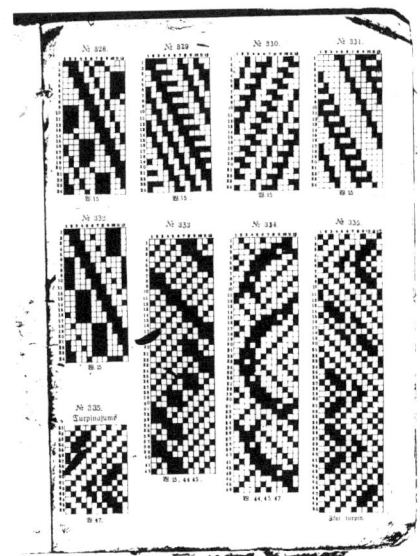

13.13. Page of twill drafts from Vilumsons' third book.

147

14.A. "Traces of Summer " rug is an example of freeform weaving on four shafts, using the 2:1 tied-Beiderwand draft. The weaving method follows the directions on page 166. 1991; warp 12/6 cotton, brown; pattern weft, wool, singles (1300 m/kg), greys and browns, used triple; tabby weft same as warp; 3 e/cm (8 epi); 3 p/cm (8ppi). Designed and woven by Jane Evans.

CHAPTER FOURTEEN

Modified Compound Weaves

The following structures have more than one set of warp and/or weft threads, and thus are *compound weaves*. These weaves are based on traditional tied-unit threadings that have been modified for either a loom-controlled or a freeform approach to creating patterns. The loom-controlled approach often requires a multi-shaft loom. Many weavers prefer this sort of technique and its resultant patterns. The freeform weaving method is described for weavers who seek flexibility of design beyond the limits of their loom's shafts. There are many choices for both types of weaving.

Three weaving terms which recur in many of these modifications are *freeform design*, *stuffer warps*, and *split-shed weaving*.

1. Freeform Design.

Four-shaft tied units adapt well to uncomplicated, freeform methods of patterning in which each threaded unit of the chosen structure can be woven independently from every other unit across the warp. Freeform weaving combines weaver-control and loom-control features, with a trade-off of speed for freedom in forming images. A smaller number of shafts is needed, and an increased amount of hand control is used, which allows the broadest range of patterning possibilities. It also has the advantage of the loom's mechanical control of structures that are more complex than plain weave.

Among freeform applications the concepts of *stuffer warps* and *split sheds* are often employed. Their general principles are given here and more specific details will be included as needed in describing projects.

2. Stuffer Warps.

A stuffer warp is mentioned in *Chapter Eight*. Stuffers are based on the fact that tied-unit drafts have both tie warps and pattern warps in each threading unit. On particularly heavy fabrics such as rugs, the pattern warp ends are held at higher tension than the tie warp ends. The tighter ends run unseen through the center of the rug without bending over wefts. This creates extra density in the rug, which usually is increased by the stuffer warps being either grouped threads or thicker than the tie warps.

Tie warps need less tension and greater length than stuffer (pattern) warps, because the tie warps do bend around wefts. The two warps' differing tensions and lengths are best handled by two warp beams, although the tie warp could be hung independently from the back beam and weighted for small projects.

3. Split-shed Weaving.

Many weavers would like the same freedom of design on their four-shaft loom as is associated with more complex looms. For fabrics woven with fairly large elements there is an efficient, uncomplicated way to weave complex images on only four shafts. The weaver uses the shuttle, or sometimes a pick-up stick, to individualize each weft's path. Exactly what constitutes an adequate size of threads or sett for weaver-control is a personal decision.

An integral aspect of such specialized shedding is a *split shed*, pictured from the side view in fig. 14.1. Split-shed weaving as described herein is done on tied-unit threadings containing two tie shafts plus one or two pattern shafts. The split shed is formed by creating a shallow shed both above and below the pattern warp ends. One tie shaft's warps form the top layer of the upper shed while the second tie shaft's warps form the bottom layer of the lower shed. These two shafts alternate positions at appropriate times.

Pattern warps form the center layer of the split shed. They are often shorter and held under greater tension than the tie warps, as in the stuffer warp setup previously described. The pattern warps may or may not be larger than the tie warps, depending on the project.

Looms with jack, countermarch, and counterbalanced actions all can form split sheds. On jack looms one treadle lifts the upper warps, a second treadle partially lifts the center (pattern) warps, and the lower warps are left unmoved. A typical tie-up with tabby is in fig. 14.2. For countermarch looms, the tie-up given in fig. 14.3 segregates rising shafts (dark symbols) on some treadles and sinking shafts (*X*'s) on others, and leaves the center warps (blanks) unmoved on pattern sheds.

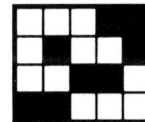

14.2. (upper) Jack loom tie-up with tabby.
14.3. (lower) Countermarch tie-up with tabby.

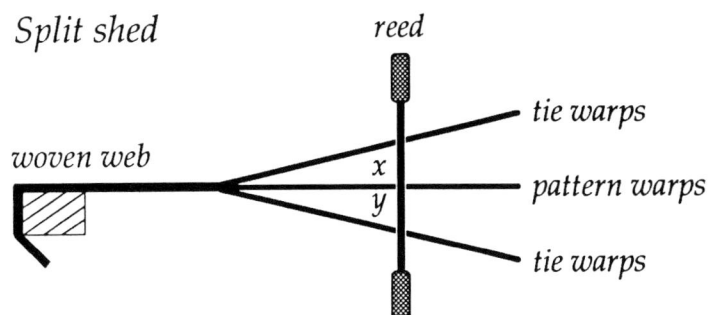

14.1. Side view of split shed containing two small sheds, x (upper shed) and y (lower shed).

Counterbalanced looms may not weave as well as the other two types of looms for all the weave structures given here. A counterbalanced loom can be adapted either by tying unbalanced sinking sheds (*X*'s) as in fig. 14.4, or by not threading pattern warps through heddles and tying as in fig. 14.5. The latter process can be done for summer/winter or tied-Beiderwand drafts. During threading, warps on shafts 1 and 2 are put through heddles. Warp ordinarily on shafts 3 and 4 are not in heddles, but run freely from back to front beams.

14.4. (upper) Counterbalanced loom tie-up.
14.5. (lower) Alternate tie-up for counterbalanced loom. See text for details.

Both tabby and pattern sheds can be formed with the tie-up in fig. 14.5.

On the tied-Beiderwand threading the pattern warp ends will group to become a thick stuffer warp.

Whatever the loom's action, during weaving the shuttle passes in the shallow sheds either above or below the pattern warp ends, as required by the design. See fig. 14.1. In areas where the weft is to be visible on the upper surface, the upper shed (*X*) is used. Selecting the lower shed (*Y*) places the weft on the back surface. For equal fabric density from selvage to selvage the shuttle travels across the whole width of warp, sometimes in the upper shed and sometimes in the lower. In a few of the following examples *brocade* wefts travel in the upper shed, within only a limited area across the warp, creating *inlaid* weft patterning.

An outline of the design can be drawn on lightweight cloth and placed under the web to help position the motifs.

The logic of weft placement during split-shed weaving becomes clear with a bit of practice. There often is flexibility on where to change sheds as long as the cloth's structure remains sound. The sense of creativity is reinforced with every weft row because designs can be freeform, released from most of the constraints of loom-controlled threading and treadling.

Compound Weaves with Supplementary Wefts

The following structures are based on threadings of tied units. A background cloth is formed by one set of warp threads and one set of weft threads. Patterning is due to one or more supplementary wefts which are regularly held by tie-down warps across the cloth.

Discontinuous supplementary wefts could be used in any of these structures. Discontinuous wefts, also called *brocade* or *inlaid* wefts, can be added over all or part of a tied-unit cloth's surface. Held only by the ties, these patterning wefts can change colors at the weaver's will. On items like rugs, brocade wefts create extra thickness. Brocading could be used to add texture or even a full-width extra layer. This means of patterning will not be specifically mentioned in most cases.

Most of the patterning described below deals with *continuous supplementary wefts* which weave *selvage-to-selvage* and create an even density in the cloth.

1:1 Drafts

Tied-unit drafts with a 1:1 ratio have alternating pattern warp ends and tie warp ends. The tie ends bind floats of supplementary, patterning weft which pass over a ground cloth. Two traditional Latvian 1:1, tied-unit drafts lend themselves well to supplementary-weft patterning. One is best known in North America as a *summer/winter* draft, and the other is a *twill-tie* draft.

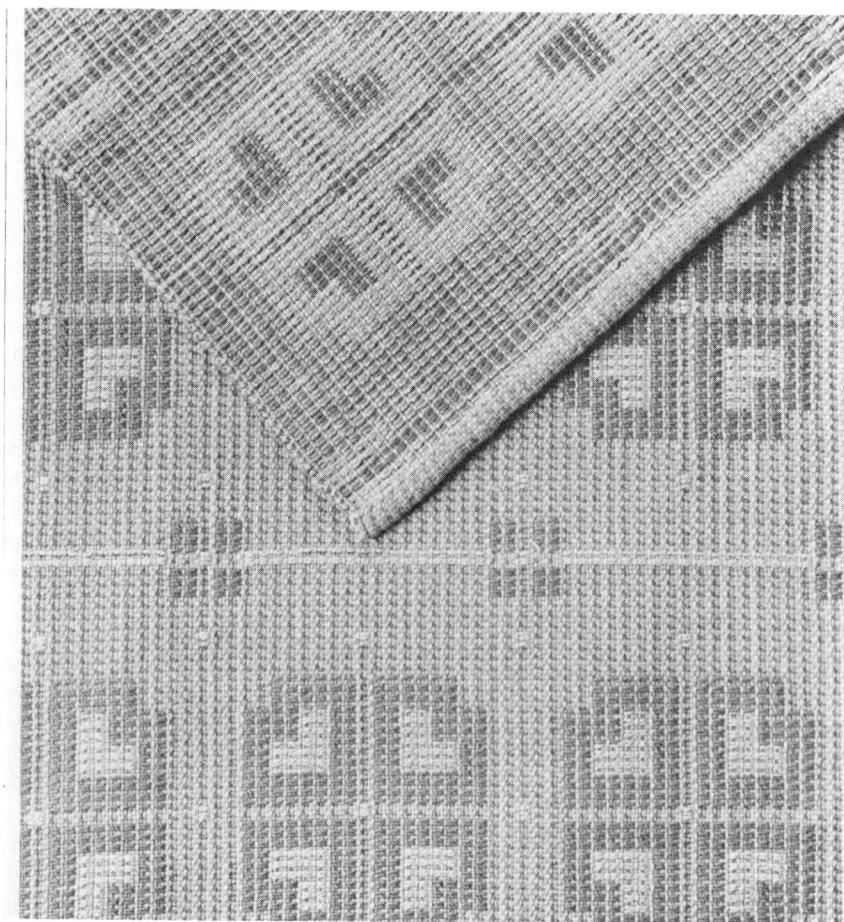

14.6. Three-color or polychrome fabric with two supplementary pattern wefts over a tabby ground cloth. Only one tie warp is used on each surface. 1983; warp, cotton, 8/2, gold; weft, cotton, perle 5, yellow, and 10/3, orange; 8 e/cm (20 epi); 19 p/cm (48 ppi). Designed and woven by Jane Evans.

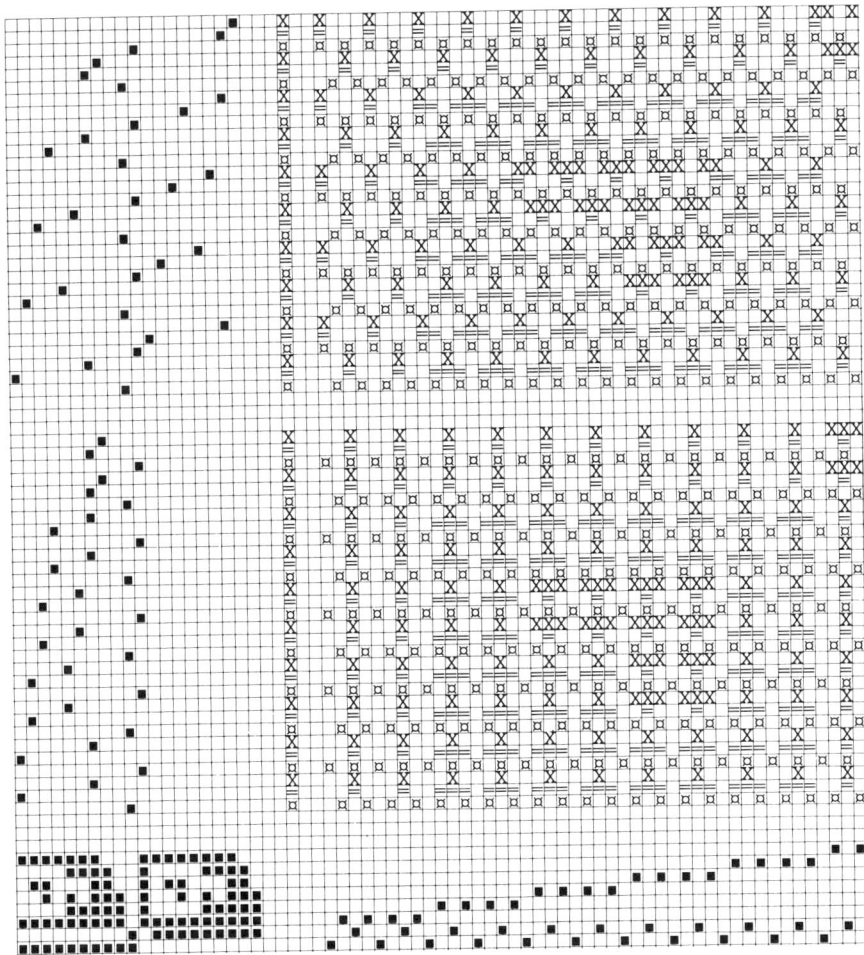

SUMMER/WINTER DRAFT

Loom-controlled version. *Summer/winter* weave is frequently woven with a ground fabric patterned by a single supplementary weft. It also was discussed in *Chapter Six* as a *tied-float weave with two or more wefts*, where more than one supplementary weft is woven between alternate tabby picks. For example, a three-colored design is shown in fig. 14.6. Patterning with more than one supplementary weft is sometimes called *polychrome weaving* in North America. Either a single warp or alternating tie warps may be used to tie down pattern wefts. Figure 14.7 displays both structures on one-half of the draft for the runner in fig.14.6, where only one tie was used.

If fine threads are closely sett for a summer/winter draft, it is generally best to have loom-controlled blocks of pattern like the example above, rather than weaver-controlled ones.

Freeform version. When a summer/winter draft is woven with large elements it may have either loom-controlled or weaver-controlled designs of supplementary weft(s). Loom-controlled work would be handled exactly like the example above, with appropriate sett and sizes of elements. Freeform patterns can be controlled by the weaver on a split-shed arrangement. Rugs and other sturdy fabrics work up well in this method.

14.7. (above left) One-half repeat of draft for cloth in fig. 14.6. Upper section of draft uses alternating tie warps, lower section uses one tie warp on upper surface. In this draft symbols indicate three colors of weft threads and blanks are warp threads.

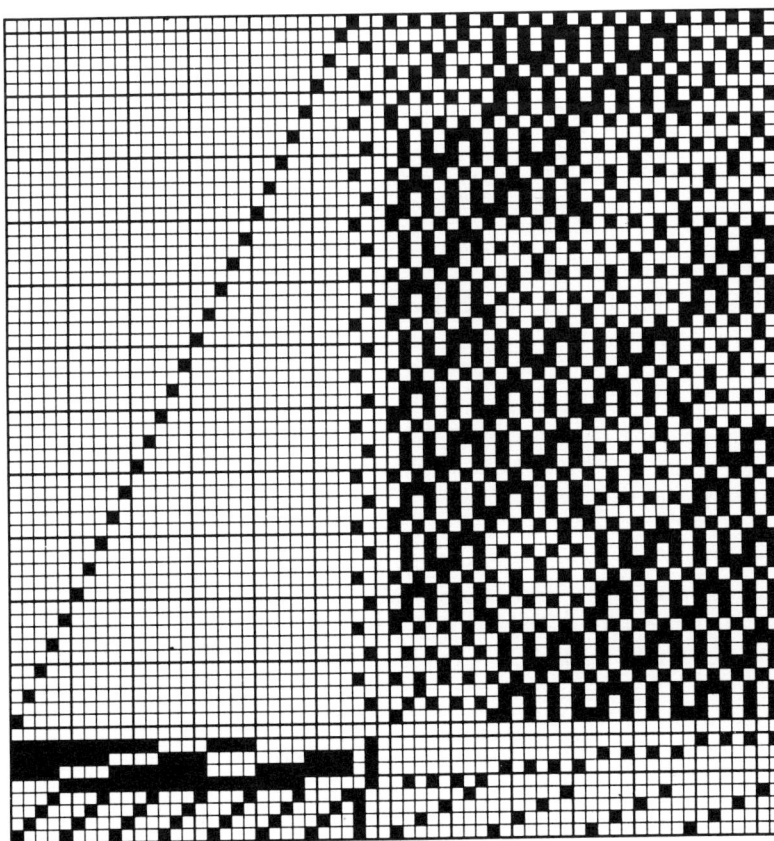

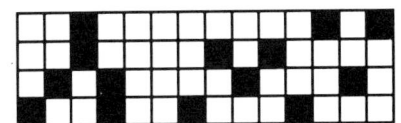

14.8. (above) Four-shaft tie-up and threading for freeform weaving of summer/winter weave.

14.9. (left) Eight-shaft draft for four units of twill-tie interlacement of supplementary weft over a plain-weave ground.

SUMMER/WINTER, TIED-BIEDERWAND, AND PAIRED-TIE WEAVES WITH SUPPLEMENTARY WEFT(S)

TIE-UP

Select an appropriate tie-up from figs. 14.2-14.5.

WEAVING

1) *Treadle a split shed* with shaft 1 on top, 3 and 4 in the center, and 2 on the bottom, as in fig.14.1.
   - Pass the pattern shuttle above and below the pattern warps in the center of the two sheds, x and y. The weft to be visible is in shed x (above the pattern warps but below the raised tie warps on shaft 1); the weft to be hidden is in shed y (below the pattern warps but above the lowered tie warps on shaft 2.) (See *Selecting Sheds* notes below.)
   - Beat.

2) Lift shafts 1 and 3 (3 and 4 for summer/winter draft).
   - Weave the tabby weft.
   - Beat.

3) *Treadle a split shed* with shaft 2 on top, 3 and 4 in the center, and 1 on the bottom.
   - Pass the pattern shuttle above and below the pattern warps as in step 1, forming whatever pattern is desired.
   - Beat.

4) Lift shafts 2 and 4 (1 and 2 for summer/winter draft).
   - Weave the tabby weft.
   - Beat.

SELECTING SHEDS

In summer/winter and tied-Beiderwand weaves, the shuttle passes to the top or bottom shed in one of two ways. *Either or both systems can be used in a piece.*

1) Enter all sheds at the gaps formed by whichever tie is raised, which will give brickwork edges to columns.

2) Alternate using gaps from raised ties versus lowered ties on alternate sheds. This results in a feathered edge of half-blocks along columns, which looks straighter than a brickwork edge.

In paired-tie weaves, the shuttle always moves into the upper or lower shed, x or y, at the gap caused by the tie warps being in the highest and lowest positions of the split shed. Only whole blocks (4 pattern ends) are between tie ends. There are no half-blocks such as with summer/winter or tied-Beiderwand weaves.

WEAVING NOTES

- With most tied-unit drafts thread warps on each of the two tie shafts at each selvage.
- Use wefts of equal size, one for tabby and one or more for pattern.
- Beat each shed firmly.
- Use all wefts throughout a weaving to keep density even. If a supplementary weft is not to show on the surface, it passes behind all raised ends and is held in place by the back surface's tie ends.
- At the selvages whichever weft is forming the surface color should be turned into the next shed such that it remains on the surface. In areas where the pattern weft travels on the back surface, small spots of that weft may show where lower-surface tie warps bind it.
- One tension is usually adequate for all warp threads.
- Summer/winter weave has a different tabby from the other weaves, as noted in the directions.
- *Polychrome weaving*, using two supplementary wefts, is also possible in this method.

The freeform threading draft (right side) and jack-loom tie-up (left side) are in fig. 14.8. Alternate tie-ups are in figs. 14.2-14.5. Weaving technique follows the directions on page 152. A suggested sett for 12/6 cotton rug warp is 2 to 3/cm (5 or 6 ends/inch).

This summer/winter structure often is distinguishable from the *tied-Beiderwand* structure only by the number of warp ends between tie warps, three or five respectively. The desired firmness of a fabric and its length of weft floats determine which draft to use.

TWILL TIE DRAFTS

The 1:1 draft in fig. 14.9 has four tie-down warps which form a straight twill, and one pattern shaft in each threading unit. The tie warps are treadled in four successive pattern sheds, alternating with plain-weave ground sheds.

The units of this structure are easier to control by the loom than by hand, and for weaving efficiency double treadling is preferable.

Figure 14.10 shows a ground cloth with one supplementary pattern weft woven on units of the above draft. An attractive, satin damask-like effect is possible due to the twill line that occurs across the pattern blocks. This structure is particularly effective when woven in fine threads.

2:1 and 4:1 Tied-Beiderwand Drafts

Traditionally, Latvian units of 2:1 tied-Beiderwand consist of one tie warp plus two pattern warps, and the tie warps alternate across the threading. In North America these three-end units are sometimes called *half-units*, assuming that a full unit

14.10. Twill-tie cloth with supplementary weft over plain-weave ground. The four units in fig. 14.9 are threaded to various widths.

includes both tie warps. Half-units of 2:1 or other ratios give extra possibilities in block designing.

WARP-FACED/WEFT-FACED WEAVE

A loom-controlled variation on the traditional *4:1 tied-Beiderwand* draft combines both warp-faced and weft-faced surfaces on each side of the cloth, as shown in Plate 39 and figs. 12.A and 14.11. Motifs on one side of this rug are weft-faced blocks, and on the other side they are warp-faced blocks. Figure 12.A shows the striped, warp-faced side of this rug with its weft-faced pattern blocks. This 12-shaft, loom-controlled rug is woven by substituting 5-end half-units into the profile draft in fig. 14.12. Only the sett and the relative sizes of weft threads differentiate this piece from a standard, supplementary-weft tied-Beiderwand fabric.

The tabby weft used in the rug is the size of the warp. The pattern weft is a cloth strip.

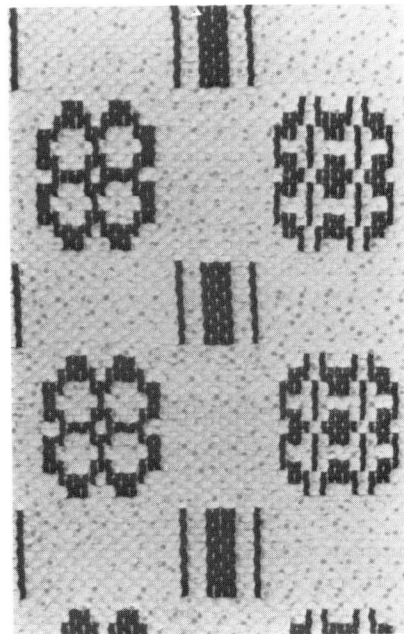

14.11. Detail, weft-dominant side of "Majolica Rug," also shown in Plate 39 and fig. 12.A.

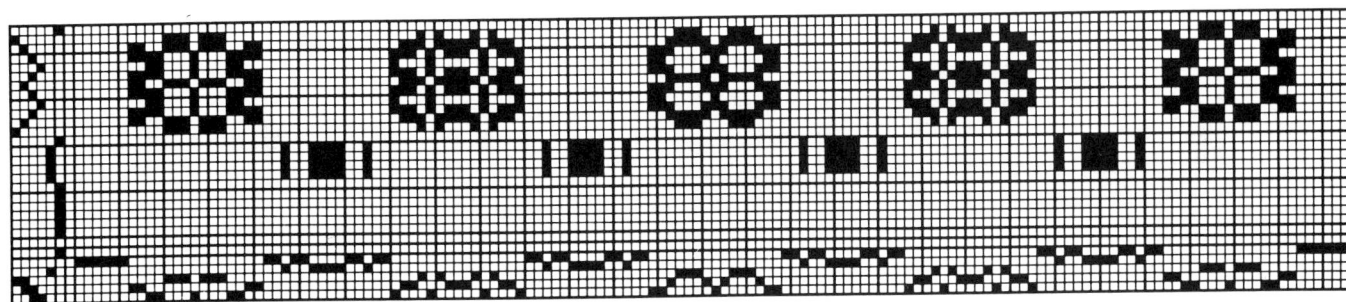

14.12. Profile draft for rug in fig. 14.11. The sixth "block" of the tie-up indicates only tie warps are woven on the surface, for a weft-faced effect.

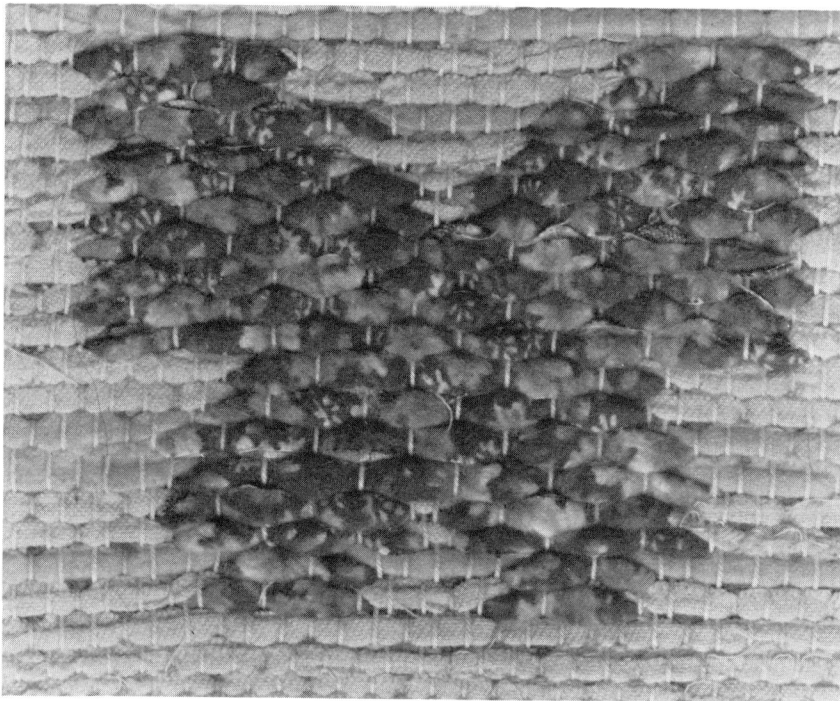

14.13. *Detail of weft-faced effect, "Butterfly." 2:1 tied-Beiderwand woven with two large wefts of cloth strips. 1985; warp, cotton, 12/6, white; wefts, cotton, flannel, 1 cm (.4"), brown print, yellow tabby; 3.5 e/cm (9 epi); 4 p/cm (10 ppi). Designed and woven by Jane Evans.*

14.15. *Detail, showing pattern and ground of "Heron II," a freeform design in the same structure as in fig 14.13. 1986; 91.5 cm (36") L X 57 cm (22.5") W; warp, cotton, 12/6, white; wefts, cotton, flannel, 1.3 cm (.5") W, grey-blue, pale green; 3.5 e/cm (9 epi); 4.5 p/cm (12 ppi). Full rug is shown in Plate 37. Designed and woven by Jane Evans.*

This 4:1 weave is not suited to freeform patterning. The 4:2 paired-tie draft discussed below is a preferable draft for that weaving method. See pages 158-161.

WEFT-FACED WEAVE

Loom-controlled version. Small warp and weft threads are the traditional elements used for weaving a *tied-Beiderwand* draft. If large wefts are used, woven on a widely-sett warp, a nearly weft-faced fabric like the one in fig. 14.13 results. This 16-shaft butterfly design, drafted in fig. 14.14, is completely loom- controlled to weave a ground of plain weave under the patterning supplementary-weft floats. Double-treadling is a useful aid in weaving this draft.

Close inspection shows that this draft contains both "full units" and "half-units" in threading, to adjust the size of the image. If a profile draft of such a pattern allowed one block per half-unit, the motif would be a mirror image. In actual threading and weaving, the alternating tie warps create full-and half-units that are not in mirror image across the two halves of the butterfly. This result is inevitable, but seldom troublesome unless single full- or half-units are dominant in a design.

Freeform version. Using the split-shed technique, four shafts can produce weft-faced, freeform designs

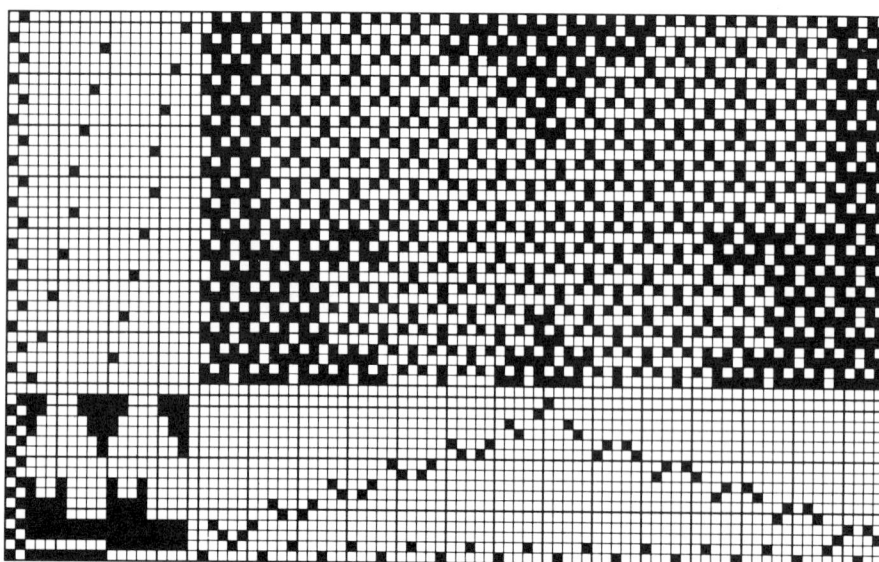

14.14. *2:1 tied-Beiderwand draft with single treadling for motif in fig. 14.13.*

14.16. *Four-shaft tie-up and threading for freeform weaving of 2:1 tied-Beiderwand weave.*

such as the "Heron II" rug in Plate 37 and fig. 14.15. Figure 14.16 shows the tie-up (left side) and threading (right side) draft for this rug on a jack loom. Treadling follows the weaving directions on page 152.

The same information noted about full-units and half-units in the preceding loom-controlled version (fig. 14.13) pertains to freeform work with this draft.

4:2 Paired-tie Draft

Fig 14.17 shows the traditional threading of the *paired-tie* draft with six warp threads per block - two warps on the tie shafts and four warps on two pattern shafts. Adjacent placement of the two tie warps creates columns of ties vertically in the fabric. Pattern areas therefore have straighter edges than when the *summer/winter* or *tied-Beiderwand* drafts are used.

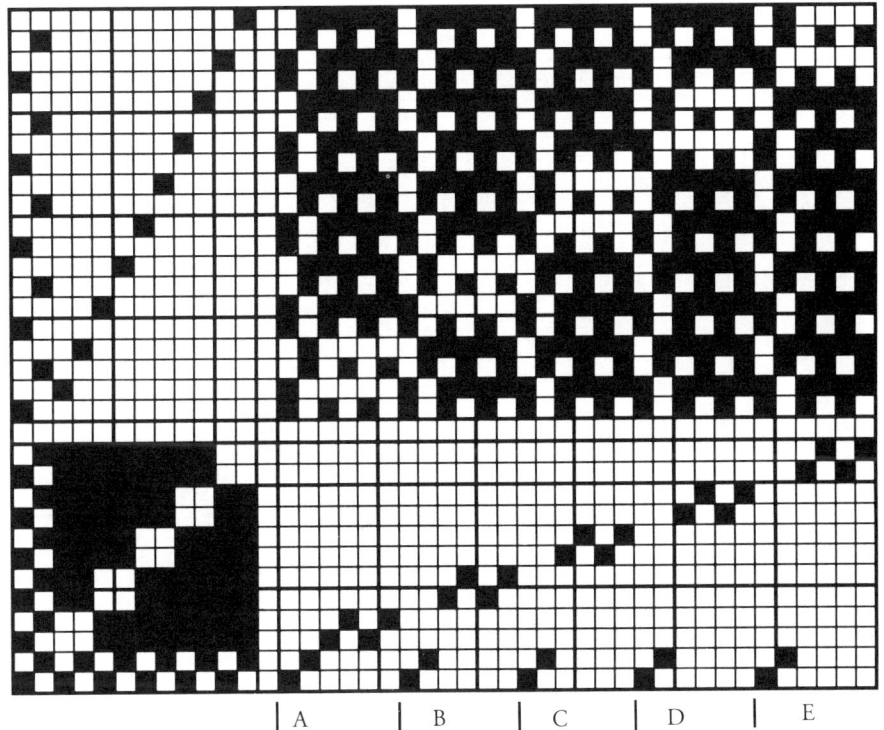

14.17. Five units of a paired-tie draft with six warps per unit.

14.18. Woven in 1986 in Latvia, this tablecloth is true to the time-honored patterning method of supplementary weft over a plain-weave ground cloth. The conventional 4:2 ratio of pattern warps to ground warps is modified to an 8:2 ratio. This deviation and some irregularities in the number of wefts woven in each block are the only changes from the old, singularly Latvian way of weaving the paired-tie structure in fig. 14.17. 222.5 cm (87") L X 150 cm (59") W; warp, cotton, 2-ply, S-twist, natural; tabby weft, same as warp; pattern weft, linen, singles, Z-twist, used triple; 20 e/cm (51 epi); 24 p/cm (61 ppi). Collection of Liena Kaugars.

14.19. One and one-half repeats of profile draft from tablecloth in fig. 14.18.

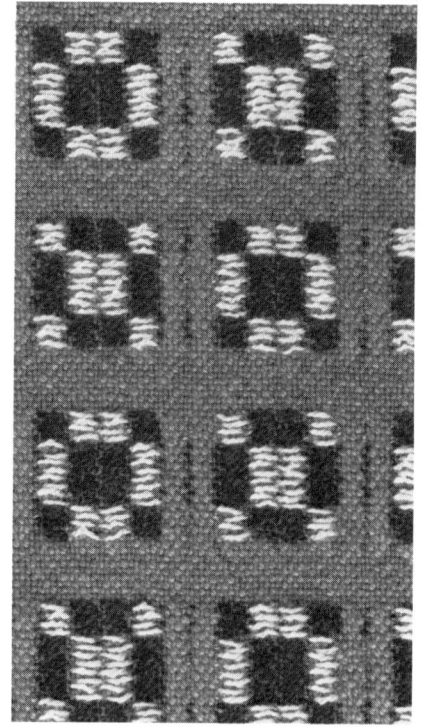

14.20. Polychrome fabric on 4:2 paired-tie draft. 1989; warp, cotton, 8/2 for pattern ends and 16/2 for ties, rust; weft, viscose, 8/2, red, white, brown; 9.5 e/cm (24 epi); woven to square. Designed and woven by Jane Evans.

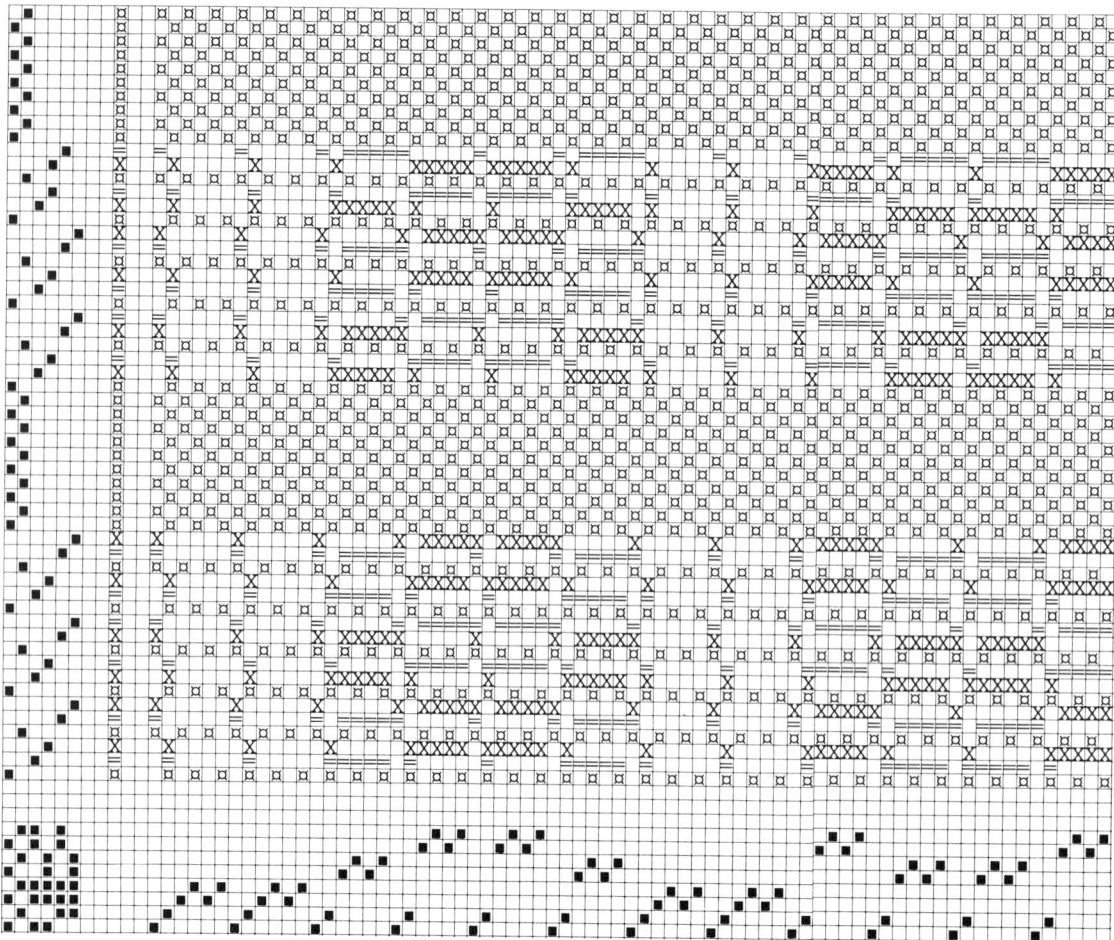

14.21. Bands of tabby and three-colored motifs in fig. 14.20. Three colors of weft are represented by symbols beside treadling.

14.22. Detail, runner woven with 4:2 draft arranged to emphasize supplementary weft. Warp, cotton, 8/2, beige; tabby weft, same as warp; pattern weft, cotton, slub singles, natural; accent pattern wefts, cotton, 8/2, black, rust; 9 e/cm (22.5 epi); 8 p/cm (20 ppi). Designed and woven by Jane Evans.

LOOM-CONTROLLED VERSIONS
Balanced weaves. The following fabrics retain the balanced warp/weft relationship in the ground cloth that is found in traditional 4:2 block-weave examples.

Figure 14.18 shows an elaborately-patterned tablecloth in a paired-tie weave with an 8:2 ratio. Figure 14.19 is the profile draft for this lovely design.

Loom-controlled *polychrome weaving* on 4:2 units works well, as shown in fig. 14.20. The draft in fig. 14.21 rotates two supplementary weft colors in successive blocks as noted in the draft.

Textured threads can be displayed attractively in four-shaft fabrics threaded to repeats of a single 4:2 unit. Figures 14.22 and 14.24 show two such fabrics. The first interlacement, drafted in fig. 14.23, emphasizes the supplementary weft thread. The second weave, drafted in fig. 14.25, highlights textured warp threads. Colored warp ends,

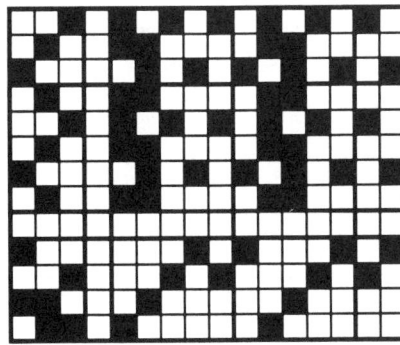

14.23. Two repeats of draft for fig. 14.22.

threaded on one or both of the tie shafts, also can be featured by either of these weave structures. Textiles made from these drafts are suitable for garments, table linens, towels, cushions or draperies.

Reducing the pattern:tie warp ratio to 2:2 is another alternative for loom-controlled block patterns. Figure 14.26 shows part of an 11-block pattern, whose whole profile draft appears in fig. 14.27. Treadling is based on the standard method for 4:2 units, shown in fig. 14.17.

A novel variation on a paired-tie draft is woven on a double-harness drawloom and pictured in fig. 14.28. Its interesting use of weft accents in the background cloth comes from modifying the paired-tie draft while keeping its 4:2 ratio. The upper part of the sample has the same tie shaft lifted on all pattern sheds. In the lower portion of the sample an 11-end float occurs in background areas. This is possible by having four shafts designated for tie warps instead of two, and by placing the ties in alternate blocks. The front (ground) harness of the drawloom had countermarch action and was tied to lift shaft 4, sink shafts 1 and 3, and leave shaft 2 neutral during all pattern picks. A very similar structure is possible on a rising shed, single-harness loom arranged as in the fig. 14.29 threading. Such treatments and threadings give wide latitude for further explorations of these weave structures.

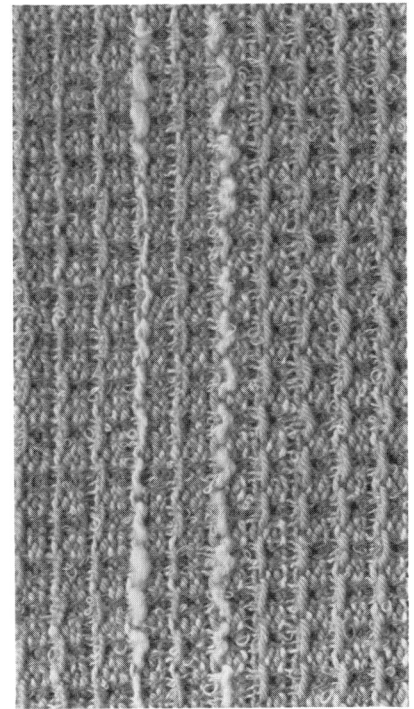

14.24. (left) Detail, fabric on 4:2 draft arranged to emphasize textured warp threads and supplementary weft. Warps, cotton - 8/2, beige, tan, ivory - flake, cream - gimp, white; weft #1, cotton/linen, 20/2, green; weft #2, linen/acrylic loop, beige; 7 e/cm (18 epi); 8.5 e/cm (22 ppi). Designed and woven by Jane Evans.

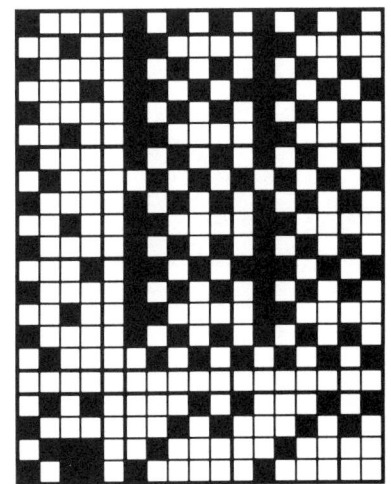

14.25. Two repeats of draft for fig. 14.24. Weft #1 (smooth) always weaves in odd-numbered picks; weft #2 (loop) always weaves in even-numbered picks.

Weft-faced weave. Wide contrast between the sizes of warps and wefts produces a sturdy, reversible cloth used in "Sunset" rug shown in Plate 46. This rug uses a 12/6 cotton warp sett at 4/cm (10 epi) and wefts of wide cotton cloth strips for both tabby and pattern. The threading units drafted in fig. 14.17 were threaded in the following order across the width: 7A, 1B, 31A, 1C, 3A, 1B, 3A. Sturdy, loom-controlled rugs or other fabrics can be woven this way in any chosen block design.

Warp-faced/weft-faced weave. The warp-faced/weft-faced "Mary Ann's Rug" shown in Plate 35 results from strong contrasts in sizes of elements along with dense sett and beat. In this arrangement the warp is sett to be warp-faced, the tabby weft is the same size thread as the warps, and a much larger fabric strip is the supplementary weft. Loom-controlled patterns are threaded, tied-up, and treadled in traditional units just

14.26. Example of 2:2 paired-tie structure. 1985; warp, cotton, 8/2, white; tabby weft, same as warp; pattern weft, wool, singles, rust; 8 e/cm (20 epi); 16 p/cm (41 ppi). Designed and woven by Peggy Hoyt.

14.27. (right) Profile design for fig. 14.26. The 12th "block" represents the pick where the supplementary weft passes on the back of the cloth only.

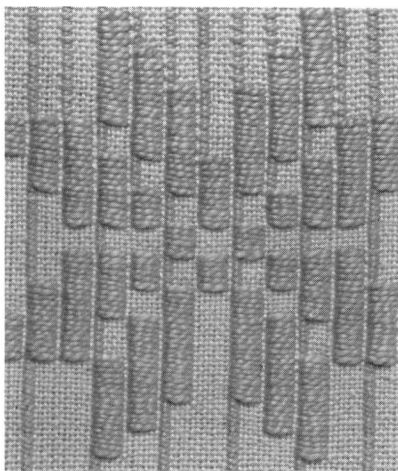

14.28. (above) 4:2 draft variation for (upper) 5-end floats and (lower) 11-end floats of supplementary weft in background areas.. Warp, cotton, 8/2, natural; tabby weft like warp; pattern weft, cotton, 3/2, lavender; 8 e/cm (20 epi); 16 p/cm (41 ppi). Designed and woven by Peggy Hoyt.

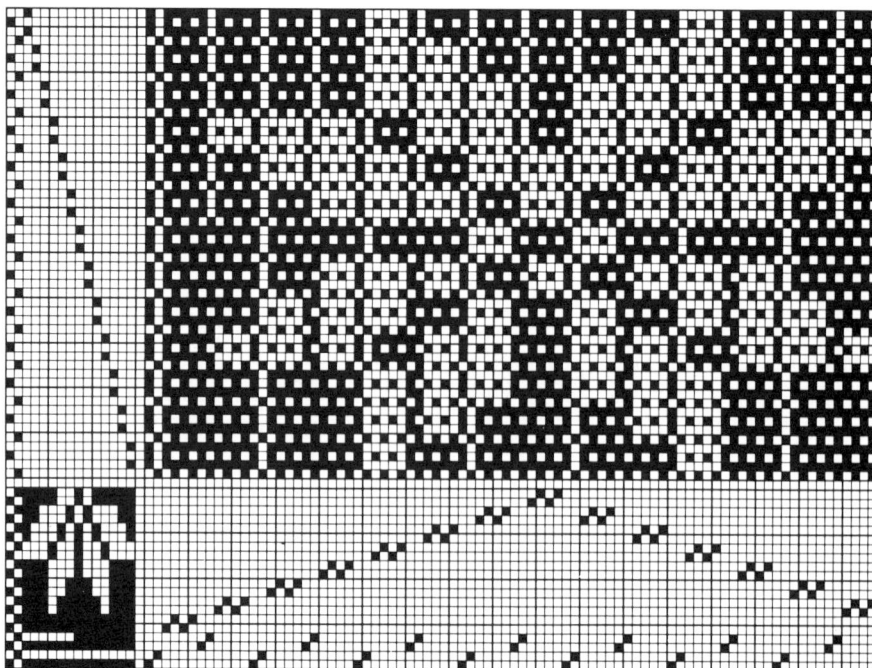

14.29. Draft on single-harness loom for results similar to lower half of motif in fig. 14.28.

14.30. Detail, "Ripple II" reversible rug with warp painting and freeform patterning on 4:2 draft in fig 14.31. 1989; 140 cm (55") L X 103 cm (40.5") W; warp and tabby weft details in text; pattern weft, cotton, flannel, 1.3 cm (.5") W, golds; 4 p/cm (10 ppi). Designed and woven by Jane Evans. See Plate 36.

like in the basic draft, fig.14.17. To gain loft and solidity, this rug's tie warps need to be longer and held at lighter tension than the pattern warps. There is significant take-up in both warps, especially the tie ends.

FREEFORM VERSIONS

Warp-faced/weft-faced weaves. The same warp-faced/weft-faced structure of Plate 35 also can be used effectively for freeform weaver-controlled patterning. Plate 36 and fig. 14.30 show a rug woven on four shafts. Figure 14.31 gives the threading (right side) and rising-shed tie-up (left side) for it. The 8/4 cotton warp is sett at 10/cm (24 epi), sleyed at two ends per dent in a 50 dents/10 cm (12 dent/inch) reed. Double-sleying is arranged to group the tie warps together in one dent, so that during weaving of the closely sett warp the blocks are visibly differentiated between gaps caused by the two tie warps.

After the loom is threaded and the warp tied to the front rod, the warp can be painted, as was done in this case. Note that the tie warps take up more quickly than the pattern warps, causing a shift in relationship of the painted warps. This can be

ignored, used to advantage, compensated for by selective painting during weaving, or avoided by not painting the tie warps.

Wefts are of contrasting sizes. The tabby thread is equal in size to the warp.

Patterning is done with a large, supplementary weft, fabric strips in

FREEFORM WEAVING METHOD

PAIRED-TIE DRAFT

WARP-FACED/WEFT-FACED WEAVE

1) Lift shafts 3 and 4.
   - Use the pick-up stick to choose any blocks of warps to remain above the supplementary weft on this pick.
   - Pass the stick from selvage to selvage, always going above or below the pattern warps only at a gap formed by the tie warps (which are all down).
   - Drop shafts 3 and 4. Push the stick, flat side down, to the reed.

2) Lift shaft 2.
   - To form a pattern shed along with the raised tie warps, it may be necessary to hold the stick with one hand against the reed while passing the shuttle through this shed. Warp strain is eased by slightly lifting shafts 3 and 4.
   - Put in the supplementary weft.
   - Remove the stick and adjust the weft's position at the selvage and across the warp.
   - Slightly "bubble" the weft by making waves of it across the warp, so it does not pull in at the selvage.
   - Beat firmly.

3) Lift shafts 2 and 4.
   - Weave the fine, tabby weft.
   - Beat firmly.

4) Lift shafts 3 and 4.
   - Use the pick-up stick to chose a new pattern row. This may be the same one as in step 1 or wholly different.
   - Pass the stick above or below the blocks of warps only at tie warps' locations.
   - Drop shafts 3 and 4. Push the stick to the reed.

5) Lift shaft 1.
   - Repeat the shedding process in step 2 for the pattern weft.
   - Beat firmly.

6) Lift shafts 1 and 3.
   Weave the fine, tabby weft.
   Beat firmly.

Hems of tabby, woven with the tabby weft, are an appropriate finish.

this case. The tie-up and method in this weave differ from a split-shed

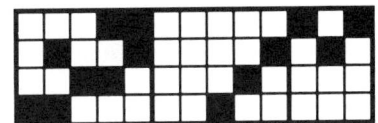

14.31. Four-shaft tie-up(left) and threading (right) for freeform work on 4:2 paired-tie draft.

tie-up and technique because the close warp sett obscures a clear view of the sheds. In dealing with the close sett, it is also easier to manipulate the shed with a pick-up stick rather than the shuttle. The stick should be smooth, slightly wider than the warp's overall width, about 3 cm (1.5 inches) wide, flat, and rounded at its tip. Weaving follows the directions on page 159.

Weft-faced weaves. In the rug in fig. 14.32 the pattern is formed in *polychrome* weave with two supplementary wefts, and it is woven freeform on a four-shaft loom. A warp sett of 4/cm (10 epi) is for 12/6 cotton, and all wefts are fabric strips. The tie warps should have less tension and be slightly longer than the pattern warps. Fig. 14.31 gives the draft. Weaving follows the method described on page 152.

14.32. "Medallion" rug in three colors or polychrome wefts, woven freeform on draft in fig. 14.31. 1985; 96.5 cm (38") L X 71 cm (28") W; warp, cotton, 12/6, natural; wefts, cotton, flannel, 1.6 cm (5/8") W, blue, brown, orange/beige print; 4 e/cm (10 epi); 3.5 p/cm (9 ppi). Designed and woven by Jane Evans.

14.33. "First Hill" - Painted warp and inlay wefts create a detailed picture in this mural. 1987; 81 cm (32") L X 51 cm (20") W (turned 90 degrees to hang); 7+inlay picks/cm (18+ ppi). Designed and woven by Jane Evans. See Plate 38.

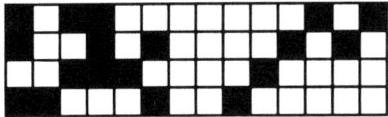

14.34. Tie-up (left) and threading (right) on 4:2 draft used for mural in fig. 14.33.

Pictorial weaves. Using the basic threading unit of the 4:2 draft, fig. 14.34, and changing the functions of supplementary wefts makes it possible to weave detailed, pictorial pieces such as in fig. 14.33. While this piece uses very fine threads, exactly the same structure can be woven in the same method with much heavier warp and weft threads for large, sturdy murals.

In "First Hill" the pattern warps are of 8/2 viscose and the tie ends are of 30/3 cotton. Together the warps are sett at 15/cm (36 epi) and dented so both ties and two pattern ends are in one dent of the reed to minimize gaps between blocks. A tabby weft of 30/3 cotton is hidden by the warp-faced sett. A continuous supplementary weft of 8/4 cotton passes only at the back of the fabric where it interlaces alternately with the two tie warps and adds stability. On the front surface discontinuous supplementary wefts are laid in under tie warps where desired, creating linear designs against the ground cloth, which may be painted as it was in this case. Inlay wefts are small groups of several colored strands of size 50 cotton sewing thread. Since the tie warps bend over the supplementary wefts of both surfaces, they need to be longer and of a looser tensioning than the pattern warps.

Treadling for this pictorial weaving takes six steps. See instructions at right which include a treadling variation.

FREEFORM WEAVING METHOD

PICTORIAL WEAVING ON PAIRED-TIE DRAFTS

TREADLING #1

The back weft is bound only by the tie warps.

1) Lift shafts 1, 3, and 4.
   Weave with backing supplementary weft. Beat.

2) Lift shaft 1.
   Place inlay wefts for front surface. Be careful not to distort ties at weft turns. Beat *gently.*

3) Lift shafts 2 and 4.
   Weave tabby weft. Beat *firmly.*

4) Lift shafts 2, 3, and 4.
   Weave with backing supplementary weft. Beat.

5) Lift shaft 2.
   Place inlay wefts on front surface where desired. Beat gently.

6) Lift shafts 1 and 3.
   Weave tabby weft. Beat *firmly.*

TREADLING #2

The back surface interlaces only with the non-tie warps. This reduces the take-up of tie warps in treadling #1.

1) Lift shafts 2 and 4.
   Weave front surface weft.

2) Lift shafts 1, 2, and 4.
   Weave back surface weft. Beat.

3) Lift shaft 2.
   Weave inlay weft(s) where desired. Beat.

4) Lift shafts 1 and 3.
   Weave front surface weft.

5) Lift shafts 1,2, and 3.
   Weave back surface weft. Beat.

6) Lift shaft 1.
   Weave inlay weft(s) where desired. Beat.

NOTES FOR BOTH METHODS

• Hide ends of inlay weft in the preceding tabby shed.
• Keep tension on tie warps loose to reduce grooves in the fabric.
• Allow for extra take-up on the tie warps.
• Hems of plain weave are suitable at the ends of the cloth.

14.35. Two versions of weaving on the 4:2 paired-tie threading draft, Latvian (top) and Lithuanian (bottom).

LITHUANIAN-STYLE TREADLING

It was mentioned in *Chapter Six* that Latvia's neighboring Lithuanian weavers use a slightly different treadling on this paired-tie draft. Figure 14.35 shows the two versions, the Latvian one above the Lithuanian one. Figure 14.36 compares both countries' treadlings. In Latvia, the two tie warps are used alternately with supplementary wefts' picks. In Lithuania, only one tie warp is lifted during all pattern wefts' picks.

The wool fabric in fig. 14.37 is threaded to seven paired-tie units and treadled in the Lithuanian interlacement. The profile draft for it is in fig. 14.38.

In Lithuania weft floats or overshots in cloth are called *dimai*. This paired-tie structure is called *su pervarai*, or *float overshot with 'stitching' tie-downs*. The vertical "paths" formed by the tie-down threads are an important characteristic in the weave.

Lithuanian weavers often produce patterns in the paired-tie structure through the use of supplementary heddles, drawlooms, or

14.36. Draft of both interlacements in fig. 14.35, Latvian (upper) and Lithuanian (lower).

sticks. The Lithuanian method of stick patterning is similar to the Latvian "stick weaving" of lace, *Chapter Eleven*. In both cases shafts threaded to plain weave have the old type of string heddles with somewhat long eyes. (Meek correspondence 1987.)

Sticks are inserted in the warp behind the shafts, and non-tabby sheds are formed by moving sticks forward. While similar in setup, the stick weaving applications are quite

different. The Latvian one is used for a simple weave (lace), and the Lithuanian one is used for a compound weave such as the one in fig. 14.39. In this linen pillowcase the "paths" are very clear between columns of supplementary weft floats. The linen runner in fig. 14.40, decorated with fig.14.41's intricate profile design, could be woven with sticks or on 12 shafts.

14.37. *Clothing fabric woven on 16 shafts in Lithuanian treadling of 4:2 paired-tie draft. Warp and weft, wool, 20/2, various reds; 10.5 e/cm (27 epi); 18 p/cm (46 ppi). Designed and woven by Jane Evans.*

Compound Weaves with Complementary Wefts

All the following tied-unit weaves have three or more sets of threads. One set of warp threads interlace with two or more sets of wefts. The latter are co-equal in the construction and hence are complementary. These wefts weave in a cycle called a *pass*, within which each weft pick is a *lat*. The cycle is incomplete until all the lats of one pass are interlaced.

On the drawdowns that follow, blank squares indicate warps and symbols indicate wefts.

Many of these weaves make a double-faced fabric, one in which the front and back surfaces have the same structure. If two wefts form one pass's cycle, the design often has negative/positive reversibility on the two surfaces. When a pass is composed of more than two wefts, only one color shows in some blocks and the other colors combine in other blocks on one or both surfaces. This characteristic of color blending can be used as a design feature, or it can be relegated to the back of a non-reversible cloth. It is best to use all wefts throughout a weaving's length, so that the density of fabric is even. If a weft is not to show on the surface at all for part of a design, it can pass behind all raised tie and pattern ends and be held in place by the tie ends on the back surface. At the selvages whichever weft is forming the upper surface color should be turned into the next shed such that it remains on the top surface.

Most of the following examples include tabby picks of single threads the size of the warp, between passes. Tabbies add flexibility to the fabric.

With the exception of the *Paired-tie, Two-faced Weave*, the following weft-faced constructions all have *stuffer warps*, described at the beginning of this chapter. Tie warp ends should be longer and held under less tension than pattern warp ends. The latter are held tightly so they run virtually straight through the center of the cloth and are wholly covered

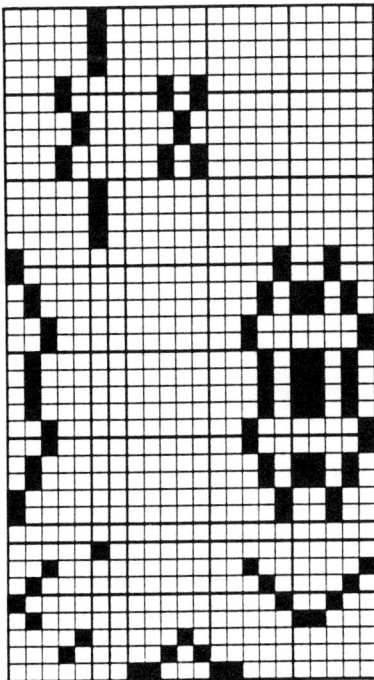

14.38. *Seven-block profile draft for design in fig. 14.37. The sixth "treadle" represents areas where pattern wefts weave wholly on back of fabric.*

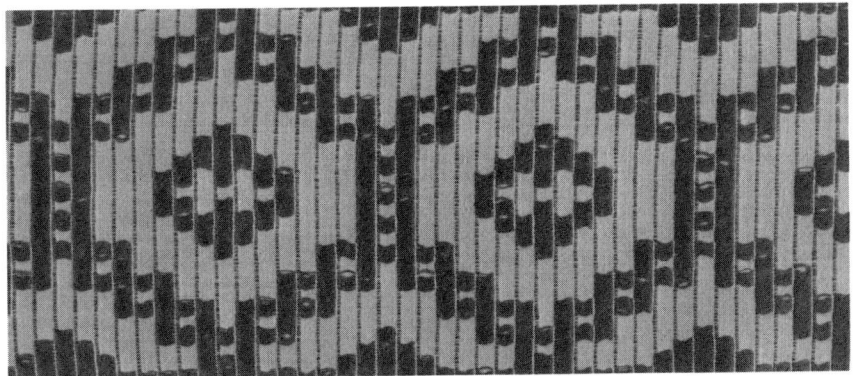

14.39. (upper) *Pillowcase with decorative band in su pervarai weave. Warp and tabby weft, linen, 40/2, bleached white; supplementary weft, cotton sewing thread (400/3), blue; 12 e/cm (30 epi); woven to square. Designed and woven by M. Kati Meek.*

14.40. (lower) *Decorative band on runner which could be woven as a loom- controlled design on the Lithuanian version of the 4:2 paired-tie draft in fig. 14.36. Warp and tabby weft, linen, 45/3, white; pattern wefts, cotton, 40/2 and 50/3, blue; 12 e/cm (30 epi); woven to square. Designed and woven by M. Kati Meek, who has generously shared her Lithuanian studies.*

by wefts. Selvages are neatest if a floating selvage thread is placed outside two warps which are threaded on the two tie shafts.

1:2 Drafts

LOOM-CONTROLLED VERSION

Two units in a 1:2 pattern:tie warp ratio are drafted with loom-controlled weft picks in fig. 14.42. This structure offers extensive design possibilities on looms with relatively few shafts, because only one pattern shaft is required per design block and only two shafts are needed for tie-downs.

A number of loom-controlled examples, such as blankets, which used two or three complementary wefts were described in *Chapter Eight*.

FREEFORM VERSION

Freeform patterning is a rewarding option on a 1:2 tied-unit threading. There is no true tabby available in this draft, so only complementary wefts are woven. The *lats* which comprise a *pass*, or *cycle*, may be in two or three colors of wefts. The resulting cloth is reversible. If only two weft colors are used, there is a positive/negative reversing of the design on the two sides.

The threading draft and the rising-shed tie-up on the left of fig.

14.42 are used. Treadling follows the method described on page 166.

The "Prairie Sky" rug pictured in Plates 47 and 48 and fig. 14.43 has two contrasting sides. It uses this 1:2 structure with two hand-dyed wefts in each pass. Treadling could be loom-controlled on 16 blocks (18 shafts) or the design could be woven on four shafts through use of the split-shed method.

A 12/6 or 8/4 cotton warp sett of 3/cm (8 epi) is appropriate for rugs in this weave. The hidden, stuffer warps can add dimension to a block if they are composed of several threads per warp end. The tie warps appear less obvious if made of a single, strong, rather fine thread of a neutral color.

1:1 Drafts

SUMMER/WINTER DRAFT

The draft in fig. 14.44, generally called *summer/winter* weave in North America, weaves well with complementary wefts. Like the preceding 1:2 weave, this 1:1 draft uses one pattern shaft per block of design and two shafts for ties. A major difference is that on the summer/ winter threading, a true tabby weave is possible.

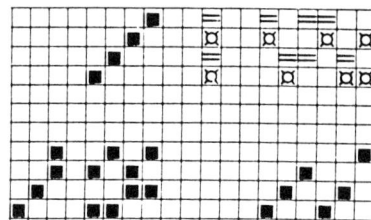

14.42. Two units of 1:2 draft. Alternate weft colors shown by different symbols. Split shed tie-up is at far left.

A fine weft added in one tabby pick after each cycle of lats will contribute flexibility to a heavy fabric. In this example, also, two or three large wefts constitute each *pass* (cycle). If two colors are used the fabric will be fully reversible, with a negative/positive change in design. Polychrome weaving with three colored wefts can give further pattern possibilities.

An appropriate sett for rugs in 12/6 or 8/4 cotton warp is around 3/cm (8 epi).

Rugs with graphic designs such as the one in Plate 43 and fig. 14.45 are possible by either loom-controlled or freeform, weaver-controlled methods. Block patterns are loom-controlled as in fig. 14.44, often on more shafts.

14.41. One and one-half repeats of ten- block profile draft for design in fig. 14.40. Right side "treadle" represents bands of plain weave.

14.43. Detail, "Prairie Sky" rug woven with wefts of dyed cotton flannel, one surface in blues, one in reds. 1983; 94 cm (37") L x 68.5cm (27"). Designed and woven by Jane Evans. See Plates 47 and 48.

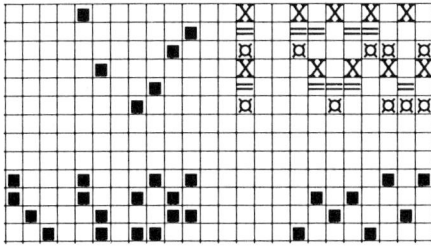

14.44. Two units on four shafts of summer/winter draft. Two tie-ups are shown. On the right is the tie-up for loom-controlled weaving. The tie-up on the left is for freeform weaving. Three weft colors represented by different symbols in the center.

Freeform Version. For freeform patterning the threading and rising-shed tie-up are in fig. 14.44 (on the left side). Treadling is described on page 166 .

An example of freeform, poly-chrome patterning on this draft is seen close-up in fig.14.46. Three weft colors form one pass's cycle. The lower section is woven as loom-controlled blocks without tabby picks. The center section also is loom-controlled blocks, this time with a fine tabby pick after each full pass. The number of wefts and the plain-weave picks spread the inter-lacement vertically so that warps show. The upper section is a freeform, three- color pattern with no tabby picks. Part of the reverse side of the fabric is also shown, displaying whichever two wefts are not present in pattern areas on the front of the cloth.

TWILL-TIE DRAFT

Eight warps form each unit of the 4-shaft, twill-tie based draft in fig.14.47, called *samitum* or *weft-faced compound twill*. (Becker, 1987.) As explained in *Chapter Eight*, in Latvia this draft is usually woven weft-faced with two or three complementary wefts. The number of tie warps and the 1:1 ratio of pattern:tie warps makes it difficult to use freeform control on this weave, so it is best done as a loom-controlled fabric.

Shown in Plate 40 and fig. 14.48 is an 8-shaft rug with buckle design, using the block threading, block tie-up, and color weaving order of fig. 14.49.

Each pass, or cycle, of three blocks is woven as high as desired, and then the next pass of three blocks is begun. Units are threaded to the draft in fig. 14.47. Within units four tie shafts are threaded to a straight twill and one pattern shaft is threaded with four pattern warps. Each pattern block requires one pattern shaft. Treadling progresses in groups, each lift of a 2/2 twill combining with all wefts before the next twill lift is treadled. The 2/2 twill sequence can be seen across the lower four shafts of all the treadles in fig. 14.47. With three colors of wefts there is a total of 12 picks per tread-ling sequence. Two colors give eight picks in a series. See fig. 8.17.

Double-treadling is useful to reduce the large numbers of treadles used in this tie-up. Four treadles are tied to the four tie shafts in 2/2 twill sequence. Three other treadles are tied for each different row of pattern. The ties are arranged so that only one weft shows on the surface within any given block. Figure 14.50 shows the tie-up and treadling order for 13 treadles that will produce all 36 necessary lifts for weaving this rug design.

14.45. Summer/winter weave can be woven in reversible, two-color designs like this "Victorian House, Eastlake Style" rug with the tie warps slightly showing on the weft-faced surface. 1981; 155 cm (61") L X 100 cm (39.5") W; warp, cotton, 8/4, black (used double for pattern ends), gold, orange; weft, cotton, flannel, 1.6 cm (5/8") W, reds, white print; 2.5 working e/cm (6 wepi); 5.5 p.cm (14 ppi). Designed and woven by Jane Evans. See Plate 43.

14.46. Sample of freeform, polychrome results on the four-shaft summer/winter threading in fig. 14.44.

1:2, SUMMER/WINTER, TIED-BEIDERWAND, AND 4:2 PAIRED-TIE WEAVES WITH COMPLEMENTARY WEFTS

1) Treadle a split shed with shaft 1 on top, 3 and 4 in the center, and 2 on the bottom, as in fig. 14.1.
   • Pass the first pattern shuttle across the warp in either the upper or lower shed, x or y, depending on which surface is to show that weft. (See notes on *Selecting Sheds* below.)
   • *Beat lightly.*

2) Continue to treadle the same shed as in step 1.
   • Pass the second pattern shuttle across the warp through the x and y sheds in a path exactly opposite to the first wefts. Blocks which the first weft went over, the second weft goes under, and vice versa. All pattern warp ends are covered with wefts, both front and back.
   • Close the shed and *beat firmly.*

3) Lift shafts 1 and 3 (1 and 2 for the summer/winter draft only).
   • Weave tabby with a weft the size of one warp thread.
   • *Beat firmly.*

4) Treadle a split shed with shaft 2 on top, 3 and 4 in the center, and 1 on the bottom.
   • Pass the first pattern shuttle across the warp in either the upper or lower shed. This weft's path may be the same as in step 1 or may be different.
   • *Beat lightly.*

5) Continue to treadle the same shed as in step 4.
   • Pass the second shuttle across the warp in exactly the opposite pattern sheds to the preceding weft's. All blocks the weft in step 4 went over, the current weft goes under, and vice versa.
   • Close the shed and *beat firmly.*

6) Lift shafts 2 and 4 (3 and 4 for summer/winter draft only).
   • Weave tabby weft and *beat firmly*.
   Repeat the above six steps in sequence to correspond to the desired design.

SELECTING SHEDS

• In summer/winter and tied-Beiderwand weaves, the shuttle passes to the top or bottom shed in one of two ways. Either or both systems can be used in a piece.
1) Enter all sheds at the gaps formed by whichever tie is raised, which will give brickwork edges to columns.
2) Alternate using gaps from raised ties versus lowered ties on alternate sheds. This results in a feathered edge of half-blocks along columns, which looks straighter than a brickwork edge.
• In paired-tie weave, the shuttle always moves into the upper or lower shed, x or y, at the gap caused by the tie warps being in the highest and lowest positions of the split shed. Only whole blocks (4 pattern ends) are between tie ends. There are no half-blocks such as with summer/winter or tied-Beiderwand weaves.

WEAVING NOTES

• For 1:2 drafts, leave out steps 3 and 6; no tabby is used.
• Summer/winter weave has different tabby sheds than the other weaves have, as noted in the directions.
• These constructions all have stuffer warps, described at the beginning of this chapter. Tie warp ends are longer and held under less tension than pattern warp ends.
• Thread a warp on each of the two tie shafts at each selvage.
• Use pattern wefts of large, equal size; tabby weft is a fine thread.
• At the selvages whichever weft is forming the surface color should be turned into the next shed such that it remains on the surface.
• *Polychrome weaving,* using three wefts, is also possible in this method.
• Use all wefts throughout a weaving to maintain density. If a weft is not to show on the surface, it passes behind all raised ends and is held in place by the tie ends of the back surface.

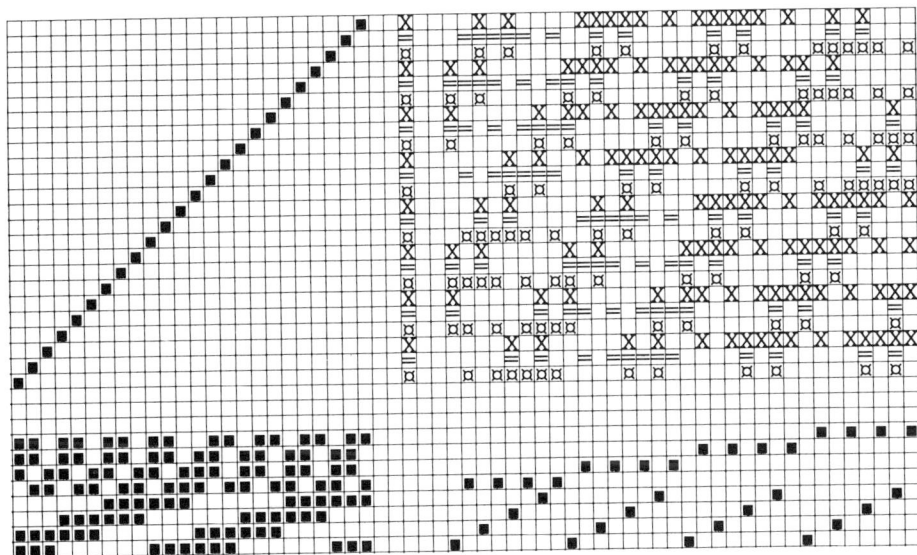

14.47. Four units threaded with ties in four-shaft twill order, then woven two units high with three colors of wefts. The left-hand twelve treadles weave one unit in height. Various symbols represent different weft colors.

In this piece three lats (picks) are within each pass (cycle), even if sometimes two lats are of the same color. The same number of lats should be continued within passes throughout the length of the weaving to give full warp coverage and even density overall. Each pass of three wefts is comparable to one pick in a 2/2 twill fabric.

All four tie treadles (a 2/2 twill) must weave in succession with all three members of each group of pattern treadles, before moving on to the next set of pattern treadles.

The pattern series is not complete until all 12 picks are woven. The color sequence of lats may be changed within the treadling order of 12 picks.

A close-up of the construction is shown in fig. 14.48 at the point where all blocks interchange. Only the fine, tie warps are visible. The multi- strand, stuffer warp formed by pattern ends is not seen. On the upper surface one weft appears within each block. On the back of the rug there is a combination within each block of the two colors that are not on the front of the block. This gives a blended, shadowy effect which could be exploited in a design on the front.

This draft does not need floating selvages or other special edge threadings, although attention to shuttle sequence is important. Plain weave is available for hems at each end. This weave does require two warp lengths and tensions, due to its stuffer warp construction. Some possible variations could be a three-tie or five-tie twill base, or a broken-twill interlacement for the tie warps.

2:1 Tied-Beiderwand Draft

Loom-controlled units of the draft in fig. 14.51 weave well with two, large complementary wefts and a fine tabby weft. Two shafts serve tie-downs warps and two shafts hold pattern warps in each block. A pair of pattern sheds may be repeated with each tie, giving six-pick units as in the lower section of the drawdown, or may be changed after a tabby pick, giving three-pick units as shown in the upper section of the figure. A

14.48. Close-up of twill-tie interlacement in "Buckle Rug." The motif on this rug is possible because three colors of wefts contribute to each row seen on the surface. 1987; 93 cm (36.5") L X 68.5 cm (27") W; tie warp, cotton, 12/3, brown; pattern warp, cotton, 12/6, grey, used double; 3 working e/cm (7.5 wepi); 7 p/cm (18 ppi). Designed and woven by Jane Evans. See Plate 40.

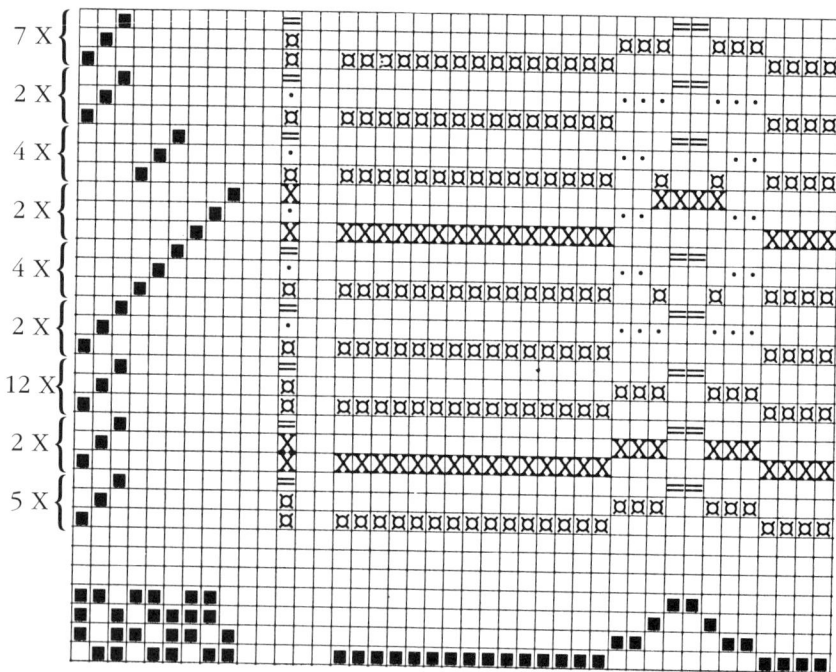

block may consist of one tie warp and two pattern warps (a half-unit) or two tie warps and four pattern warps. Blocks can be woven singly or combined.

FREEFORM VERSION

This threading adapts well to freeform patterning. The draft in fig. 14.53 gives the four-shaft threading (right side) that is repeated across the warp, and the split-shed tie-up for a rising shed loom (left side). Weaving directions are on page 166.

The rug in Plate 44 and fig. 14.52 show "Starflowers" rug in a pattern of complementary cloth-strip wefts, with the finer tabby picks wholly hidden. With only two pattern wefts, the rug has full negative/positive color reversing on its two sides.

Three pattern wefts may be used for *polychrome* patterning, as was done in the rug shown in fig. 14.54. This wool rug was woven on the same warp as the preceding rug. Treadling follows the method described on page 166.

14.49. Block weave draft for "Buckle Rug" in fig. 14.48 and Plate 40. The four symbols in the draft are weft colors on the surface of each block. Three rows or twelve picks compress to form one block in height when woven

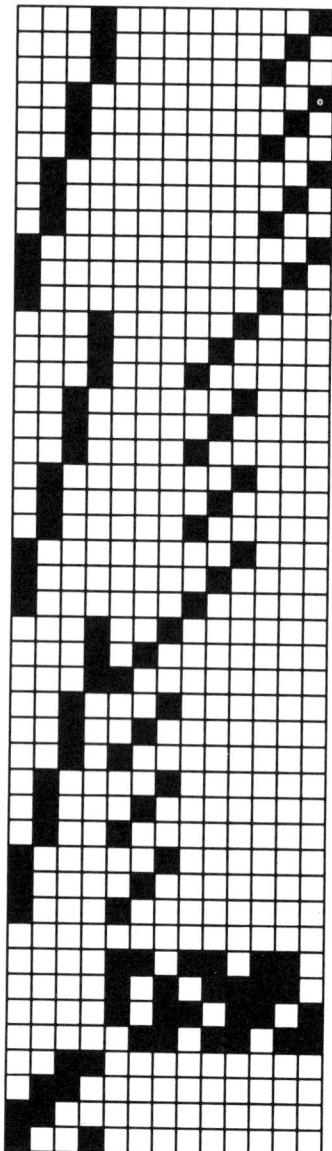

14.50. (left) Tie-up and double-treadling for all 36 weft picks required within the "Buckle Rug," fig. 14.48. Each group of twelve picks (1-12,; 13-24; 25-36) must be woven in order so that the straight twill line is retained along the tie warps.

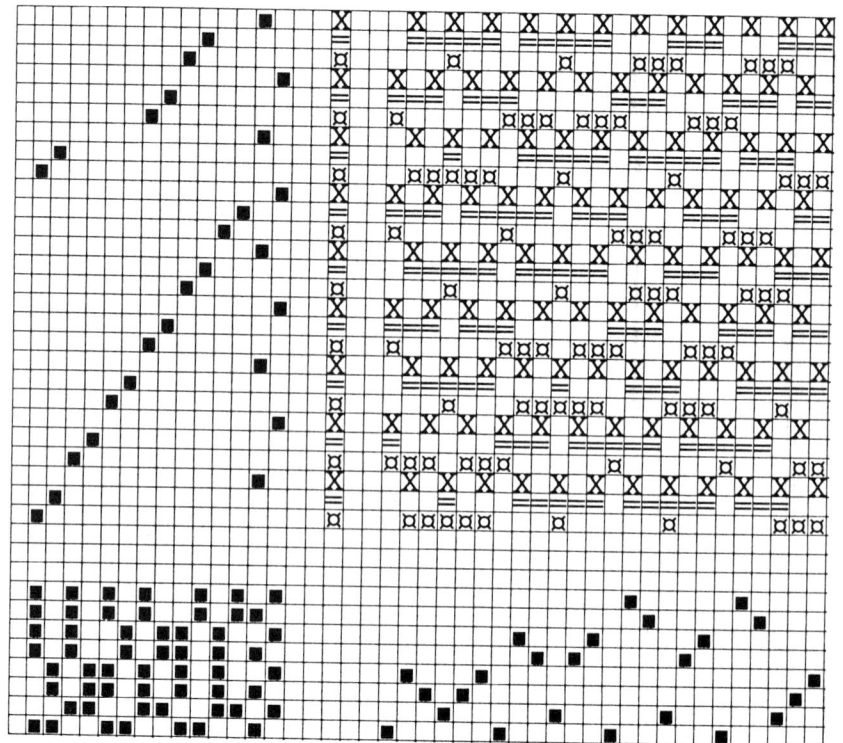

14.51. 2:1 tied-Beiderwand draft woven with a tabby and two complementary wefts, shown by three symbols.

168

14.52 Detail, "Starflowers" rug features variations on Latvian motifs, woven freeform on draft shown in fig. 14.53. 1988; 147 cm (58") L X 86 cm (34") W; warp, cotton, 12/6, tan; tabby weft, same as warp; pattern wefts, cotton, greens, tans; 3.2 cm (1.25")W; 3 e/cm (8 epi); 4 pattern, 2 tabby p/cm (10 pattern, 5 tabby ppi). Designed and woven by Jane Evans. See Plate 44.

14.54. Detail, "Flickering" rug of polychrome wefts in freeform 2:1 tied-Beiderwand. In each block one weft appears on the surface and two wefts are on the reverse side. 1988; 150 cm (59") L X 87.5 cm (34.5") W; warp, cotton, 12/6, tan; tabby weft, same as warp; pattern wefts, wool, 3ply, used triple, golds, browns, white; 3 e/cm (8 epi); 5 p/cm (12 ppi). Designed and woven by Jane Evans.

4:2 Paired-tie Draft

DOUBLE-FACED WEAVES

The paired-tie draft, customarily woven with supplementary wefts, also gives versatile patterning with complementary wefts. Figure 14.55 is a two-colored motif that could be woven loom-controlled (partially shown in fig. 14.56) on 14 shafts or weaver-controlled on one four-shaft unit, as in fig. 14.57.

Two large pattern wefts and one fine tabby weft are used for a weft-faced fabric.

Horizontal edges of block designs threaded in 4:2 units will change in increments equal to one unit's float - five warp ends. This should be taken into account when planning a design and deciding on a sett because it may make smooth curves difficult to achieve on wide warp setts. A suitable sett for rugs ranges around 3-4/cm (8 epi) for 12/6 or 8/4 cotton, giving weft floats of 1.5 cm (5/8 inch).

Loom-controlled version. Designs woven in loom-controlled blocks are threaded to units such as the one in fig. 14.56. Treadling is in the order noted, with two large pattern wefts followed by one pick of a fine tabby weft. The pair of pattern sheds may be repeated and, along with two tabby picks, be considered one unit in height, as shown in the lower section of the figure. Or a unit may be a pair of pattern picks and one tabby, as shown in the upper section, as long as the tie warps are alternated

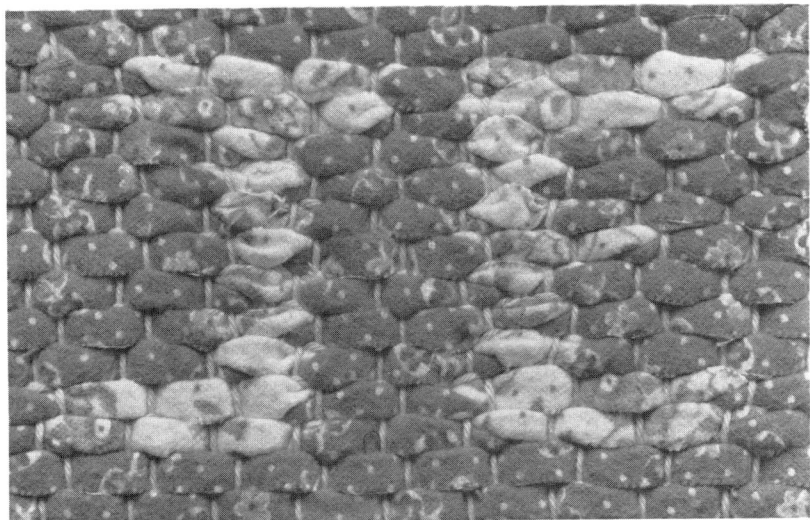

14.53. Four-shaft tie-up (left) and threading (right) for freeform tied-Beiderwand.

14.55. Example of two complementary wefts of fabric strips woven on a 4:2 paired-tie draft.

169

between these units. A firm beat should place the wefts so the tabby does not show.

It is possible to weave three or perhaps even four colors of wefts for *polychrome* patterning, if careful balance between warp sett, weft size, and beat is established to maintain clarity in the pattern. Plates 42 and 45 are of a loom-controlled polychrome rug woven on 12 shafts.

Freeform version. The four-shaft, freeform patterning method is particularly accommodated by this draft because the paired placement of tie warps makes individual blocks readily apparent.

One unit, drafted in fig. 14.57, is repeatedly threaded across the warp, with two warps threaded to the tie shafts at the concluding selvage. Freeform weaving follows the steps outlined on page 166.

There may be a broadened range of design possibilities by applying the freeform technique on a paired-tie draft reduced to a 2:2 ratio. One unit of such a draft looks like a straight twill threaded 1,2,3,4. By treating shafts 1 and 2 as tie shafts, the float length is reduced and patterns can have more gradual curves than with the 4:2 unit.

TWO-FACED WEAVE

Weaving in colored pairs of picks gives a flat, firm cloth with two very different faces, figs. 14.58a and b. Figure 14.59 shows three blocks of the paired-tie draft woven in this structure. It is one form of a weave called *Bedford cord* in English-language texts. (Nelson, 1945.)

Two picks of one colored weft float in one or more blocks and make plain weave in any other block(s). Then two picks of a second colored

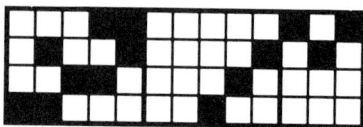

14.56. Three units of 4:2 paired-tie draft as woven loom- controlled with a tabby and two complementary wefts, shown by different symbols.

weft make floats or plain weave in the opposite blocks from the one(s) woven by the first pair of wefts. These four picks or lats are all components of one pass or cycle. Across all picks any blocks not woven as floats are woven in plain weave. The two pairs of wefts may be repeated at will to form columns of color, as long as all four wefts are included in each pass.

Warp and weft threads are of the same size in this weave, and the warp is sett for plain weave. The warps, which must be kept taught during weaving, all are of one length and can be wound on one warp beam. It is possible to change the 4:2 pattern:tie warp threads' ratio, affecting the width of blocks and therefore the length of the floats.

14.57. Four-shaft tie-up (left) and threading (right) for freeform weaving on 4:2 paired-tie draft.

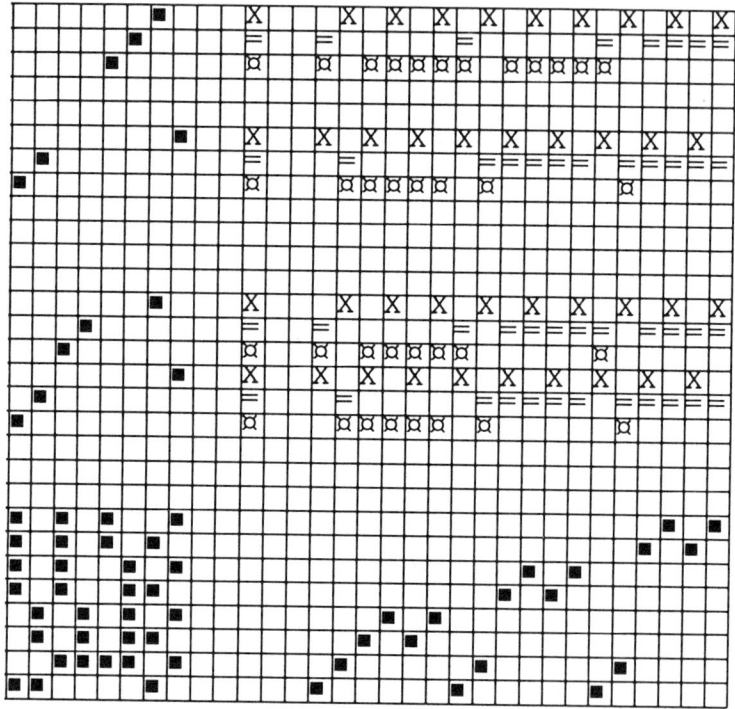

14.58a. Top surface of upholstery fabric woven in blocks on 4:2 draft.

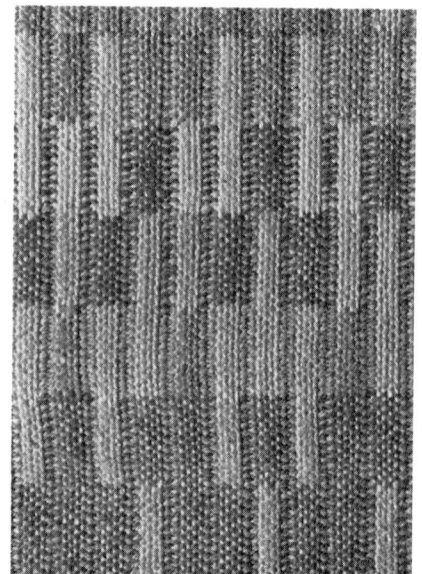

14.58b. Back surface of fabric in fig. 14.58a with long weft floats.

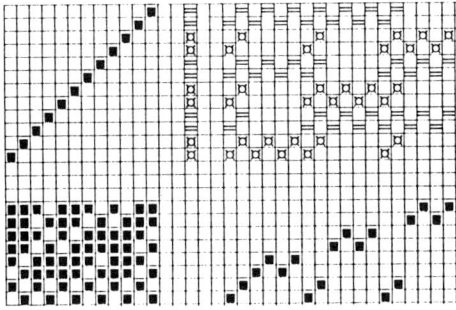

14.59. Eight-shaft draft for three blocks woven in two-faced weave for upholstery in figs. 14.58 a and b. Two weft colors, represented by different symbols, alternate after every two picks.

14.60. Detail, both sides of "Goldenrod Rug." Double cloth is patterned by an inlay, or brocade, weft held by tie warps. The rug's reverse surface has horizontal stripes from rotated weft colors. 1985; 127 cm (50") L X 79 cm (31") W; warp and tabby weft, cotton, 12/6, pale green; pattern wefts, cotton, strips flannel, 1.6 cm (5/8") W, greens and yellows; 3.5 e/cm (9 epi); 3 pattern, 1.5 tabby p/cm (8 pattern, 4 tabby ppi). Designed and woven by Jane Evans.

When the cloth is firmly beaten its back surface will show as pseudo-plain weave in blocks of two colors across the fabric, as in fig. 14.58a. Both wefts interlace with the tie warps and form a groove down the pseudo-tabby surface.

This surface is suitable for applications with much wear, such as upholstery or cushion covers. The floats form a backing which pads the fabric slightly. The opposite surface with floats, fig. 14.58b, is also attractive and could be used for items where floats are not a concern.

Double cloth

Layering two fabrics produces a double thickness of cloth. This outcome is useful for very sturdy textiles like the rug in figs. 14.60 and 14.61. It utilizes two fine warps and two large wefts for its two strata. A third, fine weft binds the otherwise separate fabrics by combining all the warps in tabby picks. There also is a fourth weft, of medium size, inlaid for the pattern motif on one surface.

This multi-faceted interlacement all takes place on a four-shaft threading of the 4:2 paired-tie draft. Figure 14.62 gives one unit's threading, tie-up, and treadling. Weaving instructions are given on page 172.

Warps on shafts 3 and 4 weave with one large weft for the back fabric. Another large weft weaves with the warps on shafts 1 and 2 for the front fabric. These warps also hold the brocade, or inlay patterning wefts on the front. A fine weft the size of the warp threads is barely noticeable between the large weft pickss.

Horizontal stripes are easily added on either surface by changing weft colors.

Inlaid wefts need attention at turns to control tension and bulk. The ends of inlaid wefts can be hidden in the center of the rug, in the back weft's shed. If a great deal of inlay is added the warps on shafts 1 and 2 may need to be longer than the warps on shafts 3 and 4.

Weft sizes should be chosen so that warp floats are reduced in length to a functional span.

As with virtually all the traditional and modified weaves from Latvia, this rug gives immediate rewards as it grows under the weaver's hands. If woven carefully, it will also give long service and satisfaction.

14.61. "Goldenrod Rug." A detail is shown in fig. 14.60.

DOUBLE CLOTH WITH INLAY

There are eight lats in one pass, treadled as follows. See fig. 14.62 for draft and tie-up.

1) Depress treadle 1.
   - Weave front ground weft.
   - Do not beat.

2) Depress treadle 2.
   - Weave back surface weft.
   - Beat.

3) Depress treadle 3.
   - Inlay pattern wefts.
   - Beat gently in place.

4) Depress treadle 4.
   - Weave a fine tabby binder.
   - Beat firmly.

5) Depress treadle 5.
   - Weave front ground weft.
   - Do not beat.

6) Depress treadle 6.
   - Weave back surface weft.
   - Beat.

7) Depress treadle 7.
   - Inlay pattern weft.
   - Beat gently in place.

8) Depress treadle 8.
   - Weave fine tabby binder.
   - Beat firmly.

This completes one pass.

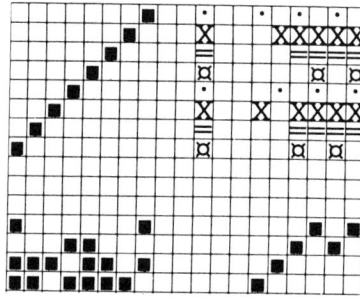

14.62. Draft for the rug in fig. 14.61. Four shafts are threaded to repeat this block of 4:2 paired-tie draft. Three wefts are woven as indicated by the different symbols. Inlay work is done as described in the text.

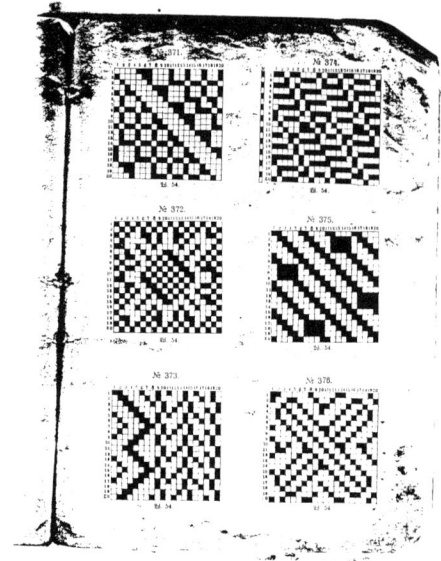

14.63. Page of fancy twill drafts from weaving text by P. Viļumsons.

Binder Any warp or weft thread that fastens a float to a ground cloth.

Block A design unit which represents a group of warps and wefts interlacing. Several independent blocks can be combined to form a pattern.

Card weaving A weaving method, also called tablet weaving, using a set of flat cards or tablets with holes through which warp threads pass. Rotating the cards produces sheds for a weft. Usually card weaving is used for narrow bands.

Counterbalanced loom A loom designed to raise and lower shafts simultaneously and in equal numbers. Usually this is a four-shaft loom.

Countermarch loom A loom designed to raise and lower shafts simultaneously in equal or unequal numbers. This loom can have few or many shafts.

Double-faced An interlacement by complementary sets of weft (or warp), giving identical structures on both sides of the fabric.

Double-harness loom A loom with two sets of shafts. Each set is called a harness.

Double treadling Combining two treadles to form the shed for one weft pick.

Draw-shaft device A set of shafts controlled by cords which a weaver pulls or draws to create pattern. This set of shafts is the back set on a double-harness loom

Front harness A set of shafts at the front of a double-harness loom, usually holding long-eyed heddles, for the control of the basic structural interlacement of the cloth.

Ground harness The same as a "front harness."

Ground shafts The shafts on a "front harness."

Jack loom A loom designed to raise shafts to create a shed. It can have few or numerous shafts which may be raised in equal or unequal numbers.

Lat One weft pick within a "pass."

Leno Also called gauze weave, this is a structure formed by twisting adjoining single warp threads or groups of warp threads around each other and securing the twist with a weft. Often this is done by hand manipulation.

Long-eyed heddles Heddles which are on the front shafts of a double-harness loom, and which have eyes longer than those on normal heddles. The length of an eye is equal to the depth of a shed.

"On opposites" sheds Sheds used in a method of weaving where two alternate wefts pass through sheds which have threads raised and lowered in exact opposition to each other.

Pass The total set of complementary wefts used as one cycle to structurally complete one row of weft.

Pattern shafts The shafts on a "rear harness."

Pattern harness The same as "rear harness."

Pick One weft in a shed.

Rear harness A set of shafts at the rear of a double-harness loom. These hold normal, short-eyed heddles which control the block design of a cloth.

Rigid heddle A tool for weaving relatively narrow pieces of fabric. There are vertical slats with one hole in each slat's center, and the slats are separated by narrow spaces. Individual warps pass through one hole or one space. When the rigid heddle is raised or lowered one of two sheds forms for a weft.

Shaft A frame holding heddles of string or metal with an eye in the center. Threaded through individual heddles, warp ends on a shaft move to form a shed.

Shed The opening across a warp where a pick of weft passes.

Tied unit A threading unit which contains both warps that are ties and warps that control the pattern interlacement of the cloth.

Tie warp In a tied-unit weave, a warp thread that occurs regularly within each threading unit to fasten the weft at regular intervals.

Turned weave An interlacement where a weave structure and its reverse surface both appear on the same face of a fabric, making a pattern of one against a background of the other. This also is called counterchanged weave.

Unit A specific number of warps and wefts which interlace in a specific way to produce either pattern or background structure, independent of but identical to other units threaded on the same warp. Units are the woven equivalent of a design's "blocks."

apakšaudi reinforcing wefts (supplementary weft on backed cloth)

apakšvelki reinforcing warps (supplementary warps on backed cloth)

atlass satin

atvasinātie sējumi derived weaves

audumi ar ielocītieu rakstiem cloth with folded-in patterning

audu rakstoti audumi weft-patterned cloth (supplementary weft patterning)

audu rakstoti audumi saisīttiem pārstaipiem weft-patterned cloth with tied floats (supplementary weft patterning on drafts with tie warps)

bārksts knotted pile or fringe

caurumotais raksts leno

četrnīšu drellis four-heddle or "crackle" weave

cilpainais pinums tufting

daļas parts (blocks of design)

dalītais pinums inlay

diagonālripss diagonal repp

divkāršie audumi double cloh

drellis blocks, especially in turned satin or turned twill weaves

dreļļu audumi block weaves (all as turned weaves)

dreļļu nītis block heddles, long-eyed heddles

dreļļu trizulis block pulley on loom

Gobēlena audums Gobelin weave

kaneva sējums canvas weave

kelima kilim or slit tapestry

krāsu maiņas raksti audumā color- and weave effects

krepa sējumi crepe

mežģinaudums gnarled weave or honeycomb

nātns linen

panama sējums basket weave

pārstaipu drellis float-block weave

pastiprinātie atlasa sējumi reinforced satin weave

pastiprinātie audumi reinforced weaves

pērlišu raksts looped or tufted pattern

plāces sējums basket weave

pubuļainie audumi lace weaves

pusdrellis half-block or M's & O's weave

rakstoti ripsaudumi patterned repp clorh

rakstots divkāršais skalu audums double cloth patterned with a pick-up stick

retinātā vienkārtņa audums spaced plain weave

ripsa sējumi derived repps

ripss unbalanced plain weave, either warp-faced or weft-faced

sakopotie sējumi combined weaves

siena wall; also a measure of length during preparing a warp; also a straw mat used on the wall.

skalu audums stick weave, a lace weave

slīpais ripss - sloped repp

šūniņaudumi waffle weave

trinītis twill

trīzuļu stāviem pulley loom

vadmala felted or fulled cloth

vagotais drellis ribbed block weave

vagotais pinums ribbed plaiting (inlay)

velku rakstoti audumi warp-patterned cloth

vienkārtnis plain weave

Alexandrovitch, Peter. Letter to author, 11 June 1987.

_____. Letter to author, 3 March 1988.

_____. Letter to author, 16 August 1988.

_____. Letter to author, 9 October 1988.

_____. Letter to author, 22 March, 1989.

Alsupe, Aina. *Audēji Vidzemē: 19. gs. otrajā puse un 20. gs. sākuma* (*Weavers in Vidzeme: Second half of the nineteenth century to the beginning of the twentieth century*). Riga: Zināte, 1982.

_____. Letter to author, 25 September 1987.

Antens, Anna [Anna Skuja-Antēne]. *Rokas grāmata audējam* (*Handbook for Weavers*). Dusseldorf: Apgāds J. Alksnis, 1949. [Originally published as *Aušana* (*Weaving*). Riga: N.p., 1931.]

Atwater, Mary. *Shuttle-Craft Book of American Handweaving*. New York: Macmillan Publishing Co., 1973.

Becker, John. *Pattern and Loom*. Copenhagen: Rhodos, 1987.

Burnham, Dorothy K. *Warp and Weft: A Textile Terminology*. Toronto: Royal Ontario Museum, 1980.

Čepelyté, E. *Ausk, Sesele, Drobeles*. Vilnius: State Publishing House of Political and Scientific Literature, 1960.

Collingwood, Peter. *Techniques of Rug Weaving*. New York: Watson-Guptill Pub., 1968.

Cyrus-Zetterström, Ulla. *Manual of Swedish Handweaving*. Translated by Alice Blomquist. Newton Centre, Mass.: Charles T. Branford Co., 1956.

Dzērvītis, Aleksandra. *Latvju raksti* (*Latvian Design*). Toronto: N.p, 1973.

_____. Letter to author, translated by Nora Priverts, July 1987.

Emery, Irene. *The Primary Structures of Fabrics: An Ilustrated Classification*. Washington: The Textile Museum, 1966.

Gabrans, Monika. Telephone conversation with author, 23 September 1987.

Grosicki, Z. *Watson's Textile Design and Colour: Elementary Weaves and Figured Fabrics*. Boston: Newnes-Butterworths, 1975.

Hilts, Patricia. "An Eighteenth Century German Court Weaver: Johann Michael Frickinger." *Shuttle, Spindle and Dyepot* (Fall 1980), 16-19, 58-59.

_____. "Ligetuhr Arbeit: A Seventeenth-Century Compound Mounting and a Family of Associated Weaves." *Ars Textrina* 7 (1987): 31-60.

_____. "Roses and Snowballs: the Development of Block Patterns in the German Linen-weaving Tradition." *Ars Textrina* 5 (1986): 167-248.

Johansson, Lillemor. *Damask and Opphämta with Weaving Sword or Drawloom*. Tranlated by Susan Jones. Stockholm: LTs forlag, 1982.

Kerans, Laima. Letter to author, 7 June 1987.

Kivicka, Elga. *Aušanas pašmācība : Aušanas technoloģija un audumu sējumu mācība* (*Teach Yourself Weaving: weaving technology and cloth set-up instruction*). Germany: Andr. Ozolina apgads, 1955. [Originally published in Latvia, 1934.]

Kurtz, Carol S. *Designing for Weaving: A Study Guide for Drafting, Design and Color*. Loveland, CO: Interweave Press, 1981.

Laansoo, Mrs. August. Telephone conversations with author, 24 and 25 September 1987.

Ligers, Z., A. Dzervite, and R. Legzdins, eds. *Latvju raksti (Latvian Design)*.Vols 1-2. Germany: Andreja Ozolina apgads, 1957-1959.

Meek, M. Kati. Correspondence with author, 1987.

Mednis, Velta. Letter to author, 12 June 1987.

Nelson, T. *Practical Textile Designing*. Charlotte, NC: Clark Publishing Co., 1945.

Oelsner, G. H. Translated and revised by Samuel S. Dale. *A Handbook of Weaves*.New York: Dover Publications, Inc., 1952.

Petrovis, Ada. Conversation with author, 23 June 1984.Pyysalo, Helvi. *Kankaiden sidokset*. Helsinki: Kustannusosakeyhtio Otava, 1965.

Robinson, A.T.C., R. Marks. *Woven Cloth Construction*. Manchester: The Textile Institute, 1973.

Šēfers, Dzidra. Telephone conversation with author, 26 October 1987.

____. Letter to author, 25 May 1988.

Sīmanis, Vito Vitauts, ed. *Latvia*. St. Charles, Ill.: The Book Latvia Inc., 1984.

Sinka, Juris. *Latvia and Latvians*. London: Central Board "Daugavas Vanagi," 1988.

Skuja-Antēne, Anna. *See also* Antens, Anna; Skujas, Anna

Skuja-Antēne, Anna. *Macies aust: Rokas grāmata skolotājām , instruktoŗem un audējām (Learn to weave: handbook for teachers and instructors and weavers)*. Riga: Latvju Sieviešu Nacionalās Līgas Izdevums, 1936.

Skujas, Anna [Skuja-Antēne, Anna], ed. *Paraugi audumiem (Samples for weaving)*. Riga: Latvju Sieviešu Nacionalās Līgas Izdevums, 1940.

Smits, Anna. Conversation with author, 10 October 1986.

Staubergs, Janis, *Rīgas vēsture,* N. D., Grāmatu Draugs, N. p.

Stepermanis, Redigejis M. *Latviešu tautas māksla (Latvian Folk Art)*. Vols 1-3.Riga: N.p., 1961-1967.

Tidball, Harriet. *Contemporary Satins*. Freeland, WA: HTH Publishers, 1962.

____. *Summer and Winter and Other Two-Tie Unit Weaves*. Santa Ana, CA: HTH Publishers, 1966.

____. *The Handloom Weaves*. Freeland, WA: HTH Publishers, 1957.

Vidbergs, Signumds, *Latvija zīmerjumos*, P. Mantnieka, Kartografiskā Institūta Izdervums, N.d., N.p.

Veveris, Ervins, and Martins Kuplais. *Latvijas Etnogrāfiskajā brivādabas muzejā (In the Latvian ethnographic open-air museum)*. Riga: Avots, 1989.

Viļumsons, Pēters. *Ceturtdienas rīts (Thursday Morning)*. Jelgava: P. Viļumsons, N.d.

____. *Otrdienus rīts (Tuesday Morning)*. 2nd edition. Riga: P. Viļumsons, N.d.

____. *Pirmdienas rīts (Monday Morning)*. Riga: P. Viļumsons, N.d.

____. *Trešdienas rīts (Wednesday Morning.)* Riga: P. Viļumsons, N.d.

Zulerons, Joan. Letter to author, 18 September 1984.